POWER PLAYS

The real stories of Australian politics

LAURIE OAKES

HACHETTE AUSTRALIA

My thanks to Matthew Kelly, whose idea this book was, and who did most of the heavy lifting to bring it into being. And to Ali Smith for help in retrieving 20 years of columns from the archives. Thanks also to my former colleagues on *The Bulletin* for their help and support over the years.

All the articles in this book have appeared previously in *The Bulletin*, as have the headings. Thanks are due to ACP Magazines. Acknowledgments and thanks are also due to those who wrote the headings – which were right then, and are still so appropriate now.

Laurie Oakes

HACHETTE AUSTRALIA

Published in Australia and New Zealand in 2008
by Hachette Australia
(An imprint of Hachette Livre Australia Pty Limited)
Level 17, 207 Kent Street, Sydney NSW 2000
Website: www.hachette.com.au

National Library of Australia
Cataloguing-in-Publication data

Oakes, Laurie.
  Power plays : the real stories of Australian politics /
  Laurie Oakes.

  9780733623653 (pbk.)
  Includes index.
  Political parties – Australia.
  Australia – Politics and government.

320.994

Cover and text design by Darian Causby, Highway 51
Cover photography by Nationwide News
Typeset in 11.5/14.5pt Sabon by Post Pre-press Group, Brisbane
Printed in Australia by Griffin Press, Adelaide

Hachette Livre Australia's policy is to use papers that are natural, renewable and recyclable products and made from wood grown in sustainable forests. The logging and manufacturing processes are expected to conform to the environmental regulations of the country of origin.

Introduction

An American politician summed it up years ago. Richard Lamm, a former governor of Colorado, said: 'There's this symbiotic relationship between the press and politicians. It's like the great apes that sit around and pick the fleas off one another.' The pages that follow reflect some of this mutual flea-picking over two decades.

Given that I wrote close to one thousand *Power Plays* pieces for the now (sadly) defunct *Bulletin* magazine between 1987 and 2007, the selection has had to be somewhat random. This collection therefore does not pretend to be a comprehensive record of either the times or the column. I hope, however, that it may help to explain some of the more significant events of the period and provide some insights into the personalities and motivations of those involved. Perhaps, too, there are lessons to be learned from the politics of these years that are relevant to the future.

One of those lessons is that political journalists can be as fallible as those they write about. A number of the predictions in these pieces proved to be wrong; some of my judgments, with the benefit of hindsight, were clearly faulty. But that is the nature of the business. Circumstances change; more information comes to light; character flaws or strengths can take time to emerge; political fortunes ebb and flow.

Before I began reporting on politics, I worked for a time on police rounds for the old *Daily Mirror* in Sydney. Crime was the bread and butter of afternoon tabloids back then, and I was involved in covering some good stories – particularly on the midnight-to-dawn shift, when Sydney's underbelly was on display. One night a prison escapee surrendered to me. Another time, a photographer and I beat the cops to the scene of a gangland shooting in Kings Cross. But when I got my first taste of politics, the die was cast. For interest and excitement, as far as I was concerned, it left the crime beat for dead.

Politics is human drama writ large. The ruthless drive for power, the emotion and the cold calculation, the wheeling and dealing and plotting, the backstabbing and brawling, the triumphs and failures, and the betrayals – a journalist cannot ask for anything more. I have watched it all with fascination, and tried to record it and explain it, since becoming a political reporter in the mid-1960s.

In the end, of course, politics is about policy. It is about how the nation should be governed, how the security and economic well-being of its citizens can best be ensured and enhanced. But to implement policy it is necessary to win office and retain it, and this is what gives politics such a wonderful multidimensional quality.

Deception and manipulation are central to it all. Machiavelli tells us that. So a truly effective politician needs to be a master of intrigue and psychology. 'It's *all* psychology,' Paul Keating once told me, but that's not true. A politician must be an actor, too. One of my favourite books on British politics is by Norman Shrapnel, a parliamentary sketch writer who was also a drama critic. He saw the parliament – accurately, in my view – as a stage where national conflicts and traumas are acted out as a form of expressionist theatre. Most of all, success in politics requires the qualities of a warrior. Petro Georgiou, former prime ministerial adviser and Liberal Party machine man who is now a prominent MP, got it right 30 years ago when he described politics as 'war without blood'.

Opinion polls show that Australians are distrustful of politicians and political institutions, and this is frequently reflected in the media. A sneering tone creeps into much of the political commentary. But, while a bit of scepticism is healthy, and journalists in particular need to be sceptical about those who wield power, we should not lose sight of the fact that our system actually works pretty well. It might cut across conventional wisdom to say so, but most politicians are well motivated.

Most importantly, perhaps, when you look back over a period like that covered in this book, it is clear that the electorate almost always gets it right. It twigged to John Hewson's manic character ahead of the pundits. It was awake to Mark Latham's true nature before he put it on open display in his poisonous diaries. The 'It's time' judgment was spot-on in both 1996 and 2007.

But for those who get to the top – or near it – in Australian politics, the burden is heavy and the price is high. That was brought home to me in a phone call from Paul Keating in 1990, when the then-treasurer was under fire over the recession he'd told Australians they had to have. 'Mate, don't ever despise me or my position,' he said, 'because I live a life…it's a shocking burden. Hours of pain and responsibility. I go to bed with these things and I wake up with them. They hang around my head like a bad smell, you know?'

This was the great bully of Australian politics, whose aggression and vicious turn of phrase struck fear into the hearts of all those who dared oppose him. And here he was, in the depths of despair and self-pity. It was unexpected, it was moving, and it was sad. Keating and I had our moments. We still have them, on occasion. There is not a lot of love lost between us. But I certainly do not despise him or – with a few exceptions – the other politicians I have dealt with and reported on in my years in the federal parliamentary press gallery. I have more than a sneaking admiration for most of them.

To me, the marvel is that intelligent, worthwhile people still choose a political career. When Kim Beazley was toppled from the Labor leadership by Kevin Rudd, he told caucus: 'I am heartbroken.' And he was. John Howard, commenting on the downfall of his old foe, summed it up. 'It's a brutal game, politics.' A year later, Howard's own brilliant career ended in tears.

The 20 years this book spans saw: Bob Hawke ruthlessly toppled from the prime ministership by an ambitious Keating; Howard rolled as opposition leader by Andrew Peacock; Hewson humiliated and cut down after losing the 'unlosable' election; his successor, Alexander Downer, reduced almost to a laughing stock before handing the Liberal leadership back to Howard; Keating driven from office by an electorate that had come to loathe him; Beazley rejected twice by voters and three times by his party; Simon Crean dispatched as opposition leader without even getting to fight an election; Latham imploding spectacularly after an election loss his fragile ego could not handle; and Howard becoming only the second prime minister since Federation to lose his seat.

But, while the participants come and go, many of the themes remain constant. I suspect most people would believe that global warming became an issue in Australian politics recently. In fact, though, legendary powerbroker Graham Richardson as environment minister was thinking about it back in 1989 – considering a referendum to give the federal government constitutional power to deal with what was then called the 'greenhouse effect'.

The problem of how to make Australia's federal system of government work more effectively is a recurring theme. When in 1991 Hawke proposed a 'new federalism' that would have returned some taxation powers to the states, Keating – arguing that Canberra's control of the national purse-strings should not be weakened – used it brutally against him in their leadership battle. At around the same time the Liberals held an 80th birthday party for John Gorton to welcome him back into the fold. Gorton had been deposed from the prime ministership in a party room coup 20 years earlier, largely because he had angered two powerful Liberal premiers with his nationalist views and contempt for state parochialism. Howard would have been regarded by most Liberals as a states' righter when he won office, but became the great centraliser, outdoing even Gough Whitlam. His wholesale takeover of industrial relations powers from the states did more than anything else to bring him down. Now Rudd is dependent on the success of his own version of cooperative federalism to implement the health and education policies that got him elected.

There is material here on Keating's high mortgage rates and the recession of the early 1990s. The theme of the ambitious deputy threads its way through these pages, illuminating both the similarities and the differences between Keating and Peter Costello. Associated with it is the theme of the leader who does not recognise when it is time to go. Howard was privately critical of Hawke's failure to arrange an orderly succession, but proved incapable of applying the lesson to his own situation. There are, too, observations – many from politicians themselves – about the nature of leadership and power. The simplest lesson is one that Richardson learned from former NSW ALP president John Ducker – you get power by exercising it. Also, Howard's views on the miseries of opposition, expressed from the comfort of the Lodge in 1996, are unlikely to console his erstwhile coalition colleagues now.

From time to time I have voiced concern that the individuality is slowly being squeezed out of our politicians to the detriment of the democratic process. The retirement of former National Party leader Tim Fischer from parliament in 1999 was one excuse for me to complain that colourful, *interesting* politicians were becoming rare.

Modern Australian politicians, I wrote, were afraid to chance their arms, to say anything spontaneous, or even to be themselves. And I blamed media training, which resulted in mantra politics. ('Ignore the questions,' the pollies are told. 'Keep repeating the message.')

For every Barnaby Joyce there are dozens of Mogadon MPs. There are no more Mick Youngs, bringing shearing shed vernacular and humour into the parliament. Keating's larrikin attitude and creative use of language has been replaced by Rudd's buttoned-down, cliché-spouting style. Treasurer Wayne Swan discusses the economy in rehearsed sound-grabs. Discipline and risk-avoidance are the priorities, and woe betide any MP who steps outside the party-approved talking points. This undoubtedly contributes to public cynicism about politicians and results in disengagement from the political process. Television's preference for the 10-second grab is sometimes blamed, but it's a bum rap. As I wrote in the Fischer retirement column, '*interesting* works on television, *boring* does not'.

Extraordinarily, in what is billed the information age, it seems to me that politicians are losing the ability to communicate. The focus on focus groups, with its 'feed back to them what they want to hear' imperative, is part of the reason. So is the growing reliance of our political leaders on jargon and glib phrases which sound impressive but mean little. You can almost hear voters crying out for some straight talk. It is why some independents, free from party constraints and with the spine to say what they really think, do so well.

Spin – the way politicians and their minders use public relations techniques to sway opinion – is a related issue. Not that media manipulation is anything new. When Keating put compliant journalists on the Treasury information drip, and removed from the drip those who displeased him, he was using a tactic as old as political journalism itself. But Keating was also a master of modern spin.

One of his advisers let the cat out of the bag in 1993. In a scholarly article on Keating's economic policy, Dr John Edwards wrote that it had 'involved a good deal of opinion management, often of a sophisticated kind, especially the exploitation of public fear or widely held misconceptions to advance objectives which would otherwise be difficult to attain'. Edwards actually used the word 'manipulation', and continued: 'Very often the personal success of politicians or the continued electoral success of government depends on the ability of the cabinet member and their officials to persuade us to see the world as they wish us to see it and then, when reality intrudes, to persuade us to see it in a somewhat different way without noticing the change or being annoyed by the contradiction.' That is as good a description of 'spin' as you will find anywhere. Tony Blair's spinmeister, Alastair Campbell, would have been proud of it.

Fortunately, voters are not nearly as naive about this sort of thing as they used to be. An increasingly media-savvy electorate tends to be more alert to the manipulative techniques used by politicians and public relations people – spin doctors, if you like. Spin is not nearly as effective if people know it is happening. And when they do know it is happening it becomes another factor undermining trust in politicians and political institutions.

Which brings me back to my starting point – the relationship between politicians and the media. We may work in close proximity, constantly exchange information, socialise with each other, in some cases even develop friendships. But that does not mean we are on the same side. We have conflicting interests. Politicians want to control information and the way it is presented to the public. The journalist's job is to dig out information the pollies want to keep buried, and to try to see past the spin to get at the truth. It is a constant battle, and sometimes it seems that the politicians are winning.

The 2001 'children-overboard' scandal showed how politicians, with the help of bureaucrats, can avoid responsibility for their actions. In Canberra these days there are a lot more public relations people than reporters. Freedom of information laws have largely been turned into a joke. Restrictions on the media have been tightened. Leakers are pursued with increasing vigour. (Federal police recently sifted through my telephone records as part of a leak hunt.)

But the good news is that leaks have proved hard to plug, embarrassing documents still fall off the backs of trucks, and a new generation of young and energetic press gallery members continues to fight and frustrate attempts at control. Lamm was right – politicians and the media need each other. But Richard Nixon was also right when he said, speaking for all politicians: 'The press is the enemy.' It's important to keep it that way.

1987

Joh's crusade could be the making of John Howard

17 February 1987

Sir Joh Bjelke-Petersen talks of annihilating John Howard and Ian Sinclair. He may do it. But the very threat could have the reverse effect, at least as far as Howard is concerned. The Queensland Premier on the rampage provides the federal opposition leader with an opportunity to show his stuff, to demonstrate whether he is a leader or not. Howard, once regarded as a tough political scrapper, has looked increasingly wimpish over the past year. Now he is involved in the political fight of his life. If he is to survive in the Liberal leadership, and if the coalition is to have any chance in the next election, he has to take on Sir Joh and break him. 'It's Howard's chance to redeem himself as a leader,' one of the shrewdest political observers in the government remarked last week. Embroiled in a battle he cannot avoid, Howard is being compelled to show strength. Ironically, he is also being compelled by Sir Joh's attacks on Liberal 'wets' to behave for the first time as leader of the whole Liberal Party rather than simply of the dominant 'dry' faction.

The Bjelke-Petersen crusade to realign conservative politics in Australia got off to an astonishing start. The way it gained momentum following his Wagga speech surprised supporters almost as much as opponents. 'He's gone a lot further and a lot faster than we expected,' says one of the people involved in putting Sir Joh's campaign together. The damage being done to the coalition is obvious enough. Equally obvious is the boost the conservative brawling has given to morale in the Labor Party. In this climate, speculation about the possibility of an early election is inevitable – especially since people close to Sir Joh claim a snap federal election in the next few months is the only thing that could foil his plans. He needs time to get his organisation ready. A May election would be too early for him.

The Prime Minister remains adamant that there will be no poll until late this year or early 1988. But there is starting to be heard in Canberra – not yet with any force at cabinet level – a view that the tough budgetary situation facing the government could make the early election option more inviting. According to this argument, such savage and electorally unpalatable spending cuts will be required this year that a post-budget election might not be winnable. If warnings from Treasury really are this grim, and if the conservative parties start to disintegrate to the point where a coalition victory in the present circumstances looks impossible, Bob Hawke could come under pressure to change his mind and consider a double dissolution election. If Labor's election strategists see a window, the temptation to go through it may prove irresistible. Hawke would, of course, need the Australia Card legislation to be rejected a second time by the Senate to provide a double dissolution 'trigger'. Interestingly, a conservative politician pointedly reminded me the other day that the government would lose its 'trigger' if a few coalition senators crossed the floor and allowed the legislation to pass. The unmistakable implication was that this could probably be arranged, if necessary.

One of the intriguing questions to arise as the drama unfolded last week was whether Andrew Peacock had been involved in a conspiracy with the Queensland Premier. Peacock's gratuitous intervention – calling on the opposition leader to hold peace talks with Sir Joh – convinced some of the more ardent Howard supporters of the existence of a plot. Peacock and Sir Joh, they suggested, were working together to destabilise Howard so that Peacock could regain the federal Liberal leadership. Like most conspiracy theories, this one does not hold water. And Howard, to his credit, at no stage accepted it. Certainly it is true that Sir Joh's backers favour the idea of a Bjelke-Petersen/Peacock leadership double, because their polling shows it would be electorally popular. But Peacock himself has had no involvement with them. He did, however, make it his business to pick up as much intelligence as possible about what the Queensland Premier was up to, and shortly before Christmas he warned Liberal Party federal director Tony Eggleton to expect an assault from the north.

The absence of a conspiracy of course does not mean Sir Joh's activities might not result in the Liberal leadership again changing hands. There is no doubt Peacock wants the job back, and he will try to take it if the battle with Sir Joh leaves Howard looking vulnerable. He has to tread warily, however. As Tasmanian Premier Robin Gray found when he cast doubts on the security of Howard's leadership last Friday, many Liberals are in no mood to tolerate anyone rocking the boat at the moment. Gray got a pasting from party members in his own state, and phoned Howard within 24 hours to square off. There is, however, muted criticism among Liberal MPs of Howard's failure to anticipate the crisis. It is possible that, had he acted in time and with a degree of subtlety, it might have been headed off. This may have been what Peacock had in mind when he suggested that the federal coalition leaders should meet Sir Joh and try to work out a solution. People who have had political dealings with the Queensland Premier often observe that the private Joh is quite different from the public one. He is the most stubborn man in the country if you take him on publicly, they say. But when you sit down with him in private his approach is much more reasonable.

Howard, according to some of his Liberal Party critics, should have tried to arrange a quiet meeting with Sir Joh before criticising him publicly. A compromise of sorts might have been worked out, even on the crucial tax issue, if they had sat down together and talked over their differences. Now, of course, with both sides hurling abuse in public, it is probably too late. Having missed the chance to negotiate a truce, Howard has to fight. He has to assert the authority of a leader, and somehow force Sir Joh to back down. If he fails, if the old Queensland warrior comes out on top, a move to topple him as leader will not be long delayed. Howard, however, would not give up the leadership as easily as Peacock did in 1985. 'If anyone wants the job,' he has told friends, 'they'll have to blast me out.'

Puny opposition tries to bucket the referee

21 April 1987

John Howard's opposition has been getting a pasting in parliament. Day after day, Bob Hawke, Paul Keating and the government's other frontliners inflict dreadful punishment on the would-be heavy-weights on the coalition side. It is disastrous for morale in Liberal ranks. Journalists watching from the gallery are influenced in their political judgments by the one-sided contest. Voters, listening to audio 'grabs' of parliamentary proceedings in radio and television news services, are presumably influenced too.

This is the background to the extraordinary attack on Speaker Joan Child in a Liberal strategy committee document leaked last week. Author of the document, shadow attorney-general John Spender, wrote: 'The plain fact is that the Speaker's bias...is unmistakable.' What is extraordinary is not that Spender should believe Mrs Child is biased in favour of the government but that he should think such a situation is at all unusual.

Under our parliamentary system it is unrealistic to expect Speakers to be impartial. In the House of Commons, a Speaker relinquishes party affiliations and in return is guaranteed not to be opposed in his seat, but in Australia, where there is no such guarantee, a Speaker has to retain party membership and endorsement. Impartiality is a myth and in Mrs Child's defence it can be said that she gets as close to it as any of her predecessors – Labor and Liberal – over the 20 years or so I have been closely studying politics.

Opposition complaints about the Speaker, which have been getting increasingly heated since the beginning of the year, reflect the frustration of Liberal and National party MPs at their inability to get on top of the government at Question Time – and at the ease with which the government stays on top of them. But lashing out at Mrs Child will not help and Howard and his team have to improve their performance. At least, when parliament resumes after its Easter break, Howard will have a reshuffled, revamped shadow ministry. That may lead to a more aggressive and effective use of the parliamentary forum – but a change in approach will be needed.

Spender, who heads the strategy committee, recognises this in his document and suggests more concentrated attacks on weak ministers – and names Aboriginal Affairs Minister Clyde Holding, Health Minister Neal Blewett, Sport and Tourism Minister John Brown, Local Government Minister Tom Uren and Territories Minister Gordon Scholes. It is good advice, but hardly enough to turn the opposition's parliamentary fortunes around. If they are to do that, it is clearly necessary for Howard and Co to find a way to deal with Hawke, Keating, Dawkins, Button and Walsh, strong ministers in important economic portfolios who are inflicting damage on the opposition and cannot be ignored.

It is never easy for oppositions to score points at Question Time. Standing orders impose no real requirement on ministers to be brief or relevant, but – since the coalition made no attempt to change those Standing Orders during its years in office – Spender and his colleagues are not on strong ground when they whinge about the situation.

The Spender document says, correctly, that 'the phrasing of questions has to be reconsidered – questions should have a greater political bite'. Hawke and Keating get a run on radio and television by using colourful, vigorous language tailored to make audio 'grabs'. There is no reason why those questioning them should not do the same, nor is there any reason why the filibustering and evasiveness of ministers cannot be exposed through skilful follow-up questioning by the opposition leadership.

But the best way to use Question Time is to be armed with information embarrassing to the government and to surprise ministers with that information. It is also possible to use Question Time to expose contradictions in government statements or – even better – to provoke contradictory statements from ministers. Gough Whitlam in opposition was devastatingly effective with this sort of approach. Bill Hayden was good at it, too, and gave the Fraser government much more trouble in parliament than Howard or Andrew Peacock have ever managed to give Hawke. The present opposition has not shown the ability or the will to do the necessary work.

The opposition's biggest problem in the parliamentary battle, though, is that it is vulnerable to attack itself. Given the state of the economy, ministers *should* be on the defensive – but they are not. Ministers attack, the opposition defends. Coalition brawling and the great split caused by Sir Joh Bjelke-Petersen is part of the reason, of course, and Hawke and his senior colleagues have exploited it gleefully. But a much greater opposition weakness is the lack of consistent policies – most importantly a detailed, consistent taxation policy. Howard and his frontbenchers are not in a position to launch an effective onslaught on the government's economic policy if they are open to ridicule themselves in the same area. The strategy of delaying the public release of the opposition's tax policy until close to an election is being exposed as politically stupid. This is something to which the Spender committee should turn its attention, rather than sniping at the Speaker. The coalition row, of course, has made it much harder for Howard to get agreement on a tax policy but that is his problem and one which Hawke and Keating have not failed to highlight. The leaked Spender document says that the opposition should be 'demonstrating we have an effective alternative to the government'. Exactly! But so far it has been demonstrating just the opposite. That is why the Howard team gets a daily parliamentary bath and only Howard and the shadow cabinet – not a strategy committee – can do anything about the situation.

Ambition drives the deputies to the limelight

4 August 1987

Normally in politics attention focuses on leaders. The recent presidential-style election campaign was an example of this. It was Hawke versus Howard. Other politicians were minor players. And the deputy leaders of the major parties – Lionel Bowen and Neil Brown – were barely heard of. But, over the next few years, deputy leaders can be expected to grab headlines, and the role of a deputy leader will be much discussed. One reason is Andrew Peacock's surprise decision to become deputy Liberal leader to his long-time rival John Howard. Another is Bowen's plan to step down as deputy prime minister, probably next year. Paul Keating no doubt considers he has a right to move into the job.

'Keating as deputy to Hawke will be like Gough Whitlam as deputy to Arthur Calwell,' a Labor staffer said a few days ago. It was a massive over-statement. The successful Hawke is not to be compared with the unelectable leader the ALP stubbornly stuck with through a large part of the '60s. But the Keating/Whitlam comparison has validity. Like Whitlam, Keating will become impatient if his chance at leadership is delayed too long. Keating expects Hawke to make way for him before the end of the current parliamentary term but it is by no means clear that the Prime Minister sees things in precisely the same way. Keating would be a thrusting deputy, dominating his leader and increasingly looking like a rival. In the view of many in the Labor Party, it would be an inherently unstable situation.

'Inherently unstable' is a description used frequently to describe the Howard/Peacock leadership team, too, and for much the same reason. It is difficult to imagine the ambitious Peacock smothering his own ego and putting Howard's interests ahead of his own. 'Andrew is no Phil Lynch or Lionel Bowen,' is the way one Liberal put it last week. Bowen and the late Sir Phillip Lynch are held up these days as the ideal deputy leadership role models.

According to Bowen, the requirements of the deputy leadership position are not the same in government as in opposition. In both situations, of course, Bowen believes a deputy leader has to provide loyalty and support to the leader. 'But in opposition a deputy leader needs to be attacking all the time, taking a high profile in parliament, giving his leader a chance to be out and about campaigning,' Bowen says. 'In government, it's the reverse of that. A deputy prime minister needs to take a subdued role. If a deputy goes after a high profile in government, he will endanger the popularity of the prime minister. He'll be portrayed as a rival.' It is clear from those comments that Bowen would have serious reservations about Keating becoming deputy prime minister to Hawke. He declines to be drawn on the issue, but the logic of his position would favour someone such as Immigration Minister Mick Young succeeding him. Young would be much more in the Bowen/Lynch mould than Keating. Not having obvious prime ministerial ambitions himself, Young could play the role of 'fixer' on Hawke's behalf, act as his eyes and ears in the party and the electorate, and never be seen as a threat.

The conventional wisdom is that successful deputies do not aspire to the top job themselves. Interestingly, though, this was not true of either Lynch or Bowen. Despite appearances, Lynch was an extremely ambitious politician who would dearly have loved to lead the Liberal Party. He was regarded as the loyal offsider, first to Sir Billy Snedden and then to Malcolm Fraser. The truth, however, was that Lynch frequently plotted or manoeuvred against them when he disagreed with what they proposed or had some plan of his own he wanted to push.

Bowen, too, had leadership aspirations. Indeed, for a period in late 1974 and early 1975, Whitlam had decided Bowen should be groomed as his successor. He stood unsuccessfully against Whitlam after the 1975 election defeat, and would have liked the Labor leadership when Hayden got it two years later. Eventually Bowen might have challenged Hayden – had Hawke not appeared on the parliamentary scene.

Peacock, when the current situation was reversed – when he was

Liberal leader and Howard was his 2IC – had very definite views on how a deputy leader should behave. He wanted absolute loyalty, absolute support – and because Howard fell short of what he expected, Peacock precipitated the crisis which saw Howard installed as leader in his place. Now Peacock will have to apply the same standards to himself.

Few people closely involved with politics believe he will be able to do so. There is an expectation in large sections of the Liberal Party as well as in the government and the press gallery that the Howard/ Peacock partnership will not work. But one of the Liberal MPs closest to the new deputy leader says: 'There is a political imperative on Howard and Peacock to make it work. If they don't, both of them are kaput.'

Peacock and Lynch were bitter rivals for years. Lynch beat Peacock for the deputy leadership in the first place. Fraser ensured that Lynch stayed in the deputy leadership to keep Peacock out. Now Peacock will have to try to model himself on his old foe. He seems genuinely determined to do it, despite the irony.

Keating, on the other hand, assuming he becomes Hawke's deputy, will not model himself on Bowen. The two are friends. In Keating's early days in politics, Bowen was one of his most important mentors. But Keating is much hungrier for power than Bowen ever was – and certainly much hungrier for it than Bowen was by the time he became deputy prime minister. There is now so much momentum behind the Keating career that it would be impossible for him to throttle back – even if he wanted to.

1988

Howard looking good in spite of Elliott

8 March 1988

When John Elliott ran for the presidency of the Liberal Party last year his most important supporter was John Howard. Considerable opposition had built up within the party to the takeover bid by the Elders boss. Many traditional 'old money' Liberals did not approve of Elliott's brash 'new money' style. The strong puritan element in the Liberal Party disliked the idea of a brewer as president. And Liberal MPs were suspicious of Elliott's motives. But Howard, the federal parliamentary leader, went in to bat for him.

Howard argued that the Liberal Party would look ridiculous if it rejected a businessman of such obvious ability. Elliott, he said, with his powerful personality and high public profile, could be a considerable asset politically. To knock back Elliott would be to confirm claims that the party was dominated by an out-of-touch parliamentary club. There was another argument which Howard did not articulate, but which undoubtedly weighed on his mind. The only alternative to Elliott on offer was Malcolm Fraser, who was completely unacceptable. 'Malcolm would have been constantly on John's back,' says a Howard supporter.

Surprisingly, despite Elliott's growing reputation as a foot-in-mouth exponent, Howard would probably still support him for the presidency today. Certainly, the opposition leader has told friends that he has not lost hope that Elliott can be effective in the role. Howard believes that he, Elliott and deputy Liberal leader Andrew Peacock should be an ideal team because between them they embody all the Liberal Party's key constituencies. Peacock represents traditional Liberals, Elliott big business, and Howard the vital middle-class element. If the team is to work, though, Elliott has to change. On the day the NSW election date was announced, Howard appeared on the *Sunday* program on the Nine network. It should have provided him with a platform from which to attack Labor and push the cause of Nick Greiner and the NSW Liberals. Instead he spent a large part of the interview being questioned about Elliott's most recent gaffe and looking like a wimp because of the need to avoid headlines suggesting an intra-party brawl at the start of a crucial election campaign. By the end of the program Howard was livid – not with the interviewers, but with Elliott.

Howard is fed up with being put on the defensive by his own party president. In contests with Prime Minister Bob Hawke and the federal Labor government this year, Howard has been coming out on top. He has drummed into his shadow ministers the need for aggression and persistence in parliament with the result that the opposition has been doing well in both the House of Representatives and the Senate. And Howard out-campaigned Hawke in the Adelaide by-election. A spectacular victory was his reward. Yet in parliament, Hawke has been able to score some points by quoting Elliott and portraying the Liberal president as a rival for Howard's leadership position. What ammunition the government has been able to fire at the opposition has been supplied by Elliott himself. And, in the Adelaide by-election campaign, Elliott was responsible for the only major Liberal setback when, on the eve of the poll, he told a breakfast meeting of Liberal supporters that the party would not have deserved to win had it beaten the ALP in the 1987 general election. Howard was white and shaking and banging the table when he confronted Elliott over the episode at a party federal executive meeting a few hours later. Elliott's response was to deny saying what the media reported. According to one prominent executive member: 'He genuinely didn't know what he'd said.' That is what makes Elliott such a major worry for the Liberal Party. It is the reason the NSW Liberals have been in a state of considerable anxiety when Elliott has visited the state during the election campaign.

There is a pattern to Elliott's outbursts. Most appear designed to suggest the party was a mess until he came along. The Fraser government did not deliver. The coalition did not deserve to win last July. Until now people have joined the party because it has been a good social club. There is a new determination in the party to start winning. And so on. The advent of Elliott has changed the party seems to be the constant message. Liberal MPs see it, not only as an implied criticism of Howard, but of themselves as well and most of them are unamused. Quite a few prominent Liberal MPs share Hawke's view of Elliott's intentions. 'He's definitely coming,' they say – meaning that Elliott has started manoeuvring to get himself into parliament and the Liberal leadership. These people believe Elliott's gaffes are somehow part of a plan to destabilise Howard and create a leadership vacuum which only the Liberal federal president – the 'jam man' – will be able to fill. It is difficult, however, to see how making himself regularly appear foolish can help any leadership ambitions Elliott may have. As a result of his ill-timed and ill-considered statements embarrassing the party, Elliott finds himself being ridiculed in the media. And, if he suddenly made the switch to parliament and challenged for the leadership, he would get an idea of the resentment he has aroused. He would attract only a handful of votes. There is a hard-core group of Elliott supporters in the party room, but their hero makes it very difficult for them to argue his cause. They must have despaired when he talked himself out of any credit for the Adelaide win.

Howard's supporters do not believe Elliott has an agenda, though they speculate that he 'probably hopes for the call'. But the scenario, in which a desperate Liberal Party turns to Elliott and 'drafts' him to lead it out of the wilderness, is pure fantasy when things are going well for the party, as they are at the moment. The government is in serious trouble despite the odd bit of help from Elliott – and Howard, for a change, is looking secure in the Liberal leadership. Elliott was brought into the Liberal presidency because the previous incumbent, John Valder, proved incapable of disciplining his tongue.

Valder came to be seen as a liability to the party. It must be galling to a man of Elliott's capacity to realise that he is increasingly regarded in the same light – not as the Liberal Party's saviour but as an obstacle to its success.

Keating ready to move – up or out

22 March 1988

Some of Paul Keating's colleagues believe he may be in the process of making a crucial decision – crucial for the Treasurer himself and for the federal government. They say that comments he has made recently – small hints – suggest Keating is weighing up seriously whether to continue in politics or make the great leap into a business career.

Keating's going would shake the government to its foundations. But a decision to stay on could also have enormous implications. The judgment of people who know Keating well is that if he sticks around it will be because he sees some prospect of becoming prime minister in the short term. That is, within the next year or so.

Bob Hawke has been saying bluntly that he intends to be there until the next election and beyond. So, if Keating *is* considering his future, he may well have to give some thought to whether Hawke can be pushed.

The idea of Hawke being pressured to step aside would have seemed ridiculous a few months ago. The Prime Minister was riding high while the Treasurer's image problems seemed insurmountable. Keating, it was said, was so disliked in the community that he could not win an election. But now there is serious concern about Hawke's handling of the job and growing doubt that *he* can pull off another election win. As Hawke's popularity has suffered a slump, Keating has had some success in softening his severe image.

Because many of the problems plaguing the government can be laid at Hawke's door, an opportunity may just be opening up for Keating. The Prime Minister's authority and standing within the Australian Labor Party were badly damaged by the way he botched the recent Adelaide campaign. It is accepted almost without argument that Adelaide was lost because of Hawke's gaffe over timed phone calls – but the by-election illustrated a more deep-seated problem. When Labor pollster Rod Cameron warned Hawke late last year that the seat was at risk, the Prime Minister simply laughed. What that says about Hawke's political judgment these days is disturbing indeed.

Hawke's judgment was again the issue when news broke last Friday that Mick Young, still national ALP president, had been given a lucrative appointment as a consultant to Qantas. The timing – a week before an election in which a state Labor government was battling desperately for survival in NSW – could hardly have been worse. Hawke, it transpired, had been told in advance that Young was to get the job. At the very least, for the good of the party, Hawke could have tried to have the appointment delayed. Some senior ALP figures believe it should have been blocked, full stop. But Hawke, it appears, did nothing. After the event, he even tried to defend what voters will almost certainly see as indefensible.

A brief summary of Labor's private polling in NSW and how it affected the party's state election strategy is instructive at this point.

At the beginning of December last year, Cameron's surveys indicated a swing against Barrie Unsworth's government of about eight percent. By the end of the year, the swing was down to six or 6.5 percent and that situation continued throughout January. In other words, Labor needed a movement of only one or two percentage points its way in an election campaign to win. The considerable optimism in the Unsworth camp was understandable. Then came the Adelaide by-election timed phone calls debacle, the Harris Daishowa campaign donation affair and Young's dramatic resignation from cabinet and parliament. 'The lid came off,' says a party official. Suddenly, Cameron's polling showed Labor's support in NSW a massive 10 percent down on the previous state election level. Support for the party had dropped by an astonishing four percent in eight days. For that kind of slump to happen so quickly is almost unprecedented. Young's resignation, in particular, seems to have been the trigger.

One of Labor's key strategists summed up the situation this way: 'It was as if people all at once realised the emperor and his courtiers had no clothes.'

The NSW party, hoping that time would dull the effects of the drama involving Young, delayed the state election as long as possible and set about trying to claw its way back. Its best chance of rebuilding support was Unsworth's pork-barrelling policy speech last week and Cameron's polling suggested that it had quite an impact. On the basis of surveys conducted immediately before and after the speech, campaign planners believed it had resulted in a 2.5 percent improvement in Labor's position. That gave them hope again. But two days later came the news of Young's cushy Qantas consultancy, with its obvious conflict of interest, and NSW Labor was plunged into pessimism again.

Within the party, Hawke is also being blamed for the bitter factional wrangle over the post of national secretary which has produced a week of extremely damaging headlines. Hawke seems to have put his dislike of Bob Hogg ahead of Labor's best interests.

Inevitably, too, there is muttering about the amount of time Hawke spends on the golf course these days. A growing number of ALP people see it as evidence that he is not giving his job the attention it requires.

Members of all factions condemn Hawke's clumsy handling of the privatisation issue.

Keating has provided an interesting contrast to Hawke. The Treasurer has hardly opened his mouth on privatisation, leaving the Prime Minister to cop the flak. Keating has let it be known that he considers Hogg would make a perfectly acceptable ALP national secretary.

The Treasurer has been displaying an increasing interest in social justice issues and toning down his hardline economic rationalism. The result is that even Labor left-wingers now look favourably on him. On top of this, he has started trotting out his wife, Annita, as part of an effort to present a more human image. It is working.

Labor sources say Cameron has no doubt now that Keating's image would be altered sufficiently for him to become a viable leader. It could only be done properly, however, if he were no longer Treasurer. As Prime Minister, he could be repackaged in a way which would be electorally acceptable. As that view gains currency in the ALP, it could put a great deal of pressure on Hawke.

Andrew Peacock, a shrewd observer of political wheeling and dealing, has told Liberal Party colleagues he believes Hawke will retire by November this year. His reasoning is that things will get tougher, Hawke will conclude that the game is not worth the candle and quit while he is still seen as a successful leader. If Keating decides that that kind of situation can be engineered, he will presumably abandon any thought of retirement himself.

Voting 'No' to waffle

10 April 1988

The enormous swing to the Liberals in the Groom by-election prompts a heretical thought: What if all those Queensland voters actually approved of John Elliott's straight-talking on the consumption tax issue? By all the accepted rules of politics – rules accepted in this country, anyway – the Liberal president's assertion that a consumption tax is essential should have lost votes. The divisions it caused, particularly between Elliott and the federal parliamentary leader of the party, John Howard, should also have alienated support. Why that did not happen is an intriguing question.

The intervention of Sir Joh Bjelke-Petersen on the side of the Liberals may provide part of the answer. Voter disapproval of the Queensland National Party's attempts to scuttle the federal coalition no doubt also contributed significantly. But something more had to be involved. The central issue in the campaign was the consumption tax debate sparked by Elliott – and it clearly did the Liberal cause no damage at all.

Elliott infuriates professional politicians like Howard because he says what he means, bluntly and without qualification. He does not hedge or sit on the fence or lie or try to please everyone, the way almost all politicians from all parties tend to do these days. It is unlikely that the voters of Groom want a consumption tax. But in the light of the by-election result it seems distinctly possible that they were attracted rather than alienated by Elliott's forthright style.

The Elliott honesty contrasted sharply with the mealy-mouthed approach of federal National Party leader Ian Sinclair. Increasingly 'Sinkers' seems incapable of stating a firm position on anything. Howard, too, rarely has the courage to say what he really thinks. Before he became party leader he was respected for his candour, regarded as a politician willing to push policies because they were right rather than popular. But his attempt to buy a win in last year's federal election showed he has changed.

There is growing evidence that voters are turned off by the waffle and hypocrisy they have been getting from politicians. The election of seven independents to the New South Wales Legislative Assembly in last month's state election was part of it. Elliott may have tapped into this, to the benefit of his party.

At the very least, by speaking his mind he did not cost the Liberals the by-election – as Howard and other senior Liberal MPs feared. Howard must now feel a little silly about the macho display he put up in the week before the Groom vote, hauling Elliott over the coals for raising the consumption tax issue. A fortnight earlier, when the Liberal president first made his comments, Howard's public view was that Elliott had done nothing wrong.

Bob Hawke has a similar problem to Howard's. Before becoming prime minister, Hawke was outspoken, in the Elliott mould. Because he said what he thought – or appeared to – people decided he was honest. Gradually, however, Hawke has lost that image. He has become another glib, smooth-talking politician who strings phrases together so that they sound impressive but mean little. As a result market research by political pollsters shows that voters no longer trust Hawke in the way they once did.

This is undoubtedly a major factor in the 'communications problem' which Hawke and other senior ALP strategists blame for the dramatic decline in Labor's electoral fortunes. Another factor – although Paul Keating denies it – is the use of economic jargon by the Treasurer and, to a lesser extent, the Prime Minister. Keating is much more adept at communicating with the readers of *The Australian Financial Review* than with the ordinary voters who buy Sydney's *Daily Telegraph* or *The Sun* in Melbourne.

There was a classic demonstration of this at a Keating news conference in Canberra on March 15, four days before the vital NSW election. Keating wanted to exploit the latest economic figures to help Barrie Unsworth and the NSW ALP. It should be noted, the Treasurer said, that 'the expectations data for 1988–89 showed real growth in plant and equipment of about 10 percent over the year'. That would have had them on the edges of their seats in Sydney's western suburbs. He went on: 'And I'll just mention one other factor, and that is in the disaggregation of some recent data into the investment share of those industries classified as tradeables.'

At that point Keating looked up and noticed that the cameras were no longer recording his immortal words. Only then did it dawn on him that the jargon he was using made his statements politically pointless. With a sheepish grin he said: 'When we get on to disaggregations you can switch the TVs off. For 9, 7 and 10, I know they have already been switched off.'

Keating and Hawke would do well to read (or re-read) part of the book *Afternoon Light* by the late Sir Robert Menzies in which he recalls how, invited into Winston Churchill's study one night during the war, he was able to study how the great orator prepared his speeches. Churchill was dictating to a secretary.

'While he was playing around with what might be called the "first draft" of a sentence, trying each word for weight and simplicity, he spoke in a low voice, almost a whisper,' Menzies wrote. 'When he arrived at a final version he spoke up, and down went the sentence into type. Thus I would just hear, "And so the struggle will continue, continue? until victory – has been achieved…no, no –" and then out it came: "And so we will fight on until the day has come!"'

Menzies commented: 'How many of us think in words of one syllable, only to succumb, when we speak, to the debased modern passion for long words and turgid sentences. Winston reversed the process.' Churchill was a great communicator. If a politician of Menzies' calibre could learn from him, so can Keating and Hawke.

The horrible House on the hill

17 May 1988

'It is comparable to nothing, this Parliament House. Its long firm lines have grace and strength and character; its windows and doors are purposeful things, and they suggest to us that great and mighty things are happening inside, that destinies are being wrought, and a nation made, and great faiths upheld, and terrible wrongs being righted, and tyrannies being destroyed...In future years we may remember this strong white building, and its sense of poise and majesty and purpose, with a feeling of pride and strength.'

Warren Denning, one of the early greats of Australian political journalism, wrote those words about the so-called 'provisional' Parliament House back in the 1930s, in his wonderful book *Capital City*. Like many people who have been involved with politics for a long time, I share Denning's view of the old building, soon to be superseded by the ostentatious billion-dollar-plus *new* Parliament House opened by the Queen this week but still several months away from being functional.

In recent days, quite a few of Denning's successors in the press gallery – and a host of colour writers, and TV anchor-persons – have waxed just as poetic about the strange construction which has grown up where Capital Hill used to be. It has been hailed as an architectural masterpiece, Australia's finest public building, stunning, breathtaking, an international drawcard, greater than the Opera House...The hyperbole has been endless.

There has been hardly a hint of disapproval. It is almost as though knocking a building that has cost taxpayers so much is somehow unpatriotic. But I, for one, when I look at the world's first subterranean legislature, do not think of mighty things occurring inside, faiths being upheld and wrongs righted and destinies wrought. I think of pretentious politicians trying to make themselves seem important, and governments aloof from and looking down on the people they rule. I think of pomposity and self-aggrandisement and nest-feathering rather than strength or pride or purpose.

It is not, to my eye, an attractive building. The massive four-legged flagpole which towers above the national capital is hideous – a great squatting insect. Some grace and character may be discernible when the building is approached from the front, but from other angles it looks like a factory – bottle-green windows in concrete-grey walls. I disagree with Ian Macphee's contention that the decision to conceal the new parliament inside a hill reflects the Australian cringe. Given that an American architectural firm was responsible for the design, it is more likely to say something about US attitudes towards this country. But, whatever the subconscious message, a buried building is undeniably eccentric.

Inside, the public areas are awe-inspiring, and that is exactly what is intended. The aim is to produce a feeling of awe in mere mortals who stray into the building, so that they will understand how very important are the permanent occupants – senators and MHR. Ordinary voters are meant to be intimidated by the vast spaces, the forest of pillars, the grand staircases – made to see just how insignificant they are by comparison with their rulers.

And naturally there is to be no contact between governed and governors. In the old building, parliamentarians and tourists mingle in Kings Hall. The minister for transport and communications, making his way from the cabinet room to the Senate, can be bailed up by a visitor (or a busload of visitors) from Wangaratta. In the new House, MHRs and senators will be segregated from the public. Voters will be able to see but not get near. And backbenchers will have much less contact with ministers, quarantined in a special executive wing. Anyone who believes the standard of government is likely to be improved by isolating ministers even more than they are now is sadly misguided.

And of course the access journalists have to politicians will be greatly reduced. The 'provisional' Parliament House is so compact and crowded with MPs, ministers, staff and journalists all thrown together that it is possible to sense even without being told when there is drama in cabinet or the party room. Secrecy is very difficult. The intimacy of the building contributes far more to open government than the *Freedom of Information Act* has ever done. Ministers trying to avoid questioning on controversial issues cannot get away from media stake-outs on the various doors. In the new Parliament House, by contrast, it will be possible – simple, in fact – for ministers to dodge the media. The public's right to know will be downgraded.

Some of those involved in the political process, of course, will regard this as a very good thing. Paul Keating is one who believes the 'hothouse atmosphere' of the old building has not been conducive to efficient government. I have heard him argue persuasively that the country would be better off if ministers did not work out of Parliament House at all but operated from their departments, as British ministers do.

It may be that, with ministers working in splendid isolation in their own wing of the high-tech palace under the hill, largely undistracted by voters, backbenchers, the media and other nuisances, the nation *will* be administered more efficiently. But government will not be as responsive or as answerable as it is at the moment.

1989

The fall of a super hero

28 February 1989

When the Treasurer faced the media after the release of the latest disastrous balance of payments figures, he looked and sounded like the Paul Keating of old. He appeared confident, he grinned, he bantered with journalists. It was a typically self-assured performance. But this time, the impact on his audience is different.

Afterwards, in the second floor corridors of the Senate wing of Parliament House, where the press gallery offices are located, members of the fourth estate were chuckling about the event. People who not very long ago approached Keating with something like awe had not taken seriously his attempt to convince them that, despite the spate of unfavourable figures, the economy was still basically OK and the government's strategy was still on track.

The hero worship of the Treasurer is no more. Keating is losing – perhaps he has already lost – the power to mesmerise journalists reporting on politics and economics in Canberra. He is also losing – though he may not understand it yet – the power to bully them. Keating is no longer seen as larger-than-life. Increasingly, he is regarded as just another politician and treated accordingly.

It is possible to discern a similar change in attitude towards the Treasurer among Labor MPs. It is most noticeable among members of what used to be his own faction, the right wing. Keating left the faction in a fit of pique after his ill-fated attempt to pressure Bob Hawke out of the prime ministership last year. Colleagues say it came as a terrible blow to Keating's ego when he found that, in a showdown with Hawke, he could expect no more than three members of the Right to throw in their lot with him. And they would have required some arm-twisting.

Now, right-wingers who previously took it for granted that Keating would inherit the leadership when Hawke was ready to quit, are no longer quite so sure. The way he has treated former factional colleagues has caused resentment. There are doubts about his judgment. The way he behaved when Hawke turned the screws has caused some concern about his reaction to pressure.

'You should not rule out the possibility that Paul has abandoned his leadership aspirations,' says a senior member of the Right. 'I think all that really drives him now is his absolute detestation for John Howard, his determination to stop Howard becoming prime minister at all costs.' The departure of Keating's main political adviser, Seamus Dawes, to join a merchant banking firm has given weight to the view that Keating's drive for the top has lost momentum.

Hatred of an opponent can be a dangerous motivation for a politician. Clear-thinking, not emotion, is required from someone in Keating's position. Loathing for the Liberal leader was obviously behind at least one recent Keating miscalculation – his botched attempt late last year to pre-empt the launch of Howard's *Future Directions* manifesto.

The Treasurer summoned journalists to a news conference, berated them for not pursuing Howard fiercely enough on the cost of his premises and distributed his own costing which was so rubbery it provoked nothing short of incredulity from the press gallery. It also undermined Keating's credibility, something a Treasurer can ill-afford. To Keating's astonishment – and fury – the gallery not only declined to carry out his instructions but subjected him to an unpleasant hour of impertinent questioning. He had sought to set the dogs on Howard, and got bitten himself. Keating's poisonous attitude to Howard was also behind a comment in an end-of-year interview which had fellow ministers shaking their heads in disbelief. The Treasurer described himself and Hawke as a couple of black widow spiders spinning a web to entrap the opposition leader. Presumably he intended to strike fear in the hearts of coalition MPs but it had the opposite effect. They saw it as bravado and were amused. Those around Hawke were decidedly unamused. The image of the government's leaders as venomous spiders is not likely to be electorally popular and popularity is something Hawke cares about, even if Keating does not.

It is Hawke's personal popularity which gives Labor some hope of surviving the next federal election. In a close contest, Labor MPs believe, the Prime Minister's high approval rating compared with Howard's lack of popularity will give Labor the edge. But that theory is worthless if Hawke's popularity is cancelled out by public dislike of the Treasurer.

Now that the economy refuses to do as it is told, the pressure on Keating is increasing. Many who admired him in the good old days when his budget estimates usually proved to be spot on, realise he is fallible. The super-hero aura has gone. And, with demands for policy changes coming from all directions, he is in danger of appearing isolated and stubborn.

Eventually, Keating's approach to the current economic problems may be proved right. I suspect it will. In political terms, there would be very little for the government to gain and a great deal to lose if Keating accepted the advice of the economics writers – and the opposition – to further slash public spending. In the build-up to an election, that would be crazy. The government has alienated enough interest groups already. Using monetary policy as Keating is doing has one great political virtue – the government has the ability to force interest rates down again to suit its electoral timetable.

Given their past performance, it has to be assumed that Keating and ACTU secretary Bill Kelty will put together a wage and tax deal which the unions will buy and which will be reasonably responsible economically. And the tax cuts will be put in place from July 1 no matter what.

No one, of course, should write Keating off yet. He is tough, shrewd, and – when he wants to be – personally engaging. Just the same, it is not hard to see why there is suddenly so much interest in the Labor Party in getting Simon Crean out of ACTU presidency and into parliament. There is definitely a need to have an alternative available.

A lesson too late for the learning

16 May 1989

On the day Ian Macphee was dumped by the Liberal Party as its candidate for the Victorian seat of Goldstein, John Howard moved to pre-empt the inevitable criticism. 'This suggestion about the Liberal Party and the New Right is gibberish,' he said. Unfortunately for his credibility, however, one of the most notorious and uncompromising members of the New Right, Charles Copeman, was at his elbow when he made the statement.

It was a measure of Howard's lack of political touch that he chose that day, of all days, to open the office Copeman will use as the endorsed Liberal candidate for the Sydney seat of Phillip. Macphee and his supporters had blamed the New Right for the assault on his preselection. It was obvious to anyone even remotely interested in politics that Macphee's defeat would make the New Right's influence on the Liberal Party a potentially damaging issue.

Howard was sufficiently aware of that to realise he had to issue a denial. But he was apparently too politically dense to understand that doing so at a function for Copeman sent a quite contradictory message. Howard's presence on the hustings for Copeman was a signal which effectively cancelled out the impact of his words. A smart politician would have gone somewhere else that day. Or stayed at home.

But Howard lacks political smarts to a surprising degree. That is one of the lessons of the Macphee affair. He mishandled it about

25

as badly as any leader could have done. Doing nothing in the early stages was inept. Getting involved in a last-minute intervention aimed at buying Macphee off with the possibility of a Senate seat was embarrassingly clumsy.

Howard was able to portray himself as an innocent victim of the coalition divisions which killed any chance of a L/NP victory at the 1987 election, but if the mess in Victoria helps Labor survive next time, he will rightly get much of the blame. The truth, of course, is that despite Howard's denials, the Victorian preselections were evidence of the growing influence of the New Right in the Liberal Party. Dr David Kemp, who beat Macphee, is a prominent New Right figure, barrister Peter Costello, who defeated moderate Roger Shipton for the Higgins preselection became a New Right hero in the Dollar Sweets case, when he used common law to force unionists – under threat of gaol sentences – to lift a picket line. Victorian Liberal president Michael Kroger, a close friend of both Kemp and Costello, is part of the New Right push.

And so is Howard to a degree – though he shies away from the label. 'The Liberal Party is owned by nobody,' he said at the Copeman office opening. 'We have a broad ideological membership.' But there is an unmistakable narrowing of the range of ideological positions the Liberal Party is willing to tolerate. Howard has contributed to that. And, while the New Right certainly does not own the party, it is doing its darnedest to gain control.

'These people are constructing a party that will be unelectable,' a Liberal of the old school complained on that day after Macphee got the chop. There is something in that. The unadorned New Right philosophy – minimal government activity, let the market reign supreme – has little electoral appeal. That is why Howard was so keen to dress it up in the garb of his *Future Directions* platitudes.

Australian Democrat leader Janine Haines no doubt exaggerated the extent to which the Liberal Party has moved to the Right when she described it as 'off the planet'. But, by dumping Macphee the Liberals made it easier for the Democrats, not to mention Labor, to push that line. The Democrats could benefit handsomely.

Already over the last six months, according to the Morgan Gallup Poll, support for the Democrats has increased from six percent to

10 percent. Liberal voters who share the progressive, tolerant, compassionate views of Macphee and his ilk may conclude that the Democrats now reflect their views more accurately than the Liberals do. Earlier this year, the federal executive of the Democrats approved a strategy paper recommending that the party should concentrate its efforts on attracting disillusioned Labor voters. Following the Macphee fiasco, targeting disillusioned Liberals could prove to be more productive.

Howard was not part of any conspiracy to get rid of Macphee, but he indirectly encouraged those in the Liberal Party tempted to mount a purge of the so-called 'wets'. A wink is as good as a nod in politics. When Howard refused to re-admit NSW senator Peter Baume to the shadow cabinet it was a clear signal that the Liberal leader did not want such people around him. Since Baume, a former minister, is a man of unarguable talent as well as great decency, there was no other explanation.

Leaving ideology aside, there are important machinery lessons for the Liberals to learn from the whole sorry chapter. Had such a drama occurred in the Labor Party it would not have got out of hand. The ALP's national executive would have intervened as it has done on a number of occasions where preselection battles threatened to create damaging divisions. The most recent example was the takeover of the entire preselection process for the NSW state seat of Liverpool. Now federal officers of the party are overseeing all federal ALP pre-selections in NSW.

This is not possible under the Liberal Party's current structure. Its executive does not have the power to move in on a state branch and override its rules or decisions. One of the reasons Labor has been so electorally successful in the last decade has been the national executive's ability and willingness to move quickly and decisively in such cases. While the Liberals retain their old-fashioned structure, they will be at a serious disadvantage.

An idea from the Canberra hothouse

6 June 1989

Because of the Australian electorate's renowned hostility towards proposals for constitutional change, governments normally shy away from holding referendums at the same time as election campaigns. The Hawke government, though, could break that rule when it next goes to the polls. In its all-out bid for a fourth term, the government may well gamble on a referendum proving an electoral plus.

The idea has not yet been discussed with the Prime Minister. But Environment Minister Graham Richardson, whose political savvy Hawke respects, has floated a trial balloon. A week after the Tasmanian election, which saw Green independents win the balance of power, Richardson said a referendum might eventually be necessary to give the federal government constitutional power to deal with the Greenhouse Effect.

Richardson mentioned no timeframe and gave the impression that he was thinking long-term. But senior Labor colleagues say he has in mind the possibility of running such a referendum in conjunction with the election expected to be held in the first half of next year. The aim would be to capitalise on growing community concern about the environment and, in the process, divide the opposition on an issue that could have a crucial bearing on the election outcome.

It might be a shrewd ploy. The political potency of environmental issues is obviously growing, and Greenhouse is the daddy of them all. The potential consequences of global warming are so massive that voters of all ages and in all walks of life are concerned about it. No other environmental issue is so all-encompassing or so alarming.

The next federal election campaign will undoubtedly be dominated by questions of economic management. The hip-pocket nerve will, as usual, be paramount. But, with a referendum to focus attention on it, the Greenhouse Effect could also influence a significant number of votes. In a tight election, perhaps it could be decisive.

Whatever happens, environmentalists will have an impact on the next campaign. But the government has no doubt they will do much more – that they will run candidates for the Senate and probably contest Lower House seats too. Those Green candidates would be backed by a coordinated, well-funded campaign, modelled on the one which proved so successful in Tasmania.

In NSW, for example, Peter Garrett has indicated privately that he would be available to run for the Senate as long as the election is not held this year. (Midnight Oil, the rock group for which he is lead singer, will be fully occupied until December recording a new album.) Riding the new wave of environmental concern, Garrett would probably be a shoo-in. Green Senate candidates would have good chances in other states, too – at the expense of the Australian Democrats.

The government is not worried about the Senate. It is the House of Representatives that matters: Green independents' preferences could be vital. Where there are no Green candidates, their national campaign will still make the environment an issue and major parties will by vying directly for the support of environmentally concerned voters.

That is where a referendum on the Greenhouse Effect would be important. It would demonstrate in a fairly dramatic way the Labor government's bona fides on the environment. In that regard, it would almost certainly be more effective than the major statement on the environment Hawke has foreshadowed, even in the unlikely event that it proves to be – as the Prime Minister modestly claimed – 'the most comprehensive statement that any government in the world is able to make'.

A referendum giving the federal government power to override state rights and legislation in combating the Greenhouse Effect would represent action, not simply words. The Greens would support it enthusiastically. It would decide the question of preferences, especially if the conservative parties opposed the referendum or were split on the issue. And can anyone believe that will not be the case?

A commitment to states' rights is too deeply ingrained in Liberal and National party philosophy for them to give united support to such a referendum proposal. Combined with the straight-out anti-greenie sentiment so strong among the Nationals and in the New Right faction of the Liberal Party, it would guarantee brawls and divisions in coalition ranks. Opposition environment spokesman Chris Puplick claimed recently that, under Andrew Peacock, the coalition would be prepared to override states' rights to protect the environment. A Greenhouse referendum would give Puplick a fascinating chance to put his money where his mouth is.

Importantly, there is an overwhelmingly strong case for the federal government to seek extra powers to deal with the crisis that Greenhouse threatens to become – so a referendum on the issue could not be portrayed as just a cynical political ploy. As Richardson said when he floated the idea, 'I don't think Australians want to risk having six states, two territories and a Commonwealth come up with nine solutions for something that will affect the way that Australians live and work for generations to come.'

The fact is that the federal government has to rely on a grab-bag of unrelated powers in the constitution to take any action – the foreign affairs power, the trade and commerce power, even the defence power. In dealing with something as serious as the Greenhouse Effect, this is clearly not good enough.

The miseries of an MP's wife

20 June 1989

When the wife of an Australian Democrat senator goes shopping, people feel they have the right to peer into her supermarket trolley and criticise her purchases on environmental grounds. She finds the intrusion on her privacy infuriating. The wife of a Liberal MP says she turned into a crying, shrieking shrew in the early years of her husband's parliamentary career. She could not handle the loneliness. And the husband of a woman parliamentarian is getting tired of jokes about his status. He is frequently referred to as 'Dennis', a sarcastic allusion to the husband of British Prime Minister Margaret Thatcher.

Little is heard about the spouses of our politicians but their lot is not a happy one. At least, there are aspects of the life of a parliamentarian's partner which take a lot of getting used to. Some spouses never learn to cope. Politicians' children are affected, too. Now the issue is being brought out of the closet. A seminar for the wives and husbands (mostly wives) of MHRs and senators will be held in Canberra at the start of the next parliamentary session on the subject of 'The Opportunities and Difficulties, Struggles and Joys of Being a Parliamentarian's Partner'. The emphasis is on difficulties and struggles.

It is an all-party affair. Hazel Hawke, the Prime Minister's wife, will open proceedings. Angela Chaney, wife of the deputy opposition leader, will be closing speaker. National Party and Australian Democrat wives are on the organising committee. And discussion will be led by an expert in inter-personal relationships, occupational therapist Penelope Coombes. 'I'll be talking about commuter marriages and how they can work,' she says, adding that political marriages pose particular challenges. 'We taxpayers are very unclear about what we expect of MPs' partners.'

One of the organisers, Diana Carlton, whose husband Jim is shadow defence minister, says the seminar will not be a whinge session. The aim is to be positive, to share ideas on how the problem of being a politician's partner can be overcome. 'I was a slow learner,' she says. 'I thought it was time we did something to help the younger, newer wives especially.' According to Jennie Macklin, wife of Australian Democrat senator Michael: 'The important thing is to know you are not the only one finding it difficult. Everyone does.'

Talk to the partners of parliamentarians and it becomes clear why there are so many broken political marriages. The marvel is that there are not more. It is not only that MHRs and senators are away in Canberra for so much of the time, leaving their spouses to raise the children and cope with domestic emergencies alone – though that is demoralising enough. But there is also a loss of privacy and personal freedom. And, to a surprising degree, there is animosity – including, sometimes, death threats.

Diana Carlton's seminar paper will be called *When the Crying Had to Stop*. She says that, when her husband became an MP, she suddenly found life unbelievably lonely. And, for the first time in her life, she encountered personal hostility. 'Overnight I was crying and shrieking,' she recalls. 'Jim offered to give up politics. But I couldn't let him do that. He'd wanted to go into parliament for years.' The turning point came when she went on an Outward Bound course in Queensland. Ten days of white-water rafting and trudging through the bush with a heavy pack, doing a lot of thinking while roughing it alone, helped her come to terms with the new life. 'I've grown a few extra skins now,' she says. 'And I've realised the need for Jim and I to make the most of every moment together.'

Jennie Macklin's talk will be called 'What Did We Win, Mummy?' That is the question their six-year-old daughter asked when Michael was elected to the Senate. From a family standpoint, it was not much of a prize. 'I've grown to be a stronger person, because my husband is never home,' says Jennie. 'And the children and I are much closer, because we suffer things together.' If they are the positives, the negatives must be corkers.

'The animosity you face as a member of a politician's family is extraordinary,' she says. 'There are abusive phone calls. And this week I've had a large plastic bag of household rubbish dumped at the front gate – the third time it's happened. I don't know what message this person is trying to send.'

The animosity, she says, puts immense strains on the children of parliamentarians. The sins of the fathers really are visited on them. Other children are told not to play with them. Teachers berate them over political issues. The children of ministers suffer most but backbenchers' offspring have a hard time, too.

The titles of other papers give the flavour of the seminar. Belinda Lamb, wife of a Labor MP, has chosen the topic *May Sanity Prevail*. Robin Mackellar, a Liberal wife, will call hers *Keeping the Ship Afloat*. In the words of one of the organisers: 'A lot of us got tired of hearing how we're ripping off the country. We need to get together and say it's not like that.'

But the token male on the speakers' list, Tony Vanstone, who is married to a Liberal senator, concedes the situation is much worse for the wives of parliamentarians than for husbands. 'I get sick of being called Dennis,' he says. 'And the life does impose strains on a marriage. But when Amanda's away in Canberra, people feel sorry for me and invite me to dinner. It's a lot easier for me than for the political wives stuck at home with kids.'

According to Penelope Coombes, there is research suggesting that there can be advantages in commuter marriages. Sometimes a spouse can develop her (or his) own talents and interests better away from a more powerful partner. But Coombes stresses the need for what she calls 'quality spouse time' in such marriages. 'The partners of parliamentarians have restricted free air travel to Canberra,' she says. 'They're allowed only nine trips a year. That's crazy. We should make it as easy as possible for parliamentarians and their partners to get together as often as possible. As a taxpayer, I feel embarrassed that we don't do that.'

1990

Keating shows backbone to Button

22 May 1990

The federal government reached a turning point with Paul Keating's massive public put-down of Industry and Commerce Minister John Button. As Keating said after dropping his bucket on the third most senior member of cabinet, it was overdue. Remarkable indulgence has been shown to Button in the seven years since Labor came to power, partly because he is likeable, more importantly because his role in forcing Bill Hayden from the leadership put Bob Hawke deeply in his debt. That indulgence is now ended.

Button went too far in giving credibility to Peter Walsh's criticisms of economic policy. It is one thing to have Walsh sniping from the back bench. It is quite another to have a serving minister of Button's seniority and standing, occupying a key economic portfolio, agreeing that the government had squandered opportunities for micro-economic reform, that only a marginal improvement was likely in the current account deficit in the foreseeable future, and the economic prospects were generally bleak. Button's comments amounted to an admission – as the opposition pointed out – that Labor had won the election on false pretences.

For the Treasurer it was clearly an intolerable situation. By telling Button some home truths via a news conference rather than in private, Keating precipitated a political crisis. But those who matter in the ministry and in caucus believe that was far better than the erosion of economic credibility that has been underway since the new ministry was sworn in. And for Keating there was a strong personal consideration. Walsh had been quoted four days before as saying Keating's prime ministerial aspirations were under threat because he was 'too closely associated with failed economic policies'. Ironically, until Monday's showdown, Button was regarded as a foundation member of the 'Keating for Prime Minister' push.

Defence Minister and right-wing factional heavyweight Robert Ray remarked that it was not unusual for a period of undisciplined conduct within government to follow an election. The same happened, he recalled, after Labor's 1987 victory. But such lack of discipline cannot be allowed to continue. Keating, it has to be said, has shown remarkable patience. For weeks there has been a running commentary from various ministers about the state of the economy, and he has held his tongue. One of those who has spoken outside his own portfolio – urging a speed-up of micro-economic reform and echoing some of Walsh's points – was Education and Training Minister John Dawkins. Keating is fond of Dawkins, who acted as campaign manager in his unsuccessful bid to replace Hawke two years ago, so it was no surprise that the Treasurer made no public response in that case. But Button is a long-term offender. He has an unenviable reputation as a minister with an undisciplined tongue, a politician prone to gaffes. He has a record of making statements embarrassing to the government, even during election campaigns.

In the last campaign Button made a fool of himself – and hurt the government – when, at a news conference to launch a new export incentive scheme, he was shown to have no understanding of the costing. Often his gaffes result from his failure to show discipline by getting across the government line on a particular issue. When the rest of the government had adopted a formula to deal with the potentially damaging Labor leadership question in the run-up to the election, for example, it was Button who made it a live issue by suggesting Hawke and Keating had done a deal over the succession. More recently Button helped the opposition and contradicted Keating by saying a consumption tax was on the agenda and had to be considered.

What particularly irks Keating and others is that, while he is giving gratuitous advice to the rest of the government, Button is not exactly performing well in his own portfolio. It is impossible to argue with the message Keating has now sent to him and other ministers tempted to behave in a similar manner – namely, that there are enough hard decisions to be made in each area of cabinet responsibility without anyone needing to go outside their own bailiwick. If everyone, including Button, did their own jobs properly, the kind of comments which have been getting headlines for Peter Walsh would have far less credibility.

It is an open secret at senior levels of the government that Button intends to step down from the ministry next year. It would be a good thing for the government if the clash with Keating caused him to bring forward his timetable. Whether that occurs or not, the affair has enhanced Keating's leadership claims. At a time when caucus was growing twitchy at what looked like a lack of firmness at the top, it was Keating – with the added authority of the deputy prime ministership – who took a grip on the situation.

But the lack of discipline of the last six weeks has taken its toll. Not only has it created an impression that economic policy is a mess, it has also made the task of ministers such as Kim Beazley, at the sharp end in Transport and Communications, much more difficult than it would otherwise have been. Expectations have been created by Walsh, Dawkins and to some extent Button which are simply not possible to fulfil. The risk is that no matter what Beazley achieves – and, on his past ministerial record it will be considerable – it will be seen as not good enough.

Quietly mastering a difficult art

31 July 1990

For a brief period in his youth, federal Social Security Minister Graham Richardson had ambitions to become a stand-up comedian. He even made an appearance on the talent-spotting TV show *New Faces*. So, when he was invited recently to act as guest host of the Seven network's *Tonight Live with Steve Vizard*, the producers did not have to twist his arm very hard. But Richardson wisely decided not to use the occasion to score political points, which meant he had to reject a one-liner suggested to him by comedian friend Brian Doyle – to wit: 'John Hewson had to be careful in choosing a deputy. He needed someone less exciting than himself who was still alive.'

It would have been an accurate jab at both the opposition leader and his sidekick Peter Reith. But, as the opinion polls show, being unexciting is not doing Hewson any damage with the electorate. Quite the contrary. Voters are reassured by his sober, matter-of-fact approach and his lack of grandstanding. They prefer his low-key style to the hype and phoney aggression usually associated with politics in this country.

Hewson – consciously or unconsciously – is following the advice of that political master and founder of the Liberal Party, Sir Robert Menzies. Twenty years ago, in his book *The Measure of the Years*, Menzies penned a chapter he titled 'The Gentle Art of Opposition' in which he disagreed profoundly with Lord Randolph Churchill's well-known edict that 'the duty of an opposition is to oppose'. According to Menzies: '...the duty of an opposition, if it has no ambition to be permanently on the left-hand side of the Speaker, is not just to oppose for opposition's sake but to oppose selectively. No government is always wrong on everything, whatever the critics may say. The opposition must choose the ground on which it is to attack. To attack indiscriminately is to risk public opinion, which has a reserve of fairness not always understood.'

That Hewson agrees was shown by his response to Bob Hawke's National Press Club speech on plans to improve the working of Australia's federal system. It was a good speech, stressing the need for cooperation between the state and federal governments and between the major political parties. From Hawke's standpoint, it was also good politics. The Prime Minister always looks best when he goes down the road of consensus and conciliation. The initiative is timely and important. It gives Hawke's fourth term a sense of direction that was lacking. And it gives a new relevance to Hawke himself, which may help to subdue speculation about the need for a leadership change.

The opposition leader could have carped and criticised, as one or two of his unreconstructed colleagues did. Instead, he reacted constructively, announcing that the coalition would 'support sensible initiatives to speed up the process of reform and adjustment to make Australia more efficient and reduce the size of government'.

Attempts to modernise Australian federalism, of course, have come to very little. They have been strangled by an unthinking adherence to 'states' rights' slogans and by petty-minded politicians seeking an advantage over their opponents. But this time, as a senior government source said after Hawke's Press Club performance, 'we've got a chance of succeeding because Hewson is there'.

Former Whitlam minister Clyde Cameron, in his just-published and fascinating book *The Cameron Diaries*, records in his entry for Wednesday May 5, 1976: 'During today's Caucus meeting, someone asked Gough whether the Party's attitude towards the Bill under discussion should be "responsible" or "political". Quite clearly he had not anticipated the question, yet he gave the quick and clever reply, "Our responsibility is to play politics". The reply was not only clever, it epitomised his own political style.' Fortunately, it does not epitomise Hewson's. Times have changed. An increasingly cynical and worried electorate would these days be turned off by an opposition playing politics for the sake of it.

To quote Menzies again: 'The great error of the Labor opposition in Australia, under Evatt and then Calwell, was that it tended to live in the past – on old hatreds and shibboleths...fighting old and losing battles about issues long since dead.' Much the same could be said about the Liberal–National Party opposition under John Howard and Andrew Peacock. But in recent months, there have been healthy signs of change – and not just on Hewson's part. The way the Liberals have backed away from their traditional states' rights stance on the environment, conceding at last that it is an area where the federal government must take a leadership role, is the most obvious example of the new thinking but certainly not the only one.

The next big test of the opposition's preparedness to abandon the hypocrisy to which observers of politics have become accustomed will be the federal budget on August 21. With cabinet's Expenditure Review Committee determined to cut federal spending by at least another $1.2 billion, a lot of people will be hurt and a lot of people will be unhappy. Such a situation would have been exploited to the full by an opposition, Liberal or Labor. The Whitlam principle would have been applied automatically. But, given that the opposition has been calling for even tougher spending cuts – $3 billion worth – it would be unashamedly opportunist, not to mention dishonest, for Hewson to suggest that the losers would have fared any better under a coalition government.

It is not as though there is a shortage of issues on which the government is open to attack. The struggle within the government over telecommunications policy, for example, is wide open for exploitation by the opposition.

Treasurer Paul Keating is at odds with Transport and Communications Minister Kim Beazley over what should be done and the split has been aggravated by other ministers going public with different views.

Menzies also called opposition 'the difficult art'. But embarrassing the government on this issue should not be difficult for Hewson at all.

Policy by necessity

4 September 1990

When ALP national secretary Bob Hogg first proposed a special party conference on the issue of privatisation, very few people were aware of the looming crisis over the State Bank of Victoria. But Hogg was one of those few. And he had the matter of the bank very much in mind when he argued that a better mechanism had to be found to allow Labor governments, on occasions, to make decisions possibly outside party policy.

With something as sensitive and important as the future of a bank at stake, it is simply not possible to go through all the rigmarole and lobbying and brawling involved in calling a party conference. Far from saving the institution, such a process would be just about guaranteed to start a run and destroy it.

The problem of Victoria's State Bank was solved in dramatic fashion because a new Labor premier found herself cornered and a federal Labor treasurer had the courage to seize the moment. As a result, the Commonwealth Bank – perhaps the most sacred of Labor's sacred cows – is to be partially privatised by a Labor government, and the ALP left-wingers taking an uncompromising stand against any watering-down of the party's public ownership principle have been unceremoniously run over. Just the same, Hogg's point has been made. Urgent issues can arise which require decisive action not necessarily in accord with Labor's platform and the party would do well to face the fact.

Paul Keating was criticised for doing nothing adventurous in his eighth budget. The press gallery, accustomed to Keating pulling a rabbit out of the hat at budget time, gave him the thumbs down when he failed to do so this time. But the rabbit emerged 48 hours after the budget speech, at the late-night cabinet meeting where the Treasurer presented his plan for the Commonwealth Bank to use private equity to fund acquisition of the State Bank of Victoria.

Contrary to the initial squeals from the Left, there was nothing sneaky about what Keating did. He made no attempt to disguise that partial privatisation of the Commonwealth Bank would be involved. Nor did he browbeat the cabinet. He was – in the words of a minister not normally a Keating fan – 'quietly and exhaustively rational'. His calm dissection of the arguments left cabinet with no alternative than to back his proposal.

Joan Kirner, only weeks after inheriting the Victorian premiership from John Cain, emerged with credit from what was a huge test given her Socialist Left affiliation. She took a big risk in agreeing to Keating's demand that there should be competing tenders for the State Bank. Had federal cabinet not agreed to allow the Commonwealth to bid, or had Westpac's bid been demonstrably better, she would have been in a very difficult position.

As John Button told cabinet, Kirner saw Westpac as the bad fairy and the publicly owned Commonwealth as the good fairy. Letting the bad fairy get hold of the State Bank would just about have blown apart the Victorian ALP.

Right up to the last minute there were fears in Canberra that the Victorian government might wimp on the decision, do nothing, and leave the Reserve Bank to sort out the resulting mess. But Kirner did not wimp. Guided by David White, her Minister for Industry and Economic Planning, she showed the kind of steel that will be necessary if Victoria is to overcome its huge debt problem.

The risk for the federal government is that the Commonwealth takeover of the State Bank has been portrayed – not without accuracy – as a bid by one Labor administration to bail out another that got itself into appalling financial strife. Federal ministers have tried to stay aloof from the economic disaster area that Victoria has become. The attitude of many in the federal ALP has been: 'Too bad. Stuff them! It's their problem.' But it was never a realistic approach. Ultimately federal Labor had to get involved.

Hogg was pivotal in conveying that message to key figures in the federal government. He was convinced that the party's base in Victoria could be so disastrously eroded that it would take decades to rebuild. Much more important, Hogg got to hear about the alarming size of the State Bank's debt problem and knew that the crunch would come when the auditor's reports became public. In talks with Keating,

Prime Minister Bob Hawke and others, he argued that the problem could not be contained in Victoria; that it was too large to isolate; that, when a bank got into trouble, the national government could not turn its back. Keating and Hawke took little convincing. All this behind-the-scenes activity coincided with Hogg's special conference call.

The month that followed saw some breathtaking hypocrisy and duplicity on the part of various leading lights of the Left in Victoria. At the same time as they were involved in secret meetings with the state government – headed by a premier from their own faction – discussing the sale of the State Bank, they were publicly ripping into federal ministers and threatening industrial action over proposals for partial privatisation of publicly owned airlines and competition for Telecom. It was the double standards being displayed by some fellow left-wingers, I believe, which led disillusioned Immigration Minister Gerry Hand to tell party members in his electorate he was likely to leave politics at the next election.

The Left has been badly undermined by the whole affair. As Senator Graham Richardson was quick to point out, now that a Socialist Left Premier has started selling assets because times are tough, the Left is hardly in a position to tell a right-wing federal government it cannot do the same. The unbendingly hard line the Left has been following in preparation for the conference on September 24 is now untenable. If federal cabinet is careful about what it asks of the conference – perhaps settling for a Commonwealth Bank-style partial sale of Australian Airlines rather than demanding full privatisation, for example – the Left will find it difficult to take the high moral ground. Certainly, the banks affair has changed the ALP's privatisation debate dramatically.

Six months ago, if anyone suggested the ALP would take privatisation by the throat this year, there would have been guffaws or stunned silence. Partly by accident, the whole thing has been accelerated enormously. Not even the driest of Labor's economic rationalists would have included the Commonwealth Bank on a list of privatisation priorities. It was regarded as off limits, untouchable – until necessity reared its ugly head.

Events have moved so quickly that the Labor Party is bewildered, even traumatised. But, as a prominent left-winger said resignedly on the eve of the special meeting of federal Labor MPs called to discuss the Commonwealth Bank/State Bank deal: 'They might not like it, but I don't see how they can lump it.'

'Mr Squiggle' is too blunt

27 November 1990

Paul Keating last week gave his definition of leadership. Attacking federal opposition leader John Hewson, the Treasurer told parliament: 'Leadership is about getting decisions through. That's what politicians are here for – getting the mail through, making the decisions stick and not lying over like a dirty dog.'

A few days later, on television, Hewson explained *his* view of the leadership role. 'I think leadership is, in part, pushing on occasions,' he said. 'And in part it's listening.' To a degree, of course, Hewson was making a virtue of necessity. He needed a description that explained and excused his failure to get party room endorsement for his recommendation that the opposition support the government's proposed family allowance assets test. But the point he made was valid.

There *is* more to leadership than getting your own way, forcing others to bow to your will. Keating's failure to recognise that is one of the reasons some people in the Labor Party, otherwise well-disposed towards him, have reservations about how he would perform as prime minister. Keating's style is to ram things through. He tramples over people. He wipes his feet on any opposition whether in parliament, the cabinet, the party or the electorate.

That is not to say that he does not use logical argument and seductive persuasion. The Treasurer is the Mr Squiggle of politics with the big white board in his office on which he draws diagrams and graphs to simplify issues for colleagues and, on occasions, journalists. But when that fails, it's war. The cabinet and party row over telecommunications policy showed how ruthless and unremitting he can be, even when it is clear he will not win and continuing the fight may damage the government.

On the other hand, a leader who lacks the strength to impose his will on his party when issues are sufficiently important is no leader at all. That is the way Keating and Prime Minister Bob Hawke are trying to portray Hewson. He is 'pathetically weak', says Hawke; 'a shiver looking for a spine to run up', says Keating, stealing the line from former New Zealand prime minister Sir Robert Muldoon. But the party room setback that prompted the government attack was not evidence of a lack of leadership authority on Hewson's part.

Had he regarded the issue as sufficiently important, he could certainly have bent coalition MPs to his will – especially since there are no votes at such meetings. At the end of the debate, Hewson could have declared: 'We'll stand by the shadow cabinet decision.' No one would have taken him on. Hewson has done it on other issues where debate was just as vehement and feelings just as strong. The problem was not weakness. It was naivete. Hewson did not realise the symbolic importance of failing to carry the day on an issue involving a cut in government spending – the way it would be set against his repeated calls for more spending cuts and used to undermine his credibility. Also, and incredibly, he did not expect the party room to leak. In other words, his inexperience caught up with him. That was all.

Most Liberals – including some who thought it was a mistake to make him leader after the March election defeat – are very impressed by the way Hewson is handling the job. In his dealings with coalition MPs, individually as well as collectively, he has shown more strength than any leader since Malcolm Fraser. And, unlike Fraser, Hewson has good personal relationships even with those who differ with him ideologically. 'He is showing first-rate management, including personnel management,' says a former Liberal critic. 'It's just that there's not quite enough political appreciation yet.' Presumably, that will come – especially with the kind of education in the realities of politics that Hewson received at the hands of the government and the media last week.

By the weekend, some shrewd Labor Party operators thought they could already detect a change in Hewson. After watching him interviewed on the Nine network's *Sunday* program, one of them commented that he had begun using the kind of equivocations and rationalisations and glib lines that are grist to the mill of professional politicians. 'The good doctor's now been dragged into the mainstream of politics,' he said, comparing Hewson's loss of innocence with what happened to John Howard when the need for compromise cost him his 'Honest John' image. It was inevitable that Hewson would undergo the transition eventually.

But Keating, too, needs to undergo a transition if he is to convince the doubters that he has what it takes to lead the Labor Party successfully. Hawke – to use Peter Walsh's imagery – may not have a backbone quite as strong as Keating's but he has other qualities necessary for leadership. Keating could do with some of Hawke's patience, some of his tolerance. More of Hawke's preparedness to listen to people who are disaffected would not go astray, either.

Keating – 'Mr Seven Per Cent' in the opinion polls – seems to think that his image problem can be solved quickly and easily when he decides the time is right, just by 'flicking the switch to vaudeville', but changing deeply ingrained perceptions is not as simple as that. Overcoming Keating's considerable unpopularity, if it is possible at all, will be a long and gradual process.

Part of the task was summed up by a Liberal MP after observing the Treasurer's parliamentary mauling of Hewson. 'He's somehow got to shed the street-fighter persona and project a more prime ministerial character. The problem is to do that without losing his parliamentary dominance.'

The decision of Stephen Smith, one of the Labor Party's best and brightest, to move from the post of Western Australian ALP secretary to Keating's staff is a big step in the right direction for Keating. Smith will come to the job unaffected by the suspicions and hatreds that too often motivate the Keating office. And he is strong enough and experienced enough to tell Keating when he is wrong – something the Treasurer badly needs.

Boom at the top

18 December 1990

The Labor Party leadership issue was just waiting to blow. If Paul Keating had not lit the fuse with his speech to the Canberra press gallery annual dinner, something else would have set it off sooner rather than later. Keating was not following any carefully thought-out strategy and some of his supporters were horrified that it flared up as it did. But it was always going to emerge as a major problem for the government. Prime Minister Bob Hawke could not avoid confronting the issue forever. Nor could the Labor caucus.

There have been other strong signs in the days leading up to the Keating speech that the party was beginning to focus on Hawke's position and the question of the succession. The most significant was a statement from Social Security Minister and right-wing faction leader Graham Richardson, buried on the features page of Sydney's *Daily Telegraph Mirror*. 'It is difficult to go into an election saying you are going to quit during the next term – that obviously places a fair bit of pressure on the Prime Minister,' Richardson said. 'The leadership becomes the issue...' Hawke had already said publicly that he intended to lead Labor to the next election and hand over to Treasurer Keating during the following term. Richardson was telling the Prime Minister that course was unacceptable.

What the Richardson warning boiled down to was that there were two choices. Hawke could have a public change of mind and announce he wanted another full term as prime minister after the current one, after all. Or he could step aside and make way for Keating fairly soon.

Given that Hawke would not be believed now if he backed away from his earlier comments on retirement, it was difficult not to conclude that Richardson was starting to come down on the side of those arguing for a leadership change early next year. Hawke would have been well aware that, if Richardson decided a Keating takeover was necessary for the good of the party, his days in the Lodge almost certainly would be numbered.

So the Prime Minister was conscious that the problem of what to do about his ambitious deputy was developing a degree of urgency. In those circumstances, any Keating comments suggesting criticism of Hawke's leadership – no matter how oblique – inevitably would lead to some kind of showdown, though people close to Keating are adamant that this was not what he intended. It was not that he was relying on press gallery journalists observing the 'off-the-record' ground rules for protection: he is not that naive. But, because the speech was about the general subject of leadership and made no actual mention of Hawke, he did not expect it to cause the crisis that it did. 'I didn't say anything I couldn't have said to a broader audience,' he told a radio announcer when the balloon went up. But one of Keating's right-wing allies was more realistic, saying: 'If there was one topic he should have avoided, it was leadership.'

The controversy over the speech, however, served to concentrate the minds of Labor members of parliament. For the first time, many of them began to realise that going into the next election with both Hawke and Keating may not be an option. As a Labor senator summed up the problem: 'What the party has to decide is, who can we best face an election without?'

The fear being expressed by some members of the Keating camp was that Hawke might resist a leadership change next year but then bale out closer to the election if he became convinced that the government was heading for defeat. Keating, these people argued, would be smart to get out rather than risk being sold a dump – handed the leadership when it was too late to turn things around.

Doubts about Keating's electoral saleability – even about his willingness to try to present a softer, more appealing image – had been reinforced by recent events. One was his statement about 'the recession Australia had to have'. Keating believed that, by embracing the recession as a necessary evil from which economic benefit would flow, he neutralised the opposition's attack – but, to many Labor MPs, it was an insensitive line which alienated voters. Caucus members were also concerned about the tough, apparently unsympathetic, way the Treasurer behaved when he visited a Ford plant and was approached by a shop steward about job losses.

But evidence that the government badly needs Keating has been piling up – particularly in parliament. In considering the leadership question, it was being said, Labor MPs needed to think about how the government would fare in the House without him. It was not a pleasant prospect to contemplate. But the prospect of cabinet without Keating was just as worrying. Keating might be headstrong, difficult, unpredictable, downright unpleasant at times – but he has been the government's driving force nonetheless. Without him, it would wallow. These were the thoughts of a large number of caucus members as they read the 'Labor in crisis' and 'Keating challenge' headlines.

That Hawke and Keating would at last have to discuss the leadership issue brought relief but a considerable amount of trepidation as well. The truth is, it is now easier to imagine the government without Hawke than without Keating.

It was precisely because of that kind of perception that Hawke could not ignore Keating's leadership comments. To have done so would have added to the impression that he lacked leadership authority and that Keating was the stronger personality – the real leader. Hawke's position had been badly undermined by repeated bouts of leadership speculation and – whether intended or not – the Keating press gallery speech had added hugely to the destabilisation. Hawke had no choice but to confront Keating.

The row over the speech served one useful purpose. It again focused attention on the idiocy and hypocrisy of a group of journalists hosting a 'non-reportable' function. The federal parliamentary press gallery stubbornly insists that the remarks of the guest speaker at its end-of-year dinner are 'off the record' – even though journalists object when others try to prevent the reporting of newsworthy statements by public figures. The journalist's job is to inform the public, not to encourage secrecy. The gallery dinner ground rules are clearly incompatible with the duties of reporters and undermine the credibility of the journalists' profession.

1991

Labor's out-of-tune quartet

12 March 1991

The nation's only Liberal premier, Nick Greiner, rose in the NSW parliament recently and pointed a scornful finger at the Labor benches on the other side of the chamber. 'The opposition knows that it has been disgraced by each and every Labor government with the possible exception of that in Queensland, which has only recently been elected,' he said. 'This is the first recession in which there have been clear interstate differences. It is the first recession where the policies of different state governments have clearly, beyond any doubt, beyond any argument, led to dramatic differences in the quality of economic life...'

Then, with obvious relish, Greiner related how NSW opposition leader Bob Carr had praised the Labor government in Victoria before John Cain quit as premier leaving behind a disastrous economic mess and a discredited party. 'Suffice it to say that the net effect of the policies of John Cain, whom the leader of the opposition portrayed as a model Labor premier, is a loss of about $3 billion to the people of Victoria,' said Greiner.

After references to the economic woes of two other Labor-governed states – Western Australia and Tasmania – came the clincher. 'After John Cain fell from favour, the leader of the opposition needed someone else to praise as a model premier...He decided upon another John. John Bannon...South Australia has lost a billion dollars as well.'

It was a taste of what will be a central theme when Greiner goes to the polls in the next few months. Carr will be battling not only the Liberals and their National Party coalition partners in NSW but also his interstate Labor colleagues. It will be a hopeless battle.

One of Labor's most experienced numbers men says simply: 'We'll get creamed.'

Research indicates there is not even much need for Greiner to remind voters of what Labor has wrought elsewhere – especially in Victoria, the state with which NSW relates most closely. According to the Liberals' NSW director Robert Maher: 'People are very conscious of the contrast, conscious of Victoria. They know it's there, know it's a big mess and they see NSW as having escaped from that.'

Another Liberal strategist says: 'The message has got through loud and clear without us even pushing it. People say: "Thank God Greiner was here, managing. Otherwise we'd be in the shit like Victoria, Western Australia and South Australia." In a state like NSW, where Bannon was seen as Mr Labor Party, to see him going down the gurgler, completing the trifecta...Well, thanks very much, that's all we need.'

In terms of the Labor Party's corporate image across Australia, the importance of Bannon's sudden fall from grace is difficult to over-estimate. Before the announcement of the State Bank of SA's huge loss it was possible for Labor people to find some comfort. The Victorian Labor Party was never really cut out for government, they would concede, and in WA the government had always been a bit too close to big business, no matter which party was in power. But with Wayne Goss doing well in Queensland and Bannon's solid businesslike image intact, the party as a whole could not be dismissed as managerially incompetent. That changed with those big front-page headlines on February 11: $1BN BAILOUT TO SAVE SA STATE BANK.

Bannon is no ordinary premier. As federal president of the Labor

Party he is a national figure, so the fallout was wide. In the words of a prominent federal Labor politician: 'There's only Queensland now where we can claim to have a good, competent administration. Everywhere else they've run off the rails. Victoria is terminal. WA probably is, too. SA will be lucky to survive this. It all rubs off on Carr in NSW and on the federal government.'

The cumulative effect is devastating for Labor. Had it not been for the WA Inc scandals and Victoria's financial collapses, the political consequences of the State Bank affair would not have been nearly so serious even within SA. But the climate is such that, in the words of a close friend of Bannon: 'People say it's another bloody Labor government messing things up, they're hopeless, you can't trust them. That will be the impact on the federal government, too.'

It used to be said that Australians differentiated between state and federal issues and administrations, that their feelings about a federal government did not have a big effect on how they voted in state elections and vice versa. That is demonstrably no longer the case. In the 1989 SA election, Bannon was almost defeated not because of anything his government had done but because voters wanted to send a message to Canberra.

It was because his popularity was strong that the Liberals campaigned on federal issues – interest rates and falling living standards. Advertisements pictured Bannon with Prime Minister Bob Hawke and Treasurer Paul Keating. The campaign went within a whisker of success, so there will be a degree of poetic justice if Bannon's local troubles cause electoral problems for federal Labor.

Hawke got an unpleasant taste of the crossover effect in the federal election last March. It was basically a status quo election everywhere except Victoria where Labor was so badly on the nose that it lost nine seats. 'The extent of the loss in Victoria seems to me very much a result of state factors,' Hawke said. Despite some bleats from the Victoria ALP, he was stating the obvious. Victorian voters, wanting revenge on the state Labor government but denied the opportunity with no state election due for two and a half years, took their anger and frustration out on federal Labor. And the situation in Victoria has deteriorated since.

Labor's beleaguered premiers – Joan Kirner in Victoria, Carmen

Lawrence in WA, Bannon and Tasmania's Michael Field – are in just about as much trouble as it is possible to imagine. Political observers talk of the '90s being a Liberal decade. With the Hawke government also in dire straits, there is a growing feeling that by the end of 1993 Goss could be the sole Labor leader in power.

The one cloud on the horizon for the Liberals is the quality of their state leaders. None is impressive. Looking at Victoria's Alan Brown, Barry MacKinnon in WA, Dale Baker in SA and Robin Gray in Tasmania, it is glaringly apparent that none of them is a Nick Greiner. How Brown, MacKinnon and Baker would perform in government must be a big worry for the Liberals. How former premier Gray would perform is already known – and that is a worry, too.

Kirner inherited an impossible task when she took over from Cain. 'Voters are just waiting until the time comes to even up,' says an ALP official. A senior federal Labor MP says simply: 'The Victorian ALP will be near wiped out. They'll get the worst shellacking any government has ever got.'

Victorians, having watched the Victorian Economic Development Corporation losses, the Pyramid collapse and the traumatic failure of their state bank, feel the sense of disgust and betrayal. Somebody will have to pay and Kirner is the bunny.

The worst of the management incompetence happened under Cain. It was Cain whose leadership was so weak that it could take six months to get cabinet approval for something as simple as the appointment of a department head. With an issue as big as the State Bank crisis, Cain seemed paralysed. Kirner has been far more decisive, far less afraid of tough decisions. She saw that selling the bank was the only way out. Despite her left-wing ideology, she set out on a program of asset disposals to ease Victoria's massive debt problem. She reshuffled the cabinet, appointing a finance minister to exercise tighter control over spending.

Kirner has tried – but it is not enough. What she and her key ministers are about is damage control, that is all.

In case voters' memories do become fuzzy, there are continuing news stories from the royal commission inquiring into Tricontinental, the ill-fated investment arm of the State Bank of Victoria.

Trench warfare has broken out between Labor's factions. Thousands of Victorians demanding the government's resignation brought Melbourne to a standstill for two hours in January. And the unfavourable financial headlines continue...All the opposition has to do is wait.

It is not prepared to do that, however. A bitter argument has broken out within the coalition about whether to force an election this year by blocking supply. And now it has adopted a strange strategy under which, it appears, the great bulk of government legislation is to be blocked in the Upper House – even legislation in line with Liberal Party policy. The aim seems to be to force an election by producing chaos. The opposition can hardly be said to be behaving responsibly in its impatience for power. Also to be blocked is a new industrial relations bill supported by both unions and employers.

Business leaders have not been impressed by the posturing and have said so. The result has been a public row. The Victorian Employers' Federation demanded an apology from state Liberal Party president Michael Kroger for comments he made about its executive director. And the Victorian director of the Australian Chamber of Manufacturers, Ken Crompton, said that attacks on employers would make it hard for business to deal with the Liberals under Brown's leadership. All of which would be intensely damaging if Victorians were not so single-minded about punishing Labor.

Behind all the wrangling is disquiet in the coalition about Brown's drab leadership style. A strong section of the party firmly believes former leader Jeff Kennett, more colourful and energetic, would stand a better chance of maximising the anti-Labor vote and – very importantly – would be more likely to make a successful premier. Brown's supporters argue that his cautious, unflamboyant image is exactly what voters want. Kroger has just passed up the chance to enter federal parliament via the safe seat of Menzies, vacated by Neil Brown, because of the need to keep the lid on the state parliamentary party's leadership ructions.

The next election is due, theoretically, in October 1992 but there is very little chance that Kirner will complete her full term. As far as federal Labor is concerned, the sooner the better. The incoming L/NP government will be compelled to take tough measures and that – or so Labor sources hope – may cause some voters to move back in time for the federal election in March '93.

The WA Labor Party, unlike the Victorians, has not given up hope. Some senior party figures genuinely see a chance of Lawrence's government surviving the next election. A more realistic assessment is that she will lose but may lose respectably, rather than in a landslide, if the parliament runs its full term. An election is not due until February 1993. Lawrence faces a tough fight. She can only make progress if public attention is somehow diverted from the WA Inc legacy of her predecessors Brian Burke and Peter Dowding and onto the way she is running the state.

For Labor in WA, 1990 was a year of survival. The party dumped Dowding and installed Lawrence, to avoid slaughter at the federal election and to head off a Liberal threat to block supply in the Upper House. The ploy succeeded. Not only were no federal Labor seats lost but the Liberals imploded over the supply issue and damaged their own standing with a leadership crisis. MacKinnon survived the challenge from his deputy but the incident further hurt his standing – hardly impressive to begin with, after his failure to beat Dowding in '89.

Lawrence's performance, given that she has been in parliament only since 1986 and was a minister for a mere two years before being thrust into the role of premier, has not been bad. Her budget was well received. It cut a swathe through spending while keeping increases in taxes and charges to the level of the Consumer Price Index or below. Her personal rating in opinion polls has been good. But dealing with what are coyly referred to within the Labor Party as 'the mistakes of the past' meant crisis management dominated her first 12 months as leader. Every policy initiative was overshadowed by continuing WA Inc allegations. Lawrence decided last November that, rather than see her government paralysed, she would establish the royal commission the media and the opposition had been baying for. The dangers are obvious: royal commissions can take on a life of their own, as Queensland's Fitzgerald Inquiry demonstrated so dramatically. Lawrence has gambled that her action will be a circuit-breaker, that WA voters will focus on other things. If that does not happen, if the royal commission revelations simply serve to concentrate attention further on what happened under Burke and Dowding, her prospects in 1993 are grim.

Meanwhile, the stability of her government has been undermined by a ministerial reshuffle that went wrong. The motivation was correct: to give the ministry a fresh look and to provide experience to younger MPs of the generation that will either have to rebuild the party in opposition or, if things go extraordinarily well, take it through a fourth term in office. But the three ministers Lawrence wanted out refused to go quietly. They had to be voted out by caucus, following which one left the party while another resigned from parliament – making necessary a by-election in which, to quote a well-placed Labor source: 'We'll have our arses comprehensively kicked.'

The normally unflappable Bannon has looked somewhat shell-shocked since launching his State Bank rescue package. He has taken a terrible battering in parliament and in the media and the vicious Adelaide rumour mill is grinding out stories of more sensational events to come. Stories, it should be stressed, that are emphatically denied by the government. Bannon has been made to look silly by not knowing, for example, the salary of the bank's former managing director Tim Marcus Clark. (Why should a premier be expected to know such details?) But most damaging is that people simply cannot understand why Bannon failed to look at the bank's affairs months earlier when reports of its troubles were circulating widely. He has the appearance of a politician whose luck has run out.

But he is not due to face the polls until November 1993, so he has time to recover – if he can get the bank back to financial health and if the royal commission he was forced to set up makes no serious adverse findings concerning him and his government. The people around Bannon seem confident on both counts. A big difficulty with the commission is that, because it is inquiring into a working financial institution, strict confidentiality will be required concerning clients' financial affairs. Anything less would see them leaving the bank and that would torpedo the prospect of getting it back into the black quickly. Insistence on confidentiality, though, will result in a further political mauling.

Bannon learned from the Victorian experience. Once he realised the seriousness of the problems there was no indecision. He accepted responsibility and put an indemnity package together immediately. Unlike Victoria, the government was able to find the funds from its own resources (or, rather, the resources of the South Australian Finance Authority). People close to him say, and the royal commission will determine the truth of it, that he had no indication of the seriousness of the situation until the end of January. In mid-1990, he was told the bank would not make the profit it had forecast; then he was informed that it would probably break even, and bank officials confessed in December that a $150 million loss was likely – bad but politically and financially manageable.

Then, when parliament rose in December, Bannon ordered that the matter be sorted out during the seven-week Christmas recess, telling one of his staff: 'I am not going back into parliament without getting to the bottom of it.' He was informed that the loss was probably $1 billion on the day he returned from holidays.

Since taking over the opposition leadership after the last state election, Baker had made little impact but the bank affair has changed that. Having opened the issue in parliament last year, he is perceived to have had a big win over Bannon. His credibility has been enhanced. Members of the business community who had displayed little interest suddenly want to meet Baker and his shadow ministers.

Field is in a different position from his colleagues. True, he is also embattled but Greiner including him under the 'Labor mismanagement' label was a bum rap. Tasmania does have a huge debt. Its state bank did lose money. But a Liberal government was in power when the problems were created. Field, premier for less than two years, has undertaken the task of cleaning up the shambles left by Gray and has earned praise from economist Des Moore of the right-wing Institute of Public Affairs. Field raised taxes 11 percent in last year's budget and slashed services to reduce debt, an act of considerable courage given that he heads a minority government which could be forced to the polls at almost any time.

The Field strategy is similar to Greiner's: take unpopular but necessary measures in the first two years to give time to regain support as voters realise the wisdom of your actions. That is all very well if the government runs its full term to May 1993. But Field got his budget passed, narrowly, only after a long war of nerves with the conservative members of the Legislative Council. And, since the collapse of the accord with the Green independents last October, he has been kept in office only because the Greens dislike Gray even more than they dislike Labor's forestry plan which allows an increase in the wood-chip quota. Opinion polls show the Liberals would be returned at an election now.

That may be surprising, given the condition of finances when Gray fell. But he is a cunning politician. Somehow he has convinced voters that the problems are a result not of his government's unashamed pork-barrelling but of Labor's alliance with the Greens. That Gray retains economic credibility is remarkable. But the Liberals have problems, anyway. Gray's deputy recently resigned. There is some disillusionment with Gray at senior levels of the Liberal Party organisation. And looming over everything is the royal commission established to inquire into the attempted bribery of a Labor MP in 1989 in an unsuccessful bid to keep the Gray government in office.

Revising the rules

26 March 1991

Maxine McKew: But Treasurer, you may have the parliamentary ascendancy over John Hewson –

Paul Keating: Not might – have.

McKew: Well, does that mean anything out in the electorate?

Keating: Absolutely, absolutely.

McKew: Why?

Keating: You can't win in the electorate unless you're winning in parliament.

McKew: Yes, but most Australians –

Keating: That is the golden rule of Australian public life. It has never been broken. You cannot be losing in the House and winning outside.

– Transcript from *PM*, ABC Radio (March 14)

Paul Keating emerged from Question Time that day convinced he had done well. He had taken on shadow treasurer Peter Reith and humiliated him. 'Reith is an embarrassment every time he stands up,' a very prominent coalition politician said later. 'Keating took him to the cleaners.'

Keating's starting point had been a Reith press statement quoting an academic survey commissioned by the Business Council of Australia. According to Reith, the study showed that, if a goods and services tax replaced the present wholesale sales tax system, gross domestic product would increase by between 0.5 percent and 1 percent. Producing the same study in the House, the Treasurer pointed out that the conclusion cited by Reith was based on the assumption that nominal wage rates did not change despite a rise of 1.72 percent in the Consumer Price Index.

In fact, Keating revealed, the study itself 'recognises that assuming constant nominal wage rates in the presence of such a substantial increase in the CPI is unrealistic'. Using what it regarded as the most plausible assumption given an uncompensated consumption tax – namely, real wage rates remaining unchanged – the survey found that 'the CPI increases by 2.54 percent; the government surplus falls by 0.85 percent; real GDP falls by 0.58 percent; aggregate employment falls by 0.79 percent; rural output falls by 1.21 percent; mining output falls by 1.65 percent; and the textile, clothing and footwear industry falls by 1.22 percent'.

Keating then quoted what he said was the most interesting part of the study. It read as follows: 'With wages linked to consumer prices, increases in consumer prices have strongly adverse effects on employment and output. Thus, in an environment of fixed real wages, the concentration of the goods and service tax on consumption goods is a disadvantage for this tax relative to the wholesale sales tax.'

By this point, Labor backbenchers were excitedly egging Keating on. The opposition troops were looking glum. And Keating, enjoying himself immensely, continued to hammer the hapless Reith. 'Someone in his office has written a press statement for the shadow treasurer and, being basically the hopeless amateur he is, he put it in the press boxes without reading the study – and the study comes out and boots the life out of him.'

The performance – as all such Keating performances do – boosted the morale of Labor MPs. And journalists watching from the press gallery could not help admiring the skill of the demolition. The incident, though, made not a ripple in the media. The story that day was unemployment – figures showing the biggest pool of jobless in the nation's history.

Sure, Keating had won in parliament. But he and the government took another beating out in the electorate. Despite what Keating believes, the golden rule no longer operates. It *is* possible to be losing in the House and winning outside. John Hewson's opposition is living proof of that. Day after day, they receive a parliamentary going-over by Keating, Hawke and some of the other, more articulate, ministers. Reith's shortcomings are repeatedly exposed. Scorn is heaped on National Party leader Tim Fischer, who is ridiculed by Keating as 'Huckleberry Hound'. Only John Howard really knows how to land a punch in return. But it matters not at all. The coalition maintains its healthy lead in the opinion polls and the feeling of inevitability about a change of government at the next election grows stronger.

The basic problem is the damage that has been done to Keating's economic credibility by the recession. His parliamentary victories may impress practitioners of the political trade and those of us who observe it professionally, but all the available evidence suggests the general public could not care less. Keating is saddled with the blame for what has happened to the economy, and that overshadows everything else. In the past, governments in considerably less trouble than this one is experiencing have cracked under parliamentary pressure, creating the impression that winning in parliament and winning in the electorate go together. Largely because of Keating, the Hawke government has for the most part kept its nerve in the House – but that has not stopped the electoral rot.

I used to believe that when voters could actually see Keating in action in parliament via their television screens they would, no matter how grudgingly, have to admire his parliamentary skills and his dominance of the chamber. I am no longer so sure. The feedback I get suggests that, unfairly perhaps, the cold and arrogant image many people have of the Treasurer is simply being reinforced – which is, of course, precisely what Keating and others in the Labor Party were worried about and one of the reasons they held out so long against the televising of parliament. It may also help to explain why Keating's ascendancy over Hewson and Co in the House seems to make no difference at all outside.

Another factor – less important, perhaps, but relevant – is almost certainly Keating's use of technical economic language and, often, the jargon of economics. The destruction of Reith's consumption tax press statement was a case in point. Keating's argument was, of necessity, somewhat technical and it went straight over the heads of many viewers watching the live telecast. Immediately afterwards, however, Hewson – despite being a former economics professor – delivered a 30-minute speech in reply to Hawke's industry statement which was almost entirely free of jargon and figures. It was an instructive contrast.

In the end, communicating with voters is what matters most. That is the real golden rule.

The super champ

6 August 1991

There are times when some knowledge of history comes in handy. Paul Keating's speech calling on the government to legislate for a national superannuation scheme was such an occasion. Those familiar with the way another pretender to the prime ministership set out to destabilise the incumbent 52 years ago were able to appreciate the irony of the situation.

In March 1939, Prime Minister Joseph Lyons announced that his United Australia Party government had decided not to implement key sections of national insurance legislation already approved by parliament, the most important of which would have established a contributory and compulsory retirement income scheme. Lyons's ambitious deputy, attorney-general Robert Menzies, hungry for the prime ministership and wanting to make leadership an issue, used the decision as an excuse to resign from cabinet. Having distributed a pamphlet telling voters in his electorate that the scheme was essential, Menzies said, 'I cannot, with self-respect, deny today what I wrote only a few weeks ago.'

Menzies' sincerity on the matter was widely doubted – just as Keating's motivation is questioned by Hawke supporters now. But the incident shows national superannuation is anything but a new issue.

It goes back, in fact, to the days before the Depression, when Stanley Melbourne Bruce appointed a royal commission on national insurance. The result was a bill providing for 'compulsory insurance against sickness, accident, permanent disablement, death or old age'. The government fell while it was being negotiated with the states.

Labor opposed the idea of a contributory scheme then, as it did in 1939. But Menzies, after creating the Liberal Party to replace the UAP in the mid-'40s, continued to push for it. Contributory social insurance was prominent in his 1946 policy speech and in the Liberal policy for the 1949 election which brought him to office – though over the following 17 years as prime minister he did nothing about it.

Gough Whitlam revived the idea, with an inquiry into national superannuation by a committee headed by Professor Keith Hancock. Unlike earlier schemes, the Hancock committee's recommendations would have retained a universal taxpayer-funded pension and set a new 'purchased pension' on top of it – an approach much more acceptable to the Labor Party – but the proposals were doomed when the Whitlam government was dismissed. In 1982, the introduction of 'a self-supporting, portable national superannuation scheme, providing entitlements to cover all persons' was adopted as policy by Labor's national conference and a detailed scheme was drawn up. It, too, sank without trace in the early years of the Hawke government, suggesting Keating as treasurer was anything but an enthusiast at that stage. However, the important thing is, Keating is a convert now and is pushing hard for a privately funded, employment-related, national superannuation scheme which would augment the aged pension. Being seen as the champion of such a reform no doubt suits his political ambitions but that does not mean the idea is not in the national interest. Unless the Keating scheme (or something like it) is implemented, Australia's social welfare system is going to collapse under the weight of a rapidly ageing population. The solution is either national superannuation or taking an axe to pensions, as is happening across the Tasman.

As a means of reducing Australia's current account deficit by increasing savings as well, the kind of dramatic expansion of superannuation coverage proposed by Keating has a great deal going for it. Menzies mounted a similar argument in 1939 when it was claimed that, with war looming, the need for increased defence spending made the pensions side of the *National Health and Pensions Act* unaffordable. In fact, said the future founder of the Liberal Party, national insurance would create a massive pool of funds that would be available for defence purposes.

Keating's well-publicised speech on national superannuation served four purposes for him: it kept his profile up; it enabled his supporters to portray him as an alternative prime minister with ideas and the ability to sell them; it put pressure on the government to honour a commitment he gave, while still treasurer, to ACTU secretary Bill Kelty, that there would be superannuation legislation in the budget session of parliament; and it positioned Keating to get the credit when the government does introduce such legislation, as it almost certainly will. The details may not match exactly but something very like what Keating put forward can be expected to emerge from cabinet later this year or early in 1992.

Putting his abilities as a political salesman on display was a timely exercise for Keating. The government is short of ministers who can sell effectively. The best is probably Social Security Minister Graham Richardson, with Treasurer John Kerin also valuable because of his plain-speaking credibility. Bob Hawke used to be persuasive, too, though it was more a result of his personality than the words he used. At the moment, though, he is too cranky to win people over. Deputy Prime Minister Brian Howe, responsible for the electorally important health and community services area, is not bad at policy but his fondness for jargon and officialese makes him hopeless at selling. Primary Industries Minister Simon Crean has a similar problem.

Even Keating – about whom it has been said 'he can sell anything but himself' – still alienates people with economic jargon, as he showed during his recent *Midday Show* appearance on the Nine network.

On the other side of politics, 'selling' ability is even more important as the opposition begins to realise the mammoth difficulty it faces in persuading a cynical electorate to vote for a new tax. Shadow treasurer Peter Reith, the opposition's chief spruiker for the consumption tax so far, cannot do the job. Through no fault of his own, Reith comes across – particularly on TV – like one of the Dodgy Brothers. No one is going to buy a tax from him, new or used.

Belatedly, opposition leader John Hewson has accepted that he will have to carry more of the load, but so far he has not shone as a super-salesman, either. Essentially dull, Hewson will always find 'selling' difficult. He is, however, beginning to find what could be an effective sales pitch – one which capitalises on his 'Mr Clean' image. The lesson of the last election, he tells interviewers, is that politicians ought to be open and honest and have the courage to be truthful about what is necessary to tackle the nation's problems. 'If you have to lie to get into government and you have to lie to stay there, it is a very sad situation,' Hewson says, adding that anyone who wants that sort of approach should vote for Hawke and his team. That, of course, is a reminder of the notorious Kirribilli House Agreement – which brings us back to Keating, leadership rivalry and an idea whose time at last may have come.

For Gorton, the party isn't over

17 September 1991

The quotation sounds familiar: 'I would willingly stand down if I felt it were for the good of Australia.' But, no, it was not Bob Hawke speaking – even though he has made almost identical statements recently. The words are those of John Grey Gorton, 20 years ago, just before he was toppled from the prime ministership in a party room coup.

Hawke has much more in common with Gorton than the possibility of meeting a similar political end. Like Hawke when he was president of the Australian Council of Trade Unions, Gorton was a down-to-earth, knock-about bloke, a larrikin who enjoyed grog, liked women, pleased himself how he behaved and was fiercely nationalistic.

Unlike Hawke, though, Gorton was a Liberal. Also unlike Hawke, he failed to discipline himself when he became prime minister. Hawke even stopped drinking. Gorton in the Lodge remained much as he had always been. And, while Hawke has had an eight-and-a-half-year reign and could remain at the top for a while yet, Gorton was tossed out after only 38 turbulent months.

The comparison between two of our most interesting prime ministers is prompted by a birthday. Gorton turned 80 on September 9. To mark the occasion, Liberal leader John Hewson threw a party for him at Parliament House and most Liberal and National members of parliament turned up. It says something about Hewson that he went to this trouble because Gorton and the Liberals have had nothing to do with each other for a very long time.

Gorton walked out of the party and sat in parliament as an independent for a while after Malcolm Fraser, whom he disliked intensely, rolled Billy Snedden and took over the leadership in 1975. Disapproving strongly of the way Fraser used the Senate later that year to block supply and force the Whitlam government from office, Gorton stood as an independent Senate candidate in the ensuing election but polled disappointingly and dropped out of politics. Now, though, touched by Hewson's gesture, Gorton says that he would like to rejoin the Liberal Party – 'if they'll have me'.

In his speech at the birthday party, Hewson said he was delighted to honour a great Australian and a great Liberal. Gorton, he said, was 'really the first prime minister who was Australian to his bootstraps'. And he added, 'John Gorton made it acceptable for a conservative to be Australian and only Australian.' The comments were perceptive: Gorton, with his fervent nationalism and his belief in one nation rather than six states, was ahead of his time as far as the Liberal Party was concerned. Now, the party has caught up.

The conservative leaders who came before Gorton were British-to-the-bootstraps or sycophantic towards the United States, or both. Sir Robert Menzies' best-known line referred to the Queen: 'I did but see her passing by and yet I love her till I die.' Harold Holt is remembered for his obsequious pledge to an American president: 'All the way with LBJ.' Gorton would have none of that. His trademark was a solo performance of 'Waltzing Matilda', belted out with gusto in a pub or at a Young Liberals function. His desire to have it recognised as Australia's national song outraged many in a party wedded absolutely to 'God Save the Queen'.

The Viet Cong's Tet offensive in Vietnam occurred within weeks of Gorton becoming prime minister. He was asked at a news conference, 'In view of the latest developments, is there any suggestion Australia will increase its commitment?' Australia, Gorton replied firmly, would not increase its forces in South Vietnam. Asked if that was a permanent statement, he said, 'As far as I'm concerned, it is.' The signal was unmistakable. The days of 'All the way with LBJ' were over. A great many of his Liberal colleagues were horrified but it is crystal clear with the benefit of hindsight that his decision was the right one.

If this sort of thing got up the noses of the conservative Establishment, Gorton's determination to overcome state parochialism was regarded as an even greater crime. 'We should be Australians first,' Gorton had said. As prime minister, Gorton proved to be unashamedly centralist with little patience for the traditional Liberal Party 'states' rights' attitude. That brought him into conflict with rough, tough Liberal premiers such as Victoria's Henry Bolte and Robert Askin from NSW – both of whom eventually played a part in his downfall. These days, of course, states' rights is regarded by such Liberals as Hewson and NSW Premier Nick Greiner as an outdated concept. They also put Australia first.

The old-style Liberals who fought against the direction in which Gorton tried to take the party would have been horrified to hear Hewson say, 'The goals of John Gorton are the goals of John Hewson.' They would also have been shocked to hear Hewson praise Gorton for asserting he was 'not of or in the Establishment'. The '80s, Hewson said, showed how corrupt establishments could be. Put style aside, and the buttoned-down yuppie and the extroverted former war hero are alike in many ways.

As far as style is concerned, Gorton was a cross between the early Hawke and the later Paul Keating. He once shouted at a critic, 'John Grey Gorton will bloody-well behave precisely as John Grey Gorton bloody well decides he wants to behave!' That attitude led to such embarrassments as the Geraldine Willesee incident, in which he turned up at the US embassy in the early hours of the morning accompanied by a young female journalist. There was no impropriety involved – Gorton had been invited and several members of his staff were also present – but those who wanted to discredit him had a field day. His drinking and his determination to be himself led to other indiscretions which were used against him.

Like Keating, he rejoiced in getting his hands on the levers of power and he was determined to use them to change a nation that had slumbered through the Menzies era. He trampled on the feelings of other ministers to get things done, overrode his cabinet where he disagreed with the majority, overturned long-held policies and practices. Where Keating was an economic rationalist, Gorton was an economic nationalist. But he lacked Keating's political skills. Ultimately, there was too much ad hoccery in his approach for it to succeed. As the late Alan Reid wrote, 'He wanted to enjoy the prime ministership rather than work at it.'

Just the same, Gorton's influence was significant. Although the old guard regained control of the Liberal Party for a time after his downfall, it had been changed permanently. Hewson believes that the Liberal Party has been too ready to forget or to disown its past and he wants to change that. Bringing Gorton back into the fold is part of the process.

Encouraging impure thoughts

5 November 1991

On his way to launch the poster for Adelaide's Fringe Arts Festival – the occasion on which he threw the switch to vaudeville by publicly crooning Cole Porter's 'You're the Top' – Paul Keating had an unexpected encounter during a transit stop at Melbourne's Tullamarine Airport. He told the festival audience: 'I ran into all of the bureaucrats who serve the premiers – the old premiers' conference shows that I ran at the Loan Council for nine years.' Because he was with one of his former senior staffers and a former ministerial colleague, Keating said, 'they thought something had happened overnight…They thought politically impure thoughts.'

The officials were also on their way to Adelaide, for a meeting of state leaders to prepare for another special premiers' conference, in Perth, on the so-called 'new federalism'. That is an issue the former treasurer clearly hopes will help bring impure thoughts about the Labor leadership to fruition. And there is just a chance of that happening if Prime Minister Bob Hawke mishandles the matter. Proposals to return powers to the states – including some financial powers – have created considerable unease in the federal Labor caucus. Hawke's minders and political allies are well aware of it and have urged him to tread very carefully.

Opposition leader John Hewson is being warned to tread carefully, too, with the launching of his consumption tax package. Senior Liberals who attended a weekend retreat at the exclusive Berida Manor resort at Bowral in the NSW Southern Highlands were astonished at how laid back and confident Hewson seems. The few people in the know about details of the package described it as 'a stunner' but that did not calm the fears of some others at the retreat. Tasmanian Liberals, for example, did not hide their concern about the likelihood of the package being unveiled at the height of an election campaign in that state. Hewson has boasted publicly that he would welcome an early electoral test of the consumption tax but

Tasmanian opposition leader Robin Gray was less than enthusiastic about being the guinea pig.

One canny and experienced Liberal strategist is known to believe that the first 24 hours after the tax package launch will be crucial. That period, he has told colleagues, will get it off the ground – or sink the party. If it goes badly, Hewson's grip on the leadership will become as uncertain as Hawke's. There may be no obvious challenger on the Liberal side but nor is there much personal loyalty to Hewson. A nervous Liberal member of parliament speculated last week, 'I reckon John Howard has plan "B" in his hip pocket.'

Before launching his National Press Club broadside against Hawke's new federalism, Keating phoned Labor premiers to tell them what he planned to say. There was very little hostility towards his views and surprisingly strong agreement from some quarters. Keating's warnings about the grave consequences of returning tax powers to the states or weakening the federal government's control of the national purse-strings strikes a chord with premiers of smaller states who have thought the issue through – they rate 'fiscal equalisation' as more important than 'vertical fiscal imbalance'.

Vertical fiscal imbalance – the states being responsible for spending much more than they raise – is only regarded as a problem by those who want to see state powers enhanced and federal powers reduced. Measures to give the states greater control over raising their own revenue are particularly attractive to NSW and Victoria, however, because they would undermine fiscal equalisation – the principle that revenue raised in the bigger states is used to subsidise smaller ones. This is just one of the traps in the new federalism options that have been under discussion among federal and state officials in the lead-up to the special premiers' conference in Perth.

Since Keating's speech, Hawke supporters have claimed proposals to give the states enhanced revenue-raising powers were never a serious possibility. How, then, do they explain a report in *The Australian Financial Review* on August 28 of remarks made by Treasurer John Kerin on the vertical fiscal imbalance issue? Kerin, the paper said, 'indicated the federal government was fully committed to handing substantial taxing powers back to the states'. It quoted him as saying: 'The Commonwealth is really prepared to go as far as we can in that area. We believe it will not impede our ability to manage the economy.'

It is unfair to describe the new federalism, as one Hawke critic does, as a 'make-work scheme for a prime minister without ideas'. But it is true that the plan was pushed up to Hawke by his department head Mike Codd soon after last year's federal election when the Prime Minister seemed uncertain about an agenda. Rationalising federal and state functions to reduce overlap and duplication and increase efficiency was a good idea up to a point. But, given the importance of 'tied' grants to the achievement of key Labor social policy goals, turning the clock back in that area in any genuine way was never on. At least, not without a major party brawl. Nor was significantly changing the financial balance between Canberra and the states, even though an attempt to do so was inevitable once Hawke started the review process rolling.

The process has become an industry. When the state leaders met in Adelaide, they were accompanied by about 40 officials. Special units and branches have been set up in the federal and state bureaucracies. There have been dozens of meetings of officials and political advisers and a host of working parties. There is a feeling, though, that it is not really getting very far; that, in the end, the result will be an anti-climax because no one is really serious about giving up powers. Hawke has so much riding on the new federalism initiative that such an outcome would hurt him. But if he tries to force the issue, he could be hurt more. After the way the party was heavied over the budget changes to Medicare, neither cabinet nor caucus is in the mood to be leaned on again.

The argument that Hawke must not be repudiated on a policy issue because of its leadership implications is unlikely to work again. Hawke will not get away this time with presenting decisions on a matter of great concern to the party as a fait accompli. Hewson, on the other hand, when he takes his consumption tax package to the coalition party room, will have to present it as a fait accompli, despite the talk of allowing proper discussion and consideration. He cannot afford a rebuff on any aspect of it because even minor changes would throw out all the financial calculations, and the credibility of those calculations, and the credibility of those calculations will be vital in determining whether the package bombs or gains acceptance.

Crocodile Keating

10 December 1991

The question of how to involve Paul Keating in the battle to discredit the coalition's economic package has been exercising quite a few Labor Party minds. Some backbenchers have suggested to the former treasurer that he swallow his pride and return to the ministry. Others have canvassed the possibility of his being appointed to head a taskforce with the job of undermining the goods and services tax and other elements of opposition leader John Hewson's plan. Prime Minister Bob Hawke used a television appearance to make clear that he would like to see his leadership rival join the fight.

The truth, though, is that none of this makes sense. For Keating to return to the ministry after vowing never again to serve under Hawke would leave him with no credibility. He rejected the approaches out of hand. For Hawke to ask him to head an anti-GST taskforce would be seen as a sign of weakness – an admission that the Prime Minister was not up to the job of countering the Hewson push. Hawke is not about to make that mistake.

In any case, while it sticks to its strategy of trying to take the Hewson package apart piece by piece, the government is better off with Keating on the sidelines. This is not because he would be ineffective. Quite the contrary, Keating has probably the most closely annotated copy of the coalition's 'Fightback' document in Parliament House. He has been through it line by line identifying the flaws and vulnerable spots. But if Keating did launch himself seriously into the campaign against the Hewson package, it would reopen the leadership issue with a vengeance and that is hardly likely to be in the government's interest. Comparisons of his performance with that of the Prime Minister would be almost certainly unflattering to Hawke. An effective Keating intervention in the 'Fightback' debate would destabilise Hawke to a much greater extent than the leadership pretender managed with his speeches on new federalism and interest rates.

Of course, without Keating's forensic skills, his energy, his aggression, the government is not exactly an impressive fighting unit – especially since John Kerin, his successor in Treasury, is now widely acknowledged even within the Labor caucus to be a liability. That said, the government is still capable of doing a lot of damage to the coalition plan. Hawke is supremely confident he can shoot big holes in it. Some of Keating's closest supporters in the ministry agree. One of them, commenting on Kerin's gaffe in telling a television interviewer the coalition's arithmetic would probably stand up, said scornfully: 'That's nonsense. By the time we've finished, the arithmetic will be in shreds.'

All this, of course, assumes that the strategy is correct. Few people have questioned it. The government has copped a bagging over tactics, not strategy. The way it gagged debate in parliament, the decision to wait for definitive findings from Treasury's economic modellers before launching an all-out assault, the scattergun style of its early responses to the package, silly statements by Kerin and Deputy Prime Minister Brian Howe – such things, rightly, attracted criticism. However, it is possible that the overall strategy – trying to pull the coalition plan to pieces over time – is fatally flawed.

Hewson believes he has tapped into something fundamental – a feeling in the electorate that change is needed. Some on the Labor side agree that he has hit a bull's-eye – that voters want a government willing to take the nation by the scruff of the neck and make things happen, rather than one that sits on its hands saying everything will be OK. If they are right, some kind of 'vision for change' is the element that will win the next election. And, if Hewson is the only one offering change, the result will be a foregone conclusion.

It is clear that, under Hawke, Labor is constitutionally incapable of putting itself forward at this stage as a party of change. After nine years, the government has lost the ability to engender excitement – even to make people listen. What the party really needs federally is a Carmen Lawrence figure – a cleanskin who could be moved into the leadership for a change of image and a change of policy – but no such person is available. It is Keating or no one and he is far from ideal, given the events of the past year or so.

It is easy to imagine Prime Minister Keating pointing contempt-uously at the Hewson package and saying, Crocodile Dundee style:

'That's not a plan. THIS is a plan.' Keating is capable of embracing change, generating excitement and putting forward an alternative to what the coalition is offering. What is not certain is how much credibility he would have. But if Hewson is right, if Australians really do want something radically different from Hawke-type gradualism which many see now as drift, Labor may yet have to take a chance.

Hawke and the doves

24 December 1991

The Labor Party, despite its early socialist pretensions, has never been influenced much by Karl Marx. Events in its centenary year, however, suggest it owes a great deal to the Marx Brothers. The sight of Deputy Prime Minister Brian Howe walking into a cupboard was the high point of the comedy, until the hilarious episode of the cabinet delegation which was supposed to persuade the Prime Minister Bob Hawke that it was time to depart. This conversation was overheard that day…

Senator: What's happening?
Minister: He's got the tap on the shoulder.
Senator: What's he doing?
Minister: He's refusing to go.
Senator: What happens now?
Minister: He gets the tap on the head.

Not so. Not immediately, anyway. The six amigos might have been talking tough when they went to tell Hawke he should leave town but they emerged saying he had their support to stay as long as he wanted. If Kim Beazley, Robert Ray, Gareth Evans, Michael Duffy, Gerry Hand and Nick Bolkus genuinely believed Hawke and the government could carry on as if nothing had happened, it proves they lack a sense of humour as well as political acumen.

Said one minister not involved in the farce: 'If this situation holds, a number of us will have to decide whether to continue to participate in what is a sick joke. How do we walk into cabinet and proceed with a serious meeting after this?' The official opposition, of course, could not believe its luck. How could Labor face the next election with a prime minister whose closest supporters had tried to lever him out of office?

Never again, though, would Hawke's critics be able to refer to him as 'Old Jellyback'. That damaging nickname, coined by Senator Peter Walsh, was clearly much more applicable to members of the ill-conceived delegation. By staring them down and turning them around, Hawke demonstrated he can be a very tough character when the chips are down. His natural style may be to avoid confrontation but he has never lacked spine when forced into a fight.

It was difficult not to feel sorry for Beazley, the most senior member of the lynch mob that let the condemned man walk off the gallows. His attempts to explain the group's extraordinary behaviour badly dented his credibility and may affect his career. A senior caucus figure, hitherto a Beazley admirer, said the next day: 'When Kim puts his hand up for the leadership, we'll be entitled to ask, in the light of this, how brave, tough and determined he'd be in a crisis.'

Opposition leader John Hewson struck a chord when he challenged Labor to free itself from the Hawke/Keating leadership tangle by having the courage to jump to the next generation of leaders. It worked for the Liberals when they turned their backs on the Andrew Peacock/ John Howard rivalry and installed Hewson, a relative cleanskin. A great many Labor members of parliament, frustrated and angry and disgusted with what has been going on, would dearly love to adopt a similar solution.

For Labor, however, the next generation means Beazley or Simon Crean. Beazley's shortcomings were demonstrated by the delegation disaster when one of the most dramatic and damaging 24-hour periods in Labor history turned out to be for nothing, meaningless. Beazley, in the words of a colleague, 'would have done his reputation more good if he'd stayed home in bed'. Crean, in parliament for less than two years, has proved adept at getting coverage in glossy magazines but so far has done little to advance a serious leadership claim.

So caucus was left with the same old choice, between a prime minister who stayed too long and a former treasurer held personally responsible by many voters for the recession. No matter how hard they try, Hawke supporters could never do as much damage to Keating as he did to himself with his statement that 'this is the recession Australia had to have'.

It is the recession that makes Labor's leadership paralysis unforgivable and which makes it impossible for ordinary party members to appreciate the slapstick comedy of their parliamentary representatives. Nineteen-ninety-one was supposed to be a year of celebrations for Labor. Instead, the workers' party marked its 100th year by clocking up a 10.5 percent unemployment rate. And, while Hawke and Keating wrestled like Holmes and Moriarty on the edge of the waterfall, a mesmerised government proved incapable of developing and implementing the kind of imaginative policies necessary to deal with the mess.

For that reason, the situation that existed when Beazley and his intrepid band emerged from the Prime Minister's office was not sustainable. Everyone knew that resolving the leadership issue had become a matter of urgency. There had to be a showdown and it had to be quick. Hawke having defied the tap on the shoulder, a tap on the head was necessary – if not for Hawke, then for his rival. One of them had to go. Stability, otherwise, was not possible.

Stability, now, will not win the next election for Labor. But it might minimise the massacre.

1992

Keating's public air needs a cut

18 February 1992

A few weeks ago, that old cowboy singer, Smoky Dawson, revealed that Paul Keating as a boy had been a deputy sheriff in his fan club. When this was mentioned to John Hewson by a television reporter, the comeback was immediate: 'I thought Chad Morgan might have been his hero, not Smoky Dawson,' said the opposition leader, with a big grin. 'Remember there was a song, "Oh Lord, it's hard to be humble when you're perfect in every way"?' The quip, shown in that night's Nine network prime-time news, was devastating.

It was an indication of Hewson's development as a politician, the sort of thing that has Labor Party strategists increasingly worried. A year ago, Hewson would not have been capable of a one-liner like that – which went to the heart of the Prime Minister's image problem. Hewson has come a long way. He is no longer the stilted, colourless academic. He has turned into a politician of considerable talent.

Watch Hewson mixing with voters these days. He used to look decidedly uncomfortable but now he is surprisingly good at pressing the flesh, chatting, listening, mingling. He comes across as easy-going, unaffected. He even seems to like it. Hewson has also become a pretty effective stump orator. When he addressed an open-air meeting in Perth recently, a few Labor people went along to see how he fared. What they saw did not please them. He spoke off the cuff and won a lot of points with the good-humoured, witty way he dealt with hecklers.

The 1993 election campaign will be fought over important policy issues. The debate will be serious, the differences stark. But style and image will be crucial as well, and both sides know it. This is why Keating, since becoming prime minister, has been trying to shake off his head-kicker image and why Hewson has been at pains to remind voters constantly that 'the leopard does not change its spots'.

Keating's public persona is a major problem for Labor. The emergence of his family into the limelight may have softened his image and shown him as more rounded, less one-dimensional. But the impact on his approval rating in the opinion polls has been less than spectacular. Most of those who have dealt with Keating in the round of consultations to do with his coming economic statement have come away impressed. He listened, took notes, was attentive, engaging, even humorous. One Labor source involved with one of the meetings said afterwards: 'I wanted to tell him, "For Christ's sake, be more like that in public and people would like you." '

Asked a week or so ago how he thought the government was going following the leadership change, a senior minister remarked that there were two perceptions – one internal, the other external. Within the government, the feeling was that things were going well. Keating was listening more than Bob Hawke ever did. There was a new enthusiasm around the cabinet table. The government had a sense of direction. But so far at least, this was not being reflected in the way voters viewed the government. The hope was that, with the unveiling of Keating's economic statement, the public perception might start to match the internal one.

That will depend on not only his presentation on the night but the way he goes about pushing his plan to the public and trying to demolish Hewson's in the weeks and months after that. It will involve a tightrope act for Keating. He clearly wants voters to forget the 'old' Keating, the one who snarled 'disappear, pal' to people raising inconvenient issues. At the same time, he will need his talent for invective and every ounce of aggression he can muster to do in Hewson and the goods and services tax. 'As soon as he attacks us, thousands of people will say he has reverted to type,' says a Liberal confidently.

In his notorious 'Placido Domingo' speech at the 1990 press gallery annual dinner, Keating asserted scornfully that leadership was about strength and taking the right direction, not about touring shopping malls tripping over television cables. The truth, though, is that going out among the voters, in shopping malls and elsewhere with the television cameras rolling, *is* part of political leadership. If Keating is to win acceptance for the policies he unveils on February 26, he will have to engage in such activities. It is not something that comes naturally to Keating. One of the most memorable images of the last election campaign was the then-treasurer visiting a factory and joining employees for afternoon tea. At a canteen table with perhaps 20 overall-clad workers, Keating in his immaculate Italian suit was stiff and awkward and uncomfortable and well and truly out of place. He can be relaxed, friendly and gregarious in private. To have any hope of winning the next election, he must somehow learn to project that side of his nature in public. If Hewson, the former economics professor, can make the adjustment, it should not be impossible for Keating, the professional politician.

The next battleground

17 March 1992

Prime Minister Paul Keating's 'One Nation' statement, with its pump-priming measures, signalled an important shift. The Labor government, having adopted so much of the Right's economic policy agenda in good times, has been forced by the recession to move back towards the centre. But John Hewson's opposition, instead of moving back as well to contest the middle ground, is staying out there on the Right. 'Just to be clear on policy,' Hewson told the National Press Club, 'we aren't changing anything – except that we are going to turn the policy knob up a couple more times between now and the next election.'

The principal area Hewson had in mind was industrial relations. Tax policy may be the focus of the Keating/Hewson contest at the moment but industrial relations and the question of wage fixation will be just as significant in the run-up to the federal election.

The transfer of Michael Costello from Foreign Affairs to head the Industrial Relations department shows that the government is well aware of this. Former departmental secretary Graham Glenn was a good and experienced manager, but he was concerned about the disruptive effects of rapid change and its impact on institutions such as the Industrial Relations Commission. The government does not have time for enterprise bargaining and workplace reform to be phased in gradually, so an SOS went out for someone more adventurous. Costello, the clever negotiator who crashed through barriers to a Cambodian peace settlement, filled the bill.

There are economic and political reasons for the rush.

There is no flexibility in 'One Nation' or the August budget for wages to move by any other means than productivity if the economic kickstart is to work without a surge in inflation. The government simply cannot afford a situation where some workers with particular skills are able to bid up wages. That is the economic imperative for a decisive move towards productivity-based wage fixation through enterprise and workplace agreements.

The political imperative is to take the industrial relations debate away from the Liberal–National Party coalition by getting a successful system of enterprise and workplace bargaining up and running as a fait accompli. Moreover, because it is so central to what happens to the economy, ministers recognise that the government's fate very likely depends on its handling of industrial relations reform.

Just how high Hewson would like to turn the industrial relations policy knob became evident when he addressed a Perth Chamber of Commerce and Industry lunch a few weeks ago. On the question of where a coalition government should start, he said: 'If I could have my way, almost immediately no more wage increases unless they are negotiated at a workplace-by-workplace level all around Australia. No more centralised wage determination.' Almost certainly, though, Hewson will not quite get his way. The slightly more gradualist Howard approach, involving the present system continuing for a time alongside an enterprise bargaining system operating under common law, is expected to hold sway. However, with legislative measures to weaken trade unions, individual workers able to be held legally liable for the financial consequences of industrial action and very little protection for workers in the bargaining process, the coalition policy is certain to produce confrontation.

Howard is honest enough not to pretend that considerations of economic efficiency are the coalition's prime motivation. The economic argument, he said last October, was important but the ideological argument was 'even more compelling'.

In the December 1990 issue of the *Economic and Labour Relations Review*, Howard conceded that the government and opposition programs were similar 'in as much as they are seeking increased flexibility by devolution of wage fixation to the enterprise level'. But he added: 'The differences are numerous, substantive and ideological.'

Cabinet discussions on imminent *Industrial Relations Act* amendments concentrated on such practical matters as how to prevent the Industrial Relations Commission using the 'public interest' test in the Act to impose its own views on parties trying to negotiate enterprise or workplace agreements. But there was also concern in the government at a threat by the Australian Democrats to oppose the amendments if abolition of the public interest provision were involved. Those ministers thinking ahead want to keep the Democrats totally on side on industrial relations to ensure, should Keating fail to pull off his election miracle, that there is a Senate-blocking majority against the more radical coalition proposals.

Street-fighting and psychology

24 March 1992

It's all psychology, Paul Keating once told me. He was talking about politics, of course. And of course he was right. Politics is about human behaviour. Politicians need to know what motivates people en masse. A successful politician also knows to study the mental make-up of individuals with whom he or she must deal – allies and opponents – to know how to influence or unnerve them.

Psychologist Keating is claiming to have the measure of John Hewson. 'He is rattled,' the Prime Minister has been proclaiming at every opportunity. The way Keating tells it, he has established such ascendancy over Hewson in parliament, given him such a terrible hiding, thrown such a scare into him, that the opposition leader has lost his confidence and is on the run.

The claim, though, may have as much to do with Keating's psychology as with Hewson's. Hewson did face a fierce Keating onslaught in parliament and suffered some severe bruising but there is no evidence that his confidence was seriously shaken. Hewson did not back away: he kept punching.

The Prime Minister may need to convince himself that he is the greatest but he does not have his opponent on the canvas yet. Far from it.

Keating does perform better in parliament than Hewson. The House of Representatives chamber is Keating's favourite arena, the one where he is most devastating and most at home. Hewson is not in the same class as a parliamentary scrapper. Outside among the people, however, meeting voters in street walks or at public rallies, the opposition leader is much more comfortable and effective than the Prime Minister. The point has been clearly illustrated in the Wills by-election campaign.

People *like* Hewson. In Wills, voters cross the street to shake his hand. He can address a public meeting without fearing hostile demonstrators. Keating could not afford the risk. And Hewson –

despite Labor claims that he is cold, aloof, incapable of relating to people – works the crowd skilfully with jokes and rhetorical questions. He may have been an academic but, when he wants to, he sheds the jargon and talks in simple language that ordinary Australians can understand.

On the broader question of the psychology of the electorate, just about everyone who has studied the matter has concluded that voters have short memories. Machiavelli, the greatest of all political psychologists, had this in mind when he wrote: 'Injuries should be inflicted all at once, for the less they are tasted, the less they offend, while benefits should be granted little by little, so that they might be better enjoyed.'

Keating has certainly taken the second part of this advice to heart. The electoral goodies offered in his 'One Nation' statement are rationed out – starting with the one-off payment to families nine days before the Wills by-election. The statement itself was only the first of several pre-election packages containing inducement for voters, with the budget and a policy speech and possibly another economic statement early next year to come.

Producing a regular flow of benefits in the months before an election is an old and well-tried approach. Christopher Matthews, in his book *Hardball* – the modern American equivalent of Machiavelli's *The Prince* – writes: 'Those entrusted with office must be seen providing loyal service at the time people are making their judgments on the quality of that service. In 1984, voters re-elected President Ronald Reagan by a landslide. They judged him on the strength of the brisk recovery that began in 1983, not the recession from which they were still in the process of recovering.' Keating is attempting to do a Reagan.

But the first part of Machiavelli's injunction poses a major problem for the Prime Minister. The economic injuries suffered by Australians were not inflicted all at once. The hurt has lasted for years.

On top of that, until recently Keating ignored another basic lesson in political psychology, also illustrated in *Hardball* with a Reagan anecdote. As president, Reagan maintained his ties with old-line conservative groups even when more votes were to be gained in the middle of the road. Several times, when Reagan's fortunes took a dive, the conservatives returned the loyalty and saved his political skin. According to Matthews, Reagan told a convention of right-wing ideologues in 1985: 'I always see this as an opportunity to dance with the one that brung ya.'

The people who 'brung' Keating to the political ball were working-class voters, traditional Labor Party supporters. The Prime Minister is determinedly courting them again, but they are not as easily wooed as he might have hoped. Their perception is that, for much of his time as treasurer, he took his relationship with them for granted and preferred to dance with big business and right-wing economic theorists. Wills will provide an indication of just how serious a difficulty this is.

Why the world waits on Richo

19 May 1992

You see the description all the time. 'Powerbroker Graham Richardson'. The power Richardson wields fascinates commentators, colleagues and opponents alike. 'The fact is, he is too strong to dismiss,' says Liberal frontbencher John Howard. *The Age*'s Michelle Grattan writes: 'More than almost anyone else…he has acquired and used power and influence out of proportion to his formal position.' It is because Richardson is perceived as such a powerful figure that he has been targeted by the federal opposition.

The interesting question is how he acquired such power. What is its source?

When Richardson first entered federal parliament, in 1983, he was recognised as a clever numbers man but seriously underestimated just the same. 'You look after the numbers, Graham, and leave the policy to us,' Gareth Evans once told him patronisingly. It was a silly statement. Numbers mean power. And a politician with power is bound to influence policy.

That Richardson's power is not dependent on position was shown during his four extraordinary years on the back bench. Accommodated in one of the pokiest offices in Parliament House, he received more visitors than almost any minister. Ranging from backbenchers to union leaders to journalists to captains of industry, they would sit in the corridor waiting to see him. He was seen as the fixer, the man who could get things done, who knew what was going on and had the prime minister's ear. When Bob Hawke wanted something fixed, he, too, frequently went to Richo.

Richardson learned about the accrual and exercise of power as NSW Labor Party assistant secretary and then secretary when the legendary John Ducker was president of the branch. In Fia Cumming's book *Mates*, Richardson says Ducker's power came more from his personality than from the positions he held. Close colleagues say the same thing about Richardson.

He is gregarious, good company, loyal to his friends. He is also, in the words of a senior Labor MP, 'the best one-on-one operator you'll ever see'. But then there is the anger. If someone does the wrong thing, Richardson gets a cold fury about him. Those who experience it do not forget. Richardson confirms in *Mates* that it was from Ducker that he learned how to use anger. 'He frightened the shit out of people,' Richardson told Cumming.

Richardson undoubtedly learned from Ducker, as well, that authority must be based on consequences. He saw from close range how Ducker coldly got rid of Geoff Cahill as NSW ALP secretary in 1976, creating a vacancy Richardson filled at the tender age of 27. Cahill, in Ducker's eyes, had been disloyal. 'You can't sack the general secretary of the Labor Party,' Richardson had protested. 'Just watch me,' said Ducker. Richardson did.

A few years later, radio personality Mike Carlton gave Richardson the nickname 'Robespierre' because of his willingness to whistle up a tumbril.

The most important thing Richardson learned from Ducker, though, was that 'the assumption of power gives it to you, whether you have it or not'. In other words, you get power by exercising it.

Richardson manipulated the levers of power as an assertive general secretary. Because Labor MPs and ministers got used to dealing with him in that role, he retained authority when he went to Canberra. Also contributing to the aura of power he had created was his access to

Hawke, based on long friendship and Richardson's key role in ousting Bill Hayden from the Labor leadership. No shrinking violet, Richardson did not mind helping the reputation along with a bit of boasting. Once people started saying Richo was the man to see if you wanted a policy change or some other government action, it became a reality.

There is, too, an extraordinary doggedness and drivenness about Richardson – a determination to be at the centre of things that is unusual even in politics. And he has always been prepared to involve himself in things most other politicians would not bother with. Listening to the grievances of backbenchers. Exerting himself to see that so-and-so gets the numbers in caucus for an overseas trip. 'People go to him with problems, a lot of them from caucus but well beyond that,' says a colleague. 'He sorts them out. A bit like a modern prince. It can be anything from family circumstances to a political difficulty to business problems.'

Not surprisingly, Richardson has built a formidable range of contacts. A friend says: 'He knows more people than anyone else in politics.'

Fundamental to all this is Richardson's political judgment. As one of Labor's top machine men puts it: 'He's powerful because he's got one of the smartest political brains around. In terms of reading and understanding the electorate, they don't come much better.' Coalition politicians do not disagree with that assessment. It is why they would so dearly love to drag him down.

ALP suffers mad outbreak of truth

20 October 1992

It's a tough game, politics. You can't drop your guard for a second. John Button gives up a planned weekend away with his wife to help undo damage caused by an injudicious throwaway line from the Prime Minister and commits a blunder himself – one, moreover, that makes Paul Keating's original offending comment look even sillier.

Treasurer John Dawkins dismissed the Industry Minister's expression of doubt about the budget growth forecasts as 'one of those statements for which Senator Button has become famous over the years'. You might say the same things about the Prime Minister, with bells on. Keating's unqualified assertion that we were 'out of the recession long ago' joins the 'recession Australia had to have' and his 'banana republic' warning in a trifecta of memorable comments that shook the government.

'Why does he do it?' colleagues ask, often shrugging their shoulders in bewilderment. There is, however, usually a reason for Keating's apparent indiscretions – not always a reason everyone would regard as sound, but a reason nevertheless.

The then-prime minister, Bob Hawke, was not impressed by whatever reasoning lay behind his treasurer's reference, in a 1986 John Laws interview, to the danger of Australia becoming a banana republic. Hawke was overseas when the storm hit, sending the dollar into a dive and producing a political crisis.

It was one of the early signs of strain in the Hawke/Keating relationship. But the conventional wisdom now – as summed up by Button in his headline-making *Sunday* interview – is that Keating did the nation a service.

'That was one of the seminal statements, in my view, in Australia's political history,' Button said. 'Because what he was flagging there was simply this – that if we went on the way we'd gone as a country in the 1970s and didn't make significant changes, that would be our fate.'

The reasoning behind Keating's extraordinary comment at a news conference on November 29, 1990 – the day the national account made the recession official – is not so easy to grasp, even now. But Keating, angered by a column I wrote on the 'recession Australia had to have' line, explained it to me himself the following week. He had obviously thought carefully about the phrase before uttering it. I had called what Keating said insensitive and politically stupid, but argued that the political ineptitude of shadow treasurer Peter Reith on the day had minimised the damage to the government.

Keating had a different explanation for why the media reaction had not been worse. He told me: 'The reason it wasn't was that they didn't expect me to say it was a recession we had to have. The reason the cost was diminished was the line I took. It took their breath away. They thought I was going to walk in there and say, "Aw, I'm sorry, we've got a recession." They would have been all over me like a rash.'

His point was that the policy of slowing the economy was right and necessary. To disown the recession would have been to disown that policy, so he embraced it instead. 'I say the slowdown is one we needed,' Keating said. 'When the recession comes, do I then say it's one we don't need?'

It is fair to assume that Keating also had a reason for declaring the recession over long ago – another remark branded by most commentators as insensitive and politically stupid. The slowness of the recovery must be of desperate concern to the Prime Minister, who needs a significant and demonstrable improvement in the economy to give him a fighting chance in the forthcoming election. To speed things up, consumers have to be persuaded to consume and investors to invest. A mood change is necessary; an injection of confidence. The recession may be over, technically, but Australians are still displaying a recession mentality. Keating was probably trying to jolt them out of it.

But it backfired. Keating had been winning in parliament when attention was on the coalition's policies. Opposition leader John Hewson somehow had to get the focus back onto the economy, particularly unemployment – the killer issue for the government. Keating's statement provided the means to do that. On cue, and with plenty of media coverage, welfare lobby representatives made the point that whether the recession was technically over mattered little to the almost one million unemployed. The opposition strategy is – and must be – to keep unemployment at the forefront of the political debate. Hewson and Co were suitably grateful to the Prime Minister for his assistance.

And they were almost as grateful to Button. Voters do not believe Button makes silly comments. They believe his vice is telling the truth. So – despite his rapid retraction – most people will believe he was simply being frank when he said he was not absolutely confident that the growth figures in the budget would be met. Hewson and Reith have been working flat out for two months to undermine the three percent growth estimate, without anything like the same impact. They lack Button's credibility.

1993

Bovver boy faces boot

2 March 1993

'Y ou get marks in this game for making political judgments,' Paul Keating once told me. 'At some stage I'll make the wrong one and the public will say, "We've had enough of you, mate, and we thank you but we don't need you any more."'

We were talking about the risks he had taken as treasurer before the elections in 1987 and 1990 – political risks he had judged necessary for the health of the economy. And about the risk he took embracing the 'recession Australia had to have'.

In 1987, for example, $4 billion was chopped from government outlays. As Keating remembered it, 'Everybody said, "Ooh, you shouldn't do that; the mad bastard, he's swallowed an economics textbook."' But Labor survived the poll. In the run-up to the 1990 election Keating resisted pressure for mortgage interest rate relief, Labor faced the voters with rates at 17 percent and defied history and the pundits by winning again. The political judgment Keating made was that housing interest rates were not impacting on people's pockets because banks, in the main, were extending the terms of loans.

To make such assessments, Keating said, it was necessary to 'understand the mob'. But – ever the realist – he added: 'At some stage, as sure as I stand here, they're going to catch up with me... They might catch up with me next time.'

As this campaign hits the halfway mark it looks distinctly likely that they will catch up with him. All the indications are that Keating has made the wrong judgment that he knew would bring him undone eventually. He is too tough and determined a fighter to write off yet but there appears to be a surge against the government and Labor is looking a pretty lousy bet. Labor candidates say there is not much aggro in the electorate but there is little affection for Keating and the 'time for a change' theme comes through strongly as they knock on doors and patrol shopping centres.

My conversation with Keating about political judgment occurred in November 1990, a few days after the publication of national accounts figures showing Australia had experienced two successive quarters of negative growth. The figures had provoked his now notorious 'recession we had to have' statement.

The then-treasurer's view on that subject was that if the government was to have any chance of winning another election in 1993, it had to break the back of inflation. That meant holding its nerve in the face of recession headlines and inching interest rates down rather than taking the screws off. As it turned out, keeping interest rates too high for too long was the almost certainly fatal misjudgment. Indications are that Keating is not going to be forgiven.

Labor in this election is desperately trying to emulate Malcolm Fraser's feat in the 1980 campaign. Then, realising a week from polling day that Bill Hayden was about to pull off a shock victory, the Liberals launched a massive scare based on Labor's alleged plans for a capital gains tax and got home on the strength of it. But the scare issue then was a new one. John Hewson's goods and services tax proposal has been around for a long time. People by now are fairly familiar with it. And the Liberals, unlike Labor 13 years ago, knew the assault was coming and were ready to deal with it.

Keating is trapped by his record. The great fascination of the campaign is watching his increasingly desperate attempts to escape from it. Challenging Hewson to a televised confrontation specifically on the GST was merely the most spectacular example. The tactic may have got the GST onto the front pages but the Prime Minister was badly damaged in the process.

All the effort spent turning him from bovver boy to statesman was thrown away in half an hour. And the next day – to the astonished delight of Liberal campaign planners – the government gazumped itself once more, pushing the GST out of the news again by announcing details of a new accord with the unions. Keating used to boast – and perhaps still does – of a psychological dominance over Hewson. If that were ever true, the dogfight on *A Current Affair* showed conclusively it is no longer the case.

Our 1990 discussion took place after I suggested in a column that 'Labor strategists' did not regard his statement on the recession as all that clever. Such people, Keating replied scornfully 'have basically worked off the old politics of the '60s and '70s...They don't understand the politics that's come from the new economics in Australia. The great mistake all these people make is to talk down to the public.'

Keating's simplistic anti-GST attack in this campaign, though, is about as 'old politics' as you can get.

Hewson hires a 'no' man

25 May 1993

Bob Hawke mishandled a news conference in the mid-'80s. Returning shamefaced to his office, the story goes that he sought out his political adviser, Peter Barron. 'It won't happen again, mate,' said the Prime Minister. 'It had better bloody not,' responded the adviser.

For a long time it has been obvious that opposition leader John Hewson badly needs someone on his staff aggressive enough, powerful enough and smart enough to treat him like that. Now he has that person. Petro Georgiou, the Victorian director of the Liberal Party who has agreed to take over the running of Hewson's office, is the conservative equivalent of Barron.

Georgiou is the toughest, best and most experienced of the Liberal Party's machine operators. In negotiations leading to his acceptance of the job he made it clear that Hewson had better listen to him. Otherwise the Victorian is out – and the effect of a sudden departure under those circumstances could end Hewson's leadership.

Hewson, always certain he is right and resentful of others pressing a different view, is a difficult man with whom to argue. His advisers have an unenviable task. Hewson's attitude towards preparation for the first of the election campaign television debates illustrates the point.

Liberal strategists, knowing that style can be as important as substance in such encounters, had arranged for a rough replica of the television studio to be set up at the party's advertising agency so Hewson could practise. The idea was not only that he would familiarise himself with camera positions, seating arrangements of the panel and other such detail but also that he could work on one-liners and get advice from professionals on the kind of rhetoric likely to go over best with a television audience.

At the last minute, Hewson refused to have anything to do with the exercise. His idea of preparation was to shut himself away and pore over briefing notes. In the event, most commentators scored the debate as a narrow win for Hewson but had he taken advice it might have been decisive. Apart from anything else, Hewson would certainly have learned how to get a more dramatically favourable response from the Nine network's on-screen 'worm'. 'We've worked with this technology so often we know exactly what makes the perception meter move,' a senior Liberal said afterwards. 'He wasn't interested.' The new staff appointment means Hewson will have to change.

Georgiou will be a powerful figure on the federal political scene. The deal is that as well as holding the controlling position in Hewson's office, he will have a role in matters such as advertising, normally the preserve of the federal party headquarters. According to well-placed sources, he can also be expected to take an interest in revamping the NSW Liberal Party – on the basis that Hewson (or any other Liberal leader) cannot win a federal election unless the party picks up more seats in that state.

On top of that, he will remain at the head of the Victorian Liberal organisation. The next election for Victorians will be a federal one anyway so the jobs will mesh to a certain extent. And the Victorians have the best-resourced Liberal Party branch in the country, including a substantial research capacity. Georgiou made use of that research in his battle late last year to force Hewson to exempt food from the proposed goods and services tax. (Without that change the election would have produced not just a defeat but a Liberal massacre.) Georgiou wants to continue to tap into the research in his new position.

Getting Georgiou to join his staff is quite a coup for the opposition leader. It sends a signal to potential leadership rivals that Hewson is not the lame duck they may have believed. There was a school of thought which held that Hewson, weighed down by his election loss and subsequent pressure, might want out. Some colleagues suspected he would push hard for the Liberals to adopt a republican platform at the August federal council meeting, fail – and use that as an excuse to fall on his sword.

If that was his inclination he would hardly have recruited Georgiou. The appointment means Hewson is fair dinkum about leading the opposition into the next election. It also means he recognises the need to toughen the political approach of his office. It represents an acknowledgment, at last, that – far from knowing best – he is a political tyro and needs hard-nosed, straight-talking advice.

Georgiou, too, is sending a signal. His move is a vote of confidence in Hewson, which may help to quell the destabilising leadership speculation, at least for the time being. Peter Costello, for example, the most credible alternative to Hewson, is said to welcome Georgiou's shift to the leader's office. While Georgiou remains at his elbow, Hewson's position is strengthened.

Hawke put his head on the block

13 July 1993

According to the ABC-TV publicity material, Paul Keating took part in the *Labor in Power* series with 'gusto'. The book produced as a companion to the program says that, in addition to giving two long on-camera interviews, Keating provided access to his personal files and spent hours with writer–producer Philip Chubb 'informally briefing him on how he saw the Labor years'. The Prime Minister 'wanted to be sure that the ABC series was right; right as he saw it, anyway'.

Well, after all the effort and despite the praise the series has earned from television critics and politics junkies, Keating is disappointed with the result. Given the way he was portrayed in *Labor in Power*, that will surprise many people. He emerged in a much more favourable light than his predecessor and rival, Bob Hawke. The series greatly bolstered the view that Keating provided most of the drive and creativity over Labor's decade in office and that Hawke was an increasingly unnecessary figurehead. Hawke came out of it looking weak and defensive, Keating strong and confident, if just a touch manic at times.

The irony is it was Hawke who made the whole exercise possible. He was still prime minister when agreement was reached for the ABC to produce the series. Hawke urged his colleagues to take part, presumably believing it would help to cement his place in history as the Labor Party's most successful leader. Instead, he has been greatly diminished. History, we know, is written by the victors. This is but another example.

Keating, though, believes the series distorted reality by over-emphasising the importance of the leadership issue and the divisions surrounding it. It gave, in his view, insufficient recognition to the teamwork and constructive policy achievements of Labor's period in office. And, while *Labor in Power* was superb television, there is some validity in Keating's criticisms, aired last week at a party celebrating Treasurer John Dawkins's 10th anniversary as a cabinet minister.

The truth is that the Hawke/Keating rivalry – apart from the 1988 flare-up hosed down by the secret Kirribilli Agreement – was a dominant issue only in 1991. It did not permeate the operations of the government to anything like the extent implied by the series' makers. And the impression of constant bitterness and backbiting is also inaccurate. Dawkins told guests at his party that he had forgotten some of the incidents recorded in the series, so minor had they been in the overall scheme of things. Even after Dawkins went to Hawke in 1988 and suggested he step down from the leadership to make way for Keating, the two continued to work together, closely and civilly. In the months following that confrontation, in fact, Dawkins's influence increased, if anything. Keating made his comments in a speech heaping praise on Dawkins's impressive portfolio achievements and, more importantly, his role as a cabinet minister. A true cabinet minister, Keating said, was as interested in submissions relating to other portfolios as in his own areas of responsibility. Dawkins had been part of a bright, energetic, hard-working and creative team whose achievements had not been adequately reflected in the series. *Labor in Power*, he said, had not conveyed the true flavour of a government that had been remarkably united and effective.

Keating, naively, had expected the series to be an assessment of what the government had accomplished. The ABC's book says Chubb set out to produce 'a genuine appraisal of the Labor decade'. In the end, of course, he did what any film-maker would do. In selecting from hundreds of hours of interviews and archival footage, he went with the drama, the conflict.

I am not trying to put down the result. Quite the contrary. It was fascinating, even to those of us who observe the political process every day and have close contact with the lead players. The program illustrated just how few real secrets there are in politics; despite the unprecedented cooperation Chubb received from Keating, Hawke and an array of ministers, advisers and bureaucrats, he uncovered few scoops. But to have the participants in major political events talking frankly about what happened behind the scenes – even when they were simply confirming things that leaked out at the time – was gripping.

Nevertheless, because it compressed 10 years into five hours, it was inevitably misleading. On the basis of the series, for example, one right-wing commentator has taken the parliamentary press gallery to task for leading the public to believe that Hawke and Keating used to work together as an effective team, when *Labor in Power* showed that they were at each other's throats. But they *were* a very effective team from 1983 to 1990. And, when it came to sustained bitterness and backbiting, the seven years of the Fraser government left the first eight years of the Labor period for dead.

Wanted: a new Labor deputy

20 July 1993

Labor MPs knew, when they made Paul Keating leader, that he had a difficult personality. Now the problems posed by that personality are becoming evident. Making and implementing policy is what interests Keating; getting out and about to sell those policies is a bit of an imposition on his time. Listening to the views of others and being prepared to compromise where necessary goes against his nature. And he is so suspicious, so ready to see disloyalty and plotting where none exists, that he can – unnecessarily and pointlessly – turn friends into enemies.

Keating has massive strengths and extraordinary political skills. He is capable of providing energy, drive and excitement in a way no other Australian politician can match. When he sets his mind to the job of persuasion, either face-to-face or by television and radio to voters at large, he is a superb salesman. He is a doer, not just a talker; a politician of substance, not simply style. And he is crazy-brave, daring to try things that more plodding pollies would shy away from.

But since the election the task of salesmanship has been badly neglected. Keating's appearance on the Nine network's *Sunday* program at the weekend, because it was effective, had his colleagues muttering, 'Why isn't he out there doing that more often?' For months there has been almost a communications vacuum. Mabo is the classic example. Keating has spent an enormous amount of time on the implications of the High Court ruling on native title and what to do about it. He regards it, rightly, as a matter of enormous national importance. The solution he favours is just and sensible. Yet he botched a premiers' conference on the issue and let the public debate get away from him.

In the process, he developed a paranoid notion that Queensland Labor Premier Wayne Goss had joined conservative premiers in plotting against him on Mabo. This after Goss, at some political cost in his state, had spent days on TV and radio defending and explaining Keating's approach – something the Prime Minister had not deigned to do. The Queensland Labor Party's support for Bob Hawke in the leadership struggle is clearly a factor in Keating's attitude. But perhaps there is something more – an inability on his part to tolerate easily another Labor figure of substance on the political stage.

Related to all this is a narrowing of the sources of political advice to Keating. Even Graham Richardson, the shrewdest of Labor's political operators, is on the outer, despite – or perhaps because of – his pivotal role in making Keating prime minister. (Keating once reminded me of two old political sayings. One was: 'No good deed ever went unpunished.' The other: 'Why does he hate me? I've never done him a favour.')

In the final episode of the ABC's *Labor in Power* TV series, Richardson said: 'Keating has more power in the Labor Party than Hawke ever dreamed of. He doesn't need king-makers. He doesn't need factions. I don't think he needs anybody at the moment.' Following his remarkable election win, that is certainly how Keating sees the situation. The truth, though, is that no leader can operate in isolation. Not effectively, anyway. Not for long. And especially not one with Keating's personality.

The Labor Party is not going to be able to change Keating. Probably, since the positives far outweigh the negatives, it would not want to. But it may be possible to deal with some of the problems posed by his personality through structural changes – in particular, by providing him with a more compatible, more useful and more effective deputy prime minister. Someone who can complement Keating as well as take some load off his shoulders.

Brian Howe, it has to be said, is a dead loss in the role. Keating made clear his opinion of Howe's abilities by stripping him of the health portfolio after the election. Howe's political judgment is lousy; his blunders in late 1991 helped to finish Hawke as leader. Howe no longer commands much respect in his own Left faction, let alone in the rest of the party. And as a communicator he is hopeless. One look at Howe is enough to tell you why the Labor Party expects Keating to do all the selling.

'It's a big part of the problem,' says a senior Labor MP. 'When the deputy is not on the same tram, it's a significant weakness.' Keating needs a deputy he respects, one with sensitive political antennae, someone who can act as a channel for views and advice from the party and elsewhere. He needs someone with the skills to smooth over problems such as the misunderstanding with Goss. Above all, he needs an articulate deputy who can share the hard grind of moving around the country explaining and selling what the government is doing, leaving the Prime Minister with more freedom to concentrate on what he likes to call the big picture. Kim Beazley's name immediately springs to mind.

Pea-and-fumble secrets revealed

24 August 1993

Dr John Edwards is Paul Keating's economic adviser. He is also a former journalist. Recently he combined the two roles to pen an article titled 'Economic policy in the 1980s and its implications for the 1990s'. Included in a book published by the Committee for Economic Development of Australia called *Governing in the 1990s*, it contains some useful insights into the selling of economic decisions in the Keating era.

Cabinet and the public service, Edwards says, went through a learning curve in the 1980s – one that involved 'continuous revision of the public rhetoric of government, of predictions about the economy and assertions about how it works, of the economic theories explaining outcomes, and periodic attempts to bring the theories, rhetoric and experience into accord'.

By those standards, it is clear the government is still learning. The 1993–94 budget and the lead-up to its presentation show a massive revision of the government's public rhetoric since the election. Treasurer John Dawkins's predictions about the economy are quite different from those he and the Prime Minister were putting to voters six months ago. We have a different set of economic theories underpinning the budget strategy – or, at least, a different explanation of them.

Before the election, the budget was self-repairing. It was going to 'whirr back into balance'. Now the revenue base has to be repaired through tax increases before the whirring can begin. Pre-election, Keating was promising not to put up tax. Now that has been redefined to mean the overall tax take will not be increased beyond the level it reached in the boomtime '80s. Pre-election, nary a word was said about the decline of national savings. Now it is one of the major problems facing the nation. And so it goes.

Edwards candidly confirms in his article that economic policy under Labor has 'involved a good deal of opinion management, often of a sophisticated kind, especially the exploitation of public fear or widely held misconceptions to advance objectives which would otherwise be difficult to attain'. That is quite an admission from a minder – that his political masters have exploited public fears and taken advantage of misconceptions in the community.

He goes further, referring to the process as 'manipulation', often on many different levels, 'with one rationale for action giving way to another more sophisticated one as each was successively undermined by fact and experience'.

He continues: 'Very often the personal success of politicians or the continued electoral success of the government depends on the ability of the cabinet members and their officials to persuade us to see the world as they wish us to see it and then, when reality intrudes, to persuade us to see it in a somewhat different way without noticing the change or being annoyed by the contradiction.'

The tricks Edwards writes about are in use again with the selling of the budget. Keating and Dawkins persuaded voters to see the world as the government wished them to see it before the election. Now, with the intrusion of post-poll reality, the line is very different – but the softening-up process and the rewriting of history are supposed to ensure that the change goes unnoticed.

After more than a decade, the government is getting pretty good at all this. The other side of the coin, though, is that the electorate may be waking up to what has been going on. This is what the opposition will be relying on in the budget session of parliament. John Hewson and his front bench, in their apparent determination to play hardball over the budget's tax measures, are gambling that voters realise they were dudded in the election campaign. Or that the opposition can *convince* voters that they were dudded and *make* them angry. If Hewson is any sort of politician (the jury is still out on that) he will be able to utilise Edwards's candour to help in this task.

But another part of the Edwards message may worry voters even more. He makes the point that while politicians such as Keating pretend to be in control when they are pulling on the levers of economic policy, this is often not the case. Economic management, according to Edwards, is like war – 'a sequence of decisions based on incomplete and constantly updated information in an environment of great uncertainty'. He quotes a remark by a British policy economist that because of lags and frequent revisions of data, 'we not only do not know where we are going or where we are – we often do not know where we have been'.

And then Edwards, who plays a crucial role in the government's economic policy-making, issues a warning: 'We should always be wary of crediting politicians and their officials with the control over events which they wish to claim, and which the repeated error of their predictions silently denies.'

Keep that in mind as Keating and Dawkins travel the country exuding confidence about the budget and its effects. And try to reconcile it with Keating's refusal over the years to admit even a skerrick of doubt about his economic policies and decisions.

1994

Labor's own leadership dilemma

1 March 1994

T he Liberals are not the only political party engaging in leadership speculation. It is going on among Labor politicians, too. Not noisily, not publicly and not urgently. Not with any sense of competition for the job, either. The discussion is calm and low-key. But it is serious nevertheless.

And it began well before Paul Keating's appearance on *The Talk Show* on SBS, in which he was asked how long he expected to remain prime minister. Those in the Labor Party who know Keating well were not surprised at his answer: 'Not an inordinate length of time.' Keating added that it would never be necessary for a deputation to tell him it was time to go. 'Before they come I'll be long gone.'

Among those at the top of the ALP, the talk for several months now has been that Keating would not stay long after the next election – assuming he wins it. Perhaps a year, then he'd be off. He would probably retire, in other words, at 53 – two years younger than Sir Robert Menzies was when he *began* his record 16-year stint in the Lodge.

A waste, some might think. At that age a politician should be at his peak, not getting out. But Keating wants to get out before he burns out. And he means it when he talks about the need for Labor to regenerate while in office – as he showed by insisting on the promotion of Michael Lee and Michael Lavarch straight from the back bench to cabinet. The trick, he told his SBS interviewers, is to provide a government with a life force through constant changes 'in the leadership, in the ministries, in the personnel, to get that rejuvenation in office'.

So, not much more than two years after Bob Hawke was toppled and Keating installed in his place, Labor is beginning to think about who should be its next leader. One who would have been seriously considered until very recently is now out of contention. It will not be Alan Griffiths. But those being watched and discussed and quietly evaluated are Kim Beazley, of course, Simon Crean and Lee. The imminent arrival in federal parliament of former West Australian premier Carmen Lawrence makes at least a quartet of contenders. One or two other names are occasionally mentioned in dispatches.

When *The Australian Financial Review* asked Beazley last week about his leadership ambitions, he dodged the question by saying it was not an issue because Keating 'is a long-term prospect'. But that is an answer only for public consumption; privately he knows better. Beazley also said, 'He [Keating] is virtually of my generation and there are a lot of ministers who are…younger.' Beazley is, in fact, nearly five years younger than Keating – and only two months older than Crean. His answer raises doubts about whether he really wants the job.

Crean's stocks are rising as a result of his cabinet performance; Keating, who not so long ago was dismissive of Crean, is impressed these days. Lee – a Keating protégé – is going well, but for him it is early days. And Lawrence? She has already proved herself a formidable politician and should have little difficulty adjusting to federal parliament.

The point is, Labor has choices and time to evaluate them. The Liberals are not so fortunate. The party has convinced itself that, if John Hewson is unsalvageable, the only alternatives this side of the next election are John Howard and Bronwyn Bishop. The great concern with Howard is the 'yesterday's man' label. The problem with Bishop is exemplified by the fact that her supporters want her installed in the leadership as close as possible to the next election so Labor has no time to expose her shortcomings.

If she is incapable of withstanding scrutiny as opposition leader, how irresponsible would it be to make her prime minister?

It is a pity the Liberals are not giving more thought to leapfrogging to the next generation, epitomised by Peter Costello. And it is a pity Costello is not giving more thought to making himself available. Costello is not lacking in ambition, but he and his supporters are thinking long-term. Their attitude is explained to a large extent by Andrew Olle's introduction to the *Four Corners* program which delivered the most recent blow against Hewson's leadership.

'No Liberal leader has ever lost a federal election and survived to fight the next,' Olle intoned authoritatively. He was wrong, of course. Menzies himself lost the 1946 election, two years after founding the Liberal Party, but survived to fight and win in 1949. Just the same, there *is* a view in the federal party these days (despite state examples like Nick Greiner and Jeff Kennett of losers who became winners) that a leader who loses an election is finished.

Costello, understandably, is not very interested in taking the sort of risk that could see his career end at 38.

Being Richo and famous has a price

29 March 1994

As sections of the media whipped themselves into a fever of speculation about Graham Richardson's future, I came across a videotape of a fascinating but sparsely reported speech he gave recently. It was especially interesting against the background of such headlines as 'Is the PM trying to oust Richo?' and 'The PM and his numbers man: a crunch coming?' The tone of much of the material made clear the impatience some journalists have to dance on Richardson's political grave.

For years Richardson has enjoyed a strangely contradictory relationship with journalists. He is something of a media favourite, because he is open, interesting, quotable and witty – and because of the palpable power backing his statements. At the same time, there has been an undoubted willingness among many reporters and commentators to believe the worst of him. And not just because of his role as a tough, right-wing powerbroker. Robert Ray performs a similar role with no less arm-twisting and knee-capping but without anything like the same image problem.

The image problem and how he came by it is what Richardson addressed in the speech, delivered at the Museum of Contemporary Art in Sydney, where an exhibition of works by Andy Warhol gave him an excuse to talk about fame and its consequences. 'My first brush with fame should have given me a warning about what the rest of my life would be like,' he said.

That initial taste of notoriety resulted from the brutal bashing of left-winger Peter Baldwin, now federal Minister for Social Security, 'by persons unknown but assumed to be on the same side as I was in the Labor Party'. Richardson, a very young and not very well-known NSW ALP secretary at the time, had to front a packed news conference on the matter. 'You get remembered for that. I don't think, in retrospect, that image ever left me.'

Then, when he entered parliament, 'I went in with all the bile and bitterness that was associated with the Hayden–Hawke battle…Half the Labor Party saw me as a villain, the other half as the hero. But the half who see you as the villain often have more to say.' People tended to remember him 'bringing someone down…They forget who you got up, how many elections you might have won, how much that might have been for the benefit of not just the party but the country.'

His high profile meant people constantly claimed to have seen him in places he had not been. One example: a phone call from a journalist claiming to have photographs of him drinking with a very well known criminal. Richardson, knowing there could be no photographs of a meeting that had not taken place, replied: 'Go for it, old son. That's the name of the game. You print, I sue and we see what happens.' The journalist later produced, not photographs, but a statutory declaration. Fortunately, on the night referred to in the document, Richardson was with 400 people at an official dinner. 'I could just as easily have been at home watching *Die Hard 2* in the loungeroom and finding it much harder to prove.'

Another problem: 'Your name is taken in vain by countless people who claim to be your closest friend, claim to have lunch with you twice a week, talk to you all the time on the telephone. Most of that's harmless...But sometimes it takes on a pretty nasty tinge.' Some people who claimed to know him very well boasted that any problem could be fixed, legally or illegally, with a word in his ear.

'Late last year there was an inventive chap in western Sydney who managed to steal some money from community groups in my name, claiming that the money they were giving to him would be given to me and I would make the local council change its mind on...a development application. I understand that when the bloke got the money he went straight to the TAB and put it on number four in the fifth.'

'Eventually these stories break, and every one of them manages to do you some harm.'

The notorious Love Boat affair, involving allegations (later discredited and withdrawn) about a number of Labor identities and a prostitute on a launch on Sydney Harbour, still cropped up somewhere at least once a year, Richardson said. 'If a decade further on, with a woman you didn't know and a boat you were never on, an allegation can still do you some harm, it does teach me something.' It taught him how dangerous it could be when lonely, frustrated, frightened, angry, jealous or downtrodden people tried to borrow a bit of somebody else's fame to improve their situation or to give them a standing they could not otherwise have.

Richardson explained to his audience of art lovers that, while power was something everyone feared, 'I have to tell you, it's not that big a deal.' His judgment on the parliamentary press gallery was: 'In the end, I think they'll always take the low road.' So, if he could have his time over, would he do something else?

'Absolutely no, because the 20-year ride I've had has been bloody marvellous.'

Tiny heirs to Chifley and Menzies

10 May 1994

There was never any chance that Paul Keating's white paper on employment would have anything like the significance of Ben Chifley's 1945 white paper on the same subject. Apart from anything else, the world has changed too much. No longer can a national government, particularly in a small country such as Australia, take economic decisions in isolation. Governments no longer have the same capacity to influence events. We live in a world economy where financial markets and giant corporations can pack more punch than government policy-makers. Australia has changed, too. It is a much more complex society than it was 49 years ago.

But our politicians have changed as well. In postwar Australia, our political leaders were willing to think big. Does anyone believe that the present crop of politicians, from either side of parliament, would have the imagination and the courage to create the Snowy Mountains scheme or to organise a mass immigration program? Today's politicians are small thinkers, often motivated by quite petty considerations. To expect them to think on anything like the scale Chifley did – or even Menzies – is quite unreal.

John Hewson had a crack at thinking big with his ambitious 'Fightback' program financed by a goods and services tax. But, since its rejection by the electorate, the opposition leader has joined his colleagues in the think-small brigade. Policy ideas do not come much smaller than his 'family values' and 'law and order' direction statement after the recent Liberal Party retreat at Eagle Hawk Hill near Canberra. These days, having opted out of any attempt to influence events in a serious way, Hewson is a mere critic of the government. He may as well be in the press gallery.

The way cabinet and its expenditure review committee carved up Health Minister Carmen Lawrence and the ambitious plan she presented to boost Aboriginal health services was a classic illustration of small thinking. On the simple political level, devaluing and humiliating Lawrence before she had even made her first appearance at Question Time was petty and stupid. Lawrence is very important to the government, as the desperate campaign to persuade her to switch from state to federal politics demonstrated. Labor needs her to shine. Yet the detailed leaks were deliberately malicious and intended to tarnish the Lawrence image. Someone quite senior, it seems, put personal rivalry well ahead of the government's overall interest.

And the decision itself, gutting the proposal prepared by Graham Richardson before his retirement, was the product of small minds. With the issue of South African apartheid removed from the international agenda, the spotlight of world opinion will increasingly focus on the treatment of Australia's Aboriginal population. We are going to look very bad indeed, and we will deserve the odium we attract. The way successive Australian governments have neglected the issue of Aboriginal health is a scandal. Richardson, one politician who was prepared to think ambitiously on occasions, tried to do something dramatic. The Lilliputians in the ERC, with former health minister Brian Howe leading the charge, headed off the move. So much for Paul Keating's ludicrous claims in caucus that the ERC is 'the engine room of Labor policy'.

So the white paper was never likely to attempt anything very original or brave. The best comparison is not with Chifley's Full Employment in Australia, but with Keating's own 'One Nation' statement presented soon after he toppled Bob Hawke as prime minister. 'One Nation' involved some necessary economic pump-priming, but its primary purpose was political. Hewson had a plan, so Keating needed a plan, too. The political imperative now is not to match anything the opposition is proposing – it is proposing nothing – but to show concern about a subject that still worries voters, despite the economic recovery. Keating, after all, promised in the election campaign to take action on unemployment. He has to be seen to be doing something.

But, while the white paper contains some admirable initiatives, packaged to make the maximum impression on voters, it is basically an extension of what is already being done. Ideas that would have involved real change in industry policy, for example, were given short shrift in developing the blueprint. Yet despite its conservatism, the document produced the usual whingeing from sections of the business community as details leaked in the week before its release. If our politicians are unwilling to think big, our business leaders are even worse.

The 'jobs compact' at the centre of the government's approach may not be especially adventurous, but it is eminently sensible. If nothing is done to try to bring the long-term unemployed back into the mainstream, it is not only social consequences – the development of an underclass – that Australia will have to worry about. The economic consequences will not be pleasant, either. Marginalising 350 000 long-term unemployed would raise the possibility of a wages break-out caused by a shortage of labour. If business leaders in this country do not take that seriously, they should look at what has happened in Britain.

The lamb betrayed

31 May 1994

Politics is not a blood-sport, John Hewson claimed in the middle of his final traumatic week as Liberal leader. He knows better now. It is also a grubby, nasty, unpleasant business. Having watched the political process up close for the best part of 30 years, I find it extraordinary that anyone finds the idea of a political career attractive.

It even takes its toll on Paul Keating. Several people have related recent conversations in which Keating has complained about the political life and expressed a desire to be free of it. He is said to envy Graham Richardson's escape. Jeff Kennett came away from a discursive talk in the Prime Minister's office convinced Keating longs for a normal existence and cannot wait to get the next election out of the way so he can plan his political retirement.

An extraordinary incident occurred outside the House of Representatives chamber a month or so ago. Hewson was standing alone, looking dejected, when Keating loomed up and put an arm around the opposition leader's shoulders. 'There, there,' said Keating.

Sympathy or send-up? Those who saw it were uncertain, but it hardly matters. Politics destroyed Hewson. Chewed him up and spat him out. The dazed and broken figure who limped away on Monday bore no resemblance to the bright, confident, energetic, idealistic bloke who came into parliament just five years ago.

Hewson was used shamelessly. He was shoved into the leadership reluctantly, before being given any opportunity to learn the political trade. When inexperience and a lack of political skills cost him the 1993 election, he was roundly condemned as an incompetent failure – but persuaded to stay on as leader anyway. Those who did the persuading were not intent on giving Hewson another chance. They had their own agendas.

Peacock was one of them, motivated by a determination to block a Howard comeback. Liberal Party federal director Andrew Robb was another. His motivation was to give the party time to look at alternatives – to allow other potential leaders to emerge and show their wares. Hardly anyone believed Hewson had been confirmed as the one to lead the Liberals to the next election. But Hewson – poor naive Hewson – believed it, fought the good fight and then, punch-drunk and pathetic, was betrayed by those he had thought his friends.

No doubt they had the Liberal Party's best interests at heart... the three people who, over lunch, discussed the possible leaking of party polling to destabilise Hewson not long before the material miraculously landed in Kerry O'Brien's hands...federal president Tony Staley, publicly defending Hewson as 'doing a good job' when he had already decided there had to be a leadership change...Peacock, who – as he flew to Canberra for the leadership vote – jokingly asked Foreign Minister Gareth Evans about available diplomatic posts because he would have no political future if Hewson was re-elected... and all the others who led him on and then helped bring him down.

Enter Alexander Downer. At least, as the son and grandson of prominent politicians, he knows what he is in for; knows what a dirty and double-dealing game it is. Knows how to play it, too. Knows how to double-deal. Downer's statement after Hewson called on the leadership spill – that his position had not changed, he still supported Hewson – is a case in point. He was already in the process of sewing up the ticket with Peter Costello, announced only an hour or so later, that spelt Hewson's doom.

While a justifiably paranoid Hewson watched Costello, it was Downer making the lunge for his job all the time. Much more effusive in his public support, but working away cleverly and without scruple in private. It was Downer who went to convince Kennett of his credentials while publicly claiming it was a routine call by a shadow treasurer on a premier; Downer who held what was intended to be a secret meeting with Tony Staley to lock in organisation support for an anti-Hewson coup. Downer is what Hewson could not be. A politician, pure and simple. As pragmatic as they come, with few illusions, aware that you have to soil your hands to succeed in politics, and ready and willing to do so.

All of which makes him a threat to Keating. Downer probably will have only one crack at the prime ministership. If he fails to win the next election, it will almost certainly be Costello's turn. Some in the Labor Party smugly believe that this son of the Establishment will be easy game, but they could be making a serious mistake. Downer is easy to underestimate. I underestimated him when he became shadow treasurer, writing that he was not up to the job – a judgment that proved quite wrong.

The new Liberal leader is a man with well-honed political instincts; not born to rule, but born to politics. Whereas no one believed it when Hewson claimed to be repositioning the Liberal Party, Downer has the skills to carry it off much more convincingly. Just look at the calculating way this member of the ultra-conservative faction of the party in South Australia has altered his own image and wooed moderate Liberals in recent months.

Downer carries some baggage – views expressed in the past, occasional traces of an immature boarding school manner. But Keating would be unwise to regard him as a pushover.

Keating's house of horrors

25 October 1994

When senators talk to Paul Keating about the powers of the Upper House and, particularly, the powers of Senate committees, he sings them a little song: 'Anything you can do, I can do better. I can do anything better than you.' The message is clear. The House of Representatives has the same powers. They might not be used much, but they are available if the government wants to take advantage of them.

The Senate committee system has evolved largely as an opposition tool. The late Lionel Murphy worked to get it off the ground in the 1960s and early '70s, when Labor was in opposition and the coalition government lacked the numbers to control the Senate. The Democratic Labor Party held the balance of power then. These days, when the coalition gets together with the Greens or the Democrats to use a Senate committee to embarrass the Labor government, people in the ALP curse Murphy's achievement. Ros Kelly, for example, has the threat posed by a Senate committee to thank for her fall from cabinet.

But there is nothing to stop a government taking a leaf out of the Senate's book and using House of Representatives committees for its own political purposes. They would have the same legal right to call witnesses and demand the production of documents. And, with the coalition in office in most states, there would be no shortage of targets with the potential to cause embarrassment to the Liberal and National parties. Send a parliamentary committee on a fishing expedition and you never know what might be revealed. It is no small threat.

The threat was used, very quietly, when Sydney/Melbourne rivalry boiled up over the Olympics back in July. With Melbourne Establishment figures claiming their city's bid for the 1996 games had been sabotaged to help Sydney get the 2000 Games, Victorian Liberal Premier Jeff Kennett called for a Senate committee to inquire into the financial accountability of the Australian Olympic Committee. Such an inquiry would clearly have been damaging to Australia's ability to stage the Games successfully, so the word went out to Kennett:

drop off, or there just might be a House of Representatives committee inquiry into the granting of the Melbourne casino licence.

Much the same threat was made last week, but rather more publicly and for a different reason. Stung by coalition attacks on his decision to buy a $2.2 million home in Sydney's eastern suburbs, the Prime Minister retaliated in parliament with a broadside against the Melbourne casino tendering process, comparing it with 'a dead cat in the middle of the road, stinking to high heaven'. If pressed, he said, he 'might be prepared to do a little more than have a debate about it'. Asked later what that meant, government sources told *The Age* newspaper it indicated that Keating might be prepared to launch a federal parliamentary investigation – and such an inquiry would be dominated by Labor members. He was talking, in other words, about a House of Representatives committee.

The Liberals, of course, were outraged that the Prime Minister should accuse a coalition state government of being involved in something corrupt. Kennett was apoplectic, and Alexander Downer – sputtering with phoney indignation – accused Keating of behaving appallingly. But what did they expect? The coalition, after all, had hidden behind parliamentary privilege to brand Keating, in effect, a crook. For example, Liberal Michael Baume told the Senate: 'In order to get this sort of money, he seems to have had some kind of snout in the trough.' Two other Liberal senators, Rod Kemp and Eric Abetz, made similar insinuations. They were not acting off their own bat. Downer and other senior opposition figures had given the green light.

The truth is that there is no great mystery about how Keating will pay for the Woollahra house. He has always kept an eye on the real estate market and made a smart purchase when he acquired a house in Sydney's Elizabeth Bay 12 years ago. That house, with renovations painstakingly supervised by Keating, is now worth at least half of what he has signed up to pay in 18 months for the new residence. If he then chooses to retire and live in it, the balance would be covered by his superannuation. The alternative, if Keating wins another election and decides to stay on at the Lodge, would be to lease the house. Given that a luxury home unit not far away was not long ago leased for $3000 a week, it is not likely that Keating will face an unmanageable financial burden.

So the suggestion that the Prime Minister is involved in anything untoward is merely grubby politicking. Keating is entitled to be angry at the attempt to portray him as corrupt. When Andrew Peacock, as opposition leader, called Bob Hawke 'a little crook', there was a backlash that hurt Peacock. But Downer, having approved the same kind of smear against Keating, gets away with it. At least Peacock had the guts to do his dirty work himself.

Few things are certain in politics. One certainty, though, is that if you belt Keating, he will belt you back. Sometimes it might take months, as it did over Bob Hawke's allegation that Keating opposed Australia's Gulf War commitment. And frequently it is politically counter-productive, which was undoubtedly the case with his eventual savaging of Hawke over the Gulf War claim. But that is Keating, and his opponents had better be aware of it. If they make unsubstantiated allegations of corruption against him, it is London to a brick that he will hit back hard – and use any weapon at hand. He has not used the weapon of a House of Representatives committee yet, but he is well aware that it is there if he needs it.

Coalition no longer coalesces

22 November 1994

Only one politician since Federation has occupied the post of opposition leader without going on to lead his party in an election campaign. John Latham stood aside in favour of Joe Lyons, a public hero after breaking away from the Depression-era Scullin Labor government. Lyons's wife, Dame Enid, called it 'an act of outstanding political generosity'. John Howard's backers, as the current spate of Liberal leadership destabilisation develops, hope to persuade Alexander Downer to be equally generous. But Downer is no Latham and Howard no Lyons.

Howard is desperate for another go at the leadership. You can see it in his eyes. And it is glaringly obvious from his behaviour. 'I saw you talking to Howard,' a Liberal MP said to a colleague one evening last week. 'I would have joined you, but he'd already spoken to me five times today.' The man who says he got the leadership by accident and lost it by ambush the first time around is everywhere as he tries to position himself as the only alternative to Downer.

But Howard's smartest advisers know he cannot afford to fight for the job again. If he is to become leader with any hope of unifying the coalition and going into the next election with some credibility, the party must come to him – not the other way around. Jeff Kennett nicknamed Howard 'the rodent', because of a belief that he was always gnawing away at John Hewson's leadership. While clearly aware that his supporters are taking soundings, Howard has tried very hard to avoid the perception of rodent-like activities this time.

An example: two days before the information leaked in a damaging way, a friend of mine was within earshot when Howard told one of his strongest supporters, the fanatically pro-monarchist MP Tony Abbott, that Downer was going to propose a constitutional convention. I happen to know that neither Howard nor Abbott was responsible for the leak, but that did not stop them displaying a touch of the Alan Bonds when I told them they had been overheard. 'I have no recollection of any such conversation,' was the formula each of them used.

Howard also needs to avoid a ballot. He needs Downer to admit that the job is too much for him and to quit. Downer's behaviour after his disastrous 'things that batter' gaffe gave Howard backers reason for hope. He may not have broken down and wept, as Alan Ramsey claimed in *The Sydney Morning Herald*, but he certainly suffered a huge attack of self-doubt when he realised how stupid he had been. In the immediate aftermath of that incident, Downer *did* confide to friends that if he decided he was not up to the job, he would not try to hang on to it. But, in response to the suggestion now that he should hand over to Howard, Downer's retort has been: 'What sort of a wuss do they think I am?'

It is too easy just to blame Downer for the mess the coalition finds itself in. Certainly, his gaffes have made a large contribution. 'When I became leader of the opposition, I was not well known to the Australian community,' he said in a recent interview. 'As time wears on I will become much better known.' He seemed blissfully unaware of the irony of what he was saying. It was when he was an unfamiliar figure that his poll rating soared; it plummeted as people got to know him. But Downer cannot be held responsible for the latest outbreak of brawling. That is down to Liberal and National party right-wingers, ultra-conservatives so unprepared to compromise, so determined to get their own way, that they helped to kill off Hewson and are well on the way to doing the same to his successor.

In different circumstances, Downer's initiative on a constitutional convention and racial hatred legislation would have been seen as politically astute. The constitutional convention idea makes sense as a means of defusing the republic issue and accommodating all strands of Liberal Party thought on the matter while allowing Downer to hammer a useful political point: 'Mr Keating wants to make the decisions himself. We want the people to decide.' On the question of race hate legislation, Downer deserves credit, not condemnation, for refusing to kowtow to the ultra-Right when a party room row erupted over a shadow cabinet decision that the coalition would prepare its own bill. Downer's media critics had been demanding that he show strength, but when he did demonstrate some steel they condemned him for that too. He can't win.

The reality is that when authority goes, nothing works. Downer needs to rebuild his authority, but he cannot do that while every attempt he makes at decisive action, every move he takes to position the coalition closer to the middle ground, produces public rows and destabilising leaks and new headlines about his leadership problems. Catch-22. If Downer is really determined not to follow the script Howard's people have written for him ('It is a far, far better thing that I do etc'), and the coalition is not prepared to stamp down hard on the arch conservatives and get behind him, the Liberal Party risks not just another defeat but electoral disaster.

Given the power now exercised in its ranks by Christian fundamentalists and other hardline conservatives, dragging the Liberal Party towards the centre is a tough enough task. Trying to haul along the ratbag-Right element of the National Party as well is just about impossible. If they lose the next election, the Liberals will need to consider very carefully whether being in coalition with such a group in opposition makes much sense.

1995

Ethics? What ethics?

21 February 1995

Ian Sinclair, Father of the House of Representatives because of his long service there and, in his day, one of the toughest ever federal ministers, can be disarmingly frank. I was reminded of this at the weekend when I phoned him to discuss leaks – in particular, budget leaks. I wanted his comments on the way the opposition was drawing on a leaked Finance Department document on possible spending cuts to embarrass the government. 'Sinkers' was expecting my call.

But first, some background. In 1980 the entire federal budget fell off the back of a truck and into my hands several days before it was to be delivered in parliament. For scooping the then-treasurer, John Howard, on his budget speech, I received a Thorn Award for television journalism. Sinclair, minister for communications at the time, had the task of presenting it to me – and, shunning the usual congratulatory platitudes, he did a real bucket job. The story, he said, was not worthy of an award. I had made use of a stolen document. This sort of thing was to be deplored, not encouraged. The publication of leaked documents was ethically dubious and did not, in his opinion, accord with the requirements of excellence in journalism. The motives of the informer in such a case were suspect. I gave an equally caustic speech in reply about government secrecy and the importance of leaks in keeping politicians honest.

Now, nearly 15 years later, the coalition of which Sinclair is a senior member had got its own budget leak – details of options for cuts in government spending prepared by bureaucrats in the Finance Department, Treasury and the Department of Prime Minister and Cabinet. Apparently unconcerned about the motives of the informer, and unworried by any ethical problem, Howard as opposition leader and key members of his front bench were using this stolen document for all it was worth to score political points and scare the pants off voters. What was Sinclair's reaction?

'I was thinking about how we'd crossed swords only the other day,' he said, and laughed. 'Perspectives vary depending on where you are. Governments cry foul, especially when they're vulnerable. I certainly did, and Paul Keating is doing a Sinclair in circumstances very similar to those we were in at the time.' As Sinclair sees it, the Fraser government in the early '80s was on the way down, fighting for its life, and the Keating government is in the same position now. Recalling his experience as a member of the Fraser cabinet, he said: 'Once the bureaucracy starts leaking against you, and once you start to deny doing what you know you've got to do, you are in real bloody trouble.'

The Keating government *is* in trouble. Howard's re-elevation to the Liberal leadership has put an ideological floor under the coalition and restored its will to win. Much more important, attention is being focused on the government rather than the opposition, and it is not a pretty sight. Whether the government can fight back, though, or whether its condition is terminal, will almost certainly be decided over the next three or four months. The way it handles the budget process, made much more difficult by the opposition's leak, will show whether or not it is comparable with the Fraser government in its dying days.

One crucial question is whether the Labor government is prepared to make the tough decisions that are obviously necessary in the current economic climate. The Fraser government could not resist behaving opportunistically and, in the end, failed the economic management test. Given that this is an election budget, pressure on Keating and his ministers to take soft options will be immense. Another crucial question is whether the Labor caucus is prepared to stand by the government in making difficult decisions. Fraser's 'nervous Nellies' made resolute government impossible. In this context, the cacophony of complaint from caucus members over the pre-Christmas wood-chip licence decision was ominous. If the government shows itself to be weak and undisciplined, its chance of convincing the electorate that it is worthy of another term will be slim indeed.

There are dangers for the coalition, too. Howard risks losing his 'Honest John' image by being slick and cynical over spending cuts. Whipping up a scare campaign on the issue when even the most cocooned voter is well aware that the opposition has been demanding *ad nauseam* that the government take tough measures to cut spending is so obviously hypocritical that Howard needs to take great care. This is presumably why the opposition's media manipulators, in feeding material from their leaked documents to journalists, have tried to demand that it be presented as new material and not sourced back to the coalition in any way. Another motive, perhaps, is to create an impression that there is a spate of leaks.

There is already concern in the business community that, by using the leaked document to spook caucus and cabinet, Howard is making it increasingly difficult for the government to cut spending. If the opportunism of Howard and Co leads the government to believe the coalition may oppose spending cuts in the Senate, the likely consequences certainly would not please the Liberal Party's traditional constituency.

'They could put us in a position where we have to go off and make deals with fruitcakes again,' says a Labor source. 'And the business community could end up with a tax it does not want.' In other words, if the coalition looks like blocking spending cuts, the government may have no choice but to introduce a carbon tax or environment levy which appeals to the Greens and Democrats, who hold the Senate balance of power. Howard considered resigning from the Fraser cabinet in 1982 because he regarded that year's budget as irresponsible. An opposition leader has the same obligation as a treasurer to behave responsibly.

Bradfield, on doctor's orders

9 May 1995

The original 'carpetbaggers' were itinerant bankers in the American wild west. Because they needed to travel light, they carried their money in bags made from old carpets. The term came to mean anyone on the make, and was soon appropriated for politics. As defined in William Safire's *Political Dictionary*, a carpetbagger is 'an outlander moving into a new area to seek political power at the expense of the native politicians'.

Brendan Nelson clearly resents being called a carpetbagger, but it is hard to see why. He is an outlander both geographically and ideologically. Not only has the Australian Medical Association president moved from Hobart to Sydney purely for the purpose of snatching Liberal preselection for the blue-ribbon seat of Bradfield, but, after 20 years of identification with the Labor Party, he believes he is entitled to be handed the safest Liberal seat in NSW and the second safest in the country.

One of the enduring images of the 1993 federal election campaign was Nelson on the evening television news telling a crowd four days before the poll: 'I have never voted Liberal in my life.' Not long after that election he started trailing his coat for a safe Liberal seat. First he eyed off Boothby, in South Australia, when Steele Hall announced his intention to retire. According to a senior federal Liberal, 'Brendan was chased out of SA by Steele and [opposition Senate leader] Robert Hill.'

Then Nelson's mentor and AMA predecessor, Bruce Shepherd, convinced him that Bradfield was the seat he deserved. Shepherd, whose previous major foray into federal politics involved backing the Joh-for-Canberra push that helped sink John Howard's prime ministerial hopes in 1987, is not a member of the Liberal Party. But he does have influence among Bradfield Liberals – not surprising, perhaps, given that Nelson says 1500 doctors live in the electorate. Shepherd is also able to tap into money to bankroll an all-out campaign to try to win preselection for Nelson.

Bad luck that it means toppling David Connolly, a life-long Liberal and one of the few members of Howard's shadow ministry who consistently attacks and embarrasses the government. A look at the bulging newspaper files on Connolly in the parliamentary library shows the impact he has made with issues that point up Paul Keating's imperial style. The Thai teak table fiasco and the extravagance of the cabinet room Gould bird print purchase are two examples. Now Connolly is responsible for developing coalition policy on superannuation, which will be an issue of major importance following the budget next week. But if he loses preselection somebody else will presumably have to take over immediately. Howard can hardly retain in a key front-bench position somebody rejected by the party.

Nelson is, of course, a man of considerable talent and charm. As the public face of the AMA he has shown great skill in explaining and selling policies. He has also demonstrated an ability to draw attention to important issues such as the scandalous state of Aboriginal health. As he says himself, his political skills are shown by the fact that 'I have the common touch but I can represent the most conservative organisation in the country outside the League of Rights.'

He has the potential to be a real asset to the Liberal Party. To get into government, the Liberals need to increase the seats they hold. Nelson is the kind of high-profile candidate who would be guaranteed to take a marginal seat off Labor. Lowe, Parramatta, Macquarie – he could win any of them. But Nelson argues that he would be confined to helping the Liberal Party in only one seat if he ran for a marginal whereas, if he was preselected for Bradfield, 'I would be capable of assisting the party in numerous marginal seats'.

Attempts were made by senior Liberals to persuade Nelson that he could be put into a relatively safe seat without taking on Connolly. Wentworth was suggested when John Hewson decided to quit politics, for example. And now that Don Dobie has decided to call it a day, another Sydney seat, Cook, is available. But Nelson is insisting that it is Bradfield or nothing. Peter Costello no doubt had this in mind when Shepherd phoned recently to complain about him backing Connolly. I am told Costello replied tartly: 'I'm the deputy leader and I'm on a nine percent margin. Howard's the leader and he's on three percent.

What's so special about your bloke that he can't go into a seat with a margin of less than 23 percent?'

Nelson supporters answer that their man's aim is not simply to get into politics. Fed up with coalition ineptitude, he wants to force the Liberal Party to send a resounding signal that it is changing – both in personnel and direction. The selection of someone like him for the bluest of blue-ribbon seats, he believes, would leave no doubt that the party is serious about becoming more contemporary and about winning office. False modesty is not one of the doctor's failings.

And what of his switch in political allegiance? According to Nelson, when he showed signs of youthful idealism at 14, 'my father said, "you're Labor" and joined me up'. He claims he paid his last subscription when he was 17 and did not renew his ALP membership until the late 1980s – about the same time he joined the AMA. He quickly became disillusioned with ALP branch meetings, Nelson says – but adds: 'I was trying to push things important to the AMA. There was a Labor government in Canberra so it didn't do any harm to remain in the party.'

Gerard Henderson, in *Menzies' Child*, identifies 'a lack of belief in a cause' on the part of many members as one of the Liberal Party's basic problems. At least, if Nelson wins the battle for Bradfield, he will fit neatly into that tradition.

Countdown to Christmas

22 August 1995

On the eve of the 1993 election, Paul Keating made two speeches. Telling an audience of sympathetic arts types about the government's success in combining responsible economic management with traditional Labor concerns, he boasted: 'If we win tomorrow, we'll make that binding so tight the Tories will need an oxy-acetylene torch to break into it.' Later, at a private dinner for his personal staff, he spoke of the opportunities for the government if it managed to secure another term. With inflation beaten, the hard structural adjustment decisions already taken and the international economy improving, Keating said: 'I think we have to go right out of our way to muck it up.'

Well, the coalition under John Howard got out the oxy-acetylene torch and applied it with vigour and skill. And the Prime Minister, with some help from his advisers and senior ministers, did go out of his way to muck up the politics of the economic recovery. The result is that Labor is now looking down the barrel of a very bad electoral defeat early next year. It is facing not just a loss but a massacre, a 1975-type result, unless something changes fairly soon. Two things might produce the necessary change. Keating could acknowledge the seriousness of the situation, pull himself together, focus on what needs to be done and apply himself in a tightly disciplined way. Or he could walk.

Keating has often told senior people in the government: 'You won't have to blow me out of here. I'll just go.' But, as a colleague puts it, 'I don't think Paul has it in him to see he is going to be smashed at the polls.' He would find it particularly difficult to accept that Howard, for whom he has utter contempt, is the one shaping to hand him a humiliating defeat. So the likelihood of Keating deciding a leadership change would be in the party's best interests and handing over to Kim Beazley is small indeed. The problem is that a significant change in Keating's attitude and approach looks almost as remote.

At the last caucus meeting before parliament rose in June for the winter recess, Keating listed for his troops all the fine things the government had done. When the question was raised of why, in that case, the opinion polls were not moving Labor's way, the Prime Minister had no explanation. The government, after all, at least in his view, was doing everything right. That scared a lot of Labor MPs. They were not reassured five weeks later when an extraordinary performance on John Laws's radio program showed Keating still believed the government had got it right and the fault lay with the voters. His 'What are you on about?' response to callers to the program provided the Liberals with yet another Keating-authored bumper sticker for the election campaign. Labor MPs will be very interested in what he has to say at the first caucus meeting of the new parliamentary session next week.

Keating seems unable to help himself. In the wake of the Laws fiasco, it was decided he should try to undo some of the damage by taking a more humble tone on the economy in a speech at Roma in Queensland. The whole point of the exercise was to get maximum media coverage – but the Prime Minister's office booted a pool television crew off the VIP aircraft flying him to the remote outback town. Labor colleagues could only shake their heads in astonishment. The point is that Keating could do a lot better, but won't. That is the reason for a growing anger at him among some caucus members.

Despite its disastrous electoral slump, Labor can still handle difficult problems. The way the Batman preselection row was sorted out is evidence of that. One advantage for the party will be Jennie George stumping the country in the election campaign as the new ACTU leader, presenting a softer image – and perhaps a more relevant one, given that she will be the first person from a white-collar union background to hold the position. A union movement with a woman as figurehead will be harder for the coalition to demonise. And Labor will need people like Martin Ferguson in safe seats if it goes down badly in the election and has to rebuild.

But the major problem is Keating and his failure to respond to – or even acknowledge – the sullen electoral mood. Backbenchers have now had the best part of two months in their electorates, getting a feel for what voters are thinking. 'A lot say they can't stand Paul,' says one Labor MP in a fairly typical marginal seat. 'Some say they'll never vote Labor again until he's gone.' According to another Labor MP – street-smart, not a nervous Nellie – voters say things like, 'You'll be OK, but the government…' That, he says, is code for 'I'd like to vote for you but I'm not going to'.

The big worry is that the consistency of opinion polls since May suggests the mood is solidifying. When Labor MPs and candidates go door-knocking, people are polite enough – but they have little to say. There is no engagement, an ominous sign suggesting they have made up their minds and are simply waiting to cast their vote. 'There is a limit to how long you can let people sit with the same view,' says a party strategist.

Labor has four months at the most to turn things around. If the party is not within striking distance of the coalition by the time voters switch off politics for the Christmas break, it will be all over – and a lot of Labor MPs will be tempted to use their holidays for job-hunting. The parliamentary session starting next week is all-important for Labor. 'Paul's contempt for Howard is one of the things that keeps pushing him off strategy,' says a senior government member. The hope is that if he can be jolted into realising how serious things are it may be one of the things that brings him back to his senses.

Bad for the ALP's health

29 August 1995

Say goodbye, Carmen. It may also be goodbye to the worm. Health Minister Carmen Lawrence and the squiggly electronic line that scored the televised debates between leaders in the 1993 federal election are both fighting for their political lives. Lawrence is on the ropes and the chance of her still being around for the election campaign, whenever it is held, is slim indeed. The assault on the worm is just beginning.

Lawrence was to be central to the Labor campaign. Her main task was supposed to be to make health the sort of winning issue for Labor that it was in the last election. Health is always a major concern for voters, especially women voters, and most especially young mothers and women over 50. That is why the Liberals under Howard have devoted so much attention and energy to neutralising the aspects of coalition health policy that Labor was able to exploit with devastating effect last time around.

The coalition mantra these days is: 'Bulk billing stays, no significant changes to Medicare, help with private health insurance.' Lawrence was to spearhead a scare campaign aimed at persuading the electorate not to believe those reassuring promises. The message was to be that a coalition government would still be wedded to the old 'Fightback' agenda threatening bulk billing and Medicare as we know it. The problem is that such a scare campaign can only work if the person promoting it has credibility.

Once upon a time Lawrence had credibility in abundance, but now – thanks to the royal commission into what has become known as the Penny Easton affair – those days are well and truly gone. If she is not a liar, evidence given to the royal commission so far certainly makes her look like one. Any attempt by Lawrence now to accuse Howard of telling lies about health policy, or anything else, would provoke a loud horse laugh from a large section of the community.

In any case, as the recent Queensland election showed, scare campaigns can produce a damaging backlash if they are not handled carefully. Wayne Goss's government got its fingers badly burnt when it alleged out of the blue that the coalition would privatise public hospitals if it won office. Instead of being frightened off the coalition, voters were angry with Labor for making the claim. It was not taken seriously because no groundwork had been done. A climate had not been created in which it would sound convincing. The ground for a federal Labor scare campaign on health needs to be prepared in the session of parliament starting this week, but a beleaguered and bleeding Lawrence is in no position to do it.

Lawrence is now useless as health minister. When she tries to talk health policy she is ignored by a media that scents blood and is interested only in the Easton affair. Not only is the government incapable of waging a scare campaign while she remains in the job; there is a very real risk that health as an election issue could turn against the government. The Liberals undoubtedly sense an opportunity. State and territory elections this year have seen opposition parties exploit with great success community concern about hospital waiting lists.

This could pay off at a federal level, too. The fact that the decline in private health insurance under Labor puts increasing pressure on public hospitals is not a difficult thing to get across to voters. Also, many seniors are likely to worry that the exodus from private health insurance could mean their premiums will rise. Young mothers who feel guilty about bowing out of private health insurance to save money may well be attracted by the kind of incentives proposed by the coalition. And, overall, the hospital waiting-list problem takes the gloss off Medicare as a Labor government achievement.

To get its election strategy back on track, the government needs a new minister in the vital health portfolio. Nothing could be more obvious than that. None of the available alternatives has the kind of standing and credibility Lawrence had in her old 'Saint Carmen' days, but current trade minister Bob McMullan is viewed as the best of the bunch by those in the government who are beginning to address the problem.

The fate of the worm is tied up in discussions now under way between Labor's national secretary Gary Gray and Liberal Party federal director Andrew Robb about the format of campaign debates between Paul Keating and John Howard, including whether the Nine network should be allowed to let the worm loose on screen to show how an audience of swing voters reacts, sentence by sentence, to what the leaders say.

Labor dislikes the worm, arguing that debate will be devalued and trivialised as leaders – instead of concentrating on serious argument about policy – simply produce rehearsed lines and researched sentiment calculated to cause the worm to register instant approval. Howard is said to have no strong feelings either way, but Robb is firmly in the anti-worm camp, believing the immediate emotional response registered when swing voters manipulate their dials can be quite different from the rational response people have when they think about and discuss what they have heard.

Robb bases his view on the 1990 debate between Bob Hawke and Andrew Peacock. There was no televised worm in that campaign, but as an experiment the Liberal Party arranged for 60 swing voters to watch the debate on a big screen in a Sydney theatre while hooked up to the Morgan Research Centre's equipment. Peacock was so little on top of issues that he could not even ask follow-up questions of his opponent. Just about every commentator and expert in the country pronounced it a clear win for Hawke, but the swingers with the dials scored it clearly Peacock's way – as it went along, and at the end. Later, though, after an hour's thought and discussion, they were asked to return to their dials and vote again – and they reversed their verdict.

20 years to debunk the myth

24 October 1995

In early October 1975, I was invited to dinner at the home of a United States diplomat. The other guests were the US labour attaché in Australia, who was a senior CIA operative, and a British MI5 agent working in Canberra under diplomatic cover. The reason for the dinner quickly became apparent. They wanted to talk about what would happen if the coalition used its Senate numbers to block the Whitlam government's budget; in particular, what the governor-general would do. I am not suggesting that American and British spies masterminded the events of 20 years ago, but they certainly took a keen interest. And they got their money's worth. I told them confidently that if the coalition kept its nerve and Whitlam refused to call an election, there could be only one outcome: Sir John Kerr would dismiss the Labor government.

That was my clear-headed view at the beginning of the constitutional crisis. But, as events unfolded, I revised my opinion. People who thought themselves close to the governor-general were convinced that he would only act on the advice of the prime minister. Like the ministers they were designed to mislead, I was fooled by the false clues that Kerr planted about his intentions. In common with just about everyone else close to events, I was swept along by Whitlam's supreme confidence and influenced by obvious signs of lack of resolve among some Liberal senators. Consequently, when I received a phone call at about 1.30 pm on November 11, 1975, telling me Whitlam had been sacked, I found it difficult to believe. So did the rest of the parliamentary press gallery and most politicians. It should not have been a shock, but it was.

Two decades on, it is easy to be clear-headed again, and what stands out is the way Whitlam and his government helped at almost every stage to bring about their own demise. 'Well may we say "God save the Queen" because nothing will save the governor-general,' Whitlam proclaimed in that memorable scene on the front steps of

125

Old Parliament House. Nothing did save the governor-general – Kerr died a pathetic and lonely figure – but the governor-general saved Whitlam. Had Kerr not martyred him, it is likely he would have become an embarrassment rather than a Labor hero. The Whitlam government left many lasting and important reforms, but in political terms it was an astonishingly inept – even stupid – administration.

I have often thought that someone should write a play based on the February 1975 federal ALP conference in the Florida Hotel at Terrigal, on the NSW Central Coast. It brought together just about everything that was wrong with the Whitlam government. Whitlam tried to have the conference called off because he feared it would erupt into criticism of the government's appalling economic management.

Every night, minerals and energy minister Rex Connor sat alone in his room waiting in vain for a shonky Pakistani commodities dealer named Tirath Khemlani to send a telex message saying he had lined up a US$4 billion loan from Middle East sources to finance massive development projects Connor dreamed about. Attorney-general Lionel Murphy had a procession of advisers going to his suite as he agonised over whether to accept Whitlam's offer to appoint him to the High Court. Deputy prime minister Jim Cairns reignited a damaging controversy about his glamorous office coordinator Junie Morosi by giving a newspaper interview in which he confessed to 'a kind of love' for her. And, adding to the image of an indulgent rabble, party president Bob Hawke was photographed tied to a whipping post at Old Sydney Town, being flogged by a scantily clad young lady.

That was the Whitlam government. The economy was a mess partly because Whitlam refused to appoint his most competent minister, Bill Hayden, to the Treasury portfolio until it was too late. (Whitlam later said of the men he had preferred to Hayden: 'Frank Crean – an incompetent treasurer, an unimpressive treasurer. Jim Cairns – worse. Scatterbrain. Mind not on the job. Positively harmful.')

Connor's naive pursuit of petro-dollar loans eventually provided opposition leader Malcolm Fraser with the 'extraordinary and reprehensible circumstances' he said justified blocking appropriation bills to force an election. Cairns, deprived of competent advisers as a result of the Morosi appointment, was snared by the loans affair, too. The appointment of Murphy to the High Court cost the government a

Senate seat when NSW Liberal premier Tom Lewis broke convention and refused to appoint a Labor nominee to fill the vacancy – setting an example followed eagerly by Sir Joh Bjelke-Petersen six months later. Indulgence, lack of discipline, permeated everything.

Without a by-election brought about by the appointment of former deputy prime minister Lance Barnard to a diplomatic post the dismissal might not have occurred; the huge anti-Labor swing gave Fraser the courage to block the appropriation bills. Even on Remembrance Day itself, Whitlam's miscalculations contributed to events. It is still argued, for example, that Kerr should have allowed more time for the coalition's resolve to crack. But the truth is Whitlam forced the timing on Kerr by deciding that day to recommend a half-Senate election. Then, incredibly, after he was sacked, Whitlam did not bother to notify Labor's Senate leaders. Had he done so, a Labor fightback might have been possible in the Upper House because, by then, it was Fraser and the coalition who desperately needed the appropriation bills passed.

There is no doubt Kerr was at fault for misleading Whitlam, or that the coalition's behaviour in taking the country to the brink was unscrupulous and dangerous. But as it commemorates the 20th anniversary of the dismissal, Labor would do well to take time out from the myth-making to acknowledge that much of what happened was self-inflicted.

The ghosts that walk

21 November 1995

Back in 1984, John Howard was calling for greater spending on defence. No surprise there. He still wants our defence forces strengthened. The difference is that 11 years ago he was prepared to say how it should be paid for. The necessary savings, Howard said, could come from 'getting health substantially out of the public sector'.

You can bet your bottom dollar he would not make such a statement today – and if a journalist asked him about it he would be most indignant. In Howard's view, things he has said in the past – potentially embarrassing things, anyway – are not legitimate matters for discussion now. We are supposed to rule off the book at the time of his second coming as opposition leader last February.

The bloke who believed that health should be substantially removed from the public sector is no more. In his place stands a staunch defender of Medicare and bulk billing and the status quo. Health, after all, is an issue that could cost the coalition votes if the impression got abroad that a Liberal–National Party government was likely to tamper with the fundamentals of the system.

In politics, having something you've said in the past dug up and used against you is an occupational hazard. Old pollies have a name for it. It is called 'making the ghost walk'. Howard has been in politics a long while and talked a great deal on all manner of subjects, so there are a lot of ghosts. One of them took a bit of a stroll on the Nine network's *Sunday* program at the weekend, when Howard was reminded of a statement he made in July 1984 opposing a Remuneration Tribunal recommendation extending politicians' travel allowances to de facto partners. 'Frequent references to the importance of the family are meaningless unless governments are willing to show a bias towards orthodox family arrangements,' Howard said then. In context, it was a clear enough statement. Howard believed families involving legally wedded partners should be given advantages not available to people whose living arrangements were different. Since Howard makes more frequent reference to the importance of the family than almost any other politician, it was legitimate to ask how a Howard government would apply the kind of bias he had advocated. But he would not give an answer. 'My attitude in 1995 is that I'm not going to get diverted into a debate about the definition of a family,' Howard said. He will not say, in other words, whether he still adheres to a view that has important policy implications. He simply refuses to discuss the matter.

Declaring his past statements a no-go area is a key part of the Howard election strategy – closely related to his decision to announce the very minimum of detail about coalition policy. The strategy involves focusing as much attention as possible on the government and its shortcomings, and as little attention as possible on the coalition. That contrasts with the view of the old Howard, who warned in 1983: 'The electorate will tire of a totally negative opposition. Likewise, the electorate demands from us the presentation of a clear philosophical choice.'

The new Howard heads a coalition that deliberately blurs differences with the government on key issues. It has adopted a 'me-too' approach on health and embraced – almost lock, stock and barrel – the government's superannuation policy, for example. It has abandoned or fudged ideas to which it was previously committed in areas such as education and the environment. It has even softened its industrial relations policy. And it has tried to defuse the republic issue by adopting a non-policy – promising a convention to sort the matter out. The all-important aim is to avoid jeopardising likely electoral victory by offending sections of the community. Smart politics? Perhaps – but Howard did not always think so.

In January 1985, Howard told a Young Liberals national convention that the party had to offer genuine alternative policies. 'There will be no shortage of those who will advocate a compromise, blurred approach to difficult issues,' he said. 'Government, we will be told, is just around the corner so we should avoid antagonising any part of the electorate by taking a definitive stand on sensitive questions. Such thinking is not only political cowardice; it also displays dubious political wisdom.'

Howard seems to have changed his mind about that, as he has – or said he has – about such policy issues as health, a $3-an-hour youth wage, Asian immigration, the republic, and so on. His recent attacks on Paul Keating for failing to disclose an alleged conflict of interest suggest the opposition leader has even altered his views in that area. Back in 1983 he opposed the Labor government's introduction of a register of ministers' pecuniary interests, saying: 'I am rather sceptical that a system of disclosure necessarily improves the quality and integrity of government.'

Howard would no doubt argue that people, politicians included, have the right to change their minds. But again the ghost that walks provides an interesting insight. This is the same John Howard who said in June 1983: 'The magnificent victory of the Conservative Party in the recent UK elections serves to remind us all of the enormous value of consistency in politics.'

Speaking of consistency…Howard was asked on the *Sunday* program why, as treasurer in the 1983 election campaign, he had stuck to a budget deficit prediction of $6 billion even after Treasury informed him it would be $9 billion. Howard replied: 'The $9.6 billion figure I was in fact told the night before the election.' That was 'Honest John' fudging things. The truth is that the then-Treasury secretary John Stone met Howard on Monday, February 28, five days before the election, and advised him the projected deficit was about $9 billion. There was plenty of time to come clean.

If the Libs win, Labor is lost

12 December 1995

When Paul Keating pulled off that seemingly impossible victory in 1993, the accepted wisdom was that he had secured two elections for the price of one. The last-days-of-the-recession poll was the tough one; 1996 was supposed to be easy, because it would coincide with the economic recovery. Keating told his staff precisely that at an emotional election-eve dinner. It all looks a bit silly now. As Labor MPs begin a long, hot summer of campaigning in their electorates, they are contemplating not an easy victory, but the consequences of likely defeat.

Not that defeat is a foregone conclusion. John Howard's shaky performance over the past couple of weeks is evidence of that. When Howard, in his censure motion speech on the second-last day of parliament, spoke of Keating being 'stranded' in Japan during the Weipa dispute, alarm bells must have started ringing in the Liberal Party. Keating was at the APEC summit with most of the leaders of the Asia–Pacific, involved in negotiations about trade policy vital to Australia's future. The electorate needs to take a good, hard look at an alternative prime minister who regards that as being 'stranded in…irrelevance'.

Doubts about Howard's leadership are showing up in opinion polls. His apparent confusion on key policy issues has left the opinion-makers in the parliamentary press gallery unimpressed. Labor believes it can win up to half-a-dozen seats in Victoria, is fairly happy with the situation in Western Australia, South Australia and Tasmania, and is confident of clawing back some of the ground it has lost in NSW. But Queensland is the party's black hole. Asked last week what the answer was to the Queensland problem, one of the most senior members of cabinet said: 'I don't know – but we'd better find one by January or we're history!'

A Labor loss would see the departure of Paul Keating. (The Prime Minister would deny it, but I am told he has already made soundings in the international business community about his future employment prospects.) The people who would be left to pick up the pieces are remarkably gloomy in their assessment of how the party would survive being cast into the wilderness. 'They'd be an awful government – but we wouldn't be heard of for a decade or more,' says one of Labor's shrewdest and most senior MPs.

The reasons for this pessimism are fascinating. Crucial among them is a conviction that one of Howard's first acts in government would be to dismantle Medicare. When Keating and other ministers make this charge publicly it is dismissed as election scaremongering, but key Labor strategists genuinely and fervently believe it. Howard's past commitments to get rid of Medicare are regarded as far more relevant than his recent denials. It might be thought that wiping out a popular health scheme, and in the process breaking an important and well-publicised election promise, would badly damage a Howard government. But current thinking by those who would be prominent in a Labor opposition if the party loses next year is that the ALP would be more seriously damaged in the longer term. Labor would promise to restore Medicare; given its platform and the needs of its core constituents, it would have no choice. But – the argument goes – financing the restoration of the scheme would involve a commitment to tax rises. And that, they say, would make Labor unelectable.

The same people are convinced that a Labor opposition would

suffer electorally as a result of Howard's industrial relations obsession. A Howard government, they believe, despite the relatively soft line adopted to avoid frightening the horses at the moment, would be gung-ho on freeing up the labour market and taking on the unions. The unions, in turn, would declare war. And the ensuing militancy and industrial strife would frighten the hell out of middle-class voters without whose support Labor could not regain office. Labor's vote would go up in its safe working-class seats – but it would plummet in marginal electorates.

In other words, pity poor Kim Beazley, on whom the burden of opposition leadership will almost certainly fall if the Keating government fails to get across the line next March. Beazley himself is said to regard his chances of leading Labor back to power in those circumstances as pretty slim. According to his supporters, he is realist enough to know that, if Labor loses office now, the next Labor prime minister is likely to come from the crop of talented MPs not yet on the front bench. Young NSW Labor backbencher Mark Latham is regarded as the one most likely to have greatness thrust upon him.

The Liberals, of course, given their lead in the opinion polls, tend to think more about victory than defeat. But when they do focus on the possibility of suffering yet another election rebuff, they show surprising equanimity for a party that has lost five on the trot. The view seems to be that, if they could survive the trauma of losing the unlosable election in 1993, they can survive anything. This time, at least, they have the comfort of knowing there would be no leadership uncertainty. There is a clear line of succession. If he lost, Howard would go and Peter Costello would take over. 'It would not be like last time,' says a Liberal frontbencher. 'There would not be nearly as many ghosts to lay to rest.'

At this stage of the electoral cycle, of course, detailed predictions are risky – but one intriguing scenario is being discussed in Labor ranks. A minister with a keen interest in psephology believes there is a real possibility of Labor losing 16 seats, but winning 11 from the coalition. That, he says, could leave two independents – Phil Cleary and Graeme Campbell – holding the balance of power in the House of Representatives. It would certainly make for an interesting parliament.

1996

How the biggest loser becomes a feted hero

12 March 1996

Paul Keating's future is clear. Having led the Labor Party to electoral destruction largely as a result of his own wilfulness and self-indulgence, he will become a Labor hero. And eventually, no doubt, a favourite of the Establishment as well, a leading member of the glitterati, filmed and photographed and fawned over at all the opening nights. His fate, in other words, is the fate of Gough Whitlam – another who led his party to a disaster that could have been avoided. For some reason, Labor feels a masochistic need to be abjectly grateful to such people.

Plenty of smart operators associated with the Keating government saw the hurricane approaching. Wayne Swan, for example, former Queensland ALP secretary and rising parliamentary star until last Saturday, issued warnings and was sent to Coventry for his trouble. Graham Richardson sounded the alarm bells publicly after the Canberra by-election loss and was dumped on from a great height by Keating loyalists. Geoff Walsh, one of the canniest political strategists to have served Labor, got sick of his advice being ignored and quietly left the Keating staff. And ALP national secretary Gary Gray commissioned research last April that showed Labor's primary vote was down to an unprecedented 36 percent. Keating was not interested. Nor were the disciples in his office.

In desperation, Gray sent the research to Don Russell, Australian ambassador in Washington, in the hope that it would filter back to Keating that way and bring him to his senses. Russell was a former head of Keating's office. From April to October, when Russell was recalled to Australia to take charge of the Keating re-election effort, all Labor's research was copied to the Washington embassy. The October research showed Labor's primary vote still at only 37 percent. Basically, nothing had been done. And the electorate's anti-Labor feelings had by then been locked in.

It would not have taken much to improve things. Keating could have changed his rhetoric and his behaviour without compromising policy. But, as always, he knew best. Just as Whitlam always knew best. Keating, preoccupied with the big picture, could not be bothered with mere politics – just as Whitlam refused to attend to the political basics. I remember an occasion when a couple of Whitlam advisers tried to warn him that things were deteriorating electorally. 'The government has only one thing going for it,' Whitlam said imperiously, 'and you're wasting its time.' While Keating did not thumb his nose at voters by taking a six-week overseas junket as Whitlam did, actions such as limiting his Question Time appearances in parliament to only two days a week were just as self-indulgent and similarly provocative.

Like Whitlam, Keating did some great things. But also like Whitlam, he let his party and its MPs and its workers and its supporters down. And, like Whitlam, he will not acknowledge that. The Keating concession speech, after the massive electoral tidal wave had shattered and swept away his government, contained not even a hint that he might have erred in some way. It was a good speech – but it was a speech of self-justification. His administration had been terrific, his policies great, his term in office something to be proud of. The unspoken corollary was that the voters, bless their little hearts, had got it wrong. So be it, and good luck John Howard.

In spite of all that, such a huge landslide against a scandal-free government presiding over relatively good economic times was astonishing. The only comparable events were the electoral earthquakes that laid waste the Whitlam government in 1975 and the government of James Scullin in 1931. Scullin was blamed for the Great Depression; Whitlam had a shaky economy and the scandal of the Loans Affair. The only thing that seems to explain the cataclysm of March 2, 1996, seems to be…well, Keating. People simply could not bear to have him as prime minister any longer.

The essential conservatism of the Australian electorate was no doubt also a factor. As an ALP observer remarked on Sunday: 'When they change from Labor to a conservative government, they always do it with much greater vigour than when they're changing the other way.' A slightly scary aspect of this was the result in Oxley, the only Queensland seat Labor was left with after the 1975 landslide but which fell this time with a 20 percent swing. That gigantic swing went to an independent – a woman who started the campaign as a Liberal candidate but was disendorsed because of comments she made about Aborigines. The people who gave her victory because of those comments were traditional Labor voters, which underlines the difficulties (and, it should be said, the courage) of a Labor prime minister identified with Mabo.

On election night, the only explanation offered by Labor spokespeople for what happened was the 'It's time' factor. But that does not hold water. As former prime minister Bob Hawke pointed out, Australians over the years 'have not had a disposition against keeping a party in for a long period of time at a federal or a state level'. Voters have shown they can remain relatively happy with one party in office for much longer periods than Labor served under Hawke and Keating.

Meanwhile, John Howard, who has described himself as the coalition's most conservative leader ever, moves into the Lodge. He does so with an immense amount of goodwill which – having studied the mistakes, not only of Keating but of Malcolm Fraser as well – he will be determined not to fritter away. A lot of people, not just in the Labor Party, underestimated Howard in opposition. They would be unwise to underestimate him in government. In 22 years of political ups and downs, Howard has seen a lot and learned a lot, and one of the things he learned is something Keating forgot. Howard consults and he listens, and he no longer believes that his own view should always prevail. There are justifiable doubts about some members of his team, but Howard himself may turn out to be a formidable prime minister.

The best entrances should look unplanned

19 March 1996

The second-last thing to move from the opposition leader's office to the prime minister's suite – just ahead of John Howard himself – was the flag. The same flag that featured in much of Howard's election material, which he trots out as a prop at news conferences, and which is so worn from use that parts of it are held together with masking tape. It was in place behind the prime minister's desk in time to feature in the newspaper photographs and television footage of the new prime minister settling into the seat of power for the first time.

A small incident, but symbolic of the planning that went into the coalition's transition to government. It was a steady, careful, well-thought-out process that helped to create the impression of a confident, assured prime minister who knew exactly what he was doing. To some this came as a surprise, because nothing had been said before the election about the transition process. This was in stark contrast to what had happened in the past.

Before each of the previous three federal elections, the coalition had set up 'transition to government' committees which produced detailed documents. Shadow ministers had received briefings. Before the 1990 election, there was even a shadow minister responsible for the transition to government – which proved, of course, to be pie in the sky. Howard astutely avoided such nonsense. In his view, it put opposition MPs in the wrong frame of mind – subconsciously giving them the feeling that the election was already won, encouraging complacency. In any case, it was likely to be regarded as an impertinence by voters.

Publicly, there was none of that this time. Privately, though, Howard did get advice on the process of taking office and creating the kind of government structure that would best suit the needs of an incoming coalition administration. He made individual approaches to a number of people with appropriate expertise and asked them to 'write me a note'. The material in those notes – combined with Howard's own extensive experience – provided the basis for the way the changeover was conducted, the shape of the ministry, and the departmental restructuring.

The result, overall, was impressive. The low-key approach was typically Howard, and no doubt reassuring for voters. Given the last-minute juggling he had to do to balance state representation as a result of the Liberal Party's unexpectedly big gains in NSW and Queensland, the ministry was probably the best that could be managed from the available talent. And the merging of departments and the re-allocation of functions from one department to another were, on the whole, sensible.

It was interesting, though, that the man who had so disapproved of the centralisation of power under Paul Keating in fact accentuated the process. He did this by creating a powerful, politically appointed cabinet office to decide policy priorities and ride shotgun – in an ideological sense – on the ministry and the bureaucracy. There will also be a very powerful new National Security Committee of cabinet, which – with the treasurer and trade minister as members – will have an economic focus rather than dealing with defence and foreign affairs matters in isolation.

The treatment of some senior bureaucrats – particularly Michael Costello, sacked as secretary of the Foreign Affairs Department – reflects little credit on Howard, however. Before the election, Howard denied there was any hit list, said changes at the top of the bureaucracy would be based on merit and asserted that there were always such changes when a new government took office. In fact,

Howard always intended to get rid of Costello – purely because of his political associations. Merit had nothing to do with it. Alexander Downer, the new foreign minister, is on record quite recently praising Costello's competence and saying: 'He's certainly a very professional foreign affairs officer. He's a career foreign affairs officer.' And it is not true that changes of government always see top bureaucrats axed. When the Hawke government took over, it even kept John Stone on as treasury secretary.

But the coalition's transition to government went smoothly. It will be interesting to see if Labor's transition to opposition is as trouble-free. When the ALP national executive holds its election post-mortem on March 20, it is likely to appoint a committee to develop strategies for the future – most importantly to look at how Labor can get back in touch with its base. The process of putting together a competent, well-qualified staff for opposition is already under way, with advertisements in last weekend's newspapers and agreement that a merit review panel will vet all proposed appointments. And there is a developing consensus that, irrespective of who becomes deputy leader to Kim Beazley, the job of treasury spokesman should be thrust on Gareth Evans – on the very sensible ground that Labor needs its best and most aggressive parliamentary performer up against Peter Costello.

Plans are being developed to try to give Labor in opposition a solid intellectual base by assembling small, informal think-tanks, by tapping back into university contacts that the party has largely ignored for the past 13 years, and by making use of trade union research facilities. The biggest problem will be getting some sort of system into all this.

There is also talk of getting some of the party hacks in safe seats to make way for new talent – or the return of some of the talent lost on March 2 – but this is almost certainly whistling in the wind. Even in Blaxland, being vacated by Paul Keating, despite the opportunity it offers to bolster Labor's depleted ranks, the powerbrokers are showing a marked reluctance to do what is necessary. Put your money on yet another hack.

After-hours call from parliament's Placido

7 May 1996

When Paul Keating resigned from parliament last week, a radio interviewer asked me if tapes existed of any of his famous phone calls to journalists. He would, he joked, pay handsomely. I know of no tapes, but occasionally I made detailed notes when Keating called me. As the toughest and most significant politician of our generation rides off into the sunset, it may be appropriate – in the interests of history, if nothing else – to impart the flavour of one of the most interesting of those calls.

It was in early December 1990, when Keating was still treasurer, two days before his notorious press gallery dinner speech. In fact, I got a preview. Asserting that he already had the psychological measure of then opposition leader John Hewson, Keating told me: 'Listen mate, I'm a politician. I'm a Placido Domingo. What the fuck is he? He's an usher. This is the grand stage for the grand performances, and this bloke is just an usher…I'm the only real leader Australia's had in the postwar years, and this nation's ready to do me in. They're saying, "You're our leader but thank you, we don't need you."'

Keating almost always rang because he was furious about something I had written or broadcast. In this case, it was a column in which I said Labor strategists were appalled at the insensitivity and political stupidity of his 'this is the recession we had to have' line the previous week. I also suggested the political cost of confirmation that Australia was in recession had been less than it might have been because of the failure of then shadow treasurer, Peter Reith, to capitalise on it effectively.

'The reason the political cost was diminished was the line I took,' Keating said. 'They didn't expect me to say it was a recession we had to have. It took their breath away.' I remarked that it had taken mine away, too. He continued: 'They thought I was going to walk in there and say, "Aw, I'm sorry we've got a recession." They would have been all over me like a rash…Handling this thing in media terms, which is the most difficult thing, probably, the government's had to do this year, I did with a minimum of damage. And you never even give me the bloody credit for it…This thing rolls through the door. I've said the slowdown's one we need. When the recession comes, do I say it's one we *don't* need? Obviously I'm not stupid.'

Keating was particularly angry at my claim that he should be held more directly responsible for his recession than John Howard was for the recession of the early 1980s. 'Howard was not controlling the events around him, mate. I pulled the levers in taking the place into recession and I can pull another lever and take it out. When Howard pulled the levers it was like Laurel and Hardy in a motor car. He pulled the bloody handbrake and it came off in his hand. He pulled the fucking steering wheel and it came off in his hand.'

There was some abuse. 'You're excusing Howard because of his drought and other things, but Keating, you're saying, brought this on himself. Now that's a very slovenly piece of analysis. But of course I know it's not slovenly because you're brighter than that. It's only you being a ****. See, Laurie, mate, I can spot a bit of ****ery in a fucking fog three miles away.'

That sort of thing, though, made up only a small part of such calls. Keating would get the anger out of his system and then set about explaining himself. He genuinely wanted us to understand him. It was a compliment of sorts. That was why most serious political journalists did not resent such calls in the way non-journalists might expect. They were useful. We always learned a lot about what Keating was doing and why, about how he saw things fitting together, and – always fascinating – about his mood. In this particular phone call, Keating described himself as 'crazy-brave'. He said: 'There's got to be somebody like me who says, "Listen, this country has to perform." We've got to break the inflation rate. It's not going to be done with some namby pamby **** trying to not have a recession when you ought to have one or not have a slowdown when you should. You know? So Australia, for better or worse, gets a fucking treasurer like me, but – without being too rough on it, mate – we get commentators like you to go with us.'

And, a little later, still on the need to break inflation: 'I'm prepared to chance my hand and take the whole show to the wire. I'd have been happier not to have the recession headline, but if I go out now and say to the banks, "You bastards, you've turned my slowdown into a recession, you behaved like Neanderthals", what good would it do? So I stood like a man and said, "OK, this is the recession I bloody well gave youse, because it's fucking good for you." Alright, that might be cutting a new political cloth, but I cut a new one in 1987 and a new one in 1989. Just give me a bit of credit for making political judgments.'

My reference to Labor strategists had clearly got up his nose. 'I'm the only Labor strategist who's mattered here in the last five years. I'm not arguing that. I'm asserting it…In 1987 I picked the election date, I picked the strategy. I put a $4 billion cut in the May statement and everybody said, "Ooh, you shouldn't do that. Here's Keating actually wants to go cutting outlays further. The mad bastard; he's swallowed an economic textbook." Right? I did that, and won.

'In 1989 you were reporting some of our Labor strategists who wanted to have mortgage interest rate relief and how I was unbending and unyielding, but it held the government together and made it look like a fucking government. And now people say the Greens got us back [in the 1990 election]. If we'd had the Greens without keeping the great mass of the public we wouldn't have won. Also, I talked Bob [Hawke] into an election on the high tide, before the tide started to run out.

'Labor strategists, mate. They're a dime a dozen and all the ones who were supposedly the great strategists of our party have basically worked off the old politics of the '60s and '70s which we have turned on its head in two elections. They don't understand the politics that's come from the new economics in Australia. The great mistake all these people make is to talk down to the public. I always talk up to them. I try and explain the stuff. See, they get up in the morning and see there's a recession and Keating says it's a recession they had to have. The people don't like me, they say "the bastard – but he's probably right"…At some stage, as sure as I stand here, they're going to catch up with me. I might as well do it right. I might as well do the right thing by the country and not the bloody wrong thing.

'See, I regard politics as a sort of high art. I don't believe in the art form I have any peers in this building. It might sound like a smartarse remark, but it's not meant to be.

'You get marks in this business for making political judgment…At some stage, Laurie, I'll make the wrong one and the public will say, "Well, fuck you, mate. We've had enough of you, we've had enough of the bullshit of you, and we thank you, but we don't need you anymore." Inevitably it will happen.'

Keating's mood struck me as extraordinary at the time. Of course, no one knew then about the secret Kirribilli Agreement – or that Keating had decided by then that Hawke had no intention of abiding by it and handing over the prime ministership. He seemed almost sorry for himself; his morale was low. Keating's staff attributed the tone of the Placido Domingo Press Club speech to grief over the death of treasury secretary Chris Higgins the day before – but our phone conversation preceded Higgins's death by 24 hours.

'I'm not saying, "Isn't it shocking? They're not recognising my talent." If I get dispatched I'll say, "OK, I had a good old time. I never got to be the prime minister, that's one disappointment, but all the other things have been pretty good" '…But who feels urgently about the country?

'Bob says to me sometimes, "Oh, you look a bit haggard." I say, "Why wouldn't I, Bob? I carry all the fucking worries of the joint. You carry the responsibility and so do I but I carry the fucking worries. I'm the only one of us that goes home tonight worrying about it. You don't."

'There are others who worry. Bill Kelty worries. People who don't worry, who want to occupy the position nominally, like Hewson, but don't worry – in the end, they won't do the things that are necessary.

'So, Laurie, you're entitled not to like me. Let me tell you this – I don't dislike anyone. There's not a soul I really savagely dislike. There are a few people I won't have anything to do with, I'll fight with people and kick them in the arse, but I don't hate them. And I recognise a lot of your work and I see the balances and see how you treat a story and how you've done this when you could have done that.

'All I'm saying to you is that all of us on the high, pointy end of the show have got responsibilities to the place. The responsibility is to track a path out of our troubles. In the end, if there's another path-tracker and it's plausible and do-able, well, you've got a choice and if you like us or them, that's fine…

'But honestly, I think this is still the only really competent show around. When everyone boots my credibility apart, they boot the whole thing apart.

'I'm signed up for Australia's troubles. I'm signed up for 40 or 50 years of economic sloth. And what they are really about to do to me is say, "We think we're going to let you out of the contract." They might be about to do me an enormous favour in personal terms. I didn't really ring you to abuse you. Mate, don't ever despise me or my position, because I live a life…it's a shocking burden. Hours of pain and responsibility. I go to bed with these things and I wake up with them. They hang around my head like a bad smell, you know.'

Keating had the roughest mouth in the business, but he had a silver tongue as well. He might have been arrogant, but he cared, too. And if a nation is to advance, it needs crazy-brave politicians. Good luck, Paul, I'll miss the phone calls.

Blame the poacher-turned-gamekeeper

25 June 1996

It was the 1985 Tax Summit all over again, except this time it was not Bob Hawke pulling the rug out from under Paul Keating. It was John Howard backing away from all-out war with the premiers and leaving Peter Costello to cop the flak. Hawke held a secret late-night meeting with the ACTU leadership to bury the consumption tax that Keating had been advocating. Howard met the premiers without his treasurer and abandoned the plan announced by Costello to impose wholesale sales tax on state governments and local government organisations.

At the post-summit news conference, Keating made the best of the situation, saying: 'I think it's a bit like *Ben Hur*. We have crossed the line with one wheel off, but we have crossed the line.' Costello, having as a consolation prize extracted $1.5 billion from the states to help fill the federal government's budget 'black hole', would have been justified in using similar imagery.

In purely financial terms, the result was not a bad one for the Howard government. Politically, though, it was a mess and it badly damaged Costello. The premiers and the media did quite a job on him. He became the scapegoat – portrayed as an arrogant bungler, deservedly cut down to size. The impression created was that Costello had naively accepted a plan presented to him by the hardline economic rationalists of Treasury – one they had tried unsuccessfully to sell to Keating and John Dawkins in the Labor years. The Prime Minister, it was suggested, had unsuspectingly gone along with Costello, not realising the horrendous and anomalous consequences that would follow from the removal of the states' sales tax exemption.

There are, however, a few things wrong with this version of events. To begin with, the sales tax idea on this occasion does not seem to have originated with Treasury at all. On the eve of the premiers' conference, Max Moore-Wilton, hand-picked by the new government to head the Prime Minister's department, spoke with some state officials about the issue. According to one of those state bureaucrats, Moore-Wilton made it pretty clear that the initiative came from Howard's department, not Costello's. No doubt Treasury and the Treasurer were happy to embrace the proposal but the sequence of events is important, given the interpretation that gained currency after the federal backdown.

Costello was lambasted for his political stupidity in announcing the sales tax plan two days before the premiers' conference. This was seen as a mark of his arrogance – going public before any consultation with the states. It was foolishly provocative, according to his critics. ('I don't like being king-hit before I've even sat down at the table,' said Queensland Treasurer Joan Sheldon.) If it was a mistake, however, it was a collective one. Cabinet considered the timing of the announcement, just as it considered the contents. As I understand it, Costello left the cabinet meeting – with the full knowledge of his colleagues – to hold his news conference. The premiers assiduously fed out the line that the Prime Minister had not realised the full implications of the sales tax proposal. This, they claimed, was evident when they dined with Howard at the Lodge. He had been 'shocked' – their word – when they told him how state schools would be taxed while private schools remained exempt. The revelation that public hospitals would be similarly disadvantaged in comparison with some private hospitals also allegedly surprised the Prime Minister. This picture of Howard as innocent dupe has to be hogwash; patronising hogwash, at that.

What the premiers were saying, in effect, was that Howard is a well-meaning fool. It was a plea that he should be absolved of responsibility on grounds of incompetence. A prime minister who went into such a battle with the states without getting across the detail would be a dill – and Howard is not a dill. Nor does he have dills around him. Howard would have been well aware of the consequences of the federal proposal – especially in the light of the GST debate before the 1993 election.

Costello, it is argued, should have known that the states could not possibly give in on the sales tax issue. He is accused of lacking political nous for not realising how big a fight he was getting into. It is also claimed that he was ignorant of various agreements between the Commonwealth and the states. But, as federal Finance Minister John Fahey said at the weekend, 'The matters that were taken to the premiers were actually approved by cabinet.' Fahey, NSW premier from June 1992 to March 1995 (and state treasurer for a large part of that time), took part in the cabinet discussion – so the sales tax plan was vetted by an expert, a premiers' conference veteran, someone well attuned to the likely state reaction. As a poacher-turned-gamekeeper, Fahey was in a position to spot the problems and predict the response – and, having had the benefit of his views, cabinet gave the green light.

Criticism of Costello may be warranted on the basis of his smug manner, which clearly got up the premiers' noses. The perception that the Treasurer is all too conscious of his own brilliance is a problem of style that he and his advisers need to deal with. But, putting that aside, the truth is that Howard and Costello were involved in a good cop/bad cop exercise. In such a situation, someone has to be the bastard. It makes sense for the Prime Minister to remain a little above the fray in case things go wrong. And the premiers played it cleverly by concentrating their hostility on Costello. Had they attacked Howard too, they would have locked him in and made withdrawal politically impossible.

What is remarkable is the discipline displayed by Costello, a pugnacious politician whose normal instinct when hit is to hit back harder. He was subjected to some quite vicious attacks by the premiers. The temptation to retaliate must have been almost irresistible, especially with Victoria's Jeff Kennett using the opportunity so enthusiastically to settle old scores. But Costello refrained. He took the knocks and kept his mouth shut. It was an indication of political maturity.

Happy 80th, Gough! Now, about your funeral

16 July 1996

Here's a cheerful thought for Gough Whitlam as he celebrates his 80th birthday – a spectacular funeral is being planned for him. Not that anyone is in a rush, mind you. Fortunately, the great man is in such robust health that official approval of arrangements for a state funeral fit for such a legend will very likely not be required until well after Prime Minister Mark Latham, a former Whitlam staffer and protégé, moves into the Lodge. But it is best to be prepared. Something special will be called for – not at all the sort of thing that can be thrown together overnight. So an informal group of family and friends has been discussing the matter, on and off, for some years. The plans are stowed away in a file kept by the former prime minister's eldest son, Nick. Big, wonderful, over-the-top plans, like the man himself; mostly serious, but with an element of tongue in cheek, as you'd expect.

Winston Churchill issued instructions for his own funeral. Whitlam is not that involved, even though the plans are of Churchillian proportions. In fact, apparently he goes uncharacteristically quiet when the matter of funeral arrangements is mentioned in his presence. But he has made one major contribution: his wishes on the music that should be played are part of Nick's file.

Gough Whitlam's is, after all, a remarkable life, and the occasion of his attaining octogenarian status provides a useful vantage point from which to survey it. The late Patrick White probably summed it up best when he emerged briefly from his reclusive existence to speak at a Labor Party election rally in the Sydney Opera House in 1974. White had been a close friend of Jørn Utzon, the architect who conceived the magnificent building. 'Both Utzon and Whitlam are men of vision who build on a grand scale for the future while not losing sight of everyday details,' the distinguished novelist shyly told the crowd. To be quite truthful, Whitlam did sometimes lose sight of details. That is how the Loans Affair and some of the other scandals and stuff-ups that marred his government's term in office occurred. He neglected to keep track of what his ministers were doing. I have been highly critical of Whitlam's indulgence as prime minister, the arrogance, wilfulness and political carelessness that contributed so greatly to his government's downfall. But he did build on a grand scale. Even though he was prime minister for a mere three years, his achievements were enormous. He created lasting monuments. The most important of them is the modern Labor Party.

When Whitlam became deputy leader, the ALP was just about unelectable. It was deeply divided, with the mad Left controlling the Victorian branch and powerful in other areas. The party's parliamentary leaders had to follow instructions issued from behind closed doors by a federal conference (the 36 faceless men) and a federal executive (the 12 witless men) on which the caucus was not represented. Policies imposed in this way – anti-American, implacably opposed to state aid for church schools, and so on – were electorally suicidal.

Whitlam fought through most of the 1960s and into the '70s, first as deputy and then as leader, to reform the party. He was almost expelled. He went within an inch of being tossed out of the leadership. But he did back then what Tony Blair is only now managing to do with the British Labour Party. This was the context in which he produced what is perhaps his most remembered line: 'When you are faced with an impasse, you have got to crash through or you've got to crash.' Whitlam crashed through, restructuring the ALP, opening it up, modernising its policies and broadening its electoral appeal in the process. He dragged Labor onto the middle ground and led it to victory for the first time in 23 years. For all its faults, and there were many, the Whitlam government changed Australia forever. There were great domestic initiatives such as the establishment of Medibank, the forerunner of Medicare. In foreign policy, Whitlam recognised China, made relations with Asia a priority, and insisted on a more independent relationship with the United States and Britain. There were important legal reforms. Australia's cultural insulation was broken down. Unfortunately, an almighty mess was made of economic management – but you can't have everything. To top it all off, of course, John Kerr made him a political martyr.

So...the funeral plans. One of the pieces Whitlam has selected is *Va, pensiero*, the slaves' chorus from Verdi's opera *Nabucco* which gave expression to the Italian people's aspirations for liberty and self-government. *Va, pensiero* became the theme song of Garibaldi's followers during the *risorgimento* – the uprising to unite Italy. The second piece he has nominated is more esoteric, but no less Whitlamesque – *The March of the Consular Guard at Marengo*, by an obscure French composer, celebrating one of Napoleon's great victories. Whitlam was fascinated by Napoleon even as a child, but his sister, Freda, once told me that it was not so much the warlike side of Napoleon that appealed to young Gough as the French emperor's civic achievements and the legal system he established.

Abraham Lincoln's funeral is the loose model for what is being planned. The idea is that the main ceremony would be held in Sydney Town Hall, after which a catafalque bearing the coffin would proceed to the historic Mortuary Station, built in 1869 and heritage-listed. Lincoln became the first president to lie in state at the US Capitol rotunda before being carried home to Springfield, Illinois, by train, with stops along the way for people to pay their respects. Whitlam would be carried slowly home to Canberra by train, to lie in state in King's Hall in the Old Parliament House. Indigenous Australians would stage a corroboree on the lawns outside. It is all appropriately immodest – and, with luck, a long way off. What matters for now is the achievement of Labor's folk hero in crashing through to 80. Happy birthday, Gough – and may there be many more.

Labor suffering severe relevance deprivation

17 September 1996

John Howard knows about opposition. He spent 13 years there. They were 13 very long years – but he still remembers the early months. There are, he has told friends, two stages. At first, it does not seem all that bad. There is a sense of freedom. Inexperienced ministers make mistakes while they are learning the ropes. You have a few wins in parliament, and that cheers you up. You convince yourself that it will not be too long before you get back into office.

But after the new government brings down its first budget and that budget gets a reasonable response from the media and the public... Well, things change then. You have to acknowledge to yourself that the other lot are not doing such a bad job. You are forced to accept the likelihood that they will be in power for quite a while. That is when it all sinks in. That is when the gloom really descends. That is when it becomes very hard indeed to summon up the will to carry on fighting day after day.

The Labor Party is now into the second stage. It has had political reality rammed down its throat. The Howard government's first budget has gone over remarkably well. Most of the coalition frontbenchers that Labor treated with contempt for all these years have got through their shaky start and are looking like reasonably competent and assured ministers. Labor's own performance in opposition is starting to come under scrutiny. Morale is so low that, at senior levels of the party, there is fear about the outcome of a by-election that any self-respecting opposition would be sublimely confident of winning. And

149

the deputy leader, Gareth Evans, is bleeding all over the place about the impotence and irrelevance of opposition. It hurts, he says. It is 'unquestionably miserable'. It stinks.

No doubt it does, but there is no point whingeing about it. Some other members of the Labor front bench, instead of moaning about their situation, have grasped the opportunities of opposition. They are freshening up their views, improving their political skills and approaching the task with enthusiasm. Simon Crean is a case in point. In government he was hard-working and an effective administrator and policy-maker, but had problems communicating. A former ACTU president, he tended to speak in a sort of union bureaucrat's jargon. But in opposition, he has worked on the problem, and is becoming an effective, hard-hitting communicator with the ability to simplify a political message and punch it home.

It was interesting to compare Crean and Evans when they appeared on rival television programs last Sunday. Few people who watched both performances would deny that Crean was the more impressive. An important factor, I think, is that Crean had been in cabinet for only six years. Evans, like opposition leader Kim Beazley, was there for the entire, grinding 13 years. The hard, unrelenting work of government takes its toll, and the effects of that are evident on both Evans and Beazley. It would be unfair to suggest that they are clapped out, but – although there is no doubt they are giving their all – Evans, certainly, and Beazley to a lesser extent, seem tired of politics. They have had too much of it. In opposition, politics is all there is.

Paul Keating was fed up with politics; the practice of it, that is. He was always OK on the theory, as he showed at a meeting with Bill Clinton in Bogor, Indonesia, at the 1994 APEC summit. The Democratic Party had just been routed in Congressional elections in the US, and Clinton was looking unelectable for a second term. Keating told him how to win – how to occupy the middle ground, take a conservative stand on key issues and force the Republicans well to the right of the mainstream. Clinton's top adviser, George Stephanopoulos, took notes. It was the same sort of advice Clinton later got from Dick Morris, the high-priced political consultant caught up recently in a sex scandal. The point is that Keating knew what Clinton should do, but no longer had the energy and self-discipline and enthusiasm for the game to follow his own advice. There is a touch of that about the current Labor leadership.

Keating should probably have got out earlier. If Evans is as sick of it all as he sounds, he should perhaps be thinking about greener pastures. Beazley, whose attack on the budget has been anything but punchy, may only need a good break – the sort of three-month sabbatical that Victorian Premier Jeff Kennett talks about taking. But finding time for an extended break will not be easy, especially with the by-election looming in the western Sydney seat of Lindsay.

Beazley will have no choice but to throw himself into the contest. It will be a test of both his leadership and Labor's campaign strategy. If Labor does not win, there will be no excuses for Beazley or for the party organisation. What needs to be done is obvious. Labor's task is to dissect the Lindsay electorate, target particular interest groups and use the various nasties in the budget to persuade them to vote against the government. The nursing home measures, for example, provide a lever to prise elderly voters away from the coalition. Migrants, the unemployed, students, low-income battlers, people worried about hospitals and childcare – the budget provides Labor with the means of getting to all of them. That is the theory. It is elementary politics. The question is whether Beazley and the party machine can put it into practice. If they cannot, what Evans calls the Relevance Deprivation Syndrome will get even worse.

No time for Reith to rest on his laurels

7 November 1996

Peter Reith is already working the waterfront. Even before his deal with the Democrats was sewn up, he had started talks with union and employer groups about how industrial relations practices on the wharves and in the maritime industry would need to change when his Workplace Relations Bill becomes law. Reith's 55 hours of painstaking negotiations with Democrat leader Cheryl Kernot to get the essentials of his legislation through the Senate were useful practice for the daunting task of achieving waterfront reform.

Reith now hopes to use the same techniques of negotiation and persuasion on some of the toughest union leaders in the country. There have been predictions of an inevitable crunch on the waterfront once the government gets its IR changes in place, but Reith wants to avoid that if possible. The patience and skill with which he conducted the negotiations with Kernot suggest that if anybody can pull it off, he can.

Reith, unlike some of his ministerial colleagues, realised that confrontation with the Senate was not the way to get results. He took a similar line in a recent conversation with a Maritime Union of Australia official. Despite the rhetoric of some coalition figures, he said, the government had a pragmatic view. It was determined to achieve a more efficient waterfront, and was adamant that there had to be a marked improvement on the present situation – but it was not spoiling for a fight. He did not believe confrontation was inevitable. An industrial battle would be costly to the nation.

It is typical of the Industrial Relations Minister that he was thinking ahead while the negotiations with Kernot were still going on. In opposition, Reith was widely regarded as a crude, head-kicking politician, but he was always much more than that. Head-kicking is simply one of the essential political skills that he mastered early in his career. Reith plays politics with a very cool head. He is extraordinarily disciplined. Not once during the marathon talks with the Democrats did his patience fray or his frustration show through. Goading comments from some colleagues to the effect that he was becoming 'Cheryl Kernot's public relations officer' failed to elicit any response from him other than an enigmatic smile. His eye was unwaveringly on the prize all the way through. And, having now signed the Democrats up to support his bill, he knows exactly what he wants to achieve next.

Reith believes it is not enough simply to pass the legislation. It will not, on its own, produce all the changes needed in key areas of the economy, such as the waterfront and the construction industry. The government, which means the minister, must take a 'facilitating role'. Unions and employers will need pushing and prodding – he is more likely to call it 'encouragement' – if the country is to get full advantage from the new IR laws. Far from resting on his laurels, Reith will be active in spelling out the approach the government sees as necessary to achieve better practices – and, where persuasion is not enough, waving a big stick to ensure there is progress. In the construction industry, for example, the government is in a position to make a major difference because, through its ownership of buildings and its role in the financing of projects, it is a direct player.

Reith has lived with the Workplace Relations Bill since the coalition won office. He has known for the past seven months that, to a considerable degree, his future career depends on it. If he got his reforms onto the statute books he would be made, acknowledged as a clever and effective politician, even a possible future leader. On the other hand, if he failed, it would be downhill from there. Kernot's signature on the agreement meant success – the end of the challenge that had dominated his time as a minister. But it did not signal any let-up for Reith. Another challenge, almost as daunting, was waiting. The next mountain Reith has to climb is reform of the public service.

Again, he has already started. There have been two meetings with the heads of government departments and agencies about a major overhaul of the *Public Service Act*. Another meeting is scheduled. Then Reith will produce a discussion paper covering all aspects of reform of the bureaucracy before deciding on the final form of the new legislation. It is another mammoth task. The existing Act, introduced in 1922 and amended more than 100 times since, entrenches countless practices that run counter to the kind of efficiency and flexibility and best practice the government is trying to force on private enterprise via the Workplace Relations Bill.

Max Moore-Wilton, the secretary of the Prime Minister's department, told a conference last week that the existing Act – supported by 101 pages of regulations and 2500 determinations on pay and conditions – was 'a tangible obstacle to a modern and thoroughly efficient Commonwealth public sector'. The cost of administering public service selection processes was three times best practice in the private sector. As an example of the sort of thing that prevented public service managers managing efficiently, Moore-Wilton cited public service leave and allowances. There were, he said, no fewer than 35 types of leave available to public servants. That generated about 1.5 million leave forms annually – about 12 per employee; 57 percent of the leave was for periods of one day or less. Total cost of administering these arrangements was more than $20 million a year.

Reith will need all the patience and political skill he showed with the Workplace Relations Bill, and more, to sort this one out. Negotiating with the public service unions is likely to make his sessions with Kernot look a snack by comparison. What is now beyond doubt, though, is that the Prime Minister has chosen the right man for the job.

Howard's silence is Hanson's validation

12 November 1996

This magazine used to have a slogan: 'Australia for the White Man'. It appeared each week under the masthead on the editorial page, well into the 1950s. For those of us associated with *The Bulletin* these days, it is remembered as an historical embarrassment. But if opinion polls are accurately measuring support for Pauline Hanson's views, reviving the old slogan might be a smart circulation move.

Just kidding, folks. The country has regressed in the past couple of months, but not quite that far – I hope. Hanson, though, is definitely a throwback to the '50s. It was significant that, in her notorious maiden parliamentary speech, the one politician she chose to quote was the late Arthur Calwell, of 'two Wongs don't make a white' fame. Calwell, according to Hanson, in a speech dealing with Asians and Africans, asked: 'Do we want or need any of these people here? I am one red-blooded Australian who says "No" and who speaks for 90 percent of Australians.' She added proudly: 'I have no hesitation in echoing the words of Arthur Calwell.'

The former immigration minister and Labor Party leader was a racist. The independent MHR for Oxley is a racist, too. But Calwell's views, while abhorrent, were – like *The Bulletin*'s slogan – in tune with mainstream Australian thinking at the time. If Hanson represents what today's Australians really think, we are lost. Given the realities of geography and economics, we have to assume that Australians are no longer like Calwell and Hanson, or acknowledge that we have no future. That is why the passage through parliament of a bipartisan motion denouncing racial intolerance was important. It was clear evidence that we have changed. Such a resolution would not have got off the ground 40 years ago.

What is needed now is for John Howard to follow up the resolution. It is not enough on its own. Reinforcement is necessary. The government accepts this on the diplomatic front, and a major effort is under way to ensure that our Asian neighbours are made aware of the resolution and what it means. The redoubtable Tim Fischer headed off overseas within days to beat the drum. Embassies have been instructed to spread the word. The incentive is dollars – trade and tourism are at stake. But action is needed on the domestic front, too. The Hanson phenomenon has exposed fears in the Australian community that need to be soothed, ignorance that needs to be corrected, confusion that needs to be cleared up. It is a job for the Prime Minister.

At the moment, Howard is the co-accused. He stands in the dock with Hanson charged with causing serious damage to the national interest. Hanson is the one who shouted 'Fire!' in a crowded theatre, but it was Howard who said it was OK for her to do so. Howard's mishandling of the issue – his refusal for the best part of six weeks even to acknowledge that there was a problem – was the worst leadership lapse I can recall from any prime minister in the 30-plus years I have been reporting politics. But he can and should make amends.

Howard is proud that, on the issue of gun control, he seized the moment. The race issue is even more important than guns and cries out for the same leadership approach, moral as well as political. Howard had to be dragged to the point where he agreed to move the racial tolerance resolution. That is not good enough. No one is saying that Howard should ram his views down the throats of Australians. But if he is sincere in his stated belief that there is no place for racial intolerance or a discriminatory immigration policy in Australia today, he should be prepared to explain why he holds those views.

In his speech on the resolution, he said politicians should accept that Australians 'can debate and understand things in a mature and open fashion'. Absolutely; but they need accurate information – as opposed to the half-truths and prejudices they get from talkback radio and the rubbish they get from Hanson – if they are to debate the matter sensibly. It is the responsibility of the nation's leader to provide that information, and to do so by engaging fully in the debate himself. Howard and others claim that Paul Keating did much to create the present situation by failing to explain his policies – not only on immigration, but also on Aboriginal affairs and our enmeshment with Asia – in ways that ordinary Australians could understand. They are right. It was one of Keating's greatest failures. But the obligation to explain and to educate is now Howard's. If his government genuinely believes in non-discriminatory immigration, it should tell the voters why it is a good thing – and keep telling them. If it believes Australia's future depends on close economic links with Asia, it should argue the case – including the case for not biting the hand that we expect to feed us. If it believes Aboriginal Australians are the most disadvantaged people in the country – not a privileged group, as Hanson claims – it should ensure that ordinary Australians understand how they are disadvantaged.

It is possible, though, that Howard's reluctance to engage Hanson is at least partly the result of a problem he cannot admit. There is evidence that, despite the parliamentary vote, quite a lot of the people who sit behind him on the coalition benches privately share some of Hanson's attitudes. Labor's Mark Latham has drawn attention to that evidence – a survey of candidates at the last election conducted by academics from three universities. They found that 61 percent of coalition candidates saw China as a threat to Australia's security, 71.4 percent regarded Indonesia as a threat, 54 percent thought government help for Aborigines had gone too far, and 35.6 percent believed equal opportunities for migrants had gone too far.

The survey once again shows the gap between what politicians say and what they really think. One of the big things Hanson has going for her is that there is no hypocrisy. Her views may be bigoted and ignorant, but she says what she believes.

1997

Nice work if you can get it

24 June 1997

One federal Liberal MP reckons this is the trip of John Howard's boyhood dreams. *Pussycat, pussycat, where have you been? I've been to London to visit the Queen.* And to watch the cricket at Lord's. Howard whipped through a visit to China in four days, working the whole time, refusing even to go to the Great Wall because it might look indulgent. But he does not mind a bit of indulgence on his first trip to the Old Country as prime minister. The pace is leisurely and the symbolism is wrong.

As soon as the May unemployment figures hit, showing the loss of 40 300 jobs in a month, Howard's 16 days of swanning through London, Washington and New York became a political problem. There were some in coalition ranks who unkindly recalled the 1981 episode when Malcolm Fraser did a quick and ultimately disastrous deal with the unions over wages so he could rush off to the Prince Charles/Lady Diana royal wedding. Howard might not have been able to do much about unemployment if he had stayed at home, but he certainly will not have any impact on it from the other side of the world. In a bid to counter the problem, a departure-eve line was put out claiming Howard's talks in London and Washington would encompass the unemployment issue. He would be briefed on the agreement between new British Prime Minister Tony Blair and US President Bill Clinton at their recent meeting under which officials from both countries would identify measures that had been most effective in boosting employment around the world. But clearly, if Australia House and the Australian Embassy in Washington are doing their job, there was no need for Howard to leave Canberra to plug into that.

Howard aggravated the situation by failing to keep the promise he made after BHP announced its decision to close the Newcastle steelworks in 1998 – that he would make an early visit to the Hunter and talk to the people affected. Newcastle is still waiting. Being photographed with Mark Taylor and attending a Test-eve dinner has higher priority than giving comfort to several thousand battlers about to lose their livelihoods. Minders argue, in justification of the trip, that it was important that Howard meet Blair. But Howard invited himself to the UK at a particularly busy time for the new British leader. Blair had trouble fitting him in between a European summit and a meeting of the G7 economic powers. Sources close to the new crowd at 10 Downing Street leave no doubt that Blair would have been delighted if the Australian Prime Minister had waited a while.

When Howard returns from the trip, he had better roll up his sleeves and start doing some serious work on the unemployment front – re-examining the government's policy direction and/or doing something to reassure Australian workers about their employment future (starting, obviously, with Newcastle, which has taken on considerable symbolic importance). Already opinion polls are suggesting voters believe Labor would do a better job in dealing with unemployment. There are those in the government who think the problem is being overstated, or rather that recent figures from the Bureau of Statistics are not reliable. Certainly it is highly unlikely that 40 000 people would be put on in one month and unloaded again the next. The series appears to have become unusually volatile because the bureau changed the sampling method. But there is no getting away from the fact that employment is flat and will remain so for quite a while.

Economic rationalists in the Liberal Party – Howard's soulmates before he succumbed to the temptations of pragmatism and populism – take the view that there is just one way to solve the unemployment problem. 'Proper deregulation of the labour market is the answer,' says one. 'But in Australia the political price is regarded as too high. Rather than adopt the British or New Zealand models, we basically decided to stick with the centralised model and keep high unemployment.' The two countries Howard is visiting have highly flexible labour markets. Unemployment in Britain is 5.8 percent and in the US 5.5 percent, compared with Australia's 8.8 percent. But Howard did not need to travel overseas to find that out either.

One of the key questions within the government at the moment, whispered rather than asked openly, is whether Howard will have the stomach to push for a second wave of reforms to the industrial relations system.

There was one hint before his departure that Howard just might be screwing up his courage and turning his mind towards a second wave. He told parliament: 'In order to reduce unemployment in a sustained way over a long period of time you need high growth, you need an infinitely more flexible labour market, and you also need taxation reform.' The reference to tax reform made the headlines, but shrewd observers regarded the statement on labour market flexibility as far more significant. It is difficult to read it as anything other than an admission that the government has not gone nearly far enough in freeing up the system. If Howard genuinely believes 'infinitely more' flexibility is required to deal with unemployment it would presumably be irresponsible of him not to move on it. 'A mark of how serious we get about unemployment is how serious we get about labour market deregulation,' says a prominent Liberal MP. 'Whether a second wave occurs, though, depends on the mind of the Prime Minister, how adventurous he will be. I don't think it will happen but that *was* an interesting statement.'

The Liberal 'dries' are no doubt hoping that Margaret Thatcher will put some steel into Howard on an issue dear to her heart when they meet in London for a cup of tea and a chat next Monday. If that happens, they at least will regard the Prime Minister's dream trip as a worthwhile exercise.

True believers vow to topple Gray eminence

22 July 1997

They are waiting on Gary Gray. Some powerful Labor figures who were supporters of Paul Keating are now looking for an excuse and an opportunity to do in the party's national secretary. The reason is the way Gray and his friends used Pamela Williams's election book *The Victory* to ensure that all blame for the 1996 anti-Labor landslide is laid at the former prime minister's door. Frontbencher Laurie Brereton, who was Keating's closest friend in politics, says: 'I was monumentally unimpressed with Gary.' Some other Keating loyalists, while unwilling to speak on the record, are even angrier – and determined eventually to exact retribution.

'Gary won't be forgiven for this,' says one. 'It sits there. The sheer unprofessionalism of it is what galls me. Paul had to carry the huge burden of getting done like a dinner by John Howard. You don't expect this sort of thing as well, as people reposition themselves.' Their charge against Gray is that he has rewritten history via the book to protect himself. They also see some of Williams's disclosures as proof that Keating was right to feel betrayed by Gray, Labor's national campaign director. One of the critics warns: 'I hold the strong view that he must never be allowed to do to Kim what he did to Keating.' Are there likely to be moves to oust Gray? 'We can wait!'

It is said that history is written by the victors, but sometimes people emerge as winners because they write the history. By taking advantage of the opportunity offered by *The Victory* to put his side – to present evidence showing how wilful, uncooperative, erratic, obsessive, deluded and impossible to deal with Keating was in the lead-up to the election, Gray has just about settled the issue of blame. The former prime minister will be 'Captain Wacky' forever. Gray first decided to cooperate with Williams out of self-defence because he believed Keating would use John Edwards's biography *Keating – The Inside*

Story to try to stick him with responsibility for the election loss, but when it appeared a few months after the election Edwards's book did no such thing. It would be close to impossible now for Keating's supporters to reverse the impression that has been created. Not that it is an inaccurate impression. Knowing Keating, and having reported the campaign, my sympathies have always been with Gray. Keating was out of control from 1993 onwards. No one could talk sense into him. He acted like a man determined to lose. The essential point, though, is that Gray took aim at Keating in *The Victory* – and he did not miss.

The muttering about Gray is just part of the fall-out from an extraordinary book. There is muttering on the other side about the Liberal Party federal treasurer, Melbourne businessman Ron Walker. Rightly or wrongly, Walker is being blamed, among other things, for a leak to Williams that has embarrassed and distressed Foreign Minister Alexander Downer. It concerns a meeting Downer attended with senior organisational and parliamentary Liberals when his leadership of the party was crumbling. The machine men, according to Williams, had picked up rumours that the ALP was about to circulate material on Downer's sex life, and they demanded to know if he was gay, if he had affairs. 'He vigorously denied allegations of homosexuality that purportedly went back to his student days,' Williams writes. It is a good story, but terribly humiliating – gratuitously so – for Downer who, whatever else may be said about him, behaved impeccably and with the best interests of the Liberal Party at heart by handing the leadership over to Howard in a way that ensured there was no division or recrimination.

Trying to identify the sources of a journalist who takes proper care to protect them is always dangerous. Walker may have had nothing to do with the leak. But there are a couple of reasons he is in the frame. One is that his closeness to Williams is not a secret. A few weeks before the election, for example, instructions were issued at Liberal campaign headquarters that Williams was to be allowed to sit in on a strategy meeting. Campaign staff who asked why were told: 'She's a friend of Ron's.' Another reason for suspicion is that, in the front of the book, Williams acknowledges and thanks for their help 'Andrew Robb, Tony Staley and Graeme Morris from the Liberal side' – but makes no mention of Walker at all. 'That's remarkable ingratitude when large parts of the book are clearly Ron,' says a senior Liberal tartly.

The Labor party, incidentally, never had any intention of using the Downer rumours. They were being spread by one of Downer's own backbenchers, a member of the Liberal faction known as the 'God squad' who had leadership ambitions himself. This MP took me to dinner one night and came out with a string of allegations about Downer. I have no doubt he fed the same dirt to other journalists. Corroboration, he claimed, was contained in a file in the Foreign Affairs Department, where Downer was employed before entering politics. I checked with some very good sources in the department; they found absolutely no evidence that any such file ever existed.

The Keating people will not find it easy to knock off Gray, unless he commits some new and major error or indiscretion – but he will need to keep an eye over his shoulder. What Labor has to do now is set up a campaign structure to ensure the same sort of problems do not occur next time around. They should not. Kim Beazley is sane and sensible and remarkably free of hubris. Also, Gray's close friend David Epstein, who worked out of the Labor secretariat in the 1996 campaign and was one of those frustrated by trying to deal with Keating, is now in charge of Beazley's office. There should be no fundamental conflict between the secretariat and the leader's office in the next campaign. From Gray's point of view, there had better not be, because with no Captain Wacky to blame he will not be able to escape responsibility if another campaign goes off the rails. Even one of Gray's supporters concedes: 'There has not been nearly as much criticism as a losing campaign director could normally expect because people say, "He had to deal with that lunatic." But with Paul gone he won't have an excuse. It will all be down to him.' And the Keating people will still be waiting.

PC is no PK, but he's prepared to wait

6 August 1997

The 1988 United States vice-presidential debate was memorable for Lloyd Bentsen's wonderful put-down of Dan Quayle, who had been unwise enough to compare himself to a Democratic Party hero. 'I served with Jack Kennedy,' Bentsen said. 'He was a friend of mine. Senator, you're no Jack Kennedy!' It was so effective that Gareth Evans paraphrased it in an attack on Treasurer Peter Costello in parliament last October. 'Let me tell you, I knew Paul Keating,' Evans thundered across the chamber. 'We all knew Paul Keating. And, Peter Costello, you are no Paul Keating.' The line fell flat, proving that Evans is no Lloyd Bentsen, either. But he *was* correct.

Costello's critics like to compare him to the former Labor treasurer and prime minister. They know it is damaging – unlike Evans, who for some reason thought it flattered Costello to be likened to the man dubbed 'Captain Wacky' by the Labor Party's national secretary. There are some obvious similarities between Keating and Costello. Costello is the most aggressive and easily the most effective parliamentary performer on the coalition side, just as Keating was for Labor. He is a strong treasurer, as Keating was. Also like Keating, Costello at times adopts a manner that many people interpret as arrogant. But there are fundamental differences, too – the main one being that Costello is capable of much more realistic self-assessment.

He is not in the same sort of hurry Keating was. Nor is he driven by the sense of destiny that made Keating such a manic figure. Costello is ambitious, but he also paces himself. When John Hewson's leadership of the Liberal Party became untenable, Costello – instead of running in his own right – let Alexander Downer have the job. When Downer's leadership imploded, Costello again stood back and left the way clear for John Howard's second coming. Costello knew he was not ready. He was too young, too inexperienced. It is impossible to imagine Keating making the same kind of judgment. He *always* knew he was ready, and better than everyone else, from the moment he entered parliament. Despite what his critics might say, Costello is a much more level-headed and down-to-earth politician than the bloke who even referred to himself on occasions as 'Mad Paul'.

These thoughts are prompted, of course, by recent idle speculation about the Liberal Party leadership succession – speculation sparked not by Howard's admission to hospital with pneumonia, but by his performance before he became ill. The talk is about the long-term. No one is suggesting Howard is under threat, or that he will not lead the coalition into the next election. But eventually, possibly during the next parliamentary term, the Liberals will have to choose a successor.

Costello is one candidate they are evaluating. Peter Reith is another. Journalists see a story in whipping up the idea of rivalry and tension between the two. It will be a recurring theme over the next few years, even though both Costello and Reith understand the potential risks for the government and will do their best not to feed it. Insofar as there is a contest, it will be very low-key.

Reith does not put himself forward overtly as a possible successor to Howard, and would not be shattered if he missed out. But no one should doubt that he would like the job. There are some in the party who believe Howard had an eye on the succession when he upgraded Reith's portfolio by adding small business to his workplace relations responsibilities. It is not suggested that Howard favours Reith over Costello; rather, that he sees it as important there is a choice available when the time comes for him to bow out. This may, however, be reading too much into the situation. The main reason for the change was that Reith, having got his industrial relations reforms on the statute books, did not have enough to do.

Reith has a few things going for him. While Costello is portrayed in the media as the heir apparent, Reith is happy to be seen as a quiet achiever. Also, his role as manager of government business in the House of Representatives gives him close and regular contact with backbenchers, and opportunities to do them favours. Consequently, some Liberals say that, even though Costello has the public profile, Reith has more numbers at this stage. But Costello is the one doing the big job for the government, running the economy. If he gets it right (as he appears to be doing), if the economy is humming along and unemployment is on the way down come the next election, those Liberal MPs who hold their seats as a result will presumably recognise who is responsible. The essential point is that – like him or not – Costello has 'leader' stamped all over him. He conveys strength, hangs tough on important issues, and is the coalition's most effective fighter. These are the qualities that should matter, even to those Liberals who have on occasion had their noses put out of joint by what they see as the Treasurer's offhand manner towards them.

What is interesting is the care both Reith and Costello are taking to try to minimise the public perception of rivalry between them. Each decided long ago not to do anything that could be construed as leadership manoeuvring. You will not find either of them bagging or undermining the other, even in private. When they disagree – Costello, for example, was annoyed when Reith floated the idea of a plebiscite on the issue of a goods and services tax – those disagreements are not aired publicly. A joking comment Reith made about the embarrassing South Pacific briefing paper fiasco was interpreted by some journalists as a swipe at Costello, but it had not been meant that way. The truth is that the Treasurer and the Workplace Relations Minister, while not personally friends, get on pretty well politically. They talk often, and tension between them is rare.

A ballot is a long way off. The fortunes of the two Peters will wax and wane in the meantime. Both are impressive politicians. But, whenever the leadership crunch comes, the choice should be obvious – as long as Liberal MPs end up agreeing with Labor's deputy leader that Costello is no Paul Keating.

Ministerial responsibility starts to implode

12 August 1997

The tragedy of the Canberra hospital implosion is fading from memory, overshadowed by the Thredbo disaster. An act of God has proved bigger and more dramatic than an act of man. But precisely because it was a man-made misfortune, the demolition that went wrong – taking the life of a young girl – contains lessons that should not be forgotten or ignored. Even before any of the inquiries are completed, it is clear that the bungled implosion says a great deal about changes that have occurred in our system of government. It raises questions about what has happened to the public service in this country, and the way ministerial responsibility has been diminished.

The immediate reaction of ACT Chief Minister Kate Carnell to the tragedy just about said it all. 'I had nothing to do with the decision on what sort of demolition methods would be used,' she told an interviewer. 'The decision was taken by Totalcare, which is a Territory-owned corporation.' She added: 'This was not something the government had anything to do with at all.' The same formula was repeated over and over again, every time it was suggested that the ACT government might have some responsibility. In other words, because Carnell's administration has corporatised the section of the ACT bureaucracy that deals with such matters, she no longer regards the government as accountable for it.

This is far from being a localised problem. In its enthusiasm for corporatisation and outsourcing and other changes to the way the bureaucracy operates and government services are delivered, the ACT administration has merely followed the lead of the federal government and the states. But because Canberra is so small and the hospital implosion was such a shocking event, the issues show out with stark clarity. Mistrust of the traditional public service and the drive for private-enterprise-style efficiency in the public sector have undermined the Westminster system. It has been altered fundamentally. We had better be aware of it, and of the consequences.

Had the Canberra hospital demolition occurred nine months earlier, the job of calling tenders and managing the project would have been handled by the ACT's Department of Urban Services. Carnell would not have got away then with saying it had nothing to do with the government. The situation altered when sections of the department were merged with Totalcare Industries, originally a government-owned laundry service which became a highly profitable commercial organisation after being corporatised six years ago. It was all done in the name of efficiency and improving the financial bottom line. The danger in this kind of private enterprise approach is that public interest may no longer have the priority it was given under the old bureaucratic structure. Given that Totalcare's two shareholders are the ACT Chief Minister and her Urban Services Minister, it is still part of government – but the structure it provides is enough of a wall for Carnell to shrug her shoulders when something goes wrong and say: 'It has nothing to do with me.' Ministerial responsibility ceases to exist. The politicians are no longer accountable.

The other problem with corporatising government functions is that, as commercial considerations provide the entire justification for the structure, the profit motive can dominate. Since the implosion that sent debris flying across the national capital, comparisons have been suggested in the local Canberra media between Totalcare and the old Civil Aviation Authority. As the *Canberra Times* pointed out, 'the CAA was found wanting because of an inability to balance the competing commercial and safety considerations'. Outsourcing – not necessarily relevant to the Canberra hospital incident, but symptomatic of the new attitude towards the public service – also gets ministers off the hook. The claim that it inevitably leads to greater efficiency is debatable. What is not debatable is that it runs counter to the concept of executive accountability and responsibility.

Another aspect of all this is the way the bureaucracy has been battered into submission. At the federal level the process began when the Hawke Labor government came to office in 1983. It found a group of mandarins at the top of the public service who – in the view of some of the new ministers – regarded themselves as more important than their political masters. Their attitude was that politicians come and go but public service permanent heads go on forever. Labor reacted with a series of reforms which meant permanent heads were no longer permanent. They could be sacked at the government's whim – downgraded to the rank of deputy secretary. The government's motives were understandable, but the result was a bureaucracy less inclined to give honest, independent and fearless advice. It is simply human nature that, if a piece of unpalatable advice can send your career down the gurgler, there is a great temptation to tell the minister what he or she wants to hear – or at least to modify your advice so that it causes minimum offence. This tendency was exacerbated by more reforms later in the Labor government's term which put departmental secretaries on contract, making them feel even less secure.

The same thing has happened at state level. In Victoria, senior bureaucrats know that they disagree with Jeff Kennett at their peril. Tame or intimidated bureaucrats make for bad government. This, too, became an issue in discussion of the Canberra hospital affair. Carnell can be as tough as Kennett in her dealings with bureaucrats. A spate of changes at the top of the ACT public service is evidence of that. And Carnell had shown considerable public enthusiasm for the implosion, helping to turn it into a major spectacle that was expected to win votes for her government. It is not known if any bureaucrats had misgivings – but, if they did, some guts would have been required to present negative advice on the subject.

The old public service had its virtues. The Canberra hospital tragedy shows that there are major problems with what is being erected in its place.

Red-faced government kills the messenger it ignored

21 October 1997

John Mellors is an angry man. The former head of the federal Department of Administrative Services, abolished as a result of the government's embarrassment over travel rorts, clearly believes that he and most of his former senior officers are victims of a vindictive payback.

'The manner in which a number of my former DAS colleagues are being dealt with by the government in the aftermath of the Travelgate affair is a disgrace to the traditional values of public administration in this country,' he told me. In light of the revelation that DAS argued for a root and branch review of the parliamentary entitlements system more than eight months ago, and the government failed to act on the recommendation, Mellors has reason to be bitter. The bureaucrats who wanted the system cleaned up and the potential for rorts reduced have been sacked by the very government that rejected their advice and vetoed a review. Political hypocrisy does not get much worse than that.

Mellors revealed the recommendation when I contacted him about the demise of the department and the 'night of the long knives' treatment of its former top brass. He found the denigration of DAS and its staff a bitter pill to swallow and was glad of the chance to defend the department's record.

'DAS has led and managed more fundamental commercialisation, privatisation and outsourcing of traditional public services than any other area of the federal public sector,' he said proudly. And then the statement that puts an entirely new perspective on the travel rorts saga. 'The department, and I personally, advised the former minister, David Jull, before the public controversy aroused by the so-called "Colston Affair", that the framework for determination of parliamentarians' entitlements required fundamental review.'

169

The axe has been wielded without mercy against DAS and the people who ran it. Mellors' job was automatically terminated when the department was wiped out and most of its functions handed over to the Department of Finance. Max Moore-Wilton, head of the Prime Minister's department, phoned to tell him there would be no offer of alternative employment. He was effectively given five days' notice after a public service career at senior levels spanning nearly 22 years.

One of Mellors' two former deputies has also been left in no doubt he will be out on his ear when various investigations are completed. Four or five other former DAS officers have been told bluntly that no job will be available for them under the new arrangements. All this helps to bolster the impression that the travel rorts scandal was the result of an incompetent department, the fault of the bureaucrats. That impression takes the heat off the politicians.

'There are lessons to be learned from the treatment meted out to politicians and bureaucrats respectively in this matter which bode ill for the future of public administration in this country,' Mellors said.

Before moving against DAS and its officers, Prime Minister John Howard knew – or should have known – about the department's recommendation of a review of the parliamentary entitlements system. If Howard was not told at the time – and more of that later – Moore-Wilton was reminded of it a few weeks ago. It was soon after Jull and John Sharp were forced to resign from the ministry following the disclosure that Sharp had overclaimed travel allowances to the tune of nearly $9000 and Jull had allowed him to repay it secretly. Apparently realising that moves were afoot to stick his department with the blame, Mellors wrote to Moore-Wilton pointing out that documents existed showing that DAS had wanted a review but the government had not acted on the recommendation. The government assigned DAS the scapegoat role, anyway.

DAS, in fact, had started looking at the parliamentary entitlements system back in mid-1994 – as Howard well knew, because he was the cause of it. As shadow minister for industrial relations, Howard used his parliamentary postal allowance to send letters to voters in a trade union election. He was endorsing a team of Liberal candidates in a Communication Workers' Union ballot. DAS approved the expenditure, but then the Labor minister for administrative services, Frank Walker, ordered a departmental inquiry.

The department reported that there was a pressing need to develop – preferably with bipartisan support – proper definitions for the terms 'parliamentary business', 'electorate business' and 'party business'. Walker agreed, and DAS prepared draft guidelines. In September 1995, Walker wrote to the leaders of the opposition parties seeking their support. Howard, by this time Liberal leader, replied supporting the guidelines in principle but raising a number of issues that concerned him. There the matter rested until after the election which made Howard prime minister.

Six months after the election, DAS revived the matter with its new minister. Jull circulated updated guidelines to various ministerial offices for comment. One of those to whom the proposed guidelines were sent was – according to a senior departmental source – Graeme Morris, Howard's trusted political adviser. No response was ever received from the Prime Minister's office – an indication of the low priority Howard gave to tightening up the system and reducing the opportunity for misuse of entitlements. Bureaucrats involved in the exercise say the word came down the line that this was not an issue in which the government was particularly interested.

Meanwhile, in late 1996, again according to a senior departmental source, officers in the ministerial and parliamentary services section of DAS were becoming increasingly concerned that the entitlements framework, its administration, and the way decisions were made on individual cases, 'lacked consistency, clarity, transparency and accountability'. They raised their concerns with Mellors, who in turn discussed the matter informally with Jull. In late December, those concerns resulted in the first draft of the DAS submission for the 1997–98 budget proposing a fundamental review of the whole framework of parliamentarians' entitlements.

In early February this year, a more polished draft was sent to Jull – still including the review proposal. The idea was to go back to square one and look at the whole basis of the remuneration of parliamentarians, including their allowances, and the sort of accountability that should go with the system. All this, it should be pointed out, was well before the Colston controversy erupted.

The draft submission prepared for Jull pointed out that the system had not been looked at properly for 25 years, it was complex, and it lacked the standards of accountability that were appropriate in today's circumstances. The proposal was for a committee to oversee the review. Although the draft did not specify who would carry it out, thinking in the department was that someone from outside the bureaucracy should be appointed. The understanding was, I am told, that Jull's office would 'test the waters' with others in the government about the proposal. The 'others' were thought by departmental officers to include either Howard's office or Peter Reith's office, or both.

The bottom line, though, is that after whatever consultations Jull engaged in, DAS was instructed to remove the review proposal from its budget submission. Mellors has told people he recalls Jull saying that, in the government's view, it was not a good time to draw attention to the system or to rock the boat. Consequently, the final DAS budget submission was lodged minus any reference to the proposed review. But there are, I am told, copies of the draft submission, stamped 'Cabinet In Confidence', on the departmental files. Other documentary evidence includes the brief notes Mellors made after his routine weekly meetings with Jull. This material would be available to any proper inquiry into the travel rorts affair.

It seems quite clear that Howard and his government knew the system was flawed, knew it was open to abuse, knew there were no cross-checks, knew that the bureaucrats who administered it were concerned. But they were not interested in doing anything about it, and ignored specific DAS advice to take action, until Colston hit the headlines and the spaghetti hit the fan. Then, suddenly, it became the bureaucrats' fault, and they have been made to carry the can.

Liberals long for strong leadership

11 November 1997

It was fascinating to see Paul Keating come out of his burrow, however briefly. The old bullying and brashness are gone, but some of the qualities that made him our most interesting politician in a generation were still evident when I interviewed him to launch the *Sunday Online* web site. The man who was the best phrasemaker in Australian politics punched out another memorable one with his comment that, because of the Pauline Hanson phenomenon, a substantial proportion of people in Asia think that 'we have got dark hearts'.

Keating's talent for sharp political analysis, which deserted him in his final deluded year as prime minister, was back. 'To be enjoined to be relaxed and comfortable was simply, at best, a naive hope... There is a sense abroad in the country that it's lost its way, that it's floating.' And the basic credo was unchanged: 'There is no substitute for leadership, ever.'

The reference to leadership was not made in the context of current Australian politics. We were discussing the way information technology will inevitably reduce the power of governments generally. But Keating's line would have struck a chord with Liberals involved in their own behind-the-scenes debate about leadership and John Howard. They, too, have picked up the community's sense of a country that is drifting, without direction, and they are worried about it. And the smart ones recognise that Howard's refusal to deal with Hanson back at the start was a failure of leadership which ultimately damages the Liberal Party as well as the nation. Hence the privately expressed concerns of Liberal federal president Tony Staley, the threat by Malcolm Fraser to campaign on the race issue at the next election if Hanson is not clearly rejected by the party, an article by Victorian powerbroker Michael Kroger asserting that Hanson *must* be put last on Liberal how-to-vote cards, and so on.

Leadership is a big issue in the Liberal Party now, just as it was during Howard's first unimpressive stint as opposition leader back in the 1980s. The talk then led to Howard being deposed. But – despite some overexcited media speculation – it will not happen this time, for several reasons. Toppling a prime minister is a much more serious endeavour than rolling an opposition leader, for one thing – especially when he has won a record majority. Also, there is a shortage of people with the inclination and the bottle to be coup leaders. John Moore, who was one of the leading conspirators in 1989, is a retired numbers man these days – and has become a Howard crony, anyway. Most important, while there is concern and even the occasional sign of despair, there is nothing like the active dislike of Howard now that was evident when Andrew Peacock was around to polarise the party. The inclination among the current crop of Liberals – even those who look with near terror at the opinion polls and see their seats disappearing from under them – is not to plot, but to hope desperately that Howard succeeds in getting his act together.

But the key point in all this is that Howard is seen less and less as a long-term leader, and anyone who wants clear evidence of that needs to look no further than the activities of Workplace Relations Minister Peter Reith. Suddenly Reith's program is attracting attention. 'He is campaigning – no doubt about it,' says a senior figure in the Liberal organisation. Reith has been travelling around the country attending an unusual number of functions for Liberal MPs. 'He'll do a four-day swing, covering as many electorates as possible,' according to another party insider. Reith is very active, making friends, notching up favours, his eye clearly on the leadership prize some time in the next parliament, stealing a march on his rival, Treasurer Peter Costello.

This puts Costello in a difficult position. There are complaints that he is not also out there visiting backbenchers in their electorates in the same way. Costello recently had dinner with Queensland Liberal MPs in what was presumably an attempt to counter the impression that he is aloof from the back bench. But, while Reith might not be snowed under with work, a treasurer cannot simply down tools for days at a time to gladhand backbenchers. He would return to a mountain of paper. And there is a more difficult problem. If Costello started behaving in the same way as Reith, it would make headlines immediately. The media would be full of stories about the ambitious treasurer making his move. The simple truth is that Reith can get away with it, but Costello could not. Any suggestion of Costello campaigning for back-bench support would be destabilising for the government. If he does anything at all, it has to be low-key.

That makes it very difficult for Costello to begin to make the image changes that are necessary to answer doubts about his leadership suitability. He needs to show that he is more than a tough treasurer and a parliamentary head-kicker. Those who know him see another, much more personable, side, but it rarely gets displayed publicly – or even within the party. But Reith has his problems, too. His thinly disguised positioning for the leadership has led to discussion about his previous life as deputy leader under John Hewson. It is being recalled that Reith, not Hewson, was the first to issue a manifesto calling for a GST, and that Reith was just as stubborn as Hewson when opinion polls showed the looming electoral dangers. One prominent Liberal has been saying of Reith: 'His greatest achievement in recent years was to dematerialise as the 1993 deputy leader. It is almost a case of, "It wasn't me, I wasn't there." '

Howard, meanwhile, is determined to show that he *can* lead, despite what the critics say. He scored some points in Edinburgh and his anti-drugs package was reasonably well received. If Howard remains focused, he may well turn the polls around – and Reith will be able to cut back on his travel. But remaining focused and 'on message' has not been Howard's great strength over the past eight months or so. As an experienced Liberal strategist puts it: 'He is giving everyone a scare by what is seen as an almost indulgent approach to leadership.' Indulgent, of course, is what they also called Keating. Now, there's an irony.

1998

Labor beware the sins of Saint Cheryl

3 February 1998

C heryl Kernot may prove to be a problem rather than an asset for the Labor Party in an election campaign. If Labor's heavies learned nothing else from the party's national conference in Hobart, they had that message rammed home to them. The former Democrat leader's defection undoubtedly contributed to the ALP's bounce in the polls last year, but there is a downside. Events in Hobart lead to the inescapable conclusion that Kernot is not as politically cluey as those who recruited her to Labor's ranks imagined. Unless she is carefully watched, her lack of discipline combined with a giant-sized ego could derail Kim Beazley's election strategy. Kernot stuffed up three times in 36 hours. There was her 'boo-hoo, I might quit' performance when the media showed a perfectly legitimate interest in an accident involving the family of a public figure. There was her inaccurate announcement that Beazley had put her in charge of a shadow portfolio for baby boomers. ('Not baby boomers, not a shadow ministry,' Beazley responded bluntly.) And there was her big-headed claim – in a speech prepared for the ALP conference dinner – that the electoral threat now hanging over the coalition government was entirely due to her switch of parties. A few gaffes like those in a federal election campaign would be manna from heaven for John Howard.

Since her defection last October, Kernot has been operating under the watchful eyes of two senior Beazley staffers and of Labor's Senate leader, John Faulkner. At the ALP conference, however, those people were busy with their real jobs. Kernot was let out alone – with unfortunate results. Now it has been decided at the top level of the Labor Party that Saint Cheryl (also known, courtesy of Alan Ramsay, as Princess Petal) needs her own exclusive minder. Someone she trusts who can be trusted by the party to keep her under constant supervision, impose some discipline on her, deal with her emotional ups and downs, and maintain channels of communication with Beazley's office and party HQ. Someone, in short, who can provide the political nous Kernot herself apparently lacks.

The Prime Minister was right when he characterised the ALP conference as a Cheryl Kernot soap opera. It may be that neither Kernot nor the party suffered much damage on this occasion – though any chance Beazley had of getting out a serious policy line was doomed once Cheryl went feral. A cynical Labor factional leader, speaking in the bar after Kernot's series of errors, asserted: 'It doesn't matter. She's fireproof!' Labor cannot afford too much of this kind of thing, however. Kernot can burn the party without being burned herself. And, while voters may be prepared to forgive almost anything she says or does at the moment, that will not necessarily last. Carmen Lawrence used to be considered fireproof, too. And the public eventually fell out of love with Bob Hawke, to whom Kernot has been compared in various post-conference news commentaries.

Kernot always looked pretty good in her previous incarnation, but the requirements were different. The Australian Democrats are judged more leniently by the media – and, I suspect, by the voters – than are the major parties. There is a discount for a Democrat leader which a minister or senior opposition spokesman does not get. As leader of what Peter Walsh christened the fairies-at-the-bottom-of-the-garden party, Kernot was expected to let her emotions show, to be inconsistent or imprecise, and to speak as a commentator on the other parties rather than as someone who aspired to a role in government. When she ratted on the Democrats and became a high-flier with the ALP, the rules changed. Her words and actions are now taken more seriously. She became subject to the same standards as Beazley, Howard, Evans, Costello, Fischer and the rest. And she has failed to adjust.

If Kernot accepts the lessons of Hobart, makes the necessary adjustments, and stops being so indulgent, she can still be a winner for Labor. Because she comes from outside the political mainstream, she has, at the moment, the kind of credibility most politicians can only dream about. That, and the easy way she communicates with voters, is why Beazley has given her the task of winning back to Labor the kind of people Howard attracted at the last election with his promise of a 'relaxed and comfortable' Australia – the middle-aged 'battlers' trying to cope with job insecurity and other stresses caused by the changing nature of work, family and community life. Howard, incapable of projecting warmth or sympathy, has failed to reassure these people. Labor hopes that a warm and cuddly Kernot can help a warm and cuddly Beazley do the job.

The Liberals will try to use Kernot's high profile to undermine Beazley's standing. They are already comparing the Beazley–Kernot situation with the way Labor wheeled out Bob Hawke and Neville Wran back in 1980 to bolster Bill Hayden in a kind of leadership triumvirate. But they will not find it easy to make the comparison stick. Hayden was not secure in the leadership; Beazley is totally secure. No one – and certainly not Kernot, who is still wearing her Labor Party 'L' plates – poses even a remote threat to him. More importantly, Beazley is totally secure with himself. His demeanour in Hobart was that of a bloke completely comfortable with his role. Avuncular, good-humoured, relaxed, and devoid of the paranoia that normally goes hand in hand with political leadership. Howard's leadership grip looks a heck of a lot less secure than Beazley's.

But Kernot *will* become an asset to the coalition if she continues to speak 'off message', if she persists in playing the prima donna, if she goes on believing her own publicity. Democrat senators and former staffers have been warning since her defection to Labor that she is not a team player. She had better become one. And, given the increasing likelihood of an early election, she had better become one quickly.

Republicans ride on Costello's shoulders

24 February 1998

Peter Costello is now the hope of the republican side. If next year's referendum is to have any chance of getting through, the republicans need the federal Treasurer and deputy Liberal leader spearheading the campaign. The most serious opposition will come from conservative coalition supporters. The 'yes' case will have no chance without a conservative champion. At the moment, the only coalition 'heavy' backing the republican model that emerged from the constitutional convention is government Senate leader Robert Hill. He is not heavy enough.

Malcolm Turnbull's Australian Republican Movement knows it. That is why ARM representatives are planning an approach to Costello to try to get him on side. Costello declared himself in favour of constitutional change at the convention, but baulked at the model Turnbull's team pushed through. Regarding it as an unsatisfactory 'hybrid on a hybrid', he abstained when the crucial vote was taken. The republicans can forget about signing him up, unless and until some of the flaws that concern him are ironed out.

Fortunately for those who want the referendum passed, Costello is clearly very interested in getting on board. More than that, when parliament begins the task of drafting legislation for the proposed constitutional amendment, he is prepared to take a leading role in whipping the convention's blueprint into what he regards as a more satisfactory shape. On the Nine network's *Sunday* program last weekend, he was asked: 'Are you going to do that work yourself? Are you going to try to turn it into a model that you can campaign for at a referendum?' The answer was unequivocal: 'Yes, I am.'

It was a display of leadership. Costello has now committed himself to an active role in trying to bring an Australian republic into being. On his terms, of course – but that is what leadership is about. It raises the prospect of a referendum campaign in which John Howard's deputy becomes the standard bearer for a cause the Prime Minister opposes. Howard did fairly well out of the convention. He set it up, and therefore got deserved credit for its success. But the bottom line is that he was allied with the Bruce Ruxtons, Flo Bjelke-Petersens and Alf Garlands. He stuck with yesterday. Costello – if he can secure the changes he wants in the proposed structure for a republic – will be grabbing an opportunity Howard passed up.

Nothing surfaced publicly, but there was some criticism in Liberal ranks of Howard's commitment to the status quo at the convention. One prominent party member – whose public image is that of a monarchist – told me as proceedings drew to a close that Howard should have got behind Richard McGarvie's minimalist republican model. 'The people want more than a fireworks display in 2001,' he said. 'They want an event, something to give meaning to the centenary of nationhood. Howard could have got a boost.' The truth, though, is that Howard's views are too well known for him to switch. Had he embraced McGarvie, or any other republican model, he would have been seen as a hypocrite. The last thing Howard needs as he tries to put last year's allegations of weak leadership behind him is more big headlines about backflips. Costello, however, suffers from no such restraints.

The assumption is that the republic issue will now be put on a shelf somewhere until after the next election. In terms of the public debate, that may be true. Howard wants it that way, so the government can be seen to be dealing with 'mainstream' issues such as taxation and jobs. But work on the actual drafting of a constitutional amendment bill will have to begin fairly soon if a referendum is to be held next year, as Howard has promised. It will be a complex process, not only because of the legal issues involved, but also because there will have to be quite a bit of horse-trading as the convention's wish-list is turned into something that might work. And when the referendum legislation hits parliament there will be a long debate, with the inevitable negotiations and problems with minor parties and independents in the Senate.

If Costello is to get the kind of changes he wants to the republican model that won the convention numbers game, he will have to get involved in the drafting process, he will have to use the cabinet and committee processes to shape the legislation to his liking, and he will have to play a major role in pushing the bill through parliament. He will also have to persuade the ARM to go along with the changes he wants.

But the fact that they have little chance of succeeding without him will be a powerful incentive for them to accept a redrawing of the model. The central element – approval of a president nominated by the prime minister by a two-thirds majority of federal parliament – would remain. The main problems concerning Costello and others of like mind have to do with the nomination process that was grafted on as the ARM tried in vain to win over those republican zealots demanding direct election of a president by the people. A mish-mash of political correctness and half-hearted populism, it would discourage many people of the type who have made excellent governors-general in the past from allowing their names to go forward. The kind of model Costello can accept might also get the nod from other Liberals, such as Western Australian Premier Richard Court, whose support would be crucial in a referendum.

Costello is already at the centre of political events as he prepares an election-year budget. Responsibility for the tax reform package that will make or break the government at the election falls squarely on his shoulders. Now he is taking on the republic as well. If he ends up campaigning for the referendum, and if Liberals like Court climb into the cart as a result, it will have a chance of getting up – albeit still a slim one. (A country that will vote against enshrining freedom of religion in its constitution, as Australia did 10 years ago, is not one in which constitutional reform comes easily.) But win *or* lose, Costello will have been on the side of the future. That will do his leadership credentials no harm at all.

Oh Lord, it's hard to be humbled

12 May 1998

The federal government is now involved in a major salvage operation. As soon as the High Court brought down its waterfront decision on Monday, it became a matter of John Howard and Peter Reith saving what they could from the clumsily handled attack on the Maritime

Union of Australia. 'We have to salvage some kind of improvement in work practices on the wharves so we can say it was not all in vain,' said a senior coalition source after the judges of the most senior court in the land delivered their blow. 'It's been a terrible interlude, but we have to persuade people that at least we got something out of it.'

The truth is that something *has* come out of this affair. The cause of waterfront reform has been moved forward. It was clear, even before the 6–1 dismissal of Patrick's appeal, that if the sacked wharfies returned to their jobs the MUA would have to accept cuts to the workforce and other measures to improve productivity. And the High Court made a significant concession to Patrick and the government. The administrators of the Patrick labour hire companies have to give priority to the commercial law – which means trading has to be profitable. That is not possible with the old workforce working under the old conditions. But the cost, as far as the government is concerned, has been enormous. It has looked partisan, inept and vindictive. It has appeared to connive in a shonky scheme to breach its own employment laws. It has proved incapable of winning a public relations battle against one of the most unpopular groups in the community. What moral authority the government had in the industrial relations area has been lost.

The plan that looked so clever at the start – causing Howard to proudly pat Reith on the back in parliament the morning after 1400 Patrick employees were thrown out of their jobs – collapsed with the High Court ruling. And, partly because of that very public prime ministerial pat, it was not possible for ministers to claim with any credibility that it was the company, not the government, that had miscalculated. Reith and Howard identified themselves so closely with Patrick and its chief executive Chris Corrigan when things were going well that they could not get out from under when the situation turned nasty. The result was to add to the growing impression of government incompetence. In the end, the government may win the industrial war but lose the political one because of this perception.

The coalition's hope now is that Treasurer Peter Costello can blot out memories of the waterfront debacle with next week's budget, in the first instance, and then the long-awaited tax reform package. The problem with the budget is that the waterfront row will probably still be bubbling when Costello brings it down, depriving him of the clean air he needs for a proper selling job – yet another downside consequence for the government. The tax package is much more important. Liberal and National party MPs must surely have twigged by now that if tax reform is managed as badly as the waterfront dispute has been, the government will lose the looming election. Selling tax reform, particularly a GST, is a perilous exercise, much harder than arguing the need for increased efficiency on the docks. It will require a careful strategy and a sure hand, and will be seen as a huge test of the Treasurer. But it will not be solely up to Costello. Howard will be involved, too, which hardly inspires confidence, given that he had his finger in the waterfront pie and was one of those responsible for the nursing homes fiasco. Quite a few in the coalition see him as part of the problem, not the solution.

Reith, Costello's rival for eventual leadership of the Liberal Party, is an expert at portraying defeats as victories. The Workplace Relations Minister demonstrated this talent again late last week, when the Industrial Relations Commission awarded low-paid workers a $14-a-week rise. Even though the commission rejected the government argument that anything over $8 would be disastrous, Reith said he welcomed the decision and proclaimed it a vindication of government policy. So it was no surprise that he portrayed the High Court ruling as a great government achievement. Certainly, the High Court decision was more acceptable to the government than the original Federal Court orders. But it still gave the MUA a moral victory.

For the assault on the MUA to bring the big political pay-off Reith and Howard had hoped for, the government needed a quick kill. Reith underestimated the resilience of the union. He underestimated the public disapproval that Patrick's ruthless and morally dubious tactics would arouse. He failed to recognise that unions can use the courts as effectively as can employers and the government itself. The government has presumably now learned that running an industrial dispute, from whatever side, is not as easy as it looks. As well as industrial relations knowledge, it requires an extensive understanding of the law, public relations skills and political nous. Even though the government will probably salvage quite a bit in the end, the fact is that Reith's handling of this episode has been unimpressive. If that has not knocked him out of leadership contention, it has gone close.

But the affair also suggests that too much is expected of Costello. He may be the government's best performer, but he cannot, and should not, move in every time something goes wrong. That would be usurping the leader's role. When the waterfront issue started to turn sour for the government, some fans of Costello thought he should charge into the front line. At the same time, there were Reith supporters criticising Costello for keeping his head down when things got tough. In fact, if Costello had muscled in early in the piece he would have been accused of trying to steal the limelight from a rival. By the time things went bad he was on his way to meetings in Washington. The headlines if he had cancelled the trip or cut it short are not hard to imagine.

Sweet and sour porkies litter the path to power

9 June 1998

This is a tale of two politicians. One of them tried to be honest. The other...well, the other is John Howard. In the 1980 election, Bill Hayden surprised everybody. No one thought he had a chance at the start of the campaign, but he gave Malcolm Fraser's coalition government one hell of a fright. And he would almost certainly have won, had the desperate Liberals in the final week not scared the pants off voters with a media blitz alleging homes were under threat because of Labor plans for a capital gains tax.

It began with a careless comment about capital gains tax from the then-shadow treasurer, Ralph Willis. Fraser challenged Hayden to rule out such a tax. The hard men around the Labor leader – Paul Keating, Bob Hawke and Graham Richardson among them – urged him to do exactly that. All he had to do was say that there would be no capital gains tax under Labor. But Hayden would not utter the magic words. He believed that a capital gains tax would make the Australian tax system fairer and more efficient, and therefore the option should at least be kept open so that it could be properly examined when Labor won office. Despite the pressure – Richardson records in his autobiography that Keating, in particular, was furious – Hayden refused to lie. The issue proved decisive. Fraser narrowly survived.

Contrast this with John Howard's behaviour as Liberal opposition leader in May 1995. Asked at a business lunch about a goods and services tax, Howard said: 'The fact is that the last election was a referendum on the GST. There's no way that we can have it as part of our policy for the next election. As to what happens some years in the future, I don't want to…you know, I don't know.'

Like Hayden with a capital gains tax, Howard believed a GST was necessary to reform the tax system and therefore wanted the option kept open. Unlike Hayden, though, he quickly decided honesty was not the best policy when the heat was on. As soon as reports appeared in the media that Howard was leaving open the possibility of a GST sometime in the future, Howard's advisers gave him the same advice Hayden received 15 years earlier. Forget about being honest! Rule it out! So Howard told a lie he is still lying about now. 'There is no way a GST will ever be part of our policy. Never, ever. It's dead.' It had the desired effect of removing the GST as an issue in the 1996 campaign.

It will not have escaped the notice of alert readers that the politician who refused to lie was defeated, while the one who told the big porkie and stuck to it was rewarded by a massive election victory. Therein lies the essential truth – the one Richo hinted at in his book, *Whatever it Takes*, and was pilloried over by still-practising politicians who have to lie about lying because that, too, is part of the game. Honesty and politics are incompatible. Ben Chifley used to say: 'You want to be scrupulously honest, but there's nothing to stop you being a bit bloody foxy.' That is an old-fashioned, romantic view. It is also nonsense. The scrupulously honest politician will be an unsuccessful politician, very quickly an ex-politician. Much closer to reality is the assessment of that great American investigative journalist I. F. Stone: 'Every government is run by liars and nothing they say should be believed.' All that needs to be added is: 'Ditto every opposition.' British philosopher Bertrand Russell had it pretty right when he wrote that 'an honest politician will not be tolerated by a democracy unless he is very stupid…because only a very stupid man can honestly share the prejudices of more than half the nation. Therefore any man who is both able and public spirited must be a hypocrite if he is to succeed in politics.'

It is the big deceptions like Paul Keating's 'L-A-W law' tax con that are noticed and remembered. But successful politicians behave dishonestly even in small things. Even, for example, at cards. About 10 years ago, a new Labor MP was invited to join a group of caucus colleagues who met regularly to play poker. He was an excellent player – a cut above the others – and at the end of that first night gleefully stuffed more than $400 in winnings into his back pocket. Later, Robert Ray, right-wing faction leader and one of the shrewdest pollies in the business, took the new man aside. 'You're not going to get very far in politics if you keep taking money off your mates,' Ray said. He advised the novice to use his poker skills to lose back the $400 in ensuing games, and after that to deliberately play badly enough every week to ensure he never did better than to break even. The L-plate politician took the advice, cheated every week to avoid winning, and was eventually rewarded by election to the ministry.

None of this will come as news to voters, of course. They understand that politicians are dishonest, even that they have to be. But they resent having their noses rubbed in it. Keating rubbed their noses in it with 'L-A-W law', and now Howard has done it with 'never, ever'. In the first of his so-called Headland speeches as opposition leader, Howard bemoaned a disturbing 'deterioration in the simple trust and confidence which used to exist between people and their governments'. He has now done more than his fair share to hasten that deterioration.

Resentment over politicians' lies, broken promises and breaches of trust is a major factor behind the rise of Pauline Hanson's One Nation party. Hanson has sold herself as a non-politician, and some voters have bought it. The truth, though, is that Hanson is a politician like the rest, and she and her party are no more honest than the rest. In some respects they are less honest.

A few years after urging Bill Hayden to rule out a capital gains tax, Hawke as prime minister and Keating as treasurer introduced it. Hayden no doubt regrets his 1980 attack of honesty. He got no credit for it from anyone. Better to be compromised and in the Lodge than opposition leader with integrity intact. Ask the current prime minister.

Timid, hypocritical, lacking credibility, and alone

16 June 1998

What is John Howard playing at with One Nation? Is he incapable of seeing the damage being done to the Liberal Party, to the coalition, while he wallows about? Why will he not lead? For that matter, why will he not even follow?

It is clear there is an overwhelming consensus at senior levels of the federal government that Pauline Hanson's candidates should be placed last on coalition how-to-vote cards. A powerful cross-section of ministers has spoken out publicly. Meanwhile, the Prime Minister pussyfoots around, refuses to state an attitude, but says he is 'not uncomfortable' with the decision of the Queensland coalition parties to give preferences to One Nation.

It is difficult to think of a single figure of any significance in the federal coalition who has openly urged the allocation of preferences to Pauline Hanson's weird mob. But it is a different story on the other side of the argument. Treasurer and deputy Liberal leader Peter Costello set an example with an unequivocal statement on national television that One Nation will be put last in his seat. Health Minister Michael Wooldridge, Industry Minister John Moore and even National Party leader and Deputy Prime Minister Tim Fischer have also indicated they would not allocate preferences to Hanson candidates. Other key ministers freely admit to holding a similar view. The Victorian and South Australian Liberal branches have formally decided not to give preferences to One Nation. Federal Liberal president Tony Staley belongs to the 'put One Nation last' school. The feeling is beyond doubt. But Howard will not articulate it.

Moore's declaration was particularly important because the position of the Queensland Liberal Party is often cited as an excuse for Howard's refusal to take a stand on the preferences issue. Moore is not only the senior Queensland Liberal in the federal government, he is also a former state president who knows the Queensland party organisation inside out. If Moore feels able to speak out, Queensland Liberal sensitivities would not seem to justify a prime ministerial display of timidity and hypocrisy which damages both him and the party in a national context. In a Brisbane context, too, if opinion polls taken in the run-up to the Queensland election are any guide.

Moderate opinion in the Liberal Party – and in the National Party, for that matter – is dismayed at how confused and ineffective Howard's strategy for dealing with One Nation has been. Assuming, that is, it can be dignified with the name 'strategy'. If the aim was to cause the Hansonites to fade away as a political force by 'depriving them of oxygen' (Howard's phrase), the pre-election panic in the Queensland coalition showed it up as a total failure. Perhaps, though, the real strategy was to be nice to Hanson so that the coalition parties would get One Nation preferences. If that is so, it looked pretty sick when One Nation began the Queensland campaign happy to receive coalition preferences but not intending to direct its own preferences in most seats to anyone. Where, asked disillusioned Liberals, was the gain for the coalition in that? And if the strategy *was* to be nice to One Nation in the hope of getting preferences, where did Howard's mid-campaign attack on Hanson as 'deranged' fit into the plan? In the final week there were signs One Nation might reconsider and give preferences to the coalition in some marginal seats. But that was simply a consequence of a surge in Labor support, not of any clever moves by the Prime Minister or the Queensland coalition leaders (unless the coalition brains trust decided the best way to attract One Nation preferences was to deliberately collapse the Liberal vote).

Howard and other coalition politicians tempted to play footsie with One Nation will learn eventually that they are misguided – but it may be an expensive lesson. Costello was right to warn about 'some of the advisers and some of the shadowy organisations that lie behind the One Nation party'. There are, as he said, 'some very unscrupulous people that are choreographing the One Nation party…for their own ends, which are very unsavoury'. Hanson's party has proved a mecca for the extreme Right in Australia. Anyone who has studied the way such extremists operate would tell Liberal and National party politicians that it is not possible to do deals with them.

The League of Rights ostensibly campaigns against communism, but it is clear from its literature that the League's real enemies are moderate conservatives and centre-right political parties – just as German communists in the '30s targeted the social democrats rather than parties of the Right. The idea is that, if you can destroy the centre, you polarise people. If right-wing extremists can destroy or discredit moderate conservatives, they leave people of conservative bent with nowhere else to go. That is the theory. That is what the shadowy organisations behind One Nation are all about. In the words of one long-time observer of the League of Rights and similar groups: 'They are white ants. If you try to deal with them, they eat you from the inside.' Anyone providing moderate conservative leadership is going to be their enemy. That is the way they operate, as Howard and Rob Borbidge and their colleagues are even now discovering. As the fear induced by One Nation's Queensland opinion poll ratings spread through the federal coalition, the prospect of a double-dissolution election over the Wik native title legislation had less and less appeal. And it was among Queensland National Party politicians – the people who originally did the most to force Howard into a hardline stance on Wik – that nervous talk about possible compromise to avoid a double dissolution first emerged. The danger of One Nation winning one of their Senate seats brought on a severe bout of cold feet among the Queensland Nationals. But – unless Tasmanian independent Brian Harradine recants within the next couple of weeks and decides to pass the Wik bill through the Senate – Howard is locked into a double dissolution, despite the certainty that the coalition will have its Upper House strength reduced and the near certainty that the low quota will see One Nation gain Senate representation.

It is a credibility issue, and credibility is something Howard no longer has in abundance.

Too soon for true believers

6 October 1998

After the 1996 federal election, a Reserve Bank cheque for $12.867 million arrived at Labor Party headquarters in Canberra. It was Labor's entitlement under the system of public funding for election campaigns, but it was not made out to the party. A remarkably trusting bureaucrat had simply issued it in the name of Gary Gray, the ALP's national secretary. After the horrors of the campaign he had just been through – with Paul Keating, aka 'Captain Wacky', out of control and at war with just about everybody – Gray must have spent at least a moment wistfully thinking about boarding a plane and buying a villa on Majorca next door to Christopher Skase, before he endorsed the cheque to the ALP and deposited it in the party's account.

This time, Labor's campaign has run smoothly. There has been no tension between the leader's office and the machine. There has been agreement on strategy. Kim Beazley, in stark contrast to Keating, has been disciplined and cooperative. There has been enough money for saturation TV advertising (though the early commercials were a bit too smart by half). Apart from a couple of hiccups in the first week, Labor has matched or even out-campaigned the Liberals. As a result, Labor has given the coalition a big fright, to the point where senior members of the government were openly canvassing the possibility of defeat a week out from polling day and at least a couple of Liberal backbenchers were on the phone excitedly discussing a possible 'dump Howard' move after the election.

There is no doubt the Liberals took the scare seriously. They genuinely regarded the election as very tight as the campaign moved into the final lap. Liberal treasurer Ron Walker and federal director

Lynton Crosby used the threat of a Labor government to prise extra funds out of party donors. At Liberal campaign headquarters in Melbourne not all the sweating was the result of Victoria's gas crisis shutting down the building's air-conditioning system. There was talk that if the government survived, it was likely to be by fewer than half-a-dozen seats. On the Labor side, opinion polls had generated the sort of optimism that was simply unimaginable at the start of the campaign. 'Newspoll has never been wrong about a federal election,' Labor people told each other. Even John Della Bosca, the level-headed NSW ALP general secretary who is one of the party's most respected strategists, last week gave the tick to a document predicting a minimum gain of 24 seats to Labor – just three short of victory.

It was clear that if the polls were vindicated to the extent that the coalition government survived by only a narrow margin, the Liberals would be in for another bout of leadership instability. When Howard asserted on the Nine network's *Sunday* program that he would expect to stay on as prime minister even if the coalition held onto office by only a single seat, it was pure bravado. Bob Menzies held onto the leadership in 1961 after winning by one seat, but Howard is no Menzies. Even supporters acknowledged privately that, while a razor-edge victory might not lead to his immediate demise, his departure would have to be orchestrated within a reasonably short time.

But beneath the surface optimism in the ALP camp was a feeling that it might all be too good to be true. Beazley himself confided to friends six days before the election that he wished the campaign had three more weeks to run. He could feel the ground moving his way, but believed the movement was not great enough. And when party number-crunchers looked carefully at the market research in marginal electorates, not only did they find it hard to identify 27 seats that Labor might seriously hope to win, they also had to consider the possibility that, unless everything went right on the night – preferences going the right way, swings occurring in exactly the right places – they might pick up no more than a dozen seats from the coalition. In the climate created by opinion polls showing Labor in the lead throughout the campaign, such a result would be well below expectations. Trying to portray it as a good result for Beazley would be an almost impossible task for Labor spin doctors, even though the best previous opposition performance against a first-term government was Andrew Peacock's eight-seat gain against Bob Hawke in 1984.

The party that has had the worst campaign is One Nation. Pauline Hanson's nose is out of joint because she did not get the television coverage that she expected as a result of her Queensland election experience. One Nation's attempt to produce policies on a variety of issues have been farcical. And the decision by the Labor and Liberal parties and most of the National Party to put One Nation last on how-to-vote cards has taken much of the wind out of the Hanson sails. It should prevent One Nation winning any seats in the House of Representatives, and may confine it to just one Senate place – in Queensland. But even here, the news may not be all good for Labor. ALP apparatchiks were painfully aware as the election approached that One Nation preferences could spoil things for them in some marginal seats. On one leaked Labor Party document I have seen is a hand-written note saying: 'One Nation might still fuck us over in Hunter or sabotage us in Robertson or Dobell.'

Beazley has used this campaign well to establish himself as a credible alternative prime minister. The ALP, knocked out of the ring at the last election, climbed back in and, to everyone's surprise, just about fought the Liberals to a standstill. Labor will certainly increase its nationwide vote, which means Gray will get a bigger Reserve Bank cheque this time around. But all that being said, election night may still prove to be an anti-climax for the true believers.

On his own show, Howard gets all the laughs

27 October 1998

On the day after the federal election, the Nine network's *Sunday* program ran a profile of Peter Costello, the man most likely to succeed John Howard. It contained excerpts from an interview in which the Treasurer answered questions on, among other things, leadership. The more paranoid members of the Howard supporters' club seized on this as evidence of either disloyalty or lack of judgment – or both. Costello, it was claimed in angry back-room muttering, had given the interview before the election to position himself for a takeover if things went badly for the coalition.

In fact, Costello had rejected requests for just such an interview. The 'grabs' used in the profile were library material originally aired two years ago. But the reaction shows how so much that occurs within the government at the moment is distorted by the leadership issue. This was never more evident than in the speculation preceding Howard's ministry reshuffle. There was an assumption that the Prime Minister would use the opportunity to clip the wings of a would-be challenger. In its bluntest form, this line (fed out by government sources and faithfully reported) involved the proposition that Howard would appoint a powerful new minister for revenue to take responsibility for tax matters out of Costello's hands. That would have been a highly provocative move – one any treasurer would find almost impossible to accept.

A more refined version suggested Howard would give the finance portfolio to his favourite troubleshooter, Nick Minchin, who – as a member of the Senate – would then take on the role of negotiating the tax package through the Upper House.

Nothing of the sort happened. Whether Howard seriously contemplated such action is unclear – but if he did, he was wise to resist the temptation. The Prime Minister, more than anyone, would understand how risky and counter-productive it can be for a leader to become obsessed with curbing an ambitious deputy. He can hardly have forgotten how he came to get the Liberal leadership the first time around in 1985. Andrew Peacock tried to pot Howard, then deputy leader, but shot himself instead. What Howard did in the reshuffle, very sensibly, was to shrug off paranoia and, instead, make optimum use of his available talent. He pointed his best troops at the toughest jobs. That did not stop some commentators seeing anti-Costello machinations in the result, but they were wrong.

Had Minchin been appointed to Finance with carriage of the GST legislation through the Senate, it could have been interpreted legitimately as a put-down of the Treasurer. And it might have been a possibility until John Fahey's determined resistance persuaded Howard not to move him. But in the big new portfolio of industry, science and resources, Minchin poses no problem for Costello. Indeed, the Treasurer is likely to welcome the appointment. Minchin, like Costello, is 'dry' on economic policy.

Had industry, science and resources gone to Peter Reith, however, there would have been a clear leadership message. Reith wanted out of workplace relations, and such a move would have enabled him to shake off the effects of the waterfront war and develop a less confrontationist image. It would also have put him in close touch with the big end of town, people who have a powerful influence within the Liberal Party. Howard could have given Costello's main potential rival a significant boost. Instead, admiring the way Reith handles difficult assignments, he added the poisoned chalice of employment to the Workplace Relations Minister's existing responsibilities. The good of the government was given greater priority than Reith's leadership aspirations.

Howard decided there was no point looking over his shoulder. He knows he will be judged by how the government performs, so he backed competence. Few issues proved more contentious in the government's first term than immigration, and Philip Ruddock's promotion to cabinet rank was acknowledgment that he handled it with considerable skill and subtlety – as was the decision to put him in charge of the reconciliation process. Howard was mindful, too, that Ruddock is a highly competent lawyer, a necessary qualification given that the task will involve drawing up a document of reconciliation between Aboriginal and non-Aboriginal Australians.

Howard also promoted people who have shown themselves capable of strongly arguing a political line. That is the main reason for the surprise elevation of Wilson Tuckey from the back bench to the ministry. Tuckey, once a pro-Peacock plotter, had been helpful to Howard over the past 18 months or so on such issues as Wik, the GST, and the problem of the wool stockpile. He also belongs to the faction of the Western Australian Liberal Party opposed to expelled powerbroker Noel Crichton-Browne. But most of all, Tuckey can push a political line hard – something that has been missing among the WA ministerial contingent. Judi Moylan, dumped for Tuckey, could not do it. And, while Daryl Williams has great strengths as attorney-general, he cannot do it, either.

The only area where Howard had the question of future leadership in mind concerned the National Party, not the Liberals. The new super-ministry for the bush, the transport and regional development portfolio, was designed partly to counter One Nation by delivering services to rural and regional Australia. But it was also intended, quite specifically, to broaden deputy leader John Anderson's CV, enabling him to work the grassroots and boost his popularity so he can move into the National Party leadership when Tim Fischer calls it a day.

For the rest, Howard seems to have been concerned only with how to get the best results from his team. He avoided the trap of being defensive over his own leadership position. Jack Benny used to say: 'A laugh on your show is a laugh for you, no matter who gets it.' If the government does well – Costello included – Howard will reap the benefit.

Too many chiefs, not enough democracy

24 November 1998

John Howard, like most conservative politicians, professes to believe in smaller government. The decision to chop another 5000 jobs out of Centrelink is just the latest example of the public sector downsizing that has become commonplace since the coalition won power in 1996, but which was well under way before that. There has even been a bit of a move towards downsizing parliaments. The Liberal government in Tasmania cut the size of that state's parliament before calling the recent election that saw it lose office. And Bob Carr's Labor administration in NSW has passed legislation that will see a smaller parliament there after the next state election in March.

But when most people talk about 'the government' they mean the executive – ministers, the politicians who actually run the system at state and federal level. And there is never any talk of downsizing there. Howard is happy to slash the public service, but the thought that 'smaller government' might also encompass a smaller ministry has not entered his head. Prime ministers and premiers simply do not think that way. At the time of Federation, the constitution decreed that there should be no more than seven ministers in a federal parliament of 111 (75 Members of the House of Representatives, 36 senators). But those numbers were to apply only 'until the parliament otherwise provides'. Now there are 30 ministers in a parliament where MPs and senators total 224. The number of parliamentarians, in other words, has doubled, but the number of ministers has quadrupled. The story is the same at state level. Bruce Stone, an academic at the University of Western Australia, examined the issue of the ratio of executive to non-executive members of parliament earlier this year (*Australian Journal of Political Science*, vol. 33, no. 1). He wrote of 'the striking increase in ministerial presence in Australian parliaments'. In every jurisdiction, he found, 'the proportion of ministers in the parliament has more than doubled since 1901, and...in some cases (Queensland and South Australia) it has almost trebled'. Stone argued that 'this process has contributed to the weakening of parliaments'.

Observing the first week of the federal parliament brought that warning to mind. The coalition's loss of seats at the October 3 election made Howard's 30-member front bench look even more bloated than it did in the last term, when the coalition had a huge Lower House majority. Include the dozen parliamentary secretaries and it is, quite frankly, ridiculous. As a former minister says candidly: 'There are only about 20 real jobs.' The Labor front bench – enlarged since the election – is just as ludicrously oversized with 30 shadow ministers and seven parliamentary secretaries.

A parliamentary committee – the House of Representatives Standing Committee on Legal and Constitutional Affairs – recommended last year that a limit should be placed on the proportion of members of the House and the Senate who can be appointed to executive office. It proposed that the number of ministers, assistant ministers and parliamentary secretaries should be restricted to no more than 20 percent of the total membership of parliament. The recommendation – surprise! surprise! – has been ignored by the government. The committee's concern was that open slather on executive appointments opened the way for governments to elevate a large number of MPs, 'thereby giving the executive the opportunity to wield excessive influence over the legislature'.

An eminent political scientist, Professor Colin Hughes, had referred in evidence to the committee to the danger of 'the executive buying itself excessive influence in the legislature which ought to monitor its performance and hold it accountable for actions and policies'. He added that 'unless there is a limit, scenarios could be devised under which an obviously excessive part of the governing party (or coalition of parties) is locked into uncritical support of the executive and all its works'. A case can be mounted for the proposition that we have already reached that situation, and that the 20 percent limit recommended by the committee is too high. The current ratio of ministers and parliamentary secretaries to total membership of federal parliament is nearly 19 percent. Bruce Stone argued in his paper for a constitutional limit of 10 percent.

Stone is quite right in believing that increasing the prospect of office as a reward for loyalty to the party and its leadership increases the control a party and its leadership can exercise over parliamentarians. He wrote: 'Adding to the ministry, in the absence of compensating increases in the size of parliament, increases the power of the leadership and the chance of benefits of office for all members of parliament...Australian parliaments, and particularly their lower houses, lack institutional strength in part because the incentives they provide for members are heavily conditioned by the size and influence of the executive.'

It is difficult to disagree with that analysis. Executive control is a major reason for the decline in the status of Australian parliaments. And it is a solid argument for not tampering with the system that allows the Senate to act as real parliaments should by holding governments accountable and subjecting their policies and actions to proper scrutiny. The row over whether there should be a parliamentary inquiry into the GST is a case in point. There has been no proper parliamentary consideration of the proposed new tax. It was devised by the executive and presented to the coalition party room as a fait accompli. The debate, when the legislation goes to the House of Representatives, will be tightly controlled – a result made possible, at least in part, because of the size of the executive. Only in the Senate – thanks to minor parties and independents – is the power of a bloated executive ever challenged.

1999

Brereton is showing Labor the way

16 March 1999

In a telephone conversation some months ago, Laurie Brereton told Kim Beazley he believed their fortunes were intertwined. 'Our political timetables coincide, mate,' Brereton said. 'If we can't get you up as prime minister next time, the party's going to have to start looking for someone to succeed me in Kingsford Smith.' Beazley asked: 'Who do you reckon it would be?' Brereton was astonished. 'Wrong question, Kim,' he said.

The incident is significant for two reasons. It illustrates, fairly clearly, that – far from wanting to destabilise the Labor leader – Brereton saw it as in his own interests to help put Beazley into the Lodge. That is still the case. If Labor does not win the next election, Brereton – along with Beazley – will be finished. But more importantly, Beazley's response showed up his leadership shortcomings. It assumed that Labor would lose. Leaders are supposed to exude strength and confidence. Beazley is not doing that. He is not providing direction. He is muddling along.

In this context, it is difficult to overstate the stupidity of those

Labor MPs who fed out the line that Brereton – with his criticism of past ALP governments over East Timor – is deliberately undermining Beazley as part of a long-term leadership bid. Their intention was presumably to give the shadow foreign minister a clip over the ear, but the effect of the headlines they generated was to focus attention on the weakness of Beazley's leadership performance since the election defeat five months ago.

Gough Whitlam also did Beazley no favours with his frothing-at-the-mouth attack on Brereton. 'Now, Brereton may think he's hurting me, or Hawke, or Keating, or Gareth Evans,' fumed the ageing Labor icon, 'but he's also hurting Beazley.' Not as much as Whitlam hurt him. It was the former prime minister's vicious personal attack on Brereton at a NSW state election function in Gosford that turned Labor Party divisions over policy on East Timor into a major news story. It was Whitlam's largely incoherent rave that enabled the government to turn the blowtorch on Beazley. Thanks to Whitlam, everyone could see that there was a blazing row in the Labor Party – and that Beazley lacked either the will or the capacity to do anything about it. John Howard's election campaign question about whether Beazley has the ticker to be a national leader was given new resonance. With friends like Whitlam, Beazley does not need a lot of enemies.

The ferocity and highly personal nature of Whitlam's comments on Brereton surprised many who only know the grandfatherly figure the former prime minister has become since his retirement from parliament. But they were not, unfortunately, out of character. Whitlam in his younger days was renowned for his poisonous tongue. This is the same man who once called William McMahon a 'quean' in parliament and then checked to make sure Hansard had spelt the word correctly; the man who claimed William Charles Wentworth had 'a hereditary streak of insanity'; the man who threw a glass of water over Paul Hasluck during an exchange in the House of Representatives. Perhaps Brereton can consider himself lucky to be let off with 'shallow, shabby and shonky' and a spiteful reference to a 25-year-old scandal over which charges were dismissed.

What Brereton said about Whitlam and East Timor was certainly not deserving of the fury it inspired. 'The key problem with Whitlam's approach was the contradiction between his support for integration on one hand, and on the other, his support for a process of self-determination which in all likelihood would lead to independence – an outcome Indonesia was determined to thwart,' Brereton told the Queensland branch of the Australian Institute of International Affairs. 'We will never know what might have been, but I think it is a matter of enduring regret that Whitlam did not speak more forcefully and clearly in support of an internationally supervised act of self-determination as the only real means of achieving a lasting and acceptable resolution of East Timor's status. At best, Whitlam's approach was dangerously ambiguous, and by mid-1975 increasingly unsustainable.' It was a considered, measured speech and its conclusions have been vindicated by the subsequent leaking of the official records of Whitlam's crucial 1974 and 1975 conversations with President Suharto. Whitlam's resort to abuse rather than reasoned debate may suggest he has no real answer.

Brereton is not engaging in any leadership destabilisation exercise. Rather, he seems to be trying to show the Labor Party and its current leadership the way they should be going about trying to win office in 2001. I suspect Brereton would argue that one of the reasons Labor's primary vote is so low at the moment – a mere 40.1 percent in last year's poll – is that many voters believe the party has lost its sense of idealism. All those years in government saw Labor compromise and adopt pragmatic policies on a number of emotive issues – East Timor among them. The party needs to get its idealism back. It needs to show it has changed since it lost office. It needs to differentiate itself from the current government. It needs to stand for something. Above all, it needs to take some risks. Brereton might have gone too far in his criticism of East Timor policy under Gareth Evans, succumbing to the temptation to settle old scores, but his general idea is right. It is the same kind of approach, ironically, that Whitlam followed in opposition – and, while opinions might vary about his period as prime minister, there is no doubt Whitlam was a great opposition leader.

A prime minister who deserves better

16 May 1999

It is, in a way, not surprising that the Prime Minister is the one public figure in this country who has refused to participate in the condemnation of Australian International Olympic Committee member Phil Coles. With even deputy PM Tim Fischer demanding that Coles stand down from the Sydney games organising committee, John Howard told an interviewer: 'I am not going to join that kind of...public plebiscite.' Howard no doubt sees a lot of himself in Coles, all stubbornness and grit, and determination not to buckle under pressure. Accepting gifts and perks may not be Howard's style, but refusing to give in no matter who is against him and what is thrown at him, even when the situation is apparently hopeless, is quintessentially Howard.

On May 18, Howard will celebrate the 25th anniversary of his election to federal parliament. There will be parties, tributes, toasts, a lot of back-slapping. But he will look back over a career littered with events that would have caused most other politicians to give the game away. When Howard was toppled from the leadership in 1989, friends advised him to walk away from politics. He shook his head. He received the same advice, and rejected it again, in 1993 after failing to beat John Hewson in a leadership ballot even though Hewson had just led the coalition to defeat in what was supposed to be the unlosable election. That Howard came back, that he is still there after a quarter of a century and at the very top of the political tree, is the result of sheer guts and doggedness.

I first came across Howard during the 1972 election campaign – Gough Whitlam versus Billy McMahon. The Liberals knew they had no chance of winning. McMahon was a lying incompetent. His campaign was a shambles, a series of humiliating disasters. Howard, then NSW Liberal Party vice-president and a protégé of party powerbroker Sir John Carrick, appeared on the campaign plane one day, and quietly went about the job of trying to bring some order into the chaos. Making the ridiculous McMahon look prime ministerial was a hopeless task, but Howard did his best. That he took on the assignment when most of McMahon's ministers had given up and were abandoning the sinking ship was an indication of Howard's character. He went into parliament at the next election in 1974.

His rise was rapid – a minister in 1975, treasurer in 1977, deputy leader of the Liberal Party in 1982. Then the setbacks began. Wanting to produce a responsible budget in 1982, Howard was rolled by a prime minister and a cabinet determined to increase spending in a bid to buy electoral survival. He considered resignation, but decided against it. Then, when Malcolm Fraser stepped down after the coalition's 1983 election defeat, Howard was beaten for the leadership by Andrew Peacock – the start of a rivalry that was to dominate and blight conservative politics for the next decade. Two years later, Howard showed how stubbornness and toughness could pay off. Peacock turned the blowtorch on him in an attempt to get a pledge that there would be no leadership challenge, Howard withstood the heat and in frustration Peacock moved a spill against his deputy in the party room. It failed, Peacock resigned, Howard became leader.

Howard refused to be crushed by the Joh-for-Canberra campaign which dashed his prime ministerial hopes in 1987, by the coup which restored Peacock to the leadership in 1989 and by the 1993 party room rejection. His colleagues and the media wrote him off repeatedly, but he worked away, never said die, and finally made it to the Lodge.

Peacock, ensconced as Australian ambassador in Washington courtesy of his old rival, is the first to congratulate Howard on this latest milestone. 'I'm very pleased for him,' says Peacock. 'I have developed a huge regard for him. He's earned the respect of a great many Australians.' Now in his fourth year as prime minister, Howard has proved himself the most significant figure in Liberal politics since Sir Robert Menzies, not because he is in any sense a visionary but because he is a stayer.

What is remarkable as Howard celebrates his silver anniversary is how little credit he gets. Even now, after winning two elections, he has still not put to rest all the doubts within his own party. There are Liberal MPs who speculate – foolishly, I believe – that Howard's leadership will again be under threat if the tax legislation hits the wall in the Senate. Remarkably, after presiding over a government whose policies have made Australia what *The Wall Street Journal* calls the 'roaring economy' of Asia, he is still not a popular prime minister.

Peacock is right to say he has earned respect, but he has so far failed to inspire affection. A booming United States economy saw Bill Clinton's approval rating shoot up and stay up despite a series of scandals. By contrast, with the Australian economy going gangbusters and Howard's liking for chesterfield sofas the only scandal in sight, his approval rating has declined. It has to be a problem of chemistry. He is a prime minister who deserves better.

Howard's answer, as always, is work and persistence. His schedule of travel and interstate engagements reads like an election itinerary. Government sources say his advance teams are going flat out. He never misses an opportunity to grab a headline, giving opinions on everything from Arthur Boyd to rugby league to the troubles of Phil Coles. And day after day he is on talkback radio, striving to develop some kind of matey relationship with ordinary Australians that, Hawke-like, he so obviously craves. Howard is unlikely ever to achieve the kind of bond with the electorate that, for a few years, Bob Hawke enjoyed, but it will not be for want of trying.

After Fischer, more boring identikit politicians

13 July 1999

Tim Fischer will be missed for a lot of reasons. He was decent. He was hard-working. He was competent. But, above all, he was *interesting*. That made him pretty rare in modern Australian politics. Today's pollies, by and large, are a bland and boring lot. No one would ever say that about Fischer. He was colourful and spontaneous. An individual. And, because he was a bit different, people took notice when he spoke.

It is necessary only to listen to his successor to realise what we have lost. John Anderson had a chance to show his stuff at a news conference immediately after the party meeting that installed him as the new National Party leader. He began by paying tribute to Fischer and wife Judy. 'They have run the race, fought the good fight, given it their best shot.' Oh, dear! Most of the next half-hour was clichés and platitudes and generalities. Hardly a thing worth listening to, or reporting. Anderson is bright and likeable, but he belongs to the generation of politicians who have mastered the art of saying as little as possible to avoid getting into trouble. Compared with Fischer, Anderson is Mogadon Man.

It would be an interesting experiment to take Anderson and, say, opposition frontbencher Michael Lee to a suburban shopping centre, stand them side by side, and see if the passers-by could pick which was the Nat and which was Labor. Same uniform. Same superficial, platitudinous way of talking. Much the same views when they can be coaxed into expressing them. It is more evidence of the way differences in Australian politics are disappearing. Just as there are fewer and fewer real differences between the parties, there is a grey sameness about the personnel.

One reason politicians are more boring than they used to be is that they are increasingly afraid to take risks. Even in election campaigns, parties rarely chance their arm. Everything is calculated and researched to within an inch of its life. Victorian Premier Jeff Kennett is one of the exceptions, and it is a major factor in his popularity. He is a risk-taker in both what he says and what he does. Kennett is open about what he thinks, and eschews the usual safe political phrases and code-words in favour of straightforward, sometimes colourful language. Like Fischer, he has the courage of his convictions. Like Fischer, he makes people sit up and take notice. Anderson, by contrast, like most others on both sides, is a button-down, risk-averse politician. He will perform competently, but he is not going to excite or inspire anyone.

Most of today's politicians have any inclination towards risk-taking knocked out of them early in their careers. A key part of this is the so-called 'media training' which politicians and would-be pollies from all parties are put through. The media training fraternity refer to the central lesson, euphemistically, as 'knowing how to set the agenda'. Step one is pretending to address questions, with such phrases as 'Let me answer you this way' or 'The facts are' or 'What I really want to say here is this'. Step two is to then ignore what you have been asked and put forward a carefully scripted line on whatever it is you want to get across. 'Go into an interview with three or four key messages,' media trainers will tell their students, 'and make sure you stick to the script no matter what you are asked or where the interviewer tries to take you. Basically ignore the questions – in news interviews, particularly, they don't matter, because most of the time only the answers will get to air.'

The result is mantra politics. At the very least, any spontaneity is eliminated. It is a recipe for boredom, a sure-fire way to ensure disengagement on the part of viewers or listeners.

A lot of people make a lot of money giving this sort of advice. One well-known media personality who provides such training (and who is certainly not the most expensive in the field) charges $750 per person per day, with up to six people in each course. Nice work if you can get it. Not surprisingly, journalists – and, increasingly, the public – are aware of the tricks being taught and see through them. A case in point was Kerry O'Brien's *7.30 Report* interview with Assistant Treasurer Rod Kemp on the notorious casino high roller GST exemptions. Kemp ignored the questions and repeated, over and over, the line that had been scripted for him. He had obviously been told: 'No matter what you're asked, just keep saying this.' It was embarrassing to watch. By the time it was over, a large part of the audience had concluded that Kemp was a half-wit, and the position he was trying to defend had been damaged irreparably.

It is sometimes argued that the dominance of television has eliminated much of the individuality from politics because of the over-riding importance of the 10-second sound grab. No one, it is claimed, can project their personality when all they are permitted if they want to get to air is a quick 30 or so words. But that does not hold water. The politicians who are most effective in the TV grab department are the Fischers, the Kennetts, the Keatings. Gough Whitlam, even now, is a TV news natural who frequently demonstrates that brevity is the soul of wit. Whether we are talking 10-second grabs or 30-minute interviews, *interesting* works on television, *boring* does not.

There are still some interesting politicians on the federal stage. Peter Costello, because of his sheer class, his thorough grasp of what he is talking about, the rhetorical and theatrical talent that allows him to get across a message in a colourful and effective way, and the confidence that makes him willing to take risks. Amanda Vanstone is interesting because she is gutsy, a fighter, always on the offensive. Jackie Kelly is interesting because – so far, anyway – she has not let the minders and media trainers sap her of her individuality; she is still prepared to have a laugh and occasionally say outrageous things – and may that never change. The rise of the boring, identikit, media-trained politician has undoubtedly contributed to public cynicism about politics. With Tim Fischer gone, people are likely to find the process even more of a turn-off.

Shock jocks in the dock – at last

27 July 1999

John Laws's first meeting with Bob Hawke stuck in his memory. It was before Hawke became prime minister – before he gave up drinking so that he *could* become PM. David Combe, then national secretary of the ALP, had dinner with Laws and wife Caroline in Sydney one night, then took them to Hawke's suite at the Boulevard Hotel to say hello. Despite the fact that Combe had phoned ahead, Hawke came to the door starkers. Embarrassed on his wife's behalf, Laws suggested some clothing might be appropriate, so Hawke wrapped a towel around his waist. Then, in a pugnacious mood, he proceeded to tell Caroline Laws – who had lived in Papua New Guinea for some years before her marriage to the radio king – that she knew nothing about the place.

But, when he made his run for the prime ministership, Hawke

went all-out to cultivate Laws. Graham Richardson and the Labor Party's NSW Right faction insisted on it. Do not underestimate Laws's power, they told him. It was essential to have Laws onside – or at least neutral. Hawke always went out of his way to make sure Laws and his radio program were well serviced. Paul Keating, Hawke's treasurer and successor, a product of the NSW Right, never had to be told. He worked hard at buttering up Laws from the start. Once, when he was treasurer, amid strict secrecy, Keating flew the talkback star to Canberra and had officials give him a private briefing on the economy. Just the same, every so often Laws would rip savagely into a Labor minister – Ros Kelly with her whiteboard was a classic example.

Alan Jones also had to be factored into the power equation. For the Labor Party, however, trying to get a fair go out of him, let alone favourable treatment, has been a waste of time. He is a failed conservative politician, having stood unsuccessfully for National Party preselection for a federal seat, also missed out on federal preselection for the Liberal Party, and lost to a Labor candidate when the Liberals nominated him for a state seat. Jones takes his power seriously, and does not just wield it on air. There are people right at the top level of the ALP who believe that Jones's unremitting anti-Labor views going out over the air waves every day are gradually changing the political culture of Sydney.

On the issue of political bias, Jones's and Laws's own views have been more telling than those expressed by outside critics. In 1994, with Keating in the Lodge – and showing sensible reluctance to appear on the Jones program – Jones's manager, Harry M. Miller, accused Laws of being the Prime Minister's puppet. Describing a Laws interview with Keating as 'disgraceful', Miller said: 'It is now known that the Prime Minister was pulling the strings for Pinocchio.' After last year's federal election, in which Jones's one-eyed support for Howard was a notable feature, Laws called his colleague a Liberal Party stooge, adding: 'You become a whore.' Jones was also the Lord Haw-Haw or Tokyo Rose of the election campaign. All this has suddenly become more interesting as a result of the 'money for opinions' scandal which has hit Laws and Jones and their employer, Sydney radio station 2UE.

The fact is that the secret arrangement that existed between Laws and the banks, exposure of which sparked the crisis in talkback radio, could just as easily have been negotiated between a radio host and a political party. According to the leaked memo from Australian Bankers' Association executive director Tony Aveling, the objective of the deal was to reduce negative comments about banks to nil, receive positive comments, and as a result 'shift Australians' perceptions and attitudes'. What political party would not love such a deal with a top-rating host on a top-rating metropolitan radio station? I am sure neither Laws nor Jones *has* entered into any such arrangement with a political party for money. But, given the way recent revelations have undermined the credibility of both 2UE's stars, it would be understandable if people wondered.

Some in the Labor Party are doing just that. One senior ALP figure said at the weekend: 'It raises the question of why Alan Jones editorialised so forcefully on behalf of the Liberals at the last federal election. He was implausibly biased. It would not surprise me if there was something behind it.' Jones's bias *was* astonishing. A study by the media monitoring company Rehame found that Jones, speaking to a fifth of the Sydney radio breakfast audience, had nothing positive to say about Labor or its policies during the entire campaign and made not a single negative comment about the coalition. Prominent Liberal Michael Kroger later told the ABC's *Lateline* program that Jones had been crucial in holding the line for the party in NSW. The Liberals, of course, did not pay Jones. They did not need to, and anyway, to do so would have been illegal under the *Electoral Act* unless the payment was publicly declared. But the fact that such suspicion can exist shows how the credibility of talkback radio has been undermined.

With any luck, the affair has been a wake-up call for the public. Increasingly the shock jocks of talkback radio have been taking over from political journalists the role of providing political information and questioning politicians. The difference is that political journalists are expected to abide by certain standards – among them a commitment to accuracy and an obligation to present things fairly. They may fall short, but the standards are there. Talkback hosts, on the other hand, with some honourable exceptions like Neil Mitchell in Melbourne and John Stanley in Sydney, feel themselves bound by no such constraints. Yet a recent *Bulletin* Morgan poll showed that 18 percent of Australians believe talkback announcers maintain high or very high standards of honesty and ethics, while only nine percent say that about newspaper journalists. It is to be hoped that the current kerfuffle will at least lead to a recognition that normal journalistic standards should be applied to those in talkback radio. Their role, particularly in the political process, is now too important for anyone to cop the pathetic excuse that they are simply entertainers.

How to unpack the Kelty baggage

31 August 1999

The Labor Party breathed a collective sigh of relief when Bill Kelty announced his decision to vacate the post of ACTU secretary. Kelty was a continuing reminder of the 'Captain Wacky' era of Labor leadership. When Paul Keating was prime minister, Kelty was his equally eccentric sidekick. He was not only part of the cheer squad that encouraged Keating in his self-indulgence, self-deception and arrogance, but displayed similar traits himself. Keating, though, shot through when the electorate told him he was on the nose in 1996. Kelty was like a smell that hung around.

The current ALP leadership now has a chance to build a new relationship with the trade union movement. In Greg Combet, who will take over officially next February, they will be dealing with someone free of the baggage of the Hawke and Keating years. They will not be continually damaged by association with someone who had become the easiest of targets for coalition attack. They will have an ally at the head of the union movement who has not thrown away most of his credibility – somebody prepared to appear in public to argue a case, rather than a sulky recluse. Combet may not be the most charismatic character around, but at least he is not an embarrassing relic.

The ALP may gain something else as well. A role model. Part of the approach Combet has foreshadowed to try to rebuild the union movement could be just as relevant to the Labor Party's attempts to recover lost support.

With part of Kelty's legacy a drop in union membership from nearly half the workforce in 1983 to just on 28 percent now, Combet takes over a movement in desperate straits. He clearly believes one of the most serious problems has been the centralisation that has marked Kelty's reign. The Combet blueprint is all about decentralising – moving the emphasis back to individual workplaces, ensuring there are delegates, activists and collective structures at every site where union members are employed. A major goal of the new approach, as set out in Combet's unions@work report made public last week, is 'educating delegates and activists to better recruit, service and bargain in the workplace'.

There is growing recognition in the ALP that this is the sort of thing the party needs to do as well. Like the union movement, it somehow has to energise its base. In political parties, as in unions and many other institutions, the top-down approach does not work any more. It is, in fact, a turn-off. Tony Blair recognised this in Britain. A key part of his success in rebuilding the British Labour Party was a concentration on activity at the local level. As one senior ALP figure says: 'A lot of unions had dropped the ball in terms of the interests of their membership on the shop floor, so there was no incentive to join. Labor has not been proactive enough in expanding the party either. We've been too content with what we've got. Like the unions, we need to put a lot more into the grassroots organisation.'

The ALP's problem is that it has not yet come to grips with one of the paradoxes of the era of global communication – namely that, in the words of a party thinker, 'the more impersonal things get, the more people yearn for local community'. People increasingly see institutions they deal with – banks, government, the media – as distant from them. Just as the banks are realising that branch closures have been counter-productive, some in the Labor Party are waking up to the need to go back to local-level politics. They are starting to make the point that, while using the national media is important, communicating with people at the local level and energising party activists in local communities is just as vital. Now proponents of this view will be able to point to Combet's plan to save the union movement to back their case.

In the past, Australian political parties have been able to neglect local-level organising to some extent because of compulsory voting. The need to 'get out the vote', which helps to drive precinct politics in the US and Britain, has not been a problem here. But the 'detribalisation' of politics – the breakdown in adherence to political parties – has changed the situation and added to the need for parties to build up strong local units. Up to 40 percent of voters are now regarded as up for grabs, not strongly committed to any party. Parties will have to find local means of communicating with such people. 'Mass communications will not do the job,' says one of those in the ALP arguing for change. 'We've got to be able to talk to them at work, at the shops, at P & C meetings or school fetes.' Perhaps the party should consider its own Combet-style report.

One reason for the union movement's neglect of its base was the process of amalgamation pushed by Kelty. Amalgamations meant officials of the merged unions became preoccupied with their own internal battles for power. Almost unavoidably, they became inward-looking. Internal problems took precedence over the things they should have been doing for their members. Amalgamations – the creation of super-unions – affected the Labor Party as well.

In most states, the Labor Party operates on the 60/40 principle. That means that, at state ALP conferences, 60 percent of votes are controlled by unions, 40 percent are cast by branch representatives. Union amalgamations meant fewer unions with the power of unions in the party remaining constant. In other words, a smaller number of union officials wielding proportionately greater power. One of the consequences has been considerably less diversity in leadership positions in the Labor Party as well as in the union movement. Another has been a degree of organisational atrophy. This is part of the Kelty legacy with which Labor has yet to come to grips.

Too much, too soon

6 October 1999

When Victorian voters turned so savagely against Jeff Kennett, they did not just cut a state politician off at the knees. They brought a national political figure tumbling down. Kennett had strutted the Australian stage like a colossus, lecturing the federal government and towering above other premiers. Speculation that he might one day make the move to Canberra was taken seriously – especially in business circles. Kennett was seen as an alternative power centre to John Howard in the Liberal Party. State Liberal leaders like Richard Court and John Olsen used to get sick of being criticised because they were not versions of Kennett. Paul Keating shocked and angered the Victorian ALP by commenting that there was 'much to be admired about Jeffrey'. Kennett's flair and daring put most other politicians, state and federal, in the shade. When he threw his weight around, it had an impact in Canberra and Sydney as well as Melbourne.

He was the archetypal can-do politician, against whom others were expected to measure up. No exaggeration was involved in the title of a book edited by Melbourne academics Brian Costar and Nicholas Economou and published not long before the Victorian election. They called it *The Kennett Revolution*, and wrote: 'Since its election on October 3, 1992 the Liberal–National Coalition…has proved to be the most activist, controversial and ideological administration in 20th-century Victoria.' And, in a judgment no one will query, they asserted: 'Notwithstanding some setbacks, the Kennett government's reputation as a major reforming administration of the neoclassical liberal type still outstrips the reputation of other Liberal and Coalition governments, including its national counterpart headed by Prime Minister John Howard.'

Now, of course, the voters have delivered the *ultimate* setback. Even if Kennett clings to power by his fingernails, relying on the support of independents, his revolution has been brought to an abrupt halt. And it is not only Victoria that will be affected. The lesson has not been lost on politicians the length and breadth of the nation. No matter how popular you seem to be, and despite opinion polls showing the electorate's clear preference for leaders who get things done, if you push too far and too fast with reform you meet a sticky end. Particularly in rural and regional Australia, voters have to be drawn along gradually. Revolutions make them feel insecure. Kennett's arrogance and autocratic manner were certainly major factors in the result, but it was angst over loss of services, insecurity brought about by change, that pushed the government to the brink. That, at any rate, is the way politicians who want to survive are choosing to read it.

In NSW, Bob Carr led his Labor government to a spectacular victory just months before the Kennett government so unexpectedly hit the wall. One message senior figures in the NSW government took from the anti-Kennett swing was that the unions who blocked Carr's plans to privatise the state electricity industry had done him a huge favour. Had the privatisation plans gone ahead, they say, Carr might well have found himself in electoral trouble too. Pondering Kennett's fate, Carr himself is reported to have conceded that this view contained a fair bit of truth. Electricity privatisation is now well and truly off his agenda. It underlines the extent to which Kennett's crash will inevitably weaken the reform push in Australia.

In his election night speech, Kennett warned that Victoria would be 'a very different place from today'. There was, he said, no other conclusion that could be drawn. 'A lot of the excitement, a lot of the consistency, a lot of the achievement that we have gained, a lot of the respect we have earned…will quite quickly dissipate.' But it is not only Victoria that is affected. Australia is different, too, now that – to misquote one of his election slogans – Jeff no longer fucking rules. Already the proposed deregulation of the dairy industry has been thrown into doubt. The federal government is again worrying about the mood of rural voters and their tendency to exact revenge on governments they perceive as pushing economic rationalism too far. The Nationals are more nervous than ever.

And the federal ALP is seizing on what happened in Victoria as justification for its stand on such issues as the privatisation of Telstra. In the words of a senior member of Kim Beazley's front bench: 'This is a lesson for all those trying to spook us into changing our policy on Telstra. Voters are fed up with privatisations.' Says another prominent Labor figure: 'Jeff seemed to have found a way to popularise hard economic decisions – but then he lost it. There are obvious implications for us about what used to be called reform fatigue.'

The Victorian electoral earthquake will have other significant impacts on national politics, of course. An immediate consequence is to puncture the certainty the federal coalition had started to feel about the next election. Talk about Beazley being finished and federal Labor being on its knees has died away somewhat since the Victorian poll. Some federal Liberals are instead discussing what they see as a disturbing pattern. 'It continues an anti-coalition slide across the country,' says one Liberal MP. 'We lost Tasmania, lost Queensland, came within an inch of losing South Australia, went backwards in NSW and scraped back in federally with less than 50 percent of the vote. Now this has happened in Victoria. Tell me there's not a big message there for the coalition.'

Like Wayne Goss and Nick Greiner before him, Kennett is a greatly diminished figure – almost certainly on the way out, whether or not he manages to form a government after the Frankston East by-election. Without a parliamentary majority in his own right, Greiner was gradually cut to pieces until he eventually threw in the towel, and Kennett can look forward to the same fate. One result of this is that the cut-down-to-size Kennett will no longer be taken seriously if he tries to continue his running commentaries on the federal government's performance. 'The problem was a weak prime minister who would not engage him,' according to a Liberal source. 'Kennett's public criticisms belittled Howard. He won't get away with it any more. After this election fiasco, if he tries to tell others what to do he'll be a laughing stock.'

Kennett's behaviour after Carr steamrollered the coalition in NSW was an indication of the kind of clout he wielded inside the Liberals. He called for NSW opposition leader Kerry Chikarovski and Liberal Party state director Remo Nogarotto to be sacked for losing 'an eminently winnable election'. Chikarovski and Nogarotto have displayed commendable restraint in not replying in kind following the Victorian poll. Then, before his election, Kennett again infuriated the NSW Liberals by hosting a $1000-a-head function in Sydney to raise money for his campaign – described by the NSW party as a $300 000 to $400 000 raid on their debt payments. A leading NSW politician says now: 'He came up to Sydney, got all the available conservative money, took it back to Victoria – and pissed it up against a wall.' There will be no more such swaggering through the interstate business community.

Kennett critics are now portraying him – unfairly – as an emperor exposed as having no clothes. 'His only line of argument was that there ought to be strong leadership,' says one. 'No matter what the issue was – native title, tax reform, anything – Jeff would be out there saying all we need is leadership. Strong leadership was his answer to everything.' His agenda, say the critics, was possible only because he controlled both houses of parliament. While every other government in Australia was hampered by a hostile Upper House or the lack of a clear majority in the Lower House, Kennett faced no such problem – so it was easy for him to sneer at others as weak. While this is true, there is no doubt that Kennett made the most of his control of parliament – and of a timid coalition back bench – to ram reform measures through.

The blueprint was a report, titled *Victoria – An Agenda for Change*, prepared by two right-wing think-tanks, the Tasman Institute and the Institute of Public Affairs, a year before the Kennett government won office. The report advocated fundamental change to markedly reduce the involvement of government, and called for a radical program of privatisation and contracting out. It was all spelt out in great detail. Kennett and his treasurer, Alan Stockdale, ran with it. In an unprecedented privatisation campaign, a host of enterprises were sold off. The size of the bureaucracy was slashed. Radical labour market reforms were put in place. Spending was cut, with health and education not exempted from the austerity measures – or the moves towards privatisation.

In the government's first year, according to *The Kennett Revolution*, 'some 37,000 public servants and 8000 teachers (the equivalent of 20 percent of the budget sector workforce) had lost their jobs; 35,000 employees of government businesses were made redundant; over 300 schools were closed'. By the end of its second term, the book says, Kennett had 'transformed Victoria into the small-government state that the authors of [*An Agenda For Change*] yearned for in the early '90s'. Voters – particularly those in the country and, according to exit polling, elderly voters – did not yearn for the same thing. But before the electorate rebelled, Kennett had achieved most of what he had set out to do. A member of the Kennett team says: 'We've done it all, really. The other states haven't – and now they won't. So it still gives Victoria an edge.'

According to a senior minister in a Labor state: 'What happened to Jeff proves that, even when you have what you think is a big mandate, you can't make swinging Thatcherite cutbacks. Reform has got to be stretched out. It's the timeframe that is important. Change has to be staggered.' A Liberal Party organisational figure says: 'This will show politicians the need to take the community with them – to spend time explaining things, rather than ramming them down the electorate's throat. The explanation process is going to have to be longer.' A lot longer, if you believe the Nationals.

Kernot's last chance

12 October 1999

Cheryl Kernot is a difficult woman. Democrat senators and staffers who served under her when she led their party will tell you so. Now those who deal with her in the Labor Party say the same thing. It is because she is so difficult that her job change – from transport and regional development spokesperson to shadow minister for employment – had to be handled very carefully.

It was clear to almost everyone that Kernot had to be moved. She was making no appreciable impact in regional Australia. As a national political figure, she had just about disappeared from sight. She was sounding off to all and sundry about her lot – in particular, about the impossibility of combining the travel involved in regional development with the task of trying to hold onto the second most marginal seat in Australia. And, as a result of her letting it all hang out, reports of yet another crisis in the recently accident-prone career of a one-time political star had started appearing in the media.

If it had been anyone else, Kim Beazley would have made a couple of phone calls and announced a shuffle. But this was Kernot, who attracted such huge headlines when she defected from the Democrats and switched allegiance to Labor. She had to be treated with kid gloves. The opposition leader, it appears, could not risk forcing a job change on her in case she exploded publicly and lashed out at her new party. He had to wait for her to request a portfolio transfer. She finally did that in the middle of last week, just hours after Beazley – questioned by journalists about her future – had said categorically: 'We are not considering shifts in portfolio responsibilities.'

Beazley has good reason for trying to accommodate Kernot. Despite all that has happened in the two years since she swapped parties, she still shows up in opinion polls as a positive for Labor. She is still capable of winning votes, and most caucus members know it. She is still a pretty effective parliamentary performer, too. And Labor owes her. 'Cheryl is a curious mixture of whinger and very courageous politician,' says one of her Labor colleagues. 'She did put her superannuation and future income on the line by coming to us in a marginal seat, after all. We can't say she is all take and no give.'

But the 'whinger' reputation is something Kernot needs to watch. A journalist, in a recent conversation with a Labor MP, said he'd been told by another caucus member that Kernot did nothing but complain. 'Not true,' said the Labor man. 'Sometimes she sulks.' It was a cheap shot, and unfair, but contained enough truth to be damaging.

Kernot and the small cheer squad around her are adept at finding others to blame when things do not go well. The way her profile has shrunk in the year since she scraped home in the marginal Queensland seat of Dickson is a case in point. The cry from the Kernot camp is that Labor has been hiding her – a ridiculous claim. The failure is Kernot's. Other Labor frontbenchers – Wayne Swan as shadow minister for family and community services is a good example – have attracted media attention and scored hits on the government through their own hard work and political nous.

The best-known example of Kernot seeking to blame others when things do not go according to plan, of course, was her election night dummy spit as the count went against her and it appeared she might not win Dickson. Then it was the fault of the ALP officials who had slotted her into a difficult seat rather than a safe one. Kernot seemed to forget that, at the time of her defection from the Democrats, she had publicly proclaimed that her wish was to win a marginal seat from the Liberals. Similarly, Kernot sought the transport and regional development job. If it proved too tough and was incompatible with holding a marginal seat, again she cannot pass the responsibility on to others.

While Kernot is noted for being difficult, Martin Ferguson is the opposite. When Beazley asked if he would exchange jobs with Kernot, he agreed immediately. 'If Kim wanted it, that was good enough for Martin,' says a colleague. 'He's a bloke who always does the right thing.' There is an upside for Ferguson, however. Employment was a job closely related to his old role as president of the ACTU. Moving to transport and regional development gives him a chance to get away from union issues and shake off the typecasting. In the judgment of a Liberal strategist, 'Farmers might not take to Martin but he should do OK in the towns.' Ferguson's challenge is to put federal Labor in a position to emulate the party's success in winning rural and regional seats in the NSW and Victorian elections. Kernot was making little headway at this.

But she has not been relegated to a less important job. She has, in fact, been given more responsibility. Employment is a crucial issue for Labor. By assigning her to it, Beazley has, in effect, given her a renewed vote of confidence. Kernot must know, however, that this is her last chance to revive her career; the last opportunity to show that she is a political heavyweight rather than a media creation. It is easy to criticise Kernot, but she has had a lot to adjust to in a very short time. The move from the Senate to the Lower House. The switch from a small party to a big one. The change from party leader to mere shadow minister. Not to mention the vicious treatment by some sections of the media of aspects of her private life which had no relevance to her political role. But she must now rise above all that and start performing.

2000

Man with a mission

4 April 2000

First, a declaration of interest. I brought Geoff Walsh to Canberra. We're talking 24 years ago when, as a raw young journalist on the *Albury Border Morning Mail*, he applied for a job in the Canberra bureau of the old Melbourne *Sun*, then the biggest-selling daily newspaper in the country. As bureau chief I rejected him the first time around, opting for someone with more experience. But politics was the youthful Walsh's consuming interest, and when another vacancy occurred four months later he came knocking at the door again. This time I hired him. Two other young reporters on the staff in those days were Tony O'Leary and Niki Savva. O'Leary is now the Prime Minister's main spin doctor. Savva is press secretary to Treasurer Peter Costello. And at the end of next week, Walsh will officially take over as national secretary of the Australian Labor Party.

Gary Gray, scarred and calloused from seven years in the post, will be farewelled at a dinner hosted by Kim Beazley. Walsh will grab the reins at an executive meeting the next day. And he will have just one job. Winning the next election. Gray, like any long-term party secretary, has had to devote much of his time and energy to organisational matters – disputes between the federal secretariat and state ALP offices, allegations of branch-stacking, proposals for reform of the party structure, careful management of the property portfolio, and so on. But Walsh does not see himself as long-term, and nor do those who have put him into the position. He will not get bogged down with such matters. The plan is for him to build the best campaign organisation possible, focus single-mindedly on the electioneering task, and – win or lose – bow out when the election is over.

The pattern, throughout his career, has been for Walsh to move in and out of politics. He was communications director at the ALP's national secretariat and then press secretary to the prime minister for the first three years of the Hawke government, before dropping out for a time to take a posting at the International Labour Organization in Geneva. He returned to work for Bob Hawke again as senior political adviser, then joined the bureaucracy as a Foreign Affairs officer, answered an SOS from Paul Keating in 1994 to take up the adviser's role again, and after a year went back to Foreign Affairs to become consul-general in Hong Kong. A result of all this movement is that Walsh is not a member of any faction. He has no power base. But he also has remarkably little baggage.

Gray helped to recruit Walsh as his successor. Beazley has a high regard for him. Beazley's chief of staff, Michael Costello, who headed Foreign Affairs before the Howard government came to office, became friendly with Walsh in that role and was crucial in persuading him to accept the job. But most of the key figures in today's Labor Party hardly know him. There is suspicion in some quarters, for example, that Walsh is a plant of the NSW Right – specifically, that he is close to John Della Bosca, former NSW ALP secretary and now a state minister, who is expected to become national president of the party in August and whose manoeuvrings were a factor in Gray's decision to quit. But the truth is that, until he decided to nominate for the national secretary's position, Walsh would not have spent more than half an hour talking to Della Bosca in his life.

It says something about the ALP that the party had to look outside its own organisation to find a replacement for Gray. No one on the inside was considered capable. Walsh was the only candidate interviewed.

His was the only name put before the executive in a postal ballot. Not surprisingly, the appointment was unanimous. That puts the new secretary in a very strong position. He is completely unencumbered. As a senior Labor figure puts it: 'Geoff doesn't belong to anyone. He doesn't owe anyone a debt. That unnerves some of the apparatchiks.' Walsh himself has told friends the only obligation he has is to Beazley.

One of the crunch issues for Gray was his belief that Della Bosca wanted to take control of Labor's campaign organisation. The national secretary is, automatically, national campaign director. But Della Bosca and Gray, once close mates, now have a frosty relationship. Dubbed a campaign 'genius' by NSW Premier Bob Carr, Della Bosca disagreed with Gray on a number of issues during the 1998 campaign. Gray feared his position would be usurped with Della Bosca in the presidency. But Walsh should not face the same problem. His natural inclination will be to draw on all the available campaigning talent within the ALP at both the state and federal levels. With no 'history' of intra-party rivalry and power plays, he has a much better chance than Gray did of building a harmonious team. But Walsh knows that someone has to be the final point of decision-making on campaign issues. That 'someone' will be him. Otherwise he will simply walk. Della Bosca, like everyone else who counts in the party, will be well aware of that. It is another example of how being an outsider gives the new secretary extra muscle.

As one powerbroker puts it: 'Geoff was brought in fundamentally because he's a fantastic campaigner.' In the 1983 campaign which saw Labor under Hawke win power, Walsh's role was central. When Hawke began the 1990 campaign grumpy and undisciplined, Walsh was the one who dragged him back on track and ultimately got out of him the best campaign performance of his four elections. His fascination with campaigning began when I assigned him to travel with Doug Anthony, then leader of the National Party and deputy prime minister, in 1977 – the original 'Wombat Trail' – and has never waned. Walsh began immersing himself in the latest electioneering techniques from the moment he went on the ALP payroll as secretary-elect on February 20. With Walsh on one side and O'Leary and Savva on the other, I will watch next year's election with even more interest than usual.

Dangerous edge of the wedge

11 April 2000

A brilliant American political strategist, the late Lee Atwater, coined the term 'wedge issues'. They are issues that divide, that split people. Atwater, a conservative Republican who worked for Ronald Reagan then managed George Bush's successful 1988 presidential campaign, was an expert at what is now known as wedge politics. Wedge issues used to great effect by US Republicans going back to Richard Nixon include abortion, homosexuality, feminism, racism and xenophobia.

As one of Australia's shrewdest political operators explains it: 'You find an issue that will separate a group of traditional voters from the opposing party and pull them over to your side.' The Republicans used proposals for equal opportunity and affirmative action laws to frighten into their camp blue-collar white male workers who had previously voted Democrat. Atwater and his team combined the issues of race and capital punishment to help Bush wipe out the unfortunate Michael Dukakis. Classic wedge politics aims at creating resentment among a large group against a smaller one – whites against blacks, ordinary workers against people on welfare.

John Howard and the strategists who advise him have learned a lot from Atwater and the Republican hardliners, and they are putting it into practice in an increasingly transparent way. In the 1988 US campaign, while Atwater ruthlessly applied his wedge-politics techniques, Bush was publicly espousing the theme of 'a kinder, gentler society'. Here, while the Prime Minister portrays himself as a 'compassionate conservative' and claims that 'we are a caring government in a caring society', Employment Services Minister Tony Abbott grabs headlines at every opportunity by beating up on the unemployed as 'job snobs' and welfare cheats.

And here, as in the US, the conservatives find race and xenophobia to be particularly useful wedges. When the United Nations Committee on the Elimination of Racial Discrimination had the temerity to criticise Australia's record, it was an opportunity too good to pass up. The cabinet response – a review of Australia's participation in the UN treaty committee system – looked like a silly and petulant overreaction, except when seen in the light of wedge politics. It pushed both the race and xenophobia buttons. With lines that may well have come straight out of the Liberal Party's market research focus groups, Foreign Minister Alexander Downer made no pretence that he was playing anything other than a domestic political game. 'We're all Australians,' Downer said. 'We know that this is not a country where there are serious breaches of human rights...The Labor Party, personified by Mr Beazley, is happier attacking Australia than defending it. They're happy to gang up with a politicised UN committee which includes Cuba and Pakistan and China.' Atwater could not have scripted it better.

The government Senate committee submission that sparked the bitter row over whether there was really such a thing as a 'Stolen Generation' may not have been so carefully calculated. It may simply be that Aboriginal Affairs Minister John Herron was too politically thick to realise how much outrage would be caused by its cold, insensitive, pedantic and flawed argument. Then again, it could just as easily have been deliberately provocative. Whatever the intent, the result is another political wedge based on race. 'Howard denies Stolen Generation', scream the headlines. Aboriginal anger produces a backlash in the non-Aboriginal community. Radio shock jocks pour on the prejudice. And out of the division, the coalition picks up votes. That, at any rate, is the theory.

The Labor Party, of course, is caught in the middle of all this. Kim Beazley and his frontbenchers know exactly what is going on and how dangerous it is for them. They are well aware that, by attacking the cabinet response to the UN or taking the side of the Aborigines in the Stolen Generation row, they are playing into the government's hands. But they also know they have no choice. 'These things are too important to ignore,' says a senior ALP strategist. 'It's frustrating knowing that we're fighting on their ground. But we might as well not exist as a Labor Party if we walk away from this sort of stuff.'

Another prominent Labor figure says: 'They are trying to make us look as though we are preoccupied with the UN and Aboriginal affairs and not engaged with basic issues. They also want a distraction from issues like the GST, Telstra and nursing homes. Their strategy is to block out the GST debate in particular. The fact that this coincides with Paul Keating's book tour helps them. But because there's such strong community feeling about the GST, they're not getting nearly as much traction as they'd like.'

The government needs to be careful how it plays the wedge-politics game. Howard should not forget what happened when he initially went soft on Pauline Hanson and her divisive agenda. Opinion leaders from church groups and other community organisations were alienated and divisions opened up in the Liberal Party. There is a risk the same thing could happen again. The risks for the nation are greater than those for the government. Wedge politics, by definition, damage national unity. Australia's international image and standing *are* being adversely affected by what is happening. The chances of the Olympics being smooth and peaceful *are* under threat. It is a high price to pay. No responsible government would even contemplate it. It is worth remembering that, when he was dying from a brain tumour, Lee Atwater expressed regret at some of the things he had done in the name of wedge politics. There is a lesson there for others.

Roadblock to reconciliation

6 June 2000

A fearless prediction. John Howard will come to regret missing the opportunity to be the prime minister who said 'sorry' on behalf of the nation for the wrongs done to Indigenous Australians over the years – particularly to members of the 'Stolen Generations'. He will also regret his failure to take part in Sunday's extraordinary 'reconciliation walk' across Sydney Harbour Bridge. How do I know? From his record.

In 1995, for example, Howard publicly expressed regret for statements he had made a few years earlier on Asian immigration –

statements that first called into question his attitude to issues involving race. In 1998 he expressed regret over the hectoring, hostile tone of the speech he delivered at the first reconciliation convention the year before – the occasion on which Aborigines first turned their backs on him in dignified protest. Now the government line is that, if he could have his time over, the document that caused outrage by denying there was such a thing as a 'Stolen Generation' would not be released. Another regret.

There is a strong suspicion, in fact, that Howard may already have some regrets over the apology issue. Certainly many of his strongest supporters do. In the crush of Sunday's Harbour Bridge walk, an elderly man wearing an RSL badge accosted Labor leader Kim Beazley and said: 'I won't vote for you. I'm a Liberal and I'll vote for Howard. But why won't the silly bugger say "sorry"?'

More significantly, one of the Liberal MPs closest to the PM – a foundation member of the Howard-right-or-wrong brigade – admitted at the weekend: 'A lot of us wish we'd said "sorry"…But the matter has become so fraught now that to do so would not help.'

He is right. It was simply not possible politically for Howard to give the hecklers what they wanted when he addressed Saturday's Corroboree 2000 function at the Opera House. Howard has missed the 'sorry' bus. He stubbornly allowed his opposition to the concept of a national apology to become so entrenched that to change position at this late stage would provoke not only suspicion, but scorn and derision. As that MP said: 'If the PM agreed to an apology now, people would say it was just cynical vote-buying.'

Howard could, however, have taken part in the bridge walk. The Prime Minister's supporters argue, rightly, that he showed guts in entering the lion's den of the Opera House when it was clear that protesters would disrupt his speech. But courage deserted him when it came to joining several hundred thousand of his fellow Australians marching in support of reconciliation. Or perhaps it was embarrassment rather than cowardice that caused him to flee Sydney on a glorious autumn day and hole up in Canberra, a city he dislikes, in the midst of a snowstorm.

Whatever the reason, Howard's absence from this historic event leaves him a greatly diminished figure. Those coalition MPs who claim it has not damaged him politically are kidding themselves. Corroboree 2000 was not only a turning point for Australia. It was a turning point for Howard, too. The people and the debate have moved on, leaving Howard behind. He is now exposed as a prime minister who has little relevance – except in a negative sense – to one of the most important issues facing the nation. Moreover, it has become painfully clear not only that Howard cannot contribute to the solution, but also that he is – as a number of commentators have noted – a major part of the problem.

Those who want the reconciliation issue dealt with have to acknowledge now that it will not happen while Howard is PM. Given the evidence that Australians overwhelmingly want to put the matter behind them, this is a dangerous situation for Howard. Beazley would be able to make progress. So would Liberal heir apparent Peter Costello, whose credentials on such issues were displayed when he took the lead in opposing Pauline Hanson's One Nation (earning a rebuke from Howard). Howard is a roadblock to progress. He has to be got rid of, one way or another, before anything significant can happen.

The Aboriginal leadership may have been somewhat premature in moving the debate forward to the question of a treaty, but Howard need not have responded in the same knee-jerk way that he rejected the idea of an apology. 'We make treaties with other countries,' he said. 'A treaty will create division because…a nation can't make a treaty with itself.' The PM also agreed with John Laws that 'a treaty's something you have after a war'. His Little Sir Echo, Reconciliation Minister Philip Ruddock, said the proposal was unacceptable because treaties are documents signed between separate nations. If Howard and Ruddock consulted the dictionary, however, they would find that the word 'treaty' also applies to 'any agreement or compact'. There is no reason why a compact between groups within the Australian community should not be a unifying rather than divisive influence. Beazley takes the view that some kind of a treaty – or treaties – may be a good idea. He uses the plural because he is toying with the notion that, because Aboriginal society is not as structured as was Maori society when the Treaty of Waitangi was signed, a series of regional compacts could be the way to go.

In his Corroboree 2000 speech, Mick Dodson – by showing that Aboriginal people were still being taken from their parents when Howard was a senior member of the Liberal Party – demolished the PM's anti-apology argument that what happened to the 'Stolen Generations' is not the responsibility of the present generation of Australians. Incredibly, Ruddock, Aboriginal Affairs Minister John Herron and Health Minister Michael Wooldridge joined in giving Dodson a standing ovation. It showed how bizarre the government's position is. Days earlier, after meeting a group of Aboriginal leaders, Howard told journalists: 'My attitude on some of these issues is different from what it was a couple of years ago. It could well be different in a couple of years' time. I'm sure it will be.' The nation is not prepared to wait.

The right wing always strikes twice

6 August 2000

John Howard has been musing in private for a while now about life after politics. At one dinner party, for example, he confided an interest in playing some sort of mentoring role with young people when he retires. But now he has done his musing in public, there is no going back. If he wins the next election, Howard will step down from the prime ministership a year or 18 months into the new term. Peter Costello will move into the Lodge, and Australia will have a very different government.

'Peter will apologise to Indigenous Australians for what happened to the Stolen Generations and clear that issue,' says a Costello supporter. 'He will open a new debate on the republic and clear that issue too. He'll adopt a more progressive social agenda. And he'll get back the soft Liberals who have been walking away from Howard in big numbers.' Some Liberal strategists even believe there will be an immediate electoral advantage for the government; that simply having a timetable of sorts for a change from Howard to Costello will be enough to coax many of those disillusioned voters back into the fold.

This, of course, is not the conventional wisdom. Most pundits – and probably most politicians – believe Howard made an error in stamping a use-by date on himself and opening up the question of the leadership succession. His harsher critics even suggest it is evidence of hubris. 'He's getting carried away,' says one. 'He thinks he can't lose – that he's invincible. This just shows how cocky he is.'

But a strong argument can be mounted that what Howard has done is shrewd, perhaps even necessary. The truth is that he could not have avoided the retirement issue indefinitely. He would certainly not have got through an election campaign without it being raised. Better to handle it now than in the heat of a campaign. Come the election it will be old news. And it just *might* prevent those soft Liberal voters – the ones turned off by the way Howard has dealt with reconciliation, One Nation, the republic – from defecting. This is something Labor's deputy leader, Simon Crean, should perhaps have considered before rushing onto the air waves to announce that: 'A vote for John Howard at the next election is a vote for Peter Costello.' Many waverers might not consider that an altogether bad thing.

The thought of Costello taking over as prime minister is unlikely to drive away those voters who could be regarded as Howard's natural constituency. Costello is as strongly pro-family as Howard, as dedicatedly anti-gambling, and every bit as conservative on drugs. But Costello – once a New Right hard man but these days the hope of Liberal moderates – has the potential to attract a broader constituency. As a result of his own experience, he has a more modern view of social issues such as childcare and the problems of families where both parents go out to work.

Peter Reith seems almost to have dropped out of the Liberal leadership equation. He is there now only as a fallback if anything goes wrong with Costello. Apart from anything else, Reith shows up appallingly in both Liberal and ALP polling. Kim Beazley is making use of Labor's polling every time he refers to, 'Peter Reith, who's identified with dogs and balaclavas'. But there is much more to it than polls and focus groups. One of the Workplace Relations Minister's strongest admirers in the parliamentary Liberal Party says: 'Reith is a politician of substance and he may have more maturity at this point, but Costello has star quality – more personality and political firepower.' On top of this, Costello gets the kudos for presiding over an astonishingly smooth introduction of the GST. The tussle between the two Peters is over.

There is another side to what Howard did. In the process of indicating roughly when he intends to leave politics, he put paid to the hopes of some Liberals that he might be persuaded to step down *before* next year's election. There was some talk (not involving Costello, it should be stressed) of trying to put pressure on him, but that idea has now been abandoned as futile. Howard is not ready to go yet, and no one is going to try to blast him out.

Something else has become very clear since Howard made public his retirement plans. He may have decided to get out in a couple of years, but he has no intention of easing up during that period. 'He's going to put his foot down on the accelerator,' says a confidante. 'He wants to do a lot more in the time he has left.' Howard has his cabinet working on an ambitious agenda. The nation-building side of it has been getting the headlines, but his real interest is said to be reforming welfare so that better values are built into the system and community-based organisations take over functions now performed by bureaucrats.

Howard has, in effect, publicly put in place the equivalent of the secret Kirribilli House Agreement that was supposed to sort out the timetable for Paul Keating to succeed Bob Hawke as prime minister. (Hawke, of course, welshed, precipitating a bitter and damaging Labor leadership struggle.) The Howard agreement, because it is public, is a liberating influence. Howard is free to throw himself into one final burst of political creativity before vacating the prime ministership. Costello is free to broaden his image, show more of his personality and put his leadership wares more obviously on display without being accused of undermining Howard.

Timor credibility gap

26 September 2000

John Howard likes to pose as the liberator of East Timor and to portray those on the Labor side of politics as the appeasers of Indonesia. Hence the release, six years early, of Foreign Affairs Department documents intended to embarrass Labor over Gough Whitlam's role in Indonesia's military takeover of the former Portuguese colony. Hence also Howard's claim that Australia would have behaved very differently on East Timor last year if Labor had been in office. The truth, though, is that Howard – until very recently – was so slavishly pro-Indonesian that he outdid even Whitlam when it came to brown-nosing Jakarta.

In July 1985, just 10 years after the Indonesian invasion, Howard published an article in *The Australian* newspaper headed: 'It's Time We Made It Up With The Indonesians'. The then-opposition deputy leader wrote that 'those who vehemently oppose the Indonesian takeover of East Timor in 1975 have some obligation to consider what alternatives there were'. East Timor had not been ready for self-government, he argued, and Fretilin, the party demanding independence, was 'a left-wing, pro-communist movement'.

According to the Howard article: 'It openly modelled itself on the Frelimo in the former Portuguese colony of Mozambique...Not long after Lisbon handed over Mozambique to the Frelimo there were Soviet and Cuban military advisers in the country. Similar developments could have taken place in East Timor. They would have been harmful to the security of both Indonesia and Australia.'

Howard, as he often does, is rewriting history. But back then, seeing the situation through the prism of the Cold War, he was an unashamed defender of the Indonesian takeover, and bagged the Labor Party for not accepting it as unquestioningly as he did. The Hawke government, he complained, had allowed Australia's relationship with Indonesia to fall into disrepair. Australia was paying a high price, he wrote, for the 'obsessions of a few left-wing activists' critical of Jakarta

231

because of East Timor. The central message of Howard's article was: 'Australia needs a friendly Indonesia more than Indonesia needs a friendly Australia.' So much for Howard the tough guy, upholder of a strong and independent Australian policy. When it came to being obsequious to Jakarta and the Suharto regime, Howard was up there with the best, in the gold medal class.

It should not be forgotten that Howard, as treasurer, was a very senior member of the Fraser cabinet that granted *de jure* recognition of Jakarta's sovereignty over East Timor in 1979. When he became prime minister, Howard turned for advice on foreign policy to none other than Richard Woolcott, the man who – as ambassador to Indonesia at the time of the invasion – argued persuasively and successfully for Australia to put pragmatism ahead of principle on the East Timor issue. It was Woolcott who advised that his first overseas trip as prime minister should be to Jakarta, where the praise Howard lavished on Suharto would have made Paul Keating blush. Howard was relaxed and comfortable when, in May 1996, his Deputy Prime Minister, Tim Fischer, declared Suharto the greatest figure of the second half of the 20th century.

Howard adopted the same approach as Keating, Hawke, Fraser and Whitlam before him. It was Labor's Laurie Brereton who changed things, not Howard. Appointed shadow foreign minister after Labor's 1996 defeat, Brereton reflected on this bipartisan policy towards Indonesia and decided it stank. What is more, it had little support in the ALP – on the Right or the Left – except among those Labor figures who had their fingerprints on it as a result of their activities in government. Brereton changed Labor's policy, from acceptance of Indonesian sovereignty over East Timor to advocacy of an act of self-determination.

With bipartisanship shattered, the old crawl-to-Jakarta policy being followed by Howard was no longer sustainable. But even in his December 1998 letter to Suharto's successor, President B. J. Habibie – the letter that is Howard's claim to having played a pivotal role in securing independence for East Timor – Howard wrote: 'I want to emphasise that Australia's support for Indonesia's sovereignty is unchanged.' He advocated not the immediate referendum that Habibie settled on but 'a compromise political solution to be implemented while deferring a referendum on the final status...for many years'.

The self-serving comments by Foreign Minister Alexander Downer and his department head, Ashton Calvert, suggesting that the release of the East Timor documents signals a new commitment to transparency, can be taken with a very big grain of salt. The raid on the home of an opposition adviser by federal police ordered to investigate the leak of documents from the Defence Intelligence Organisation and other agencies concerning last year's events in East Timor, and the instructions to pursue journalists for 'secondary disclosure' of the government secrets in those documents, shows that the belief in transparency does not extend to anything that might embarrass the Howard administration.

The disclosures were as embarrassing as the documents of a quarter of a century ago. One example was a record of conversation of a February, 1999 meeting between Calvert and assistant US secretary of state Stanley Roth. The American expressed concern about likely violence during the transition to independence and suggested that, without a peacekeeping force, East Timor was likely to collapse. Calvert dismissed that as 'defeatist' and said Australia's preferred approach 'was designed to avoid a military option by the use of adept diplomacy'. The subsequent bloodbath – and the eventual commitment of troops – exposed both Calvert's naivete and the shortcomings of the diplomacy he presided over. The leaked DIO documents also showed that the government, while fully informed by intelligence sources about the involvement of the Indonesian military in the violence, continued to lie about it to avoid offending Jakarta. Déjà vu?

Howard's golden debt to Fraser

10 October 2000

John Howard enjoyed himself immensely at the Sydney Olympics, cheering on Australian athletes to a record medal tally. But there was no such reflected glory for Malcolm Fraser at the 1976 Montreal Olympic Games. Australia won not a single gold medal. It came as a shock to the nation, and to its prime minister.

'I think at that time a lot of people had the idea that Australians were naturally better than others in a number of sports – as skilled amateurs, really,' Fraser says now. 'But I spoke to some of our athletes to find out why we had done so badly. The answer was very simple. A whole lot of countries – not just the East Europeans and the Russians – backed their athletes with government funding and resources. Techniques and practices were developing so fast that, unless you had the best and most professional people and facilities, you could not compete internationally any longer.'

Fraser concluded that Australia faced a clear choice. 'It almost came down to not putting people into the Olympic Games if we were not prepared to give our athletes the best possible chance,' he says. But the second half of the 1970s, as the pendulum swung back from the big-spending Whitlam period, was a time of financial stringency. That was when cabinet's 'razor gang' – the Expenditure Review Committee – was invented. Cutting government expenditure was the order of the day. It hardly seemed the ideal time to start pouring public money into sport. But the Edmonton Commonwealth Games two years later, when Australia again performed badly, convinced Fraser the federal government had to act.

Fraser called Bob Ellicott to his office. Ellicott, now one of the nation's most eminent QCs, held the lowly post of home affairs minister, after resigning as attorney-general on a matter of principle. 'We've got to get this fixed, Bob,' Fraser said. He asked Ellicott to add responsibility for sport to his portfolio and take on the job of rebuilding Australia's international sporting reputation. Without that decision, Howard's limelight-hogging in the self-appointed role of 'national cheerleader' during the Sydney 2000 Games would not have been possible. Ellicott, on Fraser's instructions, began putting together the machine that 22 years later saw Australia win 58 medals, 16 of them gold.

It was not done without opposition. 'I remember us wrestling with the question of whether it was a sensible thing for a federal government to move into sports funding in a big way,' says a member of the Fraser cabinet. 'It was quite a contentious argument in those days.'

Treasury had strong reservations, and its case was taken to cabinet by the then-treasurer – guess who? – John Howard. Fraser says now: 'It's too easy, when you're trying to cut expenditure, just to say, "Well, that doesn't give us room to do any damn thing." It's a question of the priority you give something.'

Ellicott recalls, however, that despite the priority Fraser gave this matter, 'I knew I couldn't assume there'd be a lot of money to spend. At first I couldn't see how I'd achieve what Malcolm wanted.'

Inspiration struck when Ellicott visited China in early 1978. He was taken to see an institute, set up as part of a college, where students from all over China studied to be physical education teachers. They received sports training plus a diploma of education. That became Ellicott's model – bringing athletes to a central place where they could develop their sporting talents while pursuing an education, or even working. He began to see how he could set up a national Institute of Sport in Canberra on the cheap – or, as he describes it, as 'a sort of cut-and-paste job'. As well as holding the home affairs portfolio, Ellicott was Minister for the Capital Territory. 'I don't think any of this could have happened if I hadn't held both portfolios,' he says.

As Minister for the Capital Territory, he controlled the allocation of land in Canberra. A stadium had recently been built there for the Pan-Pacific Games. Ellicott earmarked land next to it and ordered work to start on an administrative centre and sports hall for his institute. Curtains would partition the hall into separate areas for weightlifting, gymnastics and basketball. Across the road was Canberra's College of Advanced Education, with student residences that were half empty – ideal for young athletes.

The original budget was about $2m, but that blew out to $5.8m, which included construction of tennis and netball courts. Ellicott knew the institute would need a swimming pool, but no money was included in the budget for that. He overcame the problem by again donning his Minister for the Capital Territory hat and issuing instructions for a pool in the Canberra suburb of Deakin to be upgraded. It was given a roof, heating, an area for weights training – all paid for out of the ACT budget – and made available to the institute.

A government decision that Australia should boycott the 1980 Moscow Olympics after the Soviet Union invasion of Afghanistan proved another impediment to Ellicott's task. 'Cash that quickly,' he advised when presenting a big federal government cheque to the Australian Olympic Federation just before the boycott decision was announced. An Australian team eventually went to Moscow, but the issue divided the nation and the Olympic movement. 'It was not a helpful background to setting up an institute of sport,' reflects Ellicott.

Nevertheless, the Australian Institute of Sport was officially opened by Fraser on Australia Day, 1981, and has underpinned much of our sporting success since then – culminating with the Sydney Games where 74 percent of Australian medal winners were current or former AIS scholarship holders. Howard acknowledged Ellicott's role when they ran into each other at one of the Sydney Games events. But he has yet to thank Fraser.

2001

Dear John...

2 May 2001

On Monday, February 19 – two days after Peter Beattie's Labor government had all but wiped out the coalition parties in the Queensland state election – the Liberal Party federal president, Shane Stone, called on the Prime Minister in his Parliament House office. A sombre Stone presented John Howard with a scathing five-page memo prepared after an extraordinary meeting in Brisbane the day before.

Written in remarkably blunt terms, the memo was political dynamite. It warned Howard of a strongly held view in the party that he and Treasurer Peter Costello had gone out of their way to antagonise the traditional Liberal support base. It said the government had been 'too tricky' on issues such as the GST on caravan park fees, beer and fuel. It spoke of a belief among Liberal MPs that the government was dysfunctional and out of touch, and that it had to be 'dragged screaming' to fix its mistakes. In the community, the memo said, the government was seen as mean.

Such an assessment from a man he himself had hand-picked to head the Liberal Party must have come as a rude shock to Howard. Certainly the way the government has reacted since shows Stone's hand-grenade had a powerful impact. Now that it has leaked, it will also cause Howard and his senior ministerial colleagues acute political embarrassment. Labor will relish the opportunity it provides. The hard-hitting criticism contained in a document that was intended for Howard's eyes only is far more devastating than John Della Bosca's comments about Kim Beazley to *The Bulletin*'s Maxine McKew over a long lunch.

Stone, former chief minister of the Northern Territory, had flown into Brisbane unannounced on the day of the election and watched as the counting of votes showed the Liberal Party receiving its worst drubbing in Queensland. The Liberals had claimed that the defeat of Richard Court's government in Western Australia a week earlier was due almost entirely to state factors, but that clearly would not wash this time. Stone issued instructions that all the Liberal Party's federal MPs from Queensland be summoned to a meeting at party HQ in Brisbane at 11 the next morning. All but one – Kathy Sullivan, who had a major function in her seat of Moncrieff – turned up. Those who took part in the no-holds-barred discussion included two newly appointed ministers, Ian Macfarlane (Small Business) and Mal Brough (Employment Services).

Stone's memo to Howard reflected what was said at the meeting. Clearly realising the seriousness of what he was committing to paper, he wrote: 'Sorry if some of this is close to the bone, but I would be failing as federal president, your friend, colleague and supporter if I did not report accurately what our colleagues in Queensland feel at present.' Making clear the discontent was far from being a Queensland phenomenon, he added pointedly: 'Their views mirror much of what I have had relayed to me around Australia in general terms in these past few months...The upside is that we have an opportunity to come to grips with these issues NOW, and not in the aftermath of federal electoral defeat.'

Parts of Stone's memo read like a market research report on a political focus group. But never before has there been a focus group like this. And one of the things that comes across most clearly is strong discontent – outright anger, in fact – over the behaviour of Costello, Howard's heir apparent. Another particular target of anger is Deputy

Prime Minister and National Party leader, Transport Minister John Anderson. Stone wrote: 'I'll start with the one-liners.

"Our leadership is not listening." (*This was a continuous reference to Anderson and Costello. However, for you, PM, there is guilt by association. After all, you're in charge.*)

"The government won't even listen to our own people so what hope the public?" (*Again a particular focus on Costello.*)

"We are seen as a 'mean government'." (*This was a recurring comment and said with real venom. Fits with our polling of people feeling they are worse off.*)

"The 'dead hand of Treasury' is everywhere." (*Guess who?*)

"Bureaucrats are in charge. *Yes Minister* is alive and well." (*Costello and Anderson seen as captive to their departments.*)

"Government will 'rissole' you at every opportunity." ("*We the government*", *you PM, Costello et al.*)

"Government is out of touch." (*Costello seen as the main offender.*)

"Party meetings are a waste of time." (*There is a belief that you and Costello fob people off.*) We keep getting the pat answer.

"All we have achieved is to raise the anxiety level of ordinary Australians." (*A very clear view in the room that we, you PM and Costello in particular, have gone out of our way to antagonise our traditional support base.*)

'Perhaps one of the most telling and recurring comments centred on the view that we had gone out of our way to "get" the very people who put us there. The self-funded retirees, the small-business sector, self-employed, professionals, farmers – all middle Australia.'

According to the Stone memo, one of the 'hits' on the Liberal Party's traditional base was the superannuation surcharge. It had been a major issue in some Queensland polling booths – such as Sanctuary Cove and Hope Island – where the ALP had outpolled the coalition for the first time ever. 'They may be well-heeled silvertails, but they're not voting for us any more,' the Liberal president complained. Also: 'Forms, forms and more forms. We have buried our supporters under a sea of documentation. Three days before the Queensland state election, Centrelink sent out multiple 35-page forms to 500 000 self-funded retirees Australia-wide that scared them witless. Was this sabotage or plain stupidity?' The memo pinpointed entity taxation – taxing trusts as companies – as another issue alienating traditional Liberals. 'Telling the Treasurer to fix it will result in the same "go slow" approach that his colleagues now believe he has adopted for the Business Activity Statement,' Stone wrote. 'SHRED THE PROPOSALS NOW.' Stone got quick action on that. The proposals were dropped by the government within weeks.

Asserting that the BAS undermined everything done by the government on tax reform, the memo said: 'This is the greatest tragedy. You personally, PM, broke your back to deliver a fairer taxation system for Australia and yet you have been undermined (deliberately or otherwise by the "dead hand of Treasury"). All our gains and goodwill have been squandered in a way that is unforgivable.' The memo was highly critical of Costello's initial public equivocation after Howard told the party room the BAS would be simplified. 'I won't repeat in this memo what some of his colleagues have to say about him on this issue,' Stone wrote. 'There was a sense of despair that even when we fix BAS, Pauline will get the credit. There is a clear view that we are reactive rather than proactive and have to be "dragged screaming" to fix things and are just so far behind public sentiment on a range of issues.'

According to the memo, 'We have been just "too tricky" on some issues. For example, GST on caravan park fees, beer and fuel…Process of the party room was described as a farce…It is alleged there is generally a lack of scrutiny of government legislation…There is no meaningful dialogue between ministers and the rest…Ministers are largely run by their minders and departments.' Howard himself was chastised over resistance in his office to offering a special medal to all those who served in the armed forces as national servicemen. 'Get on top of this one, PM, because you're wearing it,' Stone warned. The National Service Medal, of course, was announced on the day after Anzac Day. The memo also attacked National Party ministers for not informing Liberal MPs of decisions concerning their electorates. 'We have been comprehensively "done over" by our own Coalition colleagues,' the memo said. An example was Anderson announcing all 'black spot' road funding and refusing to allow Liberal parliamentarians to 'hook into' such announcements.

A key point to come out of the meeting with the Queensland MPs, the memo said, was a need to audit government commitments as well as the performance of ministers and parliamentary secretaries against benchmarks. There was a proposal that the federal director of the Liberal Party, Lynton Crosby, take part in meetings of the parliamentary wing in future. And the document contained a warning that 'communications into the electorate including to our own membership at large have broken down and need to be fixed'. But Stone pointed out that communication was not only a matter for ministers. 'Those best able to communicate with the electorate are, in fact, the elected members themselves who have all the resources at their fingertips. I'm sure some MPs think manual labour is a Spanish tennis player – that was certainly the case among state members.' It was a strange jibe for a party president to make about his own MPs.

Summing up, he told Howard: 'The recurring theme was that government is dysfunctional, out of touch and hurting our own... There is an overwhelming view that when you and Costello say "It will be sorted out" there is no follow through. Things drift.' But, Stone added, while 'at first blush this note may appear to reflect an ugly mood', by and large Liberal MPs still believed in the Prime Minister and did not think it was too late to save the situation. The backflips and policy shifts that seem to have enabled the government to start clawing back some lost support prove that Howard read the memo and got the message. Getting Stoned may not have been a pleasant experience for the Prime Minister, but it clearly did him some good.

Howard's vote people

5 September 2001

As federal parliament debated the case of the MV *Tampa*, and the broader issue of how to discourage boatloads of asylum-seekers coming to this country via Indonesia, the gutsiest speech was made by independent MP Peter Andren. It dealt with the Border Protection Bill, which even Prime Minister John Howard conceded was an 'unusual' piece of legislation. Andren holds the NSW rural seat of Calare – an electorate where bleeding hearts on the issue of would-be refugees from Afghanistan and the Middle East are almost certainly in short supply.

'A few moments ago I spoke to a close relative and tried briefly to explain to her what this legislation was all about,' Andren told the House. 'She told me that she supports the Prime Minister right up to the hilt. Perhaps my electorate supports this legislation right up to the hilt. But I do not.' Howard, Andren said, risked fanning racial tensions within the community by taking such action just weeks before calling an election. 'If that is the way to win government in this country, then whoever exploits that way holds a poisoned chalice,' he said. 'And the victory would be political but certainly not moral.'

The legislation had been thrown together in an afternoon, and the government wanted it rushed through both Houses that evening. In a remarkable display of blind (some would say irresponsible) obedience to the executive, coalition MPs gave it the thumbs up without seeing either the bill itself or an explanatory memorandum. Howard expected the opposition to consider in less than half an hour what was clearly an important and controversial measure. Andren pleaded in vain for parliament to be given time to properly scrutinise the bill 'so we are not part of a pre-election knee-jerk reaction in response to polls and talkback radio'. Governor-General Peter Hollingworth was put on standby to give it late-night assent as soon as it passed. As it turned out, he was able to go to bed when Labor and the Australian Democrats voted to defeat the bill in the Senate. But that, of course, suited Howard just fine. He had, in his judgment, positioned Labor on the wrong side of public opinion.

Kim Beazley shared that judgment – but he, like Andren, showed courage. Howard had called Beazley to his office at 6 pm, handed him the bill, and asked if the opposition would give the government leave to introduce it at 6.30. Beazley said he would consult his leadership group about that issue of process. But on the bill itself, after quickly reading through it, he said: 'I'm not going to be able to agree to this, John.' At a meeting of senior colleagues a few minutes later, Beazley did not seek their opinion, but simply told them what he had decided. The bill was too sweeping, impossible to support on principle. Some of those present – including Beazley – acknowledged that this stand could cost Labor the election. But no one demurred. It was the kind of leadership his critics had deemed him incapable of displaying.

During the heated parliamentary debate that followed, Beazley said the bill would make it legal for a sinking boatload of unwanted asylum-seekers to be towed out to sea regardless of the risk to their lives. While acknowledging that no Australian minister would be likely to give approval for this, the Labor leader said legislation that allowed it was unacceptable. Agriculture Minister Warren Truss called out scornfully: 'There are other laws to fix that.' The interjection exposed both Truss's ignorance and the dangers inherent in whacking legislation through parliament so quickly that even ministers do not understand its contents. Truss was clearly unaware that the bill gave bureaucrats, police and defence force personnel involved in removing a ship from Australian waters total immunity from civil or criminal proceedings and that one clause said: 'This Act has effect in spite of any other law.' Informed by Beazley and deputy opposition leader Simon Crean that the bill would override any other law, Truss was reduced to the lame response that it would not override moral law.

Beazley's stand was the only one the leader of a party with Labor's traditions and philosophy could take. Not that all sections of the ALP accept this. Some party branches were furious with him. 'You don't know what things are like out here,' was the message they sent to his office. But Beazley knows all too well. No one realises more acutely than Beazley himself that his chances of becoming prime minister have taken a dive since the *Tampa* steamed into Australian waters off Christmas Island. When Captain Arne Rinnan answered that distress call and picked up 460 asylum-seekers from a sinking Indonesian fishing vessel, he would not have realised it was the Howard government he was rescuing – but that looks like being the result.

There were, of course, legitimate reasons for Howard's tough line in refusing the *Tampa* permission to enter Australian waters – and then dispatching SAS troops to board her when that instruction was disobeyed. Beazley acknowledged as much when he supported both actions. The international crisis that resulted has certainly focused attention on the issue of people-smuggling and put pressure on Indonesia and other countries to help solve it. But there is no doubt Howard has also exploited, cleverly and ruthlessly, a domestic political opportunity. He now has a popular issue he can keep alive until election day. Those extra navy ships the government has decided to deploy between Indonesia and Australia guarantee it.

Howard is using the asylum-seekers to pitch to the one million people who voted One Nation at the last election. He wants their preferences – or, better still, their primary votes. He may also succeed in taking some votes directly from Labor. Coalition strategists believe the issue will be most potent in rural and regional Queensland and NSW and in some outer-suburban electorates – precisely the areas where Labor, until now, had been confident of winning the election. If the strategy works it may produce, as Andren claims, only a political victory, not a moral one. Howard will settle for that.

A sly-dog race card

7 November 2001

I was speaking to a senior Liberal politician the other day about why – according to most opinion polls – the coalition looked to be heading for victory in the election. He was in no doubt about the reason. 'There's a lot of racism out there,' he said candidly. This was a man who had spent the previous four weeks door-knocking in the Liberal cause. He was happy to have the votes. But he added: 'There'll need to be a healing process when this is all over.'

The key feature of this election campaign has been a clever use of what professionals call 'dog-whistle politics'. A dog whistle is pitched so high that dogs hear it but humans do not. Dog-whistle politics involves pitching a message to a particular group of voters that other voters do not hear. John Howard wanted One Nation voters back.

He also saw a chance to attract some traditional 'blue-collar' Labor voters with similar concerns. The *Tampa* episode provided him with the dog whistle he needed.

Intrigued by the dynamics of the election, I went back to a column I wrote in *The Bulletin* in August, 1988, when John Howard was serving his first stint as opposition leader. Howard had just experimented with this kind of issue by referring on radio to a need to slow the pace of Asian immigration. Earlier that year he had told a Young Liberal conference: 'Our national interest will be served by a migration program which preserves and promotes the unity and cohesion of Australian society.' Howard's slogan – pre-Hanson and all his own work, not that of an advertising agency – was 'One Australia'.

That episode ended in tears for Howard, largely because Liberal moderates (there were a lot more of them in those days) rebelled. Party division became the dominant issue. The leading moderate then – how things have changed – was Philip Ruddock, who phoned Howard at home to abuse him over the Asian immigration comments. But before it all went pear-shaped, the reaction in the electorate was interesting. A Saulwick opinion poll taken at the height of the debate showed support for the coalition increasing, and no one could offer an explanation other than that Howard's hard line had struck a responsive chord. Howard's supporters were particularly buoyed by feedback from Liberal campaigners fighting a by-election in a state seat on Queensland's Gold Coast. The immigration comments, they said, had given the party a big boost.

I wrote at the time: 'This was not only because of the racist sentiment which has been evident in the Gold Coast area as a result of controversy over Japanese property purchases. It was also because Howard was perceived as showing – in the words of one Liberal – "that he had balls". The word from the electorate was that support for what Howard had said crossed party lines. That is exactly what the opposition leader wanted to hear because part of his motivation is to try to attract traditional Labor votes.'

Howard is a much more experienced, much smarter, much more subtle politician now than he was back then. He has learned from his mistakes – including the mistake of actually mentioning race. But he also learned in 1988 that his electoral instincts were sound. When the

Tampa sailed into view with its load of asylum-seekers rescued from a sinking Indonesian ferry the Prime Minister had a way of tapping into the sentiments he had tried to exploit 13 years ago. In a campaign where he planned to portray his opponent as weak and indecisive, he also had an already market-tested means of demonstrating that he was not deficient in the testicular department. The year 1988 was a useful exercise for Howard, if only as a kind of trial run.

Howard's handling of the *Tampa* and his subsequent refusal to allow asylum-seekers on intercepted boats to land in Australia succeeded in moving One Nation supporters en masse back to the coalition. 'That's where they're getting their big swings,' says a Labor machine man. (Pauline Hanson modestly reported voters asking her if she was now an adviser to the Prime Minister.) But Liberals hope it will do more, which is why they have returned to the immigration issue with a vengeance in the final week of the campaign. Electorates are being saturated with pamphlets featuring a presidential photograph of Howard and the line from his policy speech that got the biggest round of applause: 'We will decide who comes to this country and the circumstances in which they come.' A Labor strategist says: 'They'll go hard on that because it's all they've got.' But he does not deny the potency of the message.

As one of the Liberal Party's canniest operators put it at the weekend: 'Health and education may show up in the polls as being the most important issues, but they never change anyone's vote. This one [asylum-seekers] does. It's a major vote-switching issue... basically soft Labor voters in marginal seats. The big unknown factor in this election is how many votes it will change.' Why is its impact still unknown at this late stage? Because, says another Liberal source, anxiety or resentment about issues of race are not the sort of thing people admit to pollsters. The way the polls always badly under-estimated One Nation support is evidence that people do conceal their true opinions on such matters when pollsters phone or knock at the door.

Howard's dog whistle also helps to explain why Labor is doing particularly badly in the west of Sydney, where the party should have made up ground in this election. A Labor back-room boffin who has been involved in elections for 20 years says: 'Those western

Sydney seats are just very difficult for us because the reality of contemporary Australia is there for them to see.' The phrase 'the reality of contemporary Australia' is his euphemism for problems involving race. A Labor MP agrees, saying: 'There are very stark cultural differences within groups in western Sydney. They're rubbing up against it every day. That's why this is biting hard in those seats.'

Howard, clumsy 13 years ago, has been sure-footed this time. There will be consequences, though. Once something like this is opened up in a multicultural society it is not easy to close off again. Which brings us back to that point about a post-election healing process. One veteran observer of politics says: 'If the coalition wins, I guess they'll use Howard's retirement and Peter Costello's accession to the prime ministership to start the healing.'

Three-card trick

14 November 2001

When John Howard romped home in the 1996 election, there were many who said he had only got there because he was up against the supremely unpopular Paul Keating. His 1998 victory was not a clear-cut triumph either because Labor finished with more votes. This time there are those who put Howard's win down to luck – the fortuitous arrival of the *Tampa* and the events of September 11 that produced the war against terrorism.

The truth, though, is that attaining a third term is Howard's vindication – proof of his brilliance as a politician and his understanding of the electorate. Luck was certainly involved in the outcome of the 2001 election, but Howard's great achievement was in getting the coalition into a position to capitalise on it.

The feat is astonishing when you look back on the first four months of this year. The coalition rout in Western Australia. Labor's massive win under Peter Beattie in Queensland. The huge swing to

Labor in that remarkable Ryan by-election. The 'mean and tricky' critique of the government penned by Liberal Party federal president Shane Stone. The way Howard regrouped and recovered from all this – dramatically reversing policy on petrol excise, acting on small business gripes about the Business Activity Statement, reconnecting with elderly voters through hand-outs in the May budget, ceaselessly stumping the country like a man possessed – showed formidable political skills and even more formidable determination. It put him back within striking distance of the ALP. From that point on I had little doubt he would win.

Howard is a cannier, quicker-on-his-feet, more ruthless politician than Kim Beazley could ever be. He was always going to make more effective use of any opportunity that came along than Beazley. His exploitation of the *Tampa* and its load of asylum-seekers was simply dazzling politics. But if the Norwegian freighter had never gone to the aid of a sinking Indonesian ferry and tried to take the rescued passengers to Christmas Island, Howard would have found another way of wrong-footing the Labor Party. 'He was always going to throw in a dead cat,' a close confidant of the Prime Minister says. With or without the *Tampa*, border protection was going to be Howard's ticket to an election win. The government had already started campaigning on it. Party polling and his own instincts told Howard it was a potential vote-shifter. One way or another, an incident would have been created.

Howard and Liberal federal director Lynton Crosby now try to pretend the border protection issue was not central to the election win, but the coalition's advertising in the final week of the campaign gives the lie to that. It was all asylum-seekers – Howard on radio and television and in newspapers and leaflets sayings '*We* decide who comes to this country and the circumstances in which they come.' The coalition clearly pressed the boat-people button at the end of the campaign – when Labor had started to get traction on the issue of the GST – because they knew how effective it had been at the beginning.

ALP national secretary Geoff Walsh was not simply applying 'spin' to make Beazley's campaign look good when he revealed that party polling five weeks out showed Labor facing a landslide loss because of asylum-seekers. The polling had Labor a whopping 16–17 points behind the coalition in the working-class stronghold of Newcastle in NSW and facing a potential overall loss of 35 to 40 seats. Halfway through the first week of the campaign, Labor 'Godfather' Robert Ray sat in Walsh's office at ALP campaign headquarters in Melbourne, shook his head over the figures, and remarked that someone would have to go out and raise the possibility of Howard being returned with a 70-seat majority. Walsh concealed the full magnitude of the situation from Beazley and his staff. 'But the Libs were onto it,' says a Labor official. 'They were pumping material into areas that had never seen a Liberal pamphlet in their lives.'

Labor clawed back to the point where, while it lost the election, there was no 1975-style wipe-out. In fact, the change in numbers in the new parliament is hardly significant. But the massive loss of votes and seats that initially threatened may well have eventuated had the party not adopted a 'me-too' approach on asylum-seekers. While there is understandable disquiet in the ALP about what many see as an abandonment of principle, this is something that cannot be ignored in the election post-mortem process which is already exposing bitter divisions. Many Labor people disillusioned over Labor's failure to fight Howard on boat people *did* peel off and vote for the Greens in this election. 'But for every vote we lost on the Left, there were five, maybe 10, threatening to peel off on the Right,' says one MP.

Also influencing the internal argument over whether Labor was right or wrong to back Howard's stand on asylum-seekers is the fact that both the Left and Right of the party felt the full force of the issue – particularly in NSW. 'I'd be surprised if the NSW Left felt this was something they were going to really fight on when they were so singed by it themselves,' an ALP worker from that state told me the day after the election. One of the leading lights of the NSW Left, Anthony Albanese, contented himself with setting out the dilemma facing the party. 'Labor has got to work out how to repair the damage to both its bases: its working-class base and its progressive social base,' he said. While asylum-seekers remains a live issue, that will not be easy. And you can bet your boots a resurgent Howard will keep it alive.

Former senator Stephen Loosely quotes a senior Labor figure as saying that, with the hard line on boat people, Howard 'hit the country's political G-spot'. It takes a very clever politician to do that.

2002

Hypocritical oath

13 March 2002

Ah, hypocrisy, thy name is politics. In federal parliament at the moment the coalition government is arguing that it would be highly improper for ministerial advisers to be called before a Senate committee to give evidence on the 'children-overboard' affair. Cabinet has decided no one employed under the *Members of Parliament Staff Act* should appear. But in Victoria, the Liberal opposition is demanding that five ministerial advisers be instructed to appear before a state parliamentary inquiry aimed at embarrassing the Bracks Labor government. And politicians wonder why voters hold them in contempt.

At least, on this occasion, the Labor Party looks like exercising a bit of consistency. Victorian Attorney-General Rob Hulls says the state ministerial advisers have been instructed not to give evidence to the Upper House select committee because no precedent exists for them to be called. Despite the short-term political advantage it will be forgoing, federal Labor is expected to adopt the same line. No attempt will be made to force ministerial staffers involved in the 'children-overboard' scandal, or able to shed light on the question of who knew what and when, to give evidence before the quaintly named Senate Select Committee on a Certain Maritime Incident.

This was all but spelt out during the recent Senate estimates committee hearings at which senior bureaucrats and military top brass were questioned on how a false claim that asylum-seekers threw children into the sea came to be presented to voters as fact throughout last year's election campaign. At one point, government Senate leader Robert Hill commented: 'It would be highly unusual for staff of any minister to be called before a Senate inquiry.' His Labor counterpart, John Faulkner, responded: 'It would, you are right. That is not the normal way these inquiries work. I accept that. I try to be consistent about these sorts of things.'

This will come as something of a disappointment to those media and academic observers who have been expecting the 'A Certain Maritime Incident' inquiry to turn into a precedent-setting clash between parliament and the executive. It has been billed as a test of strength on the issue of 'executive privilege', sometimes referred to as 'public interest immunity' – the right of a government to withhold information demanded by parliament or a parliamentary committee. In this case, the specific question is whether ministers, ex-ministers and ministerial staff can be compelled to give evidence. There is fairly general agreement among legal authorities that members of one House of parliament are probably immune from the authority of the other. That means a minister sitting in the House of Representatives is protected from being summonsed before a Senate committee. Beyond that, however, the situation gets a bit murky.

One of Australia's foremost legal experts in this area, Geoffrey Lindell of Melbourne University, said in a 1994 paper titled *Parliamentary Inquiries and Government Witnesses*: 'The theoretical position...would seem to suggest that the power to send for persons, papers and records can be exercised in relation to any person, whether the person is a government official or a private citizen.' Lindell argued that for a minister to instruct a government witness not to give evidence to a parliamentary committee would breach the *Parliamentary Privileges Act*. But he also observed that 'there has been what virtually amounts to a history of parliamentary acquiescence in cases where the executive branch has been determined to maintain its claim of privilege'.

The 'children-overboard' Senate inquiry will not change that – and for good reasons. Consistency is one. Past Labor administrations have made use of the claim of executive privilege. A just-published book, *Parliament – The Vision In Hindsight* edited by Lindell and Robert Bennett of the Parliamentary Library, recalls a 'celebrated incident [that] occurred in 1975 when the Senate summonsed 11 senior public servants to the Bar of the Senate to answer questions at the height of the overseas loans dispute. Each declined on ministerial instruction to give a reply other than of a formal nature.' Having accused the Senate of abuse of power then, Labor would look utterly unprincipled if it tried to frogmarch ministerial advisers before a Senate committee now.

More fundamentally, though, Faulkner understands that any precedent the Senate establishes now will come back to haunt future Labor governments, and he will be driving this point home to his colleagues. (Victorian opposition leader Denis Napthine seems not to have thought things through with similar clarity.) Labor would be foolish to take a purely opportunistic or oppositionist view of this inquiry. Faulkner has no doubt that the Senate has power to subpoena ministerial staffers to appear. But, he says: 'We have to adopt a position that's acceptable to us both in opposition and from the perspective of an alternative government.' In other words, what Labor does unto the coalition now can be done unto them in the future, and they forget it at their peril.

So, while Labor would like to put the thumbscrews on people like Miles Jordana, the Prime Minister's Foreign Affairs adviser, and Ross Hampton, who was Peter Reith's media adviser, they are unlikely to face demands to appear. Faulkner and his colleagues will abide by what they regard as a convention giving a certain protection to ministerial staffers. There is a recognition that if ministerial advisers were liable to be summonsed and interrogated whenever a hostile Senate felt like making trouble – especially in circumstances where their political masters had immunity from such treatment – the workings of government would be seriously affected. Indications are that Labor may also stay its hand in the case of Reith, defence minister at the time of the 'children-overboard' incident but now retired from politics. Despite legal advice that *former* MPs enjoy no immunity, there is a great reluctance to force him to appear. He will certainly be invited to give evidence, but an attempt to subpoena him if he declines is unlikely.

It could be a different matter when it comes to one Mike Scrafton, who was a senior adviser on Reith's staff but now has a high-powered Defence Department job. Scrafton knew of serious doubts about the 'children-overboard' story when he spoke to the Prime Minister several days before the election. The question is – did he tell John Howard what he knew? Howard says no, but aroused suspicion by adding that Scrafton 'might have a slightly different recollection'. So Labor is arguing that Scrafton's current status as a serving bureaucrat makes him fair game for the committee. If there *is* to be any precedent-setting, this is where it will occur.

Four on the floor

10 April 2002

It's amazing what you come across when you have a clean-out. I sorted through a box of old papers last weekend and found a passionate letter written by Gough Whitlam to his wife Margaret nearly 58 years ago. On the evening of Saturday, July 22, 1944, to be precise. At the time, Whitlam was an RAAF navigator with Number 13 Squadron flying Venturas on dangerous bombing raids against Japanese installations and shipping. He mentioned that he was due to fly a combat mission the next morning but that was only in passing. References to his personal circumstances also were very brief. 'Darling…We continue to mix our drinks – malted milk, coffee (essence) and mostly cocoa.'

What Flying Officer Whitlam, at a remote base in northern Australia, wrote about with passion to his young wife thousands of kilometres away was a referendum campaign: Labor Prime Minister

John Curtin's attempt to amend the Constitution to give the federal government increased powers for postwar reconstruction. Whitlam was annoyed at a 'no' case pamphlet criticising the number of federal boards and bureaucratic controls established during the war.

'You know that the states have set up as many boards, etc, as the Commonwealth, and that most wartime Commonwealth bureaucrats came from the State services,' he told his bride of less than two years. 'I need hardly point out to you the unfairness of comparing Commonwealth administration in war with State administration in peace. You must conjecture what State administration would have been like in war and compare it with what Commonwealth has been. Similarly you may conjecture what Commonwealth administration may be like in the five postwar years if this Referendum is carried... The Commonwealth could hardly fail to do a better job than the States during this crucial period.' The letter concludes: 'You can hardly fail to see that the Commonwealth is better fitted to deal with such nation-wide problems. And so to bed. Love, G.'

I am only guessing but I suspect Margaret was probably persuaded to vote 'yes'. While there is a self-deprecating footnote – 'Authorized by E.G. Whitlam, above address' – the reformist zeal shines through. And, at that stage, Whitlam had not yet joined the Labor Party. What struck me as I read the letter – part of material I gathered when I was writing a biography of Whitlam in 1974 – was that no one has such enthusiasm for constitutional reform these days. Or any enthusiasm at all, it seems. Sure, some people get excited about the republic. But when it comes to changes that would improve the operation of the federation and make government more efficient and effective, there is an almost universal lack of interest.

Yet there are reforms worth trying for. One that springs to mind is a constitutional change to increase the term of federal parliament. Most politicians acknowledge that a three-year term works against good government, especially since prime ministers often go to the polls early. A government has a year after an election, 18 months at the most, to take tough decisions. After that it is back in election mode. This is a major reason why Peter Costello's May 14 budget will squeeze most areas of spending. It is the government's one chance to do things that are necessary but may be unpopular. By May next year, when Costello would hope to be prime minister, the coalition will have its eye on the 2004 election.

Four-year terms are now the norm at state level, and there is support, in principle, for a similar change federally. Howard said last year: 'Look, in the past I've supported four-year parliaments...You can afford to sort of invest in something that has a short-term difficulty to give you a long-term gain...From a governance point of view, there's probably a lot going for it.' The Australian Democrats advocate a fixed four-year electoral cycle. Spokesman on electoral matters Andrew Murray said a few months ago: 'The advantage of fixed four-year terms for a government is that they allow enough time for a policy agenda to be fully implemented. The advantage for opposition parties is that an election can't just be called because the government of the day feels it is in a winning position.' Howard, though, says: 'I think it should remain the prerogative of the prime minister of the day to choose the election date.' A reasonable compromise would be the Victorian model, where the Legislative Assembly has four-year terms and cannot be dissolved in the first three years unless there are special circumstances.

But politicians of all stripes are wary because they remember the last attempt. In 1988, Bob Hawke's government put four referendum questions to the people, one of which would have increased the House of Representatives' term to four years. The sticking point for then-opposition leader Howard was that it would also have shortened the term of senators. With the coalition opposed, the referendum went down to humiliating defeat. It will take someone with Whitlamesque zeal to arouse interest in another referendum. Ron Walker, who will move for four-year terms at this week's Liberal federal council, may have that zeal. Meanwhile, I will forward this yellowing, three-page letter to its rightful owners to be added, perhaps, to the collection of personal papers and photographs now kept at the University of Western Sydney's Whitlam Institute.

Lap of honour

17 April 2002

In the keynote address to his party's federal council, John Howard said it was 'important as Liberals to reflect upon the journey of the last six years'. If the speech had a theme, that was it. Look what we've done. Aren't we great? We're entitled to pat ourselves on the back. It was a retro-message, despite some advance spin-doctoring that promised details of a third-term agenda. 'I'd hoped there would be something new,' one Liberal MP said later. He was disappointed. Despite Howard's assertion two days earlier that 'nobody should assume I'm going to depart the scene next year', it was the speech of a leader who has run his race and is preparing to do exactly that.

There was just a small hint that Howard might be eyeing the possibility of one more triumph before he gallops off into the sunset. That was the warning that, if Labor and the Australian Democrats refuse to pass his unfair dismissal legislation through the Senate, he will whack it back to the Upper House a second time so that it provides grounds for a double dissolution. Think of it. One last election campaign. One last victory against a Labor Party not yet recovered from the 2001 defeat – possibly improving the coalition's numbers in the Senate while he is at it. Then the handover to Peter Costello. In theory, at least, it could all be done before the Prime Minister's 64th birthday in July next year, when he has promised to consider his future.

It is an unlikely scenario. As a Liberal source said: 'How could we get through another campaign with him being asked all the time when he was going to retire?' But the point is, whether the double-dissolution idea tempts him or not, Howard will pass the baton in the second half of next year at the latest. This year is for basking in a bit of glory. It is also for catching up on some junketeering. Trips to China and Eastern Europe are definite. Another visit to the US is being planned. Several other overseas excursions are under consideration. Outgoing Liberal Party treasurer Ron Walker commented during the conference that

Howard 'is revered worldwide'. Assuming the PM agrees with that modest claim, why would he not undertake an international lap of honour before stepping down? But step down he will.

Otherwise the Liberals would be in trouble. And not only because party unity could not be maintained if Howard decided to 'do a Hawke' and dud his deputy. (Even if Costello was prepared to cop it sweet, others would not.) In his speech, the PM said: 'The lesson of the last six years is that you always push forward.' All the signs are that Howard has largely run out of things to push for. His third-term agenda is, basically, some leftovers from his first-term agenda. The most important thing he can do for his party now is to arrange an orderly succession, and he knows it.

But the unstated deal is that it is not made to appear that he is being pushed. That is why Howard reacted so tartly – 'There is no vacancy!' – when Walker, in a radio interview, discussed the leadership issue and the expected transition to Costello. Some of the PM's people also have been annoyed by the claim in a couple of newspaper columns that Shane Stone some weeks ago offered to stand down as Liberal Party president at the federal council meeting in favour of Costello's closest friend, Michael Kroger. The alleged offer was interpreted as demonstrating that the transition to a Costello leadership is already under way. In fact, according to the Howard camp, Stone made no such offer. They say that, when approached by NSW Liberal Party fundraiser Michael Yabsley, Stone simply gave the same answer he has given publicly: that when there is a change of leader, the new leader will be entitled to choose the president he wants.

Costello, though, is clearly readying himself for a takeover. That is the only explanation for his out-of-the-blue 'doorstop' media conference to announce that defence would be a priority in next month's budget. There was no news in what he said. He provided no budget insights. It was merely a manufactured opportunity for the Treasurer to broaden his image by asserting over and over, Howard-style, that he, too, stands for 'strong defences and strong border protection'. It was all about building up his appeal with the constituency that gave Howard victory last November (and countering the erroneous idea held in some quarters that he is part of the moderate wing of the Liberal Party). We can expect a lot more of this.

Meanwhile, in the Democrats – the other party where leadership has been an issue – things have settled down. The rank-and-file membership has spoken, and made it clear that sniping at Natasha Stott Despoja has to stop. The membership view was delivered by the deputy national president, Liz Oss-Emer, to a meeting of all the Democrat senators in Adelaide on Monday, April 8. Oss-Emer read email and other messages received by party officers, overwhelmingly expressing the view that instability should not be tolerated and demanding that the senators get behind Stott Despoja. According to Democrat sources, they reflected a surprising degree of anger over deputy leader Aden Ridgeway's recent comment that the change from Meg Lees to Stott Despoja a year ago had probably been a mistake. Ridgeway, say colleagues, is a much-chastened man. And Lees's conciliatory appearance on *Meet the Press* – 'All members of the party room have made it very clear that we are supporting the leader the members have elected' – was evidence of the changed atmosphere.

Vale John Gorton

22 May 2002

Hidden away at the back of Ian Hancock's biography of Australia's 19th prime minister, *John Gorton: He Did It His Way*, is an intriguing footnote. It relates to Ainsley Gotto, who was Gorton's principal private secretary. There was a lot of gossip and innuendo at the time about this young and attractive woman and her boss, but Hancock's footnote brings an entirely new slant to the matter. During Gorton's prime ministership, it says: 'Gotto formed a relationship with Race Matthews who held an equivalent position to her in Gough Whitlam's office. Neither employer seemed to be worried about the association, nor did they have reason to be.'

I mention this because it illustrates something that struck me when

I heard of Gorton's death. Australian politics is a very different world today from what it was when Gorton was in the Lodge and Whitlam led the opposition. Imagine what would happen now if two such key people from John Howard's office and Simon Crean's staff 'formed a relationship'. In these paranoid times, it is unthinkable. Such an affair would cause a sensation. Neither leader could or would tolerate it. But back then, adversarial politics was less adversarial. Dealings between the conservative and Labor sides were more civil and decent. Socialising across the party divide was not only acceptable but normal.

Gorton had good friends among Labor MPs. Clyde Cameron was an example. He played his politics hard, but that did not prevent him having an affection for Gorton outside office hours. In 1991, along with Gotto and former National Party leader Doug Anthony, Cameron helped to organise a surprise 80th birthday party for the former Liberal PM. While Gorton and Whitlam were, of necessity, fierce opponents politically, they conducted their battles in chivalrous fashion compared with the nasty, take-no-prisoners approach of today's politicians.

The most vicious treatment Gorton experienced was at the hands not of his Labor opponents, but of people within his own party, the worst of them by far William McMahon, accurately described by Robert Menzies as 'a contemptible squirt'. McMahon waged an unrelenting campaign against Gorton to further his own ambitions. McMahon rang journalists at all hours of the day and night leaking information extraordinarily damaging to the prime minister and the government. When Gorton was eventually toppled from the Liberal leadership and McMahon took over, a Whitlam victory in the 1972 election became a certainty. That the Liberal Party was prepared to cut Gorton down in favour of a lying buffoon like McMahon still seems, to me, unbelievable.

Gorton was the last Australian political leader to be free of the influence of spin doctors. McMahon needed all the PR help he could get to try to hide his incompetence. Whitlam had the redoubtable Graham Freudenberg, a master of spin as well as of speechwriting. But Gorton had no time for such nonsense. What you saw was what you got with Gorton. His refusal to rein in his larrikin behaviour got him into all sorts of political strife, but it certainly made him much more interesting than today's crop of tailored, tooth-capped, focus-group-focused white-bread politicians.

And what made Gorton really different from today's politicians was that he used to say what he thought. Most of the time, anyway. Media training had not been invented then, but if someone had tried to advise him to 'ignore the questions and just keep repeating the agreed line', he could not have done it. It would have been out of character. Perhaps Gorton's greatest shortcoming as a politician – though non-politicians would consider it a virtue – was that he lacked deviousness. As a prominent MP told me when I first got into the political reporting business: 'In politics, often the best way to get to point A is to pretend you're aiming at point B.' But that was not Gorton's way. If he wanted to do something, there was no careful plotting of strategy, very little preparing of the ground. He just went ahead and did it. 'You ain't seen nothing yet!' he would boast. Many on his own side of politics saw that more as a threat than a promise, but it meant politics was never dull.

Whitlam always believed that Gorton's lack of discipline was a result of his easy ride into the prime ministership. After Harold Holt drowned he was plucked from nowhere – well, from the Senate, but that was much the same thing – without, in Whitlam's view, having paid his dues. But because Gorton was not well known it took Whitlam well over a year to start to get his measure. By the 1969 election, though, Gorton had become a big target. Thinking of that contest is another reminder of how dramatically politics has changed. It was the last Australian election campaign that was not made-for-TV. Television was dominant by 1972 – the famous 'It's Time' election – but in 1969 public meetings, often with leaders speaking from the backs of trucks, were still the focus. Gorton and Whitlam could not hide as political leaders do in today's carefully stage-managed elections. They had to deal with dissatisfied voters and hostile crowds. Old fashioned, perhaps – but much more democratic than what passes for campaigning now.

There is an assumption that someone like Gorton could never get to the top in politics now, and that may be true. But it is a pity. I would be interested to see how today's jaundiced, disillusioned voters reacted to a politician who broke the identikit mould by daring to be himself, speaking his mind, paying no heed to image and spin, relying on instinct rather than market research, owning up to normal human flaws, and telling his minders defiantly: 'I will behave as I bloody-well please!' It might just appeal to them.

The hard call

10 July 2002

Shortly after Gareth Evans took up his appointment at the International Crisis Group in Brussels two and a half years ago, anonymous messages began arriving at the organisation. The burden of those messages was that people at ICG should be aware their new president had lied to the Australian parliament about a five-year relationship with a high-profile Australian woman. He must have known then that the cover was starting to come apart.

For better or for worse, it is all out in the open now. A great deal has been said and written about my role. Fair enough. The privacy versus public interest debate is an important one. I made a judgment which I and many others believe was right. But it is not a matter of black and white, as many of those who have whipped themselves into a lather seem to believe. Two articles in *The Sydney Morning Herald* make the point.

Alan Ramsey, a friend of Cheryl Kernot, bagged me royally for breaking the story of the affair in the wake of Kernot's dishonest book, *Speaking for Myself Again*. In his view, there was no justification for making such a personal matter public. A day earlier, another *SMH* writer, Keith Austin, had also given me a bagging, but what 'disgusted' him was that I had not done it a long time ago. 'Presumably, Oakes knew [Evans] had lied to parliament,' Austin wrote. 'Presumably, he also knew both Kernot and Evans were economical with the truth when they went to Kim Beazley with the plan for her high-profile defection.' Austin then criticised 'the complicit nature of the Canberra press bureaus' relationship with the politicos'.

As a matter of fact, at the time Evans told his lie, I did not know it was a lie. I believed him. I was unaware of an affair or any suggestion of it at the time of the defection. I was not convinced there was a relationship until the second half of 1999, and I did not have the email proof until two months ago. Perhaps Austin should take up the matters he raises with his stablemate. Ramsey sat in my office on the day of Kernot's book launch and told me he had known at the time her defection was announced that she and Evans were romantically involved.

It is important to get a few things straight. One is the claim there was a cross-promotion plan involving *The Bulletin* and the Nine network, under which there would be a teasing column encouraging people to watch the Nine news, which would in turn plug the magazine. There was no such calculation. I wrote a column which I hoped would lead to Kernot speaking for herself truthfully. Simple as that, really. With the benefit of hindsight, I concede it may not have been the most appropriate way to handle the matter.

Then there is the allegation I wanted revenge for a savage mauling in the book. Not true. Actually, I don't regard Kernot's criticisms of me as savage, though some were surprising. For example, she complains that when she made a hurriedly planned trip to the UK in 2000, I arranged for a Nine journalist to ask questions about her health because of Liberal-inspired suggestions she had suffered a nervous breakdown. 'Mr Oakes was the only Australian journalist to pursue this all the way to London,' she writes.

The real situation was Kernot had disappeared without explanation while parliament was sitting. That inevitably caused media speculation. *The Australian* had a 'Kernot Missing' headline on the front page above a story reporting that Liberals were spreading rumours about her health. The story Nine put to air showed her doing her job as shadow employment minister by visiting an East End community centre for jobless youth, pronouncing herself in robust health, and looking it. A Labor staffer, one of those helping to 'mind' Kernot in those days, phoned me to say thanks for the positive spin.

Then there is the gender argument: that this is happening only because a woman is involved. Is Evans not male? It is Evans who has had to admit lying to parliament. Some members of the sisterhood resent what they see as an implication that a woman's judgment would be affected by a sexual liaison. But the matter concerns the judgment of *both* parties. To quote David Epstein, Beazley's chief of staff at the time of the defection, 'the intensity of the relationship befuddled the political judgment of those involved and, in turn, made it virtually impossible for the ALP leadership to engage in rational dialogue with them'.

Epstein's article in *The Weekend Australian*, asserting that 'the relationship affected the political fortunes of the ALP in significant ways', demonstrates that the matter involves public interest questions, not just privacy considerations. Australian Democrats founder Don Chipp told the ABC: 'For heaven's sake, you have the parliament of Australia passing laws that affect every Australian. To have such a close relationship between the leader of the [balance of power] party and a leading member of the government I think is intolerable and had to be exposed.' There is the parliamentary lie. There is the question of whether Labor's leading lights would have vetoed the defection if they had known about the affair. (Even Ramsey confirms Kernot did not come clean when then-ALP national secretary Gary Gray asked if there was anything that could come back to embarrass her or Labor.) There is the impact the gradual break-up had on Kernot's behaviour and therefore on Labor's election prospects. And there is the book, containing no mention of the relationship but promoted on the cover as 'a woman dealing honestly with the slow unravelling of her political life'.

I weighed up these and other matters against the privacy issue. Some may argue I made the wrong decision but I do not believe they can claim that the Evans–Kernot relationship had no impact on, or relevance to, recent political events.

All smirk and no play

14 August 2002

The Labor Party is keeping a close eye on Peter Costello. One of the briefs given to its polling company, UMR Research, is to track perceptions of the federal Treasurer. UMR asks questions about him in its marginal seat surveys for the ALP, and in focus groups. Details of some of the findings – in a UMR report titled *A Brief Look at Peter Costello* – have now been leaked to coincide with his well-publicised visit to outback Queensland this week.

The report concedes Costello 'is respected for his competence, particularly [in] economics'. Apart from that, it is anything but flattering. (If the news was good for Costello, Labor would keep it tightly under wraps.) A tracking program conducted in marginal seats before last November's federal election found negative sentiment about Costello at 51 percent compared with positive sentiment at only 34 percent, a 17-point deficit. Of 14 other prominent coalition MPs included in the survey, according to UMR, only Bronwyn Bishop and Michael Wooldridge showed worse results.

Further marginal seat surveys were conducted in March. Costello's lack of popularity with voters, according to the report, was confirmed in focus group studies in June. 'Soft voters are particularly turned off by the Treasurer,' the report says. 'They essentially see him as: arrogant ("smug" often used to describe him, still many references to the smirk); out of touch; and running a policy agenda that favours the better-off in the community…He has particular problems with lower-income earners, those with a household income of under $30 000, and those voters who say they are under financial pressure.' UMR finds that Costello's most serious problem is with 'what could be described as the "middle Australia" segment – the thirty- and forty-somethings, who are most likely to have dependants and responsibilities.' But, it says, while 'the intense negative reactions' to Costello occur at the lower end of the household income scale, 'surprisingly, the higher end is not convinced by him either'.

Labor clearly wanted this material in the public arena as Costello embarked on his sweep through Longreach, Blackall and Roma accompanied by a 30-strong media contingent. The Treasurer's tour was attracting greater media interest than the Prime Minister's latest overseas trip at the same time, and for obvious reasons. When John Howard turned 63 last month, the countdown began to the big decision he has promised to address on his 64th birthday: the question of whether he will retire and hand over the reins to Costello. Between now and then, everything the Treasurer does will be viewed in this light. His coalition colleagues, the media, voters – and no doubt Howard himself – will be assessing Costello's performance, judging his ability to lead the coalition into the next election.

Three days of wooing voters in the bush, out of his normal big-end-of-town environment, and dealing at close quarters with people who face genuine hardship and have real grievances, provides an ideal opportunity to make such judgments. Labor's calculation, presumably, was that if Costello performed well, it would boost his standing and help him in the process of remaking himself – giving the public a look at his more personable side. Leaking the research could be viewed as either a reality check or a spoiling operation, depending on your point of view. A Costello supporter I spoke to chose to look on the bright side, saying: 'It shows they're worried if they're doing special research and then leaking it to try to damage him.'

A briefing on the June focus group studies says: 'The word that sums up the popular view of Costello is "shifty", a judgment that has moved on from the criticism of the "smirk". If anything, this one is more potent. He is considered untrustworthy and insincere. More than Howard, Costello is considered to favour the rich, to be too close to the wealthy.' Comments on the Treasurer included 'he's not a people person' and 'he doesn't say what he thinks'. According to the briefing: 'There is emotional intensity among swingers in their views of Costello – the Keating syndrome..."He always thinks he's right"..."I don't like him at all"..."He's just after Howard's job"... He's "scary", "horrible", "worse than Keating".'

All this may sound bad but much of it can be put down to the simple fact that, as treasurer, Costello has been in something of a straitjacket. Voters like the economic stability Australia enjoys and the benefits of the economic growth that has occurred on his watch. But economics is a dry argument, and the subjects a treasurer normally deals with tend to be eye-glazing. He has had few opportunities to project a more rounded personality. Although the outback safari was not designed for the purpose, it offered such a chance. Costello needs to create others. Keating used to say that, when the time came to counter the image problems that are part and parcel of being treasurer, he would 'throw the switch to vaudeville'. Costello can leave the song and dance to Alexander Downer but he does not require Labor research to know it is time to give the wider public a look at the likeable personality his friends are familiar with. He has already started expressing views on a range of subjects not directly related to Treasury: getting heavily involved in the debate on family policy, for example, and moving into the areas of education by advocating performance tests for teachers. And, unlike Keating, he has not given voters 17.5 percent interest rates, a recession, or the finger.

Costello is not the only would-be PM with image problems. I would love to have leaked to me the research UMR has done on Simon Crean. The Labor leader is using his campaign for reform of the ALP to try to remake himself. The remaking of Costello can almost certainly be achieved by rather less drastic means.

Following the leader

25 September 2002

It is easy to understand the attitude of those coalition MPs who propelled the Liberal leadership back into the headlines last week by calling for John Howard to stay on. Things are going very well for the government. Howard is at the top of his form, relaxed and comfortable as prime minister. As near as anyone can tell two years out, the Liberals look a pretty good bet to win the next federal election. So why change things? Why risk a leadership transition next year? Why fix something that ain't broke? It sounds persuasive but it is superficial.

Peter Lindsay, the MP whose sucking up to Howard at a meeting of Queensland Liberals prompted a front-page leadership story in *The Age*, and his NSW colleague Bob Baldwin, whose public gushing kept the issue in the news, are thinking short-term. They – and others in the coalition with similar views – should refresh their memories of the Prime Minister's own comments on leadership transition in an interview in *The Australian* at the start of last year's election campaign. Arguing that the messy Labor leadership change from Bob Hawke to Paul Keating was not only 'undignified' but also served the nation badly, Howard said: 'One of the things you've got to do, which Hawke did not do though Menzies did, is you've got to think of the medium- and long-term future of the party.'

In other words, in considering the leadership, it is necessary to have in mind not just the next election but the election after, and the one after that. As Howard often says, nothing is forever. If he decides not to retire when he turns 64 next July, it will simply be a postponement. He will undertake, presumably, to look at the matter again when he turns 67. But who knows what the political situation will be like then? The circumstances are unlikely to be anywhere near as propitious for a change as they are now.

The point being missed by the junior woodchucks on the coalition back bench is that the best time to undertake such a transition is from a position of strength. The coalition's dominant position at the moment is a powerful argument in favour of a leadership change, not against it. Parties rarely have the luxury of an orderly leadership change in a favourable political climate. The fact that Labor is travelling badly under a new leader is a bonus. Howard has the opportunity to hand over a party in excellent shape to an undisputed and highly qualified successor. That might not be the case in mid-2006.

Early this year, I was invited to address the inaugural dinner of the coalition's Class of 2001, the Liberal and National MPs who came into parliament at the last election. My gratuitous advice included some thoughts on this very matter. 'I've seen John Howard develop,' I told them. 'He's now an extraordinarily formidable politician. I can see why some Liberals are saying it would be madness for him to retire next year when he's so on top of the game. And I can understand why the PM might be tempted to believe that himself. But there's the longer-term view. If Howard decides to contest another election, stays for another term, what does that do to Peter Costello? In my view, it wipes him out. And Peter Costello is your future.

'If Howard did not make way next year, Costello would have to contemplate at least three more years as treasurer, three more budgets – probably an impossible ask. There's a big chance he'd burn out. He could take another portfolio but that would be seen as a clear indication that he has peaked and he's on the way down. Or he could start planning a career outside politics. My point is that, while John Howard can win another election, if he stays on to do that you may burn off the bloke who would otherwise be expected to take you through the rest of the decade. I'm not sure that's smart.'

But, in the end, what coalition MPs think or want is not all that important. The decision is Howard's alone. So far – on this, as on so many other issues at the moment – he is playing his cards very skilfully. There is no Kirribilli-type agreement between the Prime Minister and his heir apparent but there is a tacit understanding that neither will do anything between now and July to destabilise the government by feeding leadership speculation. While some of his supporters might stir things along from time to time, Howard plays a dead bat whenever he is asked about the subject. His mantra, repeated over and over, is: 'I don't have anything to add to what I've previously said.' (Costello is also doing his best not to stoke the coals, to the frustration of some in the media. When he told a news conference that 'I am not going to add to speculation', one journalist came out with the extraordinary question: 'Isn't that just adding to speculation, Mr Costello?')

Privately, the Prime Minister is weighing up his responsibilities – to the Liberal Party, to the nation, to himself, and to his successor. Back in 1995, Howard would have been regarded as a dreamer if he had said he hoped to win three elections and then go out on his own terms, with the succession taken care of and his party well-positioned for further success. But that is the opportunity he has. Few leaders find themselves in such a position. He should be wary of the siren song from the back bench.

2003

A Carr ride to Canberra

26 March 2003

When Edmund Capon, the director of the NSW Art Gallery, lowered the Australian flag as an anti-war protest a few days before the state election, an angry Bob Carr was quickly on the phone. 'I just told him the flag will fly if I've got to go over there to the Art Gallery and haul it up with my own hands,' the Premier said later. 'If someone wants to make a protest, it should not be by diminishing a national symbol that unites us all.' Then, on the day the war in Iraq began, an interviewer asked Carr if he was worried. 'Yes,' the Premier replied. 'Worried first of all for the Australian men and women who are there and very anxious for their families back here…If I'm returned, one of the first things I'll do is ask the Commonwealth to cooperate with us…to have the families of the men and women over there at a function at Government House. With the Governor, we can offer them the nurturing and the support that make a difference to their anxiety at this time.'

Carr did not buck Labor's line opposing Australian involvement. He made it clear he disagreed with the decision to send troops to the Gulf. But – as his resounding election victory on Saturday demonstrated – Carr is no political mug. He managed to be anti-war while demonstrating that he is not unpatriotic. Simon Crean, by contrast, got himself into all sorts of trouble. His greatest stupidity came at the National Press Club on Thursday, as the first missiles were hitting Baghdad, when he was asked – twice – if he wanted the coalition forces to win. Crean waffled and would not answer. That was the moment the federal opposition leader proved beyond any reasonable doubt that he is a political mug.

Australian servicemen and women were about to go into battle, and here was an Australian political leader apparently unsure about whether he wanted them to emerge victorious. It is difficult to imagine a more monumental gaffe. Crean may be guilty of slow-wittedness rather than a lack of patriotism, but either way it is probably enough to disqualify him from becoming prime minister. Voters, given a choice between an obvious dill or someone unwilling to back Australian troops who are in harm's way, can be expected to tick the box marked 'neither of the above'.

Carr is the leader Labor needs in Canberra. He is the one premier who could make the transition. He has the intellect and the breadth of policy interests – including defence and foreign policy – required of a prime minister. Not surprisingly, he has been quietly sounded out by people who support Crean at the moment but recognise his leadership is becoming less and less viable. Carr, however, will not entertain the idea. He once planned a career in federal politics, but believes the time to make the shift has passed. 'He says his batteries are too flat after all the effort he's put into state politics to start over again,' says one friend. Another says: 'Immense effort would be required. He would have no life. And what is there for him at the end? Hardly the Elysee Palace – just boarding house accommodation at the Lodge.'

This is bad news for Labor, good news for the Liberals. Carr is the only Labor politician in sight with political abilities to match those of John Howard. His achievement – not only retaining but building on Labor's gains in the 1999 NSW poll landslide – was extraordinary. And the coalition's claim that it was solely the result of a $12m Labor campaign war chest will not wash. Carr held a big lead over the opposition for most of the last parliamentary term. And the excuse used by those who toppled Kerry Chikarovski from the NSW Liberal leadership and installed John Brogden in her place was that he would be able to raise large sums of money from the big end of town. The day after the election, ABC local radio in Sydney broadcast a program recorded with Carr last year in which, among other things, he played some of his favourite music. The song that stood out – a 'fun' song, he called it – was from the musical *Chicago*. Those who saw the recent film will recall Richard Gere singing it while performing a nifty tap dance.

Give 'em the old razzle dazzle.
Razzle dazzle 'em.
Give 'em an act with lots of flash in it
And the reaction will be passionate.
Give 'em the old hocus pocus
Bread and feather 'em...

And so on. It is clear why Carr likes it. Any good politician would. It describes the skills a successful political performer needs. Carr is a master razzle-dazzler. Crean, on the other hand, is incapable of razzling or dazzling. When he tries to tap dance, he trips over his own feet. He thought he was on a winner opposing war, but as the Iraq situation developed, he was increasingly off the pace. Everyone except the Labor leader himself could see it. He was inconsistent – arguing that Australian forces should be withdrawn but US and British forces should stay. He was slow to adjust his line – still calling for Australian troops to be brought home as they went into battle. He got the tone wrong – engaging in a parliamentary shouting match on what should have been a grave occasion as Australian troops risked their lives.

Carr's sure-footedness was shown in his victory speech on Saturday night. Instead of engaging in parochial gloating, he said: 'I ask you to reflect on the wider world, a world sadly not at peace tonight. We unite in our thoughts for our serving men and women in Iraq and for the safe and speedy return of these servicemen and women.' The last premier to become prime minister was Joe Lyons, and that was more than 70 years ago. It would take an exceptional state politician to do it now. But Carr is exceptional, and his party is desperate. What a pity he will not give it a go.

Labor's great challenge

30 April 2003

So now we watch and wait. Simon Crean knows at last who his challenger will be, if there is a challenge. And he knows there will be a challenge unless he performs well in the post-budget period and that improved performance is reflected in the opinion polls. At the same time, the out-in-the-open confrontation with Kim Beazley puts the Labor leader under intense pressure, increasing the likelihood that he will stumble. Given that voters are not impressed by disunity, it also makes it harder for Crean to engineer a lift in his own poll ratings and those of the ALP. Catch-22.

Crean's people claim their man showed a clever tactical sense when he turned on Beazley, all guns blazing, after Maxine McKew's interview with Comeback Kim in *The Bulletin* last week. 'It's the last thing they [the anti-Crean forces] would have expected Simon to do,' boasted one Creanite. That may be true, and for good reason. It is far from obvious how elevating the Beazley comments into a full-blown crisis helped the Crean cause. If the aim was to put the screws on a tickerless Beazley and make him back off, it had the opposite effect. When Crean accused him of disloyalty, the normally even-tempered Beazley saw red. From that moment, as far as Beazley was concerned, Crean was on borrowed time.

In the McKew interview, Beazley was obviously signalling a renewed interest in a return to the Labor leadership, but it fell well short of throwing down the gauntlet. Crean's reaction made it that. It locked Beazley in. Prompted him to publicly put the incumbent on notice. And those who believe the big bloke has been back-pedalling since then badly misread the situation. To the extent that there is a timetable for a challenge, it is most likely to happen towards the end of parliament's budget session. By then, the implications of continuing poor opinion polls (and Beazley-backers assume they will remain poor) will have had time to gel in the minds of caucus waverers. Those same waverers will have had plenty of opportunity to judge Crean's performance as the political debate switches to domestic issues.

'But no one can be precise about timing,' says a member of the Beazley camp. 'These things develop their own dynamic.' That was shown by the way *The Bulletin* interview created a momentum Beazley had genuinely not expected. It made the impact it did because of the climate created by two more disastrous opinion polls and an ill-judged unity call by six faction leaders which amounted to an admission that Crean was in trouble. The one thing that is certain, according to sources close to Beazley, is that he will not move without a reasonable degree of consensus among the factional heavies who count and without being sure of the numbers.

Watching a political leader fall – and the odds now certainly favour Crean being toppled – is never a pretty sight. Crean has done some good things and displayed quite a lot of courage as Labor leader. An example was the way he took on the factions to get rid of dead wood from the shadow ministry and ensure the promotion of a group of very talented younger MPs. No one believes Beazley would have done that. Crean has tried his heart out since taking over after the 2001 election loss. He has good reason to feel he does not deserve what is happening to him. But the unmistakable conclusion is that, in terms of regaining lost ground for Labor, his leadership simply has not worked. No matter what he does, voters just don't seem to like him.

That was brought home to some Labor MPs as they mingled with crowds on Anzac Day. They found a tangible friendliness and warmth towards Beazley. 'People just don't react that way with Simon,' said one. 'It's sad, but there's nothing there for him.' Another commented: 'They just think the leadership argument is a no-brainer – that of course you'd go back to Beazley.' He added: 'These are ordinary people, not letter-writers to *The Sydney Morning Herald*.' The weakest argument being put forward by the Creanites is that Beazley has had his go at the leadership and it is now their man's turn. All that should matter is who can get the best results for Labor. If Crean genuinely believes he is the one, he needs to show evidence of it very quickly.

Journalists had a field day interpreting comments made by Beazley on Sunday – four days after *The Bulletin* article appeared. Sydney's *Daily Telegraph* reported that Beazley had 'moved to end a fight he said he had not started' and Crean's critics had been subdued. The *Tele*'s sister paper in Melbourne, the *Herald-Sun*, ran the headline 'Beazley refuses to quash challenge speculation'. And *The Age* in Melbourne said that 'pressure on Simon Crean grew yesterday' as a result of Beazley's refusal to withdraw his leadership challenge. You pays your money and you takes your choice.

But the most significant aspect of Beazley's news conference was missed. Beazley set out to squash the view that Labor cannot win the next election and that the motivation for a leadership change is simply to salvage as many seats as possible. 'Let's get back to a winning mode of thinking in the Labor Party,' he told the news conference on the verandah of his Perth home. 'I see a lot of speculation around in the press that there's an attitude inside the Labor Party that John Howard is not beatable. He is eminently beatable.' That might sound like wishful thinking. The important thing, though, according to colleagues, is that Beazley really believes it.

Prime time

4 June 2003

It is probably Peter Costello's worst nightmare. Not content with breaking Malcolm Fraser's record as the second-longest-serving Liberal prime minister, or Bob Hawke's record as the second-longest-serving PM of any stripe, John Howard decides to go after the big one. It is generally assumed that Howard is too old to challenge Robert Menzies' 16-year continuous stint from December 1949 until January 1966 – but why? Menzies was 55 when he displaced Ben Chifley as PM, Howard 56 when he sent Paul Keating packing. Menzies, a lover of the good life and certainly no physical fitness fanatic, retired at 71. There is no reason to suppose that Howard, with his daily power walks and apparently boundless energy, will not still be hale and hearty at 72.

Granted, it is a highly unlikely scenario. Politics has become a tougher business. Without television, there was not the same exposure and scrutiny in Menzies' day. Voters did not tire of politicians so quickly then. But the comparison puts into perspective the question of Howard's retirement. Age is not a consideration. The fact that he is approaching 64 is essentially irrelevant. What matters is whether Howard still has the appetite for the job, whether he believes he can continue to do it better than Costello would – and whether, in his judgment, the Liberal Party's interests are better served by a continuation of his leadership than by an orderly transition to the next generation while the government is riding high.

While Howard is playing his cards close to his chest, the feeling is growing among Liberals that he will stay. Discussion has turned to the question of how Costello is likely to react to such a decision. With Howard's position in the party unassailable, the heir apparent would be in no position to make a fuss, but he would not like it. 'Things would not stay the same,' says a Costello supporter. In other words, the relationship of trust at the top of the Liberal Party which has given the government such stability would be damaged. There would be tension and resentment. The loyal deputy could be expected to be less loyal. The sourness would not remain hidden. And history shows that, when there is disunity at the leadership level of a political party, voters are usually unimpressed.

A strategy was activated several weeks ago to try to soothe Costello's feelings and minimise his frustration in anticipation of Howard announcing he is in no hurry to depart. Paul Kelly described it in *The Australian* as 'peer group backing of Costello's uncontested leadership claim into the next parliament'. In the words of a prominent Liberal: 'The idea is to make sure Peter knows that, although the wait may be longer, the result will still be as certain as these things can be.' Hence Tony Abbott's statements on the *Sunday* program that, even if Howard stays another term, the Treasurer can still be confident of succeeding him: 'One day the PM will go, and on that day Peter Costello will take over.' But Costello is unlikely to be reassured or pacified by people saying: 'Don't worry. Whatever happens, you're next.' In politics, no one can give such a guarantee three years ahead, and Costello knows it. Ambitious politicians such as Brendan Nelson, or Abbott himself, are not going to abandon their own leadership aspirations. If opportunities open up, they will grab them.

There are those in the Liberal Party arguing that another three years as deputy could be good for Costello. It would give him an opportunity to engage more with fellow Liberal MPs – something, they say, he has always neglected. 'If he is going to be a good leader he needs to develop relationships with his colleagues,' says one of this group. There is muttering about the need for Costello to appoint a strong political operator to his staff to advise on such matters and to help build bridges with backbenchers and other ministers. But, whether or not this criticism is justified, it is unlikely to impress Costello. As far as he is concerned, he has put in the hard yards as treasurer and has earned the right to move into the top job. And Howard, by publicly stating he would consider his future ahead of his 64th birthday, certainly gave the deputy every reason to expect it would happen this year.

Howard may comfort himself with the thought that any Liberal tensions caused by a decision to stay on would be more than outweighed by Labor's leadership troubles. It is true the opposition is paralysed by Simon Crean's ineffectiveness and the threat of a Kim Beazley challenge. Crean is said to be so paranoid he has banned state ALP branches that use the same market research firm as federal Labor from doing any polling on federal matters. The thinking is that polling reflecting on his leadership can't be leaked if it doesn't exist. Only the NSW ALP, which has its own research firm, is in a position to defy the Crean edict. Labor, for the time being, is a basket case. But Howard, more than most, should be aware that fortunes change quickly in politics. Sooner or later, Labor will start to get its act together.

If he stays, Howard not only will need to treat his deputy with kid gloves. He will, if he is wise, also handle the announcement in a way that avoids any impression of triumphalism. To reveal the decision amid an orgy of cheering and popping Champagne corks at the Liberal Party's national convention, for example, as well as rubbing Costello's nose in it, would risk giving voters the idea that the Prime Minister and his party are just a bit full of themselves.

Educating Brendan

9 July 2003

It would be nice to think that, when Labor's latest polling was presented to the shadow ministry, there were some red faces among the group which had been trying to force Jenny Macklin out of the education portfolio. A handful of factional wheeler-dealers had persuaded Simon Crean – in their debt because they had helped him to survive Kim Beazley's leadership challenge – that Macklin should be moved back to her former job as shadow health minister. She had been, it was claimed, an 'under-performer' in the critical education area. Melbourne's *Sunday Age* quoted some colleagues as saying she had 'not starred'. *The Sydney Morning Herald* reported that critics in caucus were 'unhappy with Ms Macklin's...inability to score a king-hit on the Education Minister, Brendan Nelson'.

What Labor's polling showed was that, for all his cockiness and naked ambition, Nelson is not travelling very well. If he has not been 'king-hit', he has certainly been damaged. Macklin must be doing something right. The research makes it quite clear Crean's attempt to humiliate his deputy was yet another political misjudgment. Even though Macklin had been scrupulously loyal and supported him in the leadership ballot, he leaned very heavily on her. Stories were leaked to newspapers that her intransigence was frustrating Crean's reshuffle plans. But it was obvious that being shunted back to health before she had a chance to put forward the education policies she has been working on would inevitably be seen as a demotion. So Macklin dug in her heels and refused to budge. Who could blame her?

The ALP's national secretary, Geoff Walsh, attended the shadow ministry meeting on the very day of the reshuffle to outline the findings of the party's polling firm, UMR Research. Not surprisingly, national security – covering defence, terrorism and asylum-seekers – was highlighted as the area of greatest concern for Labor. Health and education were the two policy areas where Labor is strongest. What Macklin's critics presumably did not expect was that the party is doing rather better in education than in health, even though most of Crean's efforts since the budget have been focused on Medicare and bulk billing. Asked which party is better to handle education, 46 percent of those polled said Labor, while only 22 percent nominated the coalition – a 24-point margin. In health the figures were 35 percent to 24 percent Labor's way, a margin of 11 points. No basis there to suggest the education spokesperson has been under-performing.

In the nationwide poll, UMR asked 1000 people whether they had a positive or negative view of Nelson. The results were: 18 percent positive, 30 percent negative. The negative percentage was higher among those with a university degree. The word most commonly used to describe Nelson was 'shifty'. A mere 20 percent of the sample were satisfied with the government's handling of higher education, while 64 percent said they were dissatisfied. The poll tested some of the government's themes on higher education against those put forward by Labor. Support for the government's lines was 20 percent, for Labor's 72 percent. And so it went on. The inescapable conclusion was that Macklin's criticism of Nelson and his policies has struck home. The public has been getting Labor's higher education message loud and clear.

In the period immediately before and after the reshuffle, much media attention was devoted to Julia Gillard, the former immigration spokesperson transferred to health and billed as Labor's 'rising star'. There is no denying that Gillard – bright, articulate and tough – is one of the more talented members of the opposition front bench. She did a good job devising a compromise policy on asylum-seekers for Labor, and in getting the so-called 'cash-for-visas' issue off the ground, even if it did boomerang to damage Labor as well as the government. But Gillard does not yet have anything like a record to match Macklin's, as she herself would no doubt acknowledge.

Gillard might have caused Immigration Minister Philip Ruddock some embarrassment, but Macklin has been given credit for destroying two ministerial careers. Her pursuit of then-health minister Michael Wooldridge in the last parliament – particularly over the so-called 'scan scam' which saw radiologists rushing to buy expensive Magnetic Resonance Imaging machines ahead of a budget change to Medicare – was regarded as a key factor in his decision to quit politics. Before that, Macklin's attacks as aged care spokesperson over nursing home bonds played a major role in destroying Judi Moylan's ministerial career. In light of the praise being heaped on Gillard for her aggression and her success in 'stinging' Ruddock, it is interesting to look back at what was being said and written about Macklin just a couple of years ago. According to one commentator back then, 'exacting pain on the government has been Macklin's speciality'. She was 'the marauding Macklin' and 'one of Labor's key spear throwers'.

No Labor frontbencher has scored a king-hit in the past 18 months but Macklin has done a fair job at getting under Nelson's skin. Some of her parliamentary questions, framed to accentuate his 'shifty' image, have produced answers that had even some on the government side laughing at him. And Labor's polling is clear evidence that Macklin's undermining of Nelson's higher education package has produced results, despite what her critics say. It may or may not be coincidence that Nelson is trailing his coat for a portfolio change if John Howard reshuffles the government front bench. Macklin's task now – as she and Crean unveil Labor's own policy bit by bit throughout this month – is to show she can do just as well at the selling job. Meanwhile, it is worth making the point that, if those who tried to shaft her were anywhere near as effective, Labor would be in much better shape.

Mark of a fighter

27 August 2003

Mark Latham has notched up two notable achievements since his elevation to a starring role on the opposition front bench. He has galvanised the Labor Party. And he has galvanised Peter Costello. In the two weeks of sittings following parliament's winter recess, Latham made no stand-out speeches, produced no significant contribution to the economic debate. But he had a major impact just the same. With

Latham muscling up to Costello as shadow treasurer and calling the shots as Manager of Opposition Business, the dynamics of the House were very different.

One unintended consequence – unintended, that is, by Simon Crean when he promoted the notorious head-kicker and arm-breaker – is that Latham overshadowed his mentor. Crean has become the incredible shrinking leader. It is not that he performed badly. Crean's attacks on John Howard over the ethanol issue and on Wilson Tuckey's use of ministerial letterhead to try to get a son off a transport fine were effective enough. But it was Latham who appeared to be driving the process, Latham who looked most aggressive, Latham who attracted attention. The phrase 'de facto leader' appeared in print more than once, and bobbed up in conversation rather more often. The effect of Latham's hulking presence has been to diminish Crean.

There is nothing subtle about Latham, no indication that he is particularly brilliant in a strategic or tactical sense. But because he is a front-foot player, he is good for party morale. He has injected a new verve into the opposition's attack. Labor MPs, for the first time in a long while, have their tails up. 'They are at least trying now,' says a prominent Liberal politician. 'They've lifted their game. They're having a go.' According to another senior coalition MP: 'Labor's been catatonic. He's waking them up.'

He has also woken up the Treasurer. After the best part of eight years in the job, Costello was cruising. On top of that, Howard's decision to stay on for at least another three years as prime minister had left the heir apparent frustrated and rather down. Some of the energy seemed to have gone out of him. Also, with the quiet and cautious – almost invisible – Bob McMullan as his shadow, Costello had no one to bounce off. In any case, the Treasurer rather liked McMullan and was disinclined to give him both barrels. But Latham is a different matter. His style demands a response. More important, he is clearly dangerous to the government and has to be dealt with. Costello has assumed that responsibility with the kind of zest he has not displayed for some time. It is obvious that Latham's elevation renewed Costello's interest in the political battle.

Not that other ministers have been reluctant to engage with Latham. It is a measure of the concern he arouses within the government that so much effort has gone into trying to discredit him. But most of the attacks have been badly directed. The government's chief bovver boy, Workplace Relations Minister Tony Abbott, in particular, has looked rather juvenile in his attempts to dig up political dirt. So far, Abbott has come off second best in their clashes.

'That's why he's called the Mad Monk,' Latham told the House at one point to emphasise the over-the-top nature of one of Abbott's interventions.

Before parliament resumed, Howard was asked how he thought the Latham–Costello contest would turn out. 'Peter does his research,' the PM said with a grin. 'He's got a lot of material.'

Costello went into parliament armed with a stack of controversial or conflicting policy ideas put forward by Latham over the years – especially during the period after he resigned from Kim Beazley's front bench to become a 'thinker' in exile. It was, Costello boasted, a treasure trove. He told the House: 'It is just a mine of unbearable riches. It never comes to an end.' And the Treasurer made effective use of these riches to ridicule his new opponent.

Sample. 'He has had a position on practically every policy, like a child in a lolly shop. You know, "I'll have one of them and one of them and one of them." Writing in September 1990, the would-be economic spokesman for Labor said: "The federal government should shed part of its funding role for basic services by encouraging the states to raise income and consumption taxes." Income taxes! Not only did he want a state GST; he wanted a state income tax... The moment "Fightback" was put forward and it became Liberal policy to have a GST, the member for Werriwa, having been a supporter of the GST, then became an opponent of it and, as we now know, advocated instead of the GST the PET – the progressive expenditure tax...I say to the back bench of the Labor Party: wait for the progressive expenditure tax, because you ain't seen nothing yet.'

Even more effective was the job Costello did on his opponent when Latham asked questions about a past business association of David Knott, chairman of the Australian Securities and Investment Commission. Costello carved Latham up with precision, eventually delivering the killer blow – the revelation that Knott's first appointment to a senior federal regulatory job had been under Keating. 'Peter was on fire,' a colleague commented later.

This is a fight that is just beginning. Latham may have suffered some bruises, but that is all. He, too, as Costello knows well, is capable of landing a heavy punch. Some of Latham's fellow MPs are concerned that, while he may have revved up Labor's attack, his crudeness is likely to antagonise voters. 'They already refer to him as "the bloke with the filthy mouth",' says one Labor source. That may be so. But it is undeniable that, in his newly prominent role, he has changed the game.

Pride and prejudice

24 September 2003

George Brandis, a lawyer before he entered parliament, has that rather supercilious manner that some barristers seem to cultivate. It was on display on the ABC television program *The Insiders* recently. The Queensland Liberal senator was gloating over problems for the Labor Party caused by Bob Carr's musings about a possible switch to federal politics. NSW Liberal leader John Brogden had reason to smile, Brandis said, and then – with a self-satisfied smirk – added: 'And John Howard? Well, he's always smiling.' Freeze-frame it there. The picture of Howard government arrogance.

The Prime Minister frequently professes to warn against arrogance and overconfidence. 'All my political life I've been a person who's never believed in overexuberance, never believed in taking things for granted,' he told Queensland Liberals at their Gold Coast conference. 'We've got to understand the inherent capacity of the Australian electorate to harshly judge any sign of complacency, any sign of hubris...' But there are now signs aplenty of both. While Howard tells his party the next election is likely to be close and the loss of only a handful of seats would put the government out of office, coalition members from the top down behave as though they can't be beaten.

It is not hard to understand why. They look at the Labor Party and see a rabble. They look at Simon Crean and see an opposition leader incapable of leading. They look at Howard and see a master politician apparently at the peak of his powers. They look at the economy and see low interest rates, high employment and a remarkable growth performance in difficult circumstances. So they swagger and indulge themselves and ignore some of the basic lessons of politics. And the punters are starting to notice; the arrogance issue is beginning to bite. Take Community Services Minister Amanda Vanstone. Her department suddenly introduces data matching that uncovers the fact that many pensioners, through no fault of their own, have been overpaid. The overpayments are small, but over the years have built up into quite large debts, and the department demands the money. The following exchange occurs on the TV program *A Current Affair* when the Minister is questioned about the difficulties some of these pensioners face:

Interviewer: So you would be prepared to sell up their family homes?

Vanstone: Well, I would be.

How is that for arrogance? Equally arrogant was Howard's attempt in parliament last week to pretend that Vanstone never uttered such a threat.

Another example involved Deputy Prime Minister and Transport Minister John Anderson. After the theft of a laptop computer exposed appallingly lax security in the headquarters of the federal Transport Department – with implications for airline safety and counter-terrorism – Anderson was asked a question in parliament. He went to the dispatch box, started to answer, but then – because of a few opposition interjections – spat the dummy and flounced back to his seat. 'Arrogant and petulant,' was the judgment of one of Anderson's Liberal colleagues.

A much bigger display of arrogance was Anderson's six-month-long semi-public flirtation with the idea of quitting politics. At a time when the government claimed to represent stability and certainty in troubled times, the Deputy PM could not make up his mind whether he wanted to do the job or not. 'When he finally decided that he would stay on, we were all supposed to be grateful and greet the announcement with sighs of relief and delight,' said another coalition MP. 'He obviously felt the government was going so well and the opposition was so weak and he was so important that he could safely engage in this extraordinary act of indulgence.'

'Arrogant' is about the only word to describe Howard's decision to stand by Wilson Tuckey. Letters were tabled in parliament showing the Regional Services Minister, who rejoices in the nickname 'Ironbar', had tried to bully a South Australian minister into intervening in a traffic case involving his son. The wrong thing to do, conceded the PM. Tuckey had been a fool – but he would remain in the ministry. In effect, an admission Howard does not mind having fools on his front bench. Which leads to another issue. Government sources are now putting it about that there is not likely to be a reshuffle of the ministry this side of the next election. Tuckey is not alone in deserving the chop. But Howard, apparently, has decided not to bother freshening up his government by promoting the half-dozen or so talented backbenchers who should be ministers if ability and performance are what counts. The judgment is that the public will put up with second-raters. Arrogance again.

Then there is the leaking of a highly classified Office of National Assessments report authored by Andrew Wilkie, the intelligence analyst who resigned over the Iraq war. I make no criticism of journalist Andrew Bolt for getting a scoop. More power to his elbow. But someone was prepared to commit a crime by giving him the material in a bid to discredit a critic of the government. That is the kind of behaviour only an arrogant administration would engage in – as was the spin put on the document by the leaker. Wilkie, it was suggested, was incompetent because the potential humanitarian disasters canvassed in the paper did not occur. The truth emerged in another context. Howard, defending himself against charges of concealing intelligence unfavourable to the case for war, told parliament: 'The Australian intelligence community, as part of the government's prudent contingency planning, undertook various assessments of what could go wrong in the event of conflict in Iraq.' That was Wilkie's brief. He was instructed to look at what might go wrong, not to predict the outcome if all went well.

A brief history of martyrdom

3 December 2003

After Bill Hayden was forced out of the Labor leadership at the start of the 1983 federal election campaign, he told a caucus meeting he felt qualified for immediate appointment as Patron of the Society of Saint Sebastian. Only one caucus member, Hayden later noted, a regularly practising Catholic, appeared to understand the imagery. Sebastian was a Christian member of the Praetorian guard in the Imperial Palace of the Roman Empire. On instructions from the Emperor Diocletian, he was tied to a tree in a courtyard while a phalanx of archers launched a hail of arrows into their human target. Although it was said his body was so riddled with quills he looked more like a porcupine than a man, he miraculously survived and was nursed back to health – whereupon Diocletian had him beaten to death and thrown into a sewer.

Simon Crean would now understand vividly what Hayden was talking about. And it is impossible not to feel sympathy for the latest Labor leader to be martyred in similar style to the saintly Sebastian. But when Crean and his cohorts start complaining he was a victim of disloyalty and treachery, that sympathy needs to be tempered with a bit of history. Specifically, it should be remembered that Crean – as one of Bob Hawke's lieutenants – played a leading role in the process that left Hayden bleeding from thousands of arrow wounds, ready for the final, fatal blow.

In his bid to unseat Malcolm Fraser's government, Hayden tried to negotiate a prices and incomes accord policy with the trade union movement. Crean, then vice-president of the ACTU, was a key figure in ensuring those negotiations got nowhere. Hayden was humiliated and frustrated at every turn. Details of one meeting – where Hawke, as shadow industrial relations minister, sprawled back with a cigar blowing smoke rings while Crean and his ACTU colleagues ripped into the accord plan and thumped the table at Hayden – were leaked to the media on the eve of the crucial Flinders by-election, helping to minimise the swing to Labor and further weaken Hayden's grip on the leadership.

Graham Richardson, in his autobiography *Whatever it Takes*, makes it clear this was all a deliberate part of the strategy to remove Hayden as leader and install Hawke in his place. After Hawke assumed the leadership, the ACTU speedily endorsed the very prices and incomes accord unacceptable under Hayden. So the whingeing about disloyalty from the Crean camp in the wake of his political demise should not be taken too seriously. Crean, like others with political ambition, played it tough, and he was not entitled to expect that others would be less tough on him. He should have had no illusions about what happens to those who live by the sword.

When Mark Latham announced his candidacy for the Labor leadership contest to succeed Crean, he tried to wrap himself in the cloak of loyalty. 'Some people unhappily in politics say that disloyalty is a virtue,' Latham said, in an unsubtle slap at Kim Beazley and his supporters.

'I don't think that. I think it's a vice. I think being loyal and sticking by the person who's in is important and that's what I tried to do with Simon Crean and that's the standard that we've got to carry forward to the future. We shouldn't be rewarding disloyalty in the modern Labor Party.' It was self-serving and hypocritical claptrap, given Latham's own behaviour in walking out of Beazley's shadow ministry in 1998 and spending three years sniping from the sidelines.

In the leadership battle against Beazley, Latham invoked the support of two Labor legends, Gough Whitlam and Paul Keating. Their records on the loyalty front are interesting. Keating and his supporters white-anted Hawke mercilessly in a campaign that eventually succeeded in bringing down the most electorally successful federal leader Labor has had. And between 1963 and 1966 Whitlam, then deputy leader, did his best to oust Arthur Calwell from the leadership so he could take over. In 1965, for example, Labor MPs were startled to read a story in *The Australian*, datelined Wellington, New Zealand, and headed: 'Whitlam Report – Calwell Too Old and Weak'. On a cross-Tasman visit, Whitlam had told a Dunedin journalist he was 'better equipped' than the 'old and weak' Calwell or any other Labor figure to lead his country. Under Calwell, Whitlam said, Labor would lose the next election. It was just one of many episodes in Whitlam's undermining of Calwell.

There can be conflicting calls on a politician's loyalty. Keating and Whitlam, like Beazley's backers, would have said their loyalty was to the party and the nation, and that this was more important than loyalty to a leader. Keating's excuse was that the Labor government was running out of steam under Hawke. Whitlam was convinced – and he was right – that sticking with the ageing Calwell simply lengthened Labor's period in the wilderness. Latham does not really believe disloyalty to a leader is always a vice. If he did, he would have to condemn both his mentors.

Politics is not an activity for gentlefolk or wimps. Queensberry rules do not apply. Saint Sebastian serves as patron saint of archers, athletes and soldiers. He should also be patron saint of Labor leaders.

Making his Mark

10 December 2003

When John Howard resumed the Liberal Party leadership in early 1995, the Labor government thought it would have a field day with his past. His comments bucketing Medicare, his statements about Asian immigration, his record as treasurer in the Fraser government, and so on. There was plenty of ammunition. But Howard's authorised biographer, David Barnett, wrote that the resuscitated leader 'inoculated himself against attacks relying on past events'. He did it by standing in the parliament and telling then prime minister Paul Keating: 'The more you talk about the past, the more you proclaim your embarrassment about the present and that you have nothing to say about the future.' Howard can hardly complain, now that Mark Latham has latched on to the same formula.

The new Labor leader is not proving the easy target the coalition expected. He is not the one-dimensional figure they thought. No sooner had the caucus votes been counted than the foul-mouthed thug morphed into sensitive family man. The volatile politician with a short fuse suddenly developed the ability to absorb attacks and insults without responding. Ministers and some in the media are now starting to catch up with a side of Latham that helped him snatch the leadership from under Kim Beazley's nose. For months, Latham had been ingratiating himself with Labor MPs, addressing dozens of fundraising functions for them, and in the process showing them that he was not as difficult, grating and unpopular with women as his critics claimed. This was how he defied all the traditional ALP power bases to win the caucus ballot.

Labor is dramatically transformed as a result. Everyone in the party is energised, although, as an ALP strategist points out: 'That may have less to do with Latham than with what a weight Simon Crean was around everyone's neck.' At a NSW candidates' seminar five days after Latham won the leadership, state ALP secretary Eric Roozendaal – previously a Beazley supporter and Latham critic – spoke enthusiastically about the changed atmosphere. Party membership applications had increased sixfold since the ballot, he said. Labor now had a genuine chance of winning next year's election. 'Talk about a backflip,' said one of those present. 'Eric bent right over.'

But Roozendaal was not exaggerating. If Latham can maintain his self-discipline, it is possible to imagine a Labor victory – something totally in the realms of fantasy before the leadership change. In the words of one of Labor's longest-serving MPs: 'For years our lifeblood has been ebbing away. We've been incapable of reinventing ourselves. Now we've given ourselves a whole new go at it.' Under Crean, Labor's national conference in late January would have been a minefield, but now there is a real prospect that it will become a launching pad. 'We'll have to change the conference backdrop we were planning under Crean,' joked an ALP wit. 'The one that said: "Please vote for us. We're not that bad. You can't let Howard get too big a majority. Come on."'

Certainly, the new leader made good use of his novelty value. He took the advice of a party veteran who said after the vote: 'There is a brief window of opportunity when the public might listen to us. If we use it, OK. Otherwise it will close.' Latham used it. He did not hold back. And clearly the public was listening. That was the big change. Where Crean put voters to sleep, Latham woke them up.

Not that the Labor Party should get too optimistic just yet. All new leaders have a honeymoon. Alexander Downer enjoyed an initial burst of attention even more rapturous than Latham's. Then, as now, it was reflected in the opinion polls. Keating's rating as preferred prime minister tumbled 15 points following Downer's election as Liberal leader. The coalition's vote immediately jumped three points, putting it ahead of Labor. Two weeks later, the coalition had 47 percent of the vote compared with Labor's 41 percent. A fortnight after that, Downer was seven points ahead of Keating as preferred PM. But very quickly Downer crashed and burned, leaving Howard to pick up the pieces. There are still those convinced that Latham will meet a similar fate. 'We won't really know how he's going until about March,' says an ALP strategist.

Latham had two immediate aims. The most important was to heal party divisions, which he did by showing generosity to those who had been his opponents. The paranoid Crean used to get bogged down over such matters, but Latham's ambition and will to win overrode all other considerations. The second thing the new leader had to do was deal with the perception that he is anti-American. This became more urgent when, on his second day as leader, he was trapped by the wily Melbourne radio host Neil Mitchell into asserting that he stood by his attack on George Bush as the most dangerous and incompetent president in US history. 'He would have been ambushed like that again and again,' says an adviser. 'He had to cut it off at the pass.' Hence the now-notorious news conference where, in front of a US flag, Latham portrayed himself as ardently pro-US and a faithful supporter of the alliance. It was a touch hypocritical and demeaning – but it was effective. 'We didn't want it going on for weeks,' says the adviser. 'A line had to be drawn. Now they'll say he's all over the place, but that's not much of a hit.'

Howard looked decidedly awkward in his initial attempts to engage his new, younger opponent. Latham's task is to make himself respectable without losing the sense of excitement his elevation has brought to politics or the straight-talking style which differentiates him from the grey, cautious politicians Australians are fed up with. If he can do that, the coalition will have a real fight on its hands. To quote another of Labor's newly enthused MPs: 'We could be in for the election of a lifetime.'

2004

Super man v the man of steel

10 February 2004

'The man of steel has feet of clay.' That was the judgment of one prominent Liberal MP after John Howard performed his extraordinary cave-in on parliamentary superannuation. Howard would like his sudden embrace of Mark Latham's policy to be seen as the action of a strong and determined leader, prepared to put up with a few days of unfavourable headlines to neutralise an issue that was winning easy points for the opposition. But it will not wash. The prime ministerial backflips on such issues as petrol excise that helped restore the coalition's electoral fortunes at the start of 2001 were carefully planned and coolly executed. Last week's super somersault bore all the hallmarks of panic.

At the first party meeting of the parliamentary year, Howard warned coalition MPs not to be spooked by Labor's new leader. By the end of the week they were well and truly spooked, not by Latham, but by their own prime minister. 'What amazed everyone was that he clearly didn't know what he was doing,' said one party room source. 'It was a shambles.' Howard was unclear about such basic details as who would be affected by the proposed superannuation changes and whether the taxpayer contribution under the proposed new scheme would be 9 percent or 15 percent. There were angry arguments, shows of hands, mass confusion. 'Who's running the government?' shouted Bronwyn Bishop. If Howard was not panicking himself, he certainly panicked many of his followers.

In politics, of course, timing is everything. Plans to exploit public resentment over highly generous parliamentary superannuation had been drawn up – but not announced – before Simon Crean was toppled from the Labor leadership. What delivered Latham a spectacular win would have bombed in Crean's hands. It would not have been taken seriously. The government could have shrugged it off. It is because Latham is seen as a credible threat to Howard that the issue gained such momentum. Then, wedged by an opponent prepared to use the same kind of populist tactics he himself has made an art form, Howard botched his response. The truth is, Latham had telegraphed the punch. Howard should have seen it coming and taken evasive action – by referring the superannuation issue to the Remuneration Tribunal for investigation, perhaps. Instead, he was caught flat-footed.

Howard's reputation as the nation's cleverest politician has taken quite a battering since he came up against Latham. After two and a half months he still has not got the measure of his new opponent. The initial personal attacks backfired. Howard's attempts to engage with Latham during the national ALP conference also proved counter-productive. Now, in the confrontation over MPs' retirement benefits, the almost universal perception is that it was Howard who blinked. The Prime Minister needs to get some runs on the board soon, or faith in his leadership within the coalition will start to slide dramatically.

Latham is not a recent convert to the cause of cleaning up MPs' perks. While Howard flip-flopped on the super issue, Latham has been consistent. He penned an interesting column in Sydney's *Daily Telegraph* at the time of the Peter Reith phone-card scandal in October, 2000, in which he singled out parliamentary retirement benefits as something requiring reform. 'Compared to the money earned by senior public servants and corporate leaders, Australia's politicians are underpaid,' Latham wrote. (In that view, at least, he agrees with

Peter Costello.) 'The system has tried to compensate for this shortfall by squirrelling away dozens of additional entitlements – such as travel and expenses allowances, free transport and generous superannuation.'

On the specific matter of phone rorts, Latham wrote: 'As a federal MP I have six taxpayer-funded telephones…The only way in which I can pay for a private call is to find a telephone box.' He then made a suggestion which may be a pointer to action under a Latham government. 'What they should do is bundle all the entitlements together and cap the overall amount,' Latham wrote. 'Every minister and MP should be given a fixed budget for running their office, covering the costs of rent, staff, telephones, postage, travel and so forth. This approach would have several advantages. Most obviously, MPs would no longer be able to abuse their open-ended entitlements. They would be responsible for keeping their costs below the capped amount, plus complying with stringent audit requirements every 12 months. Any over-spending would need to be met from the member's own pocket.'

Howard hardly covered himself with glory when he tried to defend himself on Neil Mitchell's 3AW talkback program the morning after his super cave-in. There was, basically, not much wrong with the existing system, the PM said. He had decided to dump it for reasons of political expediency because he did not regard MPs' remuneration as very important. He would 'die in a ditch' politically on some issues, but not on others. In that case, Mitchell said, 'We need a list of things about which you feel strongly enough not to change.' Howard's response was: 'Well, you can just keep asking me.' A cynic might see this as an extension of Howard's notorious concept of core and non-core promises; now, apparently, we have core and non-core beliefs.

Howard saw the super row as a distraction from debate over the Free Trade Agreement with the US – an issue he believes he can use to discredit Latham. The contest over the FTA will be fascinating, but it is unlikely to be as one-sided as the government appears to believe. Labor can draw on a respectable body of intellectual opinion that sees the deal as contrary to Australia's national interest. And Howard's recent performance makes it far from certain that he will get the better of his young opponent. At the same time, though, it would be very unwise to write the PM off at this stage. Latham has scored with an appeal to populism – but, when he puts his mind to it, there is no more populist politician in Australia than Howard.

Truth will out

18 August 2004

On Monday morning, Mike Scrafton sat in his office in Victoria's Department of Sustainability and Environment, wondering what the Howard government would do to try to discredit him. He had seen what happened to previous critics and whistleblowers. In fact, it was the way the government scornfully dismissed the views of 43 retired ambassadors, department heads and defence and intelligence chiefs – 'doddering, daiquiri diplomats', one frontbencher called them – that prompted Scrafton to break his three-year silence on the 'children-overboard' affair. Their open letter about the Iraq war, he said, had 'at its centre the vital issue of truth in government'. For that reason, he had decided to set the public record straight on the most controversial 'truth in government' issue of John Howard's term as prime minister.

According to friends, it was partly because his conscience bothered him about the matter that Scrafton gave up his job in the Defence Department. At the time – it all took place during the 2001 election campaign – he was on secondment from the Defence Department as senior adviser to then-defence minister Peter Reith. That made him a key figure. His version of events cannot be easily dismissed. Moreover, unlike the Prime Minister, whose political hide is at risk, Scrafton would seem to have no reason to lie. There is nothing in it for him except pain. The government and its spin merchants will make sure of it. In his letter to *The Australian*, Scrafton described his revelations about what he told Howard, and when, as 'a small footnote' to the history of the affair. It is much more than a footnote. With an election looming in which Howard's credibility was already set to be an issue, Scrafton's recollections of three phone conversations with the Prime Minister become very important indeed.

Howard's Sergeant Schultz impersonation – 'I know nothing' – was never credible. Within hours of ministers proclaiming that asylum-seekers on an intercepted vessel had thrown children overboard, the captain of the intercepting warship had notified his superiors it was untrue. It takes a real stretch to believe the Prime Minister would still be ignorant of this a month later when he addressed the National Press Club in the final week of the election campaign. Now that there is a detailed statement from a reputable witness that Howard was briefed before that speech, it could be a crucial turning point for the Prime Minister. While the sad truth is that voters are more likely to be angry over broken promises about tax cuts than lies about asylum-seekers, there is evidence that people are wearying of Howard's claims in moments of embarrassment that 'no one told me'. His refusal to accept responsibility at such times is part of the motivation for the 'Not Happy, John' campaign being organised against him in his own seat by former federal Liberal Party president John Valder. And an apparently straight-shooting public servant with no obvious axe to grind punching a hole in that already tattered 'Honest John' persona plays right into Mark Latham's 'can't lie straight in bed' attack on the PM.

Scrafton's letter says that on November 7, 2001, after viewing a videotape which Reith had claimed showed children being thrown overboard, he received three phone calls from Howard. 'In the course of those calls I recounted to him that: a) the tape was at best inconclusive as to whether there were any children in the water but certainly didn't support the proposition that the event had occurred; b) that the photographs that had been released in early October were definitely of the sinking of the refugee boat on October 8 and not of any children being thrown into the water; and c) that no one in Defence that I dealt with on the matter still believed any children were thrown overboard.' Scrafton also said he told Howard a report from the Office of National Assessments appearing to confirm the 'children-overboard' claim seemed to be based on nothing more than public statements of then-immigration minister Philip Ruddock. At the National Press Club the next day, Howard not only denied any uncertainty about children being thrown overboard but quoted the ONA report as his authority.

Voters will have to decide who to believe. The Howard version is that Scrafton told him nothing more than that the video was inconclusive – and he points out that the other claims in the letter were not mentioned in a statement Scrafton gave to a departmental inquiry into the affair after the election. In fact, though, Scrafton said in his statement to the inquiry that he had been 'involved in or aware of a number of discussions between Mr Reith's office and the Prime Minister's office and the Prime Minister which he could not discuss'. Professor Patrick Weller, in his book on the affair, *Don't Tell the Prime Minister*, says Howard's office later checked with the inquiry head 'to ensure this statement could not be taken further and the contents of these conversations would not be revealed'.

Other things are relevant when considering Howard's attempt to refute the Scrafton version of events. Before Scrafton made his statement to the departmental inquiry, he was pointedly asked by superiors what he was going to say. He had already been told he would not be allowed to give evidence before a Senate inquiry because the government did not regard it as proper for ministerial staffers to speak about such matters. The departmental inquiry was a simple administrative inquiry by a relatively junior officer. There was no indication at the time that statements made before it would be handed to the more important Senate committee. And, most important, Scrafton had just returned to the department from Reith's office. If he was at all interested in a future in the federal public service, he would have been a fool not to be very cautious and guarded in what he told the inquiry.

Power plays

22 September 2004

Last Saturday, a Liberal MP with a fairly healthy margin embarked on what he thought would be a routine day of gladhanding and pressing flesh at supermarkets in his electorate. He had done the same thing the previous two weekends, and had found voters relatively disengaged and uninterested in the election. But this time – at the exact mid-point of the campaign – things were different. 'People were lining up to speak to me,' he says. More than that: 'They were waiting patiently to give me a belting.' The list of gripes ranged from pension levels to higher education, from Iraq to uncertainty about John Howard's future. But the overriding theme was 'an expectation that government can fix everyone's problem – and if we don't, it's because we don't really want to'.

Three weeks out from polling day, voters were starting to take notice and get involved. And, even if little else from the campaign had registered with them before that, what had not gone unnoticed was the huge amounts of money that had appeared – almost magically – in the government's coffers. With Treasurer Peter Costello unveiling massive budget surpluses and then boasting about the GST collecting billions of dollars more than anyone had expected, who can blame the punters for catching their collective breath? For ages the Howard and Costello message was about the need for fiscal responsibility. Then suddenly the government is rolling in money. Buckets of the stuff are being thrown at various interest groups. In such a climate, trying to tell ordinary voters that the government cannot afford to deal with their concerns is bound to be met by scepticism and resentment.

On the day after my Liberal friend had his unpleasant supermarket experience, a Labor mate reported in from his seat in a different city. 'All my experience on the ground tells me that this election is going better than OK for us,' he said. 'I know that doesn't match up with the published opinion polls. But I can tell you that people are engaged in the election. There is a lot of interest. More people are talking politics than for a very long time. The commentators are claiming voters are not engaged, but I'm finding the punters are more interested than usual at this stage of a campaign.' I suspect that such anecdotal evidence, while it may appear at odds with the findings of published polls, is not inconsistent with the private polling conducted by the political parties themselves. Insiders on both sides seem genuinely convinced that the election is very close – teetering, capable of going either way. The professionals in the Liberal bunker are serious, even nervous. The mood at ALP campaign HQ is surprisingly upbeat. 'The campaign is a corker,' says a key Labor strategist. 'I think we're going to be on the edge of our seats on election night.'

The word 'corker' may be stretching things, but the campaign is fascinating. Apart from anything else, this contest is certainly less predictable than the last three elections. And the struggle between Howard and Mark Latham has an edge that was lacking in the Howard versus Kim Beazley campaigns. Now that Latham has abandoned the Mogadon Man image and reverted to the lively, aggressive style that appealed to Labor MPs when they elected him leader, the personal confrontation should become even more interesting. Unless, that is, the media succeed in shutting Latham down again. After the Labor leader showed a bit of his fiery side in an interview on the Nine network's *Sunday* program, there was an extraordinary amount of journalistic tut-tutting about him 'boiling over' and 'losing his cool'. Because he was in Darwin, a couple of scribes could not resist saying he 'went troppo'. After the boredom of the Great Debate, we should be grateful for a bit of life and colour and spirited argument. Some spontaneity instead of the stage-managed, eye-glazing stuff that passes for campaigning in modern politics. 'I thought it was a good, feisty exchange with Laurie Oakes,' Latham said later when accused of getting hot under the collar. 'That's the way he likes it, and the way I present myself on important issues...' Right on. Stick with it, Mark.

Latham's clash with *The Australian*'s Samantha Maiden at a news conference the same day was in a different category, however. The Labor leader objected to questions about whether he intended to send his children to a government or private school. Latham has exploited his two sons in the campaign, even allowing them to feature in the ALP's television commercials on tax and family policy, so he is hardly in a position to claim that questions about them are out of bounds.

And it was a mistake to allow personal pique about his family to distract attention from the guts of his education policy. The wealthy private schools that would lose funding might be squealing, but Labor's polling suggests that the policy – with its $1.9bn in extra funds for government schools and a big boost for Catholic schools – appeals to swing voters by a margin of two to one.

Howard is campaigning with his usual grim efficiency, and in the end may prove the bookies right in making him a clear favourite. But even Liberal candidates admit that quite a bit of gloss has gone off him as an electoral asset. 'I don't know who'll win,' says a canny long-time observer of the political scene. 'But halfway through the race, you'd have to say Labor's horse is well-positioned and could get there with a strong finish.'

Given the healthy state of the economy, the fact that Labor is still in the race at all is remarkable enough.

Election losers

20 October 2004

It was a miserable Saturday night for Michelle O'Byrne as she watched the election count that took away her Launceston-based seat of Bass and handed it to the Liberal Party. First thing Monday morning she was officially notified that all her entitlements ceased immediately. The car, the phone, the email account: all unceremoniously taken away. The only help the Finance Department offered was some packing cases and the loan of a shredder to help clear out her office. O'Byrne is not complaining. This sort of thing goes with the territory when you represent a marginal seat. But it shows what a brutal game politics is – especially when you lose.

Since the election, huge quantities of newsprint have been devoted to speculation about the plans of the re-elected government and what Labor needs to do to rebuild. But scarcely a thought has been spared for the losers: the MPs from both sides who suddenly find themselves without a job, consigned to irrelevance. It can be a life-changing experience, as Liberal Don Randall found out when he lost the Western Australian seat of Swan in 1998 after just one term in parliament. At the time, he says, it was 'a gut-wrenching personal tragedy'. Bob Baldwin, who lost the NSW seat of Paterson to Labor in the same year, describes it as 'the most gut-wrenching experience I've ever had'.

Randall and Baldwin staged comebacks in 2001, with the result that John Howard refers to them as his 'MacArthurists' – a reference to the World War II general's famous 'I will return' pledge. But they agree the ordeal of losing had changed them. The results of the recent election bear this out. 'Losing made me more focused,' Baldwin says. 'Between 1996 and 1998, I got involved in a whole lot of issues and travelled a lot on committee work. Not any more. These days, I don't waste time on things that are not important to the electorate.' On October 9, he increased his vote by about 5.5 percent in Paterson, much higher than the statewide swing in NSW. Randall is almost fanatically determined not to lose again. He doorknocks his current seat of Canning as no MP has ever doorknocked before. 'Even my wife can't believe how hard I work,' he says. As a result, Randall's hair's breadth 0.4 percent pre-election margin has turned into a comfort zone of 10 percent.

A few months ago, I was guest speaker at a dinner get-together of the Class of 1996, the coalition MPs elected in the anti-Keating landslide that brought the Howard government to power. During the meal, I listened as Randall delivered a pep talk to his colleagues about the forthcoming election. 'Believe me, you don't want to lose,' he warned – and proceeded to tell them how horrible his own experience had been. I got him to repeat it last week.

'It's one heck of a reality check, I can tell you,' Randall said. 'As an MP, you get invitations to lunch and dinner all the time. People keep saying if you weren't in politics, you could earn more money in private enterprise. But when you lose, they avoid you like the plague. You are barely employable. I had been promised the world by colleagues and people in business but after I lost, my phone calls went unreturned. I won't forget the ministerial colleagues who didn't return my calls.' There was huge pressure on his family, he says. His daughter cried for days. It all made him more determined to get back.

'But it may have been a good thing,' Randall reflects. 'When you get into parliament, you suddenly think you're important. You sit up the front in aeroplanes. You automatically become a member of the Qantas Chairman's Lounge. People pick you up in Commonwealth cars. You're made to think you're someone special. But you're not. Losing makes you a better person, a better MP. And it makes you very hungry. Prepared to do whatever it takes to prove you're not finished.' The day after he snatched his narrow victory in Canning in 2001, Randall's bank manager phoned to say congratulations, adding: 'If you hadn't won I'd be coming around to see about selling your house.'

Baldwin says: 'When you lose, you quickly find out there's nothing as ex as an ex-politician. It took me seven months to screw up the courage to visit Canberra again, even though I was doing lobbying work. At first when you lose, coming back is the furthest thing from your mind, because it whacks you so hard. But it made me a better politician because it made me more focused. I'd say to anyone who loses that they should keep trying.'

O'Byrne is not sure about that. 'I'm leaving my options a bit open,' she says. 'It's pretty confronting when you lose. You wonder if you want to risk putting yourself through it again. In a marginal seat, you try to prepare yourself but you still spend a lot of time thinking about why you lost. You can understand the theories of a national swing and the impact of a forestry policy, but it's hard to know how much of it was you, and you keep wondering what you might have done wrong. It knocks you around a bit.'

So far the only jobs she has been offered are unpaid ones. O'Byrne and the other defeated Labor MPs have been in constant phone contact since the election, helping each other through the experience. At this point, though, it is doubtful they would agree with Randall's proposition that losing can be good for you.

The ghost of Gough

27 October 2004

Mark Latham says he regards Gough Whitlam not as a mentor but as a tutor. Unfortunately, he appears to have been a slow learner when it comes to absorbing lessons from the Labor folk hero's mistakes. When Labor won office in 1972, after 23 years in the wilderness, Whitlam considered making Bill Hayden treasurer but sentimentality got the better of him. Frank Crean had been shadow treasurer for 20 years, and the new PM decided it would be unfair not to give him the job in government. It was a moment of weakness Whitlam came to regret. Latham displayed similar sentimentality when he gave the shadow treasury portfolio to Simon Crean, son of Frank, last December. He was warned the failed leader would be incapable of boosting Labor's stocks in the vital economic management area but Latham felt he was in Crean's debt. The consequences of that moment of weakness were reflected in the election result.

Selecting the right person as treasurer – or shadow treasurer – is one of the most important decisions a leader has to make. Whitlam stuffed it up twice. When it became obvious that Crean Snr lacked the toughness to push necessary economic measures through cabinet, Hayden was overlooked again because of a row in which he'd had the temerity to criticise the Great Man over foreign policy as well as economics. Whitlam installed Jim Cairns instead. Cairns proved weaker than Crean and earned the nickname 'Dr Yes'. Hayden did not get the nod until mid-1975. He put economic policy back on track and produced a responsible, cost-cutting budget that was widely praised, but by then it was too late to save the government. Latham, who helped his tutor produce a detailed tome called *The Whitlam Government*, should be well aware of all this.

Yet he made heavy weather of the task of naming a shadow treasurer to take on the job of rebuilding Labor's economic credibility between now and the 2007 poll. His first impulse was to promote close ally and confidante Julia Gillard but that became untenable when he invested just about all the political capital he had left in caucus in the battle to keep Simon Crean on the front bench. His authority was diminished to the point where he could no longer simply insist on getting his own way. But speculation that Gillard would get the job – and the controversy this caused within the ALP – continued for days after the leader had abandoned the idea. Why Latham allowed this to happen is as puzzling as why he allowed Crean's situation to become a crisis. Did he really expect shadow ministers from the Victorian Right faction to shoot themselves in order to save Crean? Both matters got out of hand because of Latham's lack of political management skills.

Gillard was also a victim of Latham's failure in his 10 months as leader (and six months as shadow treasurer before that) to develop any sort of relationship with members of the business community. Labor will not regain economic credibility if it is seen as incapable of engaging with business. The business community wanted a sign that Labor would engage, and that it would adopt a more centrist approach to economic policy. Appointing Gillard would not have sent such a signal. After the election debacle, Latham needed to provide evidence very quickly that he is serious about restoring Labor's economic credentials. Gillard may be talented but she is also relatively inexperienced. In the post-election climate, the party could not afford another L-plater in the key economic portfolio. It should have been obvious all along that opting for a tried and tested performer was the only way to go.

After the caucus meeting which formally elected members of the new shadow ministry, Latham told a news conference Labor needed to learn from the rebuff it received from voters in mortgage-belt areas 'and obviously do as much as we can to improve our economic policy and credentials'. He is not the first Labor leader to face a credibility gap on economic policy. Whitlam's lack of economic expertise was seen as a major problem in 1972. He solved it by announcing during the campaign that, if Labor won, respected economist and former Reserve Bank governor H. C. Coombs would join his staff as economic adviser. (The idea is supposed to have emanated from none other than Rupert Murdoch.) Such a gimmick would not work today. Latham's position is more like Hayden's after he took over from Whitlam as Labor leader in 1977.

After two landslide losses, the party Hayden inherited was in an even worse position than it is now. As Hayden wrote in his autobiography: 'After the spectacular way in which the Whitlam government breached the outer limits of prudent economic management, our most important need was to re-establish public trust in our ability to manage the economy soberly…Our task would be to persistently hammer away and create a credible set of measures over many months to demonstrate that the new management would be different and reliable.' Hayden applied himself single-mindedly to achieving that, emphasising fiscal caution and tailoring policies to economic priorities. It was a long, hard process but he restored credibility to the point where Labor almost regained office in 1980. (Hawke reaped the ultimate benefit of Hayden's hard work three years later.) Latham and his new economic team need to take a leaf out of Hayden's book. Hayden may not be a Labor folk hero like Whitlam but he is likely to be a more useful tutor in the party's present circumstances.

Captain Wacky

1 December 2004

It was great to see him back. Just when the ALP thought things could not get any worse, Paul Keating made a brief return to the political stage. There was Captain Wacky whacking Stephen Conroy and the Labor Party's national office on Mark Latham's behalf. Mad Paul lining up with Mad Mark. It was a spectacle unlikely to give much comfort to sane and sober members of caucus.

At Labor's official campaign launch a week and a half out from the election, some care was taken to hide Keating. Gough Whitlam arrived to enthusiastic applause and was hugged by Latham in front of the cameras. Keating was moved in quietly, largely unnoticed by the crowd, and Latham stayed away. A Latham–Keating hug would have been too much of a gift to the Liberals, ready-made material for another hard-hitting commercial panicking the punters over interest rates.

Keating's contribution to Latham's poll defeat was considerable – the memory of those 17.5 percent mortgage rates when he was treasurer. And yet he charged forth – in an interview with *The Age* – to blame the Labor machine for the party's dreadful result. The organisation people involved in the campaign were 'nincompoops', he said, skilled only at 'snatching defeat from the jaws of victory'. He had been a victim of these same incompetents in his 1996 loss. The solution, said Keating, was for Labor's election campaigns to be run entirely from the leader's office.

It is true that Labor's campaign machine was outperformed by the Liberal organisation. But given that Latham, in Labor's internal post-mortems, bagged his former chief of staff and admitted his office had not been adequately prepared for the election, the brilliance of Keating's proposal was not immediately apparent. And the thought of what might have happened in the 1996 election had Keating been in sole command is mind-boggling. Keating was on a different planet from the rest of us in that campaign. He was the issue. Voters could tolerate him no longer. John Howard achieved an overwhelming victory primarily because he was not Paul Keating. And yet, when the campaign began, Keating abused people in the media – this columnist included – for being too thick to understand that it was a foreign policy election and he would win it on the strength of his secretly negotiated treaty with Indonesia's President Suharto.

Keating's intervention came on the day Conroy, Labor's deputy Senate leader, offered a loyalty pledge of sorts after being accused by Latham of running a jihad against him via media leaks. 'If he wants to challenge Latham, he should at least get off Latham's front bench,' Keating thundered. 'This guy believes in having his cake and eating it too.' Pardon? Can this be the same Keating who started white-anting Bob Hawke well before launching a challenge, and who departed the front bench only when that first challenge failed? The same Keating who used to call Hawke 'Old Jellyback'? The Keating who undercut Hawke with the notorious Placido Domingo speech at a press gallery dinner? There is no doubt Latham needs allies, but whether he needs allies like Keating – encouraging his autocratic approach, his bare-knuckle aggression and his propensity to blame others for the election loss – is another matter.

Latham's leadership is now in deep trouble. Michael Costello, Kim Beazley's former chief of staff, did not miss when he invoked Monty Python's best-known sketch to dub him a dead parrot. Some Labor MPs believe it was the Costello column that tipped Latham over the edge and had him threatening to demand that caucus sack Conroy as deputy Senate leader – a course of action that would have thrust the party into a huge crisis and given Latham nothing more than a pyrrhic victory. But more significant was Michelle Grattan's *Sunday Age* column branding Latham 'a dead leader walking'. Grattan is a very cautious journalist, noted for scrupulous checking of facts and the avoidance of sensationalism of any kind. When she delivers such a judgment, it has to be taken seriously.

Latham singled out Conroy, a Beazley supporter in last year's leadership brawls, as a scapegoat for the recent flood of damaging leaks. Conroy has made no secret of his dislike of Latham and was therefore an obvious candidate. The truth, though, is that many of the most damaging stories have come from former Latham supporters. Some of them felt they were dudded by him in the post-election shaping of his shadow cabinet. Latham can't threaten to sack all the leakers. There are too many. And every time he precipitates a crisis, he damages himself and makes his leadership position even more shaky. All he can do is try to improve his own performance. He still has time – but not much.

Latham's remaining supporters argue he is not in danger because there is no alternative leader in sight. They kid themselves. Beazley means it when he says he will not challenge again, but if drafted he would serve. Stephen Smith and Wayne Swan are working loyally under Latham, but if the party's fortunes continued to head south, no one believes they would sit on their hands and do nothing indefinitely. And there is Kevin Rudd, the shadow foreign minister. While well-regarded in the community, Rudd has lacked support in the caucus, but there are signs that could be changing. If the caucus concludes that Latham really is a dead parrot walking, an alternative leader will be found. What Latham needs to survive is some un-Keating-like behaviour – consultation, teamwork, and careful people management.

The reins of King John

15 December 2004

In all the post-election profiles of a victorious John Howard, one line stood out. *The Australian*'s Paul Kelly provoked it with the suggestion that, like Malcolm Fraser before him, Howard might fail to seize the chances provided by a Senate majority. 'Just hang around and see,' retorted the PM. Thumping his chest like that is most un-Howard-like, but given that he has been one of those most critical of Fraser for wasting the opportunities inherent in control of both Houses of parliament, a tart response was probably to be expected. Howard plans to make the most of a piece of good fortune he never thought would come his way.

Winning control of the Senate was an accident. It arose out of a disagreement between the Liberals and the National Party in Queensland which saw the Nationals run a separate ticket and – against all the odds – get their man elected. Howard is not going to look a gift horse in the mouth. He has made it clear he will use the opportunity to sell the rest of Telstra, change media ownership laws, and push through industrial relations legislation hitherto blocked by Labor and the minor parties. But he intends to go a lot further when the new senators take their places in July 2005.

'There is no doubt the prospect of having the numbers in the Senate has reignited the interest of some in doing things on a policy front that previously did not seem achievable,' Howard said in one of his end-of-year interviews. The buzz within the government is that the focus will be on measures that boost productivity. 'Big items, not tinkering,' says one plugged-in Liberal MP. 'Infrastructure. More industrial relations reforms. Taxation. Productivity issues that need bold attention.' It is the success of the economy that has driven the coalition's electoral success, and Senate control is seen as a means of continuing that.

Concern that Howard might do a Fraser was sparked in some quarters by his repeated public assurances that the government will not let the increased power go to its head. But Howard does not mean that the power will not be used – merely that it will be used sensibly and in a measured way. It is about not frightening the horses. 'Managing the expectations of various interest groups now we have the Senate is going to be really hard,' says a senior coalition figure. 'A lot of people have the view that we can now do anything we want. It's not helped by the cock-a-hoop attitude of a lot of backbenchers and some ministers.' Howard has already started managing those expectations.

At the final party meeting of 2004, the PM described it as one of the coalition's best years to date. It was certainly Howard's year, and it has set him up for an even better 2005 as long as he plays his cards right. The thumping election win took even him by surprise. He told a radio interviewer during parliament's final sitting week: 'If I'd been put against a wall at half-past-four in the afternoon [on election day] and told my life depended on getting the prediction right, I would have said we'd won, probably with the loss of two or three or four seats.' Such a result, he added, 'would have produced a whole different psychology and dynamic in the aftermath of the election'. He is right. Had Labor made up ground and come within three or four seats of victory, Mark Latham would not be a pariah and the ALP would not be tearing itself apart. The coalition would be soul-searching after a narrow escape.

But the scale of Howard's win left the government in such a strong position and Labor so weakened that many Liberal and National party MPs believe they do not have to worry about opposition, at least for the next three years. It is a dangerous frame of mind and Howard, for one, knows better. Opposition will rear its head in other ways. In the 1980s when the coalition was on the ropes, other groups came to the fore to provide opposition to the Hawke government. The National Farmers' Federation and the Business Council of Australia were two of them. In such circumstances, dissenters within the ruling party are likely to emerge as an important force as well. The media, too, tends to take on more of an opposition role to help fill the vacuum.

So, even if Labor is determined to become irrelevant and the minor parties no longer pack a punch in a coalition-controlled Senate, the government will still find itself under plenty of scrutiny. Becoming too hairy-chested would be unwise. The power the government will have as of mid-2005 involves a new set of challenges not faced for 30 years. 'We have to take people with us,' says a Liberal source close to the PM. 'Even with the numbers in the Senate, we need to "sell" what we do, make a proper case for it. Apart from anything else, we could get internal division if we don't handle things carefully.'

That is particularly the case where social issues are concerned, which is another good reason why Howard intends to make his big hits in areas related to productivity. On those there is a large degree of unanimity within the coalition. This is Howard's chance to create a truly impressive legacy. Careful planning will be required. The question of his future – whether or when he should hand over the reins to Peter Costello – will be banished from his mind while he manages his new agenda through the transformed parliament. Then, in 18 months or so, he will sit back and survey what he has achieved. If he is satisfied, that is the point at which he is likely to start thinking about retirement.

2005

The comeback kid

26 January 2005

Two days after Mark Latham made his graceless exit from politics, Kim Beazley held a council of war with key factional heavies over lunch at a restaurant rejoicing in the name 'The Meat and Wine Company' in Sydney's Darling Harbour. Among those present were Mark Arbib, secretary of the NSW ALP branch, Senator Stephen Conroy from the Victorian Right, Wayne Swan from the same faction in Queensland, and Anthony Albanese from the NSW Left. As they discussed how to steamroll Kevin Rudd and lock in a majority of caucus votes behind Beazley, and agreed there'd be no deals to accommodate Julia Gillard's ambitions, a young waiter butted in to ask the would-be born-again leader to autograph a plate for the restaurant. There were frequent interruptions as diners wished Beazley well in the leadership ballot. 'The country needs you,' said one.

The most interesting question to arise from Labor's latest leadership contest is why Beazley would want the job. Having lost two elections in his first stint as opposition leader and then been twice rejected in leadership ballots against Simon Crean and Latham, why would he risk humiliation again? He must have known when he decided to run that if he lost a third leadership ballot, he'd be a laughing stock. He certainly had plenty of people – including close mate and shrewd political judge Robert Ray – telling him that, if he did make a comeback, he had virtually no chance of winning the 2007 election and would simply be derided as a three-time loser. But he went ahead. Why?

Part of the answer lies in the kind of thing that happened at the restaurant. 'Put yourself in Kim's shoes,' says a friend of Beazley. 'Wherever he goes, people have been saying they want him back. That's bound to have an effect.' But there has to be a more substantial reason than that. Perhaps he feels guilt about mistakes made and opportunities missed last time? 'It's not guilt,' argues an experienced political operator from whom Beazley has sought advice recently. 'But he does have a sense of unfinished business. He's had a long time to reflect on what might have been.' According to another member of the group masterminding Beazley's comeback bid: 'Kim does have that old-fashioned sense of service to the country. He saw this as an act of loyalty to the country and the party.'

Beazley also wanted the leadership again because of a genuine belief he is capable of winning the next election, despite the dreadful position Labor is in as a result of the Latham experiment. Not many in the ALP share this optimism. Some see Beazley's confidence as little short of delusional. But Beazley reasons that he won more votes than John Howard in the 1998 election, did well in 2001 given the impact of 9/11 and *Tampa*, and would be a more effective leader now because he has learned from his mistakes. The ascendancy Howard enjoys has a great deal to do with how the PM made just about every mistake in the book earlier in his career and honed his political instincts and skills as a result. Beazley has been around long enough to learn the tricks of the trade. Labor's other wannabes have not.

No one could doubt the strength of the Bomber's desire to return to the leadership. Strange though the phrase sounds when applied to Beazley, he was clearly hungry for it. One of those who did his dirty work in previous contests told him: 'If you want it, you'll have to go and take it without fucking around.' He took that to heart, made his own phone calls, did his own arm-twisting, personally supervised the wheeling and dealing. His willingness to risk further personal hurt and damage to his reputation belied the claim he lacks ticker. 'I hope that's the key this time around; the fact that he is really driven,' said a colleague a few days before caucus met.

Beazley promised colleagues they would see big changes if he got the leadership again. His pledge to set up house somewhere in the eastern states rather than being isolated and out of touch with the news cycle in Perth was a major concession. He undertook to seek advice more widely within the shadow ministry, caucus committees and the broader party. He promised he would recruit staff who would challenge him, fight his tendency to waffle and help him put out punchier political messages.

And certainly – a point made by his former chief of staff Michael Costello – Beazley is tougher than he used to be. For a long time, things came very easily to him in politics. He had an armchair ride into parliament, the ministry and leadership. But political life has been very tough for him in recent years. He has been battered from all directions: by the government, the media and his own party. He could have bailed out; there have been tempting job offers. But he built up scar tissue and carried on, in stark contrast to the way Latham eventually fell apart under pressure.

A former critic best summed up the hopes of realists in the Beazley camp as Rudd tapped the mat, virtually guaranteeing the Bomber's return as leader: 'Kim might not win the next election. But as long as he performs well, rebuilds Labor's vote, picks up seats, and provides some air cover for people such as Rudd, Wayne Swan, Stephen Smith and Julia Gillard while they develop, it will be no mean achievement. He will be seen as the bloke who picked up the pieces, put the show together again, and moved us back into contention.'

Rorts and all

16 February 2005

Phillip Edman is a cabinetmaker by trade, the sort of knockabout bloke who not so long ago would have been expected to vote Labor. He owns a small furniture firm in Western Australia, and a few years back bought his dream house at Shoalwater, south of Perth. After seeing boats smashed against the shore in a storm, Edman threw himself into the fight for a marina in Rockingham, agitating for funds for a feasibility and environmental impact study. As president of the Rockingham Marina Action Group, and at that stage not a member of any political party, he wrote to his local federal MP, Kim Beazley, the member for Brand, seeking support. That was in June 2003.

A few weeks later, when Beazley had not replied, Edman chanced his arm and dialled the Prime Minister's number in Canberra. He was astonished by what happened. A staffer listened to his spiel, told him about a scheme called the Regional Partnerships Program, and immediately referred him to the appropriate minister's office. Edman was informed the marina project would be eligible for a Regional Partnerships grant and given details on how to lodge an application. A few months later, he was invited to Canberra to put his case directly to De-Anne Kelly, parliamentary secretary in charge of the scheme, and got to meet John Howard. In early 2004, Justice Minister Chris Ellison turned up in Rockingham with a media entourage to hand over a large, laminated cheque for $242 000.

Beazley never did reply to the original letter – though, according to Edman, 'he invited me to his office and gave me a bear hug and a cup of tea'. In a second letter to Beazley four months after the first, Edman said: 'When I met you…I told you about Regional Solution Partnerships and how the people in Brand could apply for a federal grant for an environmental study for a marina. Your response was that you didn't think we could apply for the grant because we were not regional. Just to keep you informed, we could apply and we got the grant.' Ouch! Beazley tried desperately to get onto the bandwagon after that. It was too late.

Edman joined the Liberal Party and, with his profile boosted by the marina grant, became the party's candidate in Brand for last October's poll. He was associated with the local council in three other well-publicised Regional Partnerships grants – for an environmental walk, a plan to turn the underused Rockingham oval into a village green and the sinking of an old tuna boat as the first stage of a proposed dive park. The PM visited the electorate to announce the dive park grant with Edman beside him. Beazley was involved in none of the grant applications. In the election, his margin in Brand was cut from a safe 10 percent to a much more dicey 4.5 percent. Mark Latham may deserve some of the credit, but the prominence Edman gained was clearly of major significance.

Some of Beazley's critics claim this story illustrates how, pre-occupied with regaining the Labor leadership, he dropped the ball in his electorate. There may be some truth in this. But a more interesting and important lesson concerns the potency of the coalition's Regional Partnerships pork barrel as a political weapon. In the early 1990s, the Keating government had its own barrel of pork, the community, cultural, recreational and sporting facilities program, which enabled cash to be doled out at the community level to win votes. What became known as Sports Rorts was essentially defensive in political intent. The primary aim was to help Labor hold on to its marginals in the 1993 poll. Labor MPs could shore up support by securing grants for projects, usually sports-related, in their electorates. But coalition MPs were in the loop and could also apply for grants. Every MP was given data on how to lodge applications. Any sitting member could take advantage of the scheme and gain kudos in his or her seat. Regional Partnerships is different and not only because Sports Rorts was a penny-ante scheme by comparison.

Like Sports Rorts, Regional Partnerships helps government MPs to defend marginal seats. But it is also designed as an attack weapon to dislodge opposition MPs. Before last year's election, when grants went to seats held by Labor or independents, the sitting members were left out in the cold. Announcements were made by 'patron' Liberal or National Party senators assigned to those seats, with coalition candidates involved as prominently as possible. It was a means of boosting the profile of Liberal and National party candidates. 'A coalition candidate could be made to look like a more effective local member,' claims a Labor frontbencher.

Brand was slightly different in that Edman in the beginning was not a Liberal candidate. But when Beazley realised how effectively Edman was using the marina grant, the only way he could get into the act was to lobby the state Labor government to also grant money for the project. Beazley later told a friend: 'I thought, "My God! If that's happening here, what's it like in other places?" It's really terrible stuff.' Attacking Labor over Sports Rorts in 1994, Peter Costello told parliament: 'If governments get the idea that they can spend $30m to buy elections, that is the end of open, fair and honest elections in this country.' The Regional Partnerships price tag is about $300m.

Godfather of the Liberals

13 April 2005

One of the most deadly serious factional struggles seen in Australian politics for a very long time has now hit the tabloid headlines. 'Liberals fight religious takeover', trumpeted Sydney's *Daily Telegraph*. The story quoted moderate NSW Liberals warning of a takeover of the state party by the religious Right and vowing to wage 'an almighty war' against it. Over the preceding couple of weeks, articles on the tightening grip of Christian conservatives on the NSW Liberal Party had also appeared in broadsheets – *The Australian* and *The Sydney Morning Herald*.

The sudden burst of media coverage is generated by the moderates – the group that calls itself The Group – and the reason is obvious. 'They can't stop the juggernaut,' says a Liberal branch member allied with the Right faction that is clearly in the ascendant. 'The Left's only defence now is to go public.' Their aim, presumably, is to create concern that disunity and the possibility of a Liberal lurch to the Right will result in a damaging electoral backlash. That would put pressure on the party leadership, including the Prime Minister, to intervene. But in the unlikely event that he was tempted to buy in, even John Howard would find the process very difficult to stop.

The NSW Liberals have always been deeply factionalised, but for most of the past 25 years The Group has been in charge. Not any more. The hardline conservatives have gradually been taking over branches. They have won control of the NSW Young Liberals and the state Liberal Women's Council which used to be moderate strongholds. Now the Right is poised to flex its muscles in the election for the party's state executive next month. Understandably, moderate Liberal MPs – state and federal – are starting to feel decidedly nervous. The Group has played its factional politics hard over the years. The moderates have not gone out of their way to share the spoils. Now it looks as though the boot may be on the other foot.

The headlines suggesting that religion is playing a big part in all this – 'In God these Libs trust' in *The Australian* and 'On a right wing and a prayer' in the *SMH* – are not sensationalising the situation. They are stating the simple truth. The organisational brain behind the Right's takeover is NSW Upper House MP David Clarke, a Catholic associated – according to friends – with the ultra-conservative Opus Dei movement. Opus Dei's purpose, as described by *The Columbia Encyclopedia*, is to promote traditional Catholic values and teaching and oppose liberalism and immorality.

Churches – not just the Catholic Church – provide Clarke with recruits to take over Liberal branches. He told the *SMH*: 'I encourage Christians to get active in public life, whether they are Coptic Christians, Mormons, Catholics, Anglicans or Pentecostals.' Says a Clarke supporter: 'Christians here are getting more interested in politics, just as they have in the United States. And that has given the Right a new recruiting pond. A huge one.' The Group is not averse to stacking branches, either, but its opportunities for recruitment are limited, whereas – to quote the Clarke supporter again – 'the churches, if they really get involved…it's just bottomless'.

Clarke is more than a numbers man. He has, it is said, 'a strange charisma'. A Liberal friend told me once: 'He's got people who will spill blood for him. If David Clarke walked into a room, you wouldn't notice him. But once you start a conversation, you are drawn to him by the strength of his beliefs.' He certainly has strong beliefs on such issues as drugs, homosexual relationships, gay marriage, the age of consent and abortion. In January, at an anti-abortion forum, Clarke urged his audience to join the branches of mainstream political parties to push for a ban on 'the blackest of crimes' and to maximise their influence through preselection ballots. This hardline moral agenda, not any personal ambition, is what drives him.

Clarke's allies include such conservative federal politicians as Bronwyn Bishop and Howard confidant Senator Bill Heffernan. The moderate NSW Liberal senator Marise Payne is very definitely on the faction's hit list. But the Clarke forces do not appear to be targeting incumbent state Liberal MPs at this stage, even though a majority of them are in the moderate camp. To start knocking off sitting MPs would be provocative and possibly counter-productive. The Right seems to have concentrated instead on winning control in marginal seats that the Liberals need to win to form government. As a result, if the moderate opposition leader John Brogden is victorious at the next election, he will bring into the parliament a swag of Liberals who oppose him ideologically. That would give the religious Right considerable clout in the way an incoming Liberal government dealt with moral issues.

So far, the move by the religious Right to get control of the Liberal Party is largely confined to NSW – but it is unlikely that this will remain the case for long. What happens in the NSW party will be watched closely by Liberals elsewhere. There is, after all, no reason churches should not also provide a fertile recruiting ground for Clarke's soulmates in other states.

Broken promise = resignation

20 April 2005

Earlier this year, when a huge surf was battering most of the NSW coast, Tony Abbott grabbed his board and headed for the beach. The wave he caught was massive, and his surfing skills were not up to the task. He was smashed into the sand, the impact tearing his hamstring away from his pelvis. 'If you want to keep running,' Abbott's doctor told him, 'you'll need to have it surgically repaired.' Giving up marathons was more than the Health Minister was prepared to contemplate, so this week he went under the knife.

But the wave that put Abbott in hospital was nothing compared with the political dumper that crashed over him when the Prime Minister announced that Medicare safety net thresholds would be raised, drastically reducing the number of people who would benefit. It was a shameless breach of a core election promise, and Abbott's reputation was inextricably linked to that promise. In a TV interview before the election, he had given 'an absolutely rock-solid, iron-clad commitment' that the thresholds would not be altered. There was no wriggle room. Abbott's cabinet colleagues made a liar of him, in full knowledge of what they were doing.

His word is now worthless, his credibility shot – not permanently, perhaps, but for a long time. Future commitments from Abbott will be greeted by horse laughs. He knows it, too. 'I understand your scorn,' he said repeatedly when he appeared on the Nine network's *Sunday* program. 'This will be difficult for you but we'll all help,' John Howard had reassured him when cabinet's Expenditure Review Committee made the decision. The truth, though, is that no one can help. No surgery can repair the damage Abbott has suffered to his political standing. 'Peter Costello will be laughing,' a NSW Liberal told me. His point was that any chance of Abbott becoming a rival for the Liberal leadership is now gone. It was Costello and Finance Minister Nick Minchin who insisted the promise had to be jettisoned.

Presumably, as a religious man, Abbott likes to think of himself as principled. I believe he is that. He should have resigned. He not only had the 'rock-solid iron-clad commitment' quote to explain away. He had also told a campaign news conference: 'I absolutely guarantee that the safety net, as the government has put it into operation, will continue. I absolutely guarantee it.' In light of that, how he can stay on as Minister and retain his self-respect is a mystery. Abbott says the thought of resignation passed through his head, 'but not seriously'. Had he taken it seriously, he might have done himself a favour. By resigning, he would have enhanced his reputation – shown himself as a politician who does not take his commitment lightly, rather than just another sleazy opportunist.

And there were ways of doing it without breaching cabinet solidarity. 'The cabinet is right,' Abbott could have said. 'The cost of the safety net was blowing out to levels we did not expect. Economic responsibility required that the thresholds be raised. I support the decision. However, there is no getting away from the fact that during the election campaign I misled voters. It was inadvertent – at the time I had no reason to believe that changes to the safety net would be necessary – but I must accept responsibility for what I said.' When people got over the shock of a politician behaving honourably, he would have departed the ministry a hero. His time in the sin bin could have been brief. Having lifted himself above the grubby ruck, he might even have improved his career prospects. But politicians do not think that way any more. Once they start the climb up the greasy pole, they cling on no matter what.

Abbott should not be hung out to dry on his own. He uttered the solemn pledge that turned out to be a con, but Howard and Costello probably deserve more blame. Howard claims now that the extent of the blow-out was not evident before the election, but that is simply untrue. When Treasury examined Labor's health policy before the poll, under the so-called Charter of Budget Honesty, it estimated savings from the proposal to abolish the safety net at $1.3bn over four years – three times the government's original costing of the scheme. So Howard and Costello knew about the blow-out then. Which means they were also aware before the election that the safety net would almost certainly have to be reined in, but gave no inkling of that to voters or, apparently, to Abbott.

Howard and Costello are the government's supposed economic experts. They are the ones who spearheaded the attack on Mark Latham's economic credibility. They blasted Labor over the economic irresponsibility of its Medicare Gold policy while knowing very well that what Howard called 'the you-beaut Medicare safety net' was equally open-ended. And they let Abbott's simplistic statements about the financing of the safety net stand.

At one point in the election campaign, while admitting that the safety net was costing more than originally anticipated, Abbott said: 'This is not an indication that there's a problem with the safety net. It's an indication of the need for the safety net.' He added that 'like everything under the medical benefits scheme, it [the safety net] is not a budget-limited bureaucratically controlled program'. Had someone on the Labor side made statements like that, Howard and Costello would have torn them apart.

Abbott is a talented politician. He will keep on running, and his career may eventually recover. But the safety net saga will slow him down a lot more than the injured hammy.

Straining credibility

27 April 2005

Brendan Nelson had some strong advice for the Liberal Party when he delivered the inaugural Dame Pattie Menzies Oration recently. The first priority, he said, was that 'we should not ever lose sight of what it is in which we believe'. For those who recall the federal Education Minister's history, it was a delicious moment. This is a man who was identified with the Labor Party for 20 years, before changing sides to win Liberal preselection for Bradfield on Sydney's North Shore, one of the safest Liberal seats in the country. A man, moreover, who – on his own admission – publicly lied about his political loyalties. And here he was lecturing an audience of Liberal Party faithful about the importance of belief in politics.

When Nelson made his first overtures to the Liberal Party – he had the South Australian seat of Boothby in his sights – he was branded a 'carpetbagger'. The then-president of the Australian Medical Association bitterly resented the description, but it was apt. The original 'carpetbaggers' were itinerant bankers in the American wild west who carried their money in bags made from old carpets. The term was soon appropriated for politics. 'Carpetbagger' came to mean, as defined in William Safire's *Political Dictionary*, 'an outlander moving into a new area to seek political power at the expense of the native politicians'.

Nelson is still about seeking political power. His Dame Pattie Menzies speech was part of the power struggle in the parliamentary Liberal Party in anticipation of John Howard's departure. Most of Nelson's colleagues believe his goal is to become deputy leader of the party under Peter Costello, but some are convinced he is aiming higher than that. They see him positioning himself for the top job in the hope that Howard stays on long enough for Costello to lose either his gloss or his enthusiasm. After all, before he had even been elected to parliament, Nelson told journalists he wanted to be prime minister.

Howard and Costello are both being very careful in public to say nothing that will set the leadership hares running. The issue is being carefully managed. There is, however, a lot of background noise. In *The Australian*, for example, Dennis Shanahan – closer to the PM than any other press gallery journalist – reported that Costello was offered a portfolio swap with Foreign Minister Alexander Downer in the middle of the last parliamentary term after Howard decided against retirement. That boosted Downer's stocks in manoeuvring for the deputy leadership and fed into current speculation that 10 budgets is enough for Costello and a new job would allow a necessary broadening of his image. There was reporting of rumours that key Howard staffers were seeking employment elsewhere, aimed at planting the suggestion that their boss might not be intending to stick around for long. Malcolm Farr, covering the PM's latest overseas trip for Sydney's *Daily Telegraph*, filed a story from China headed 'Wait your turn, Pete'. It said 'John Howard is committed to a "smooth transition" to Peter Costello – but later rather than sooner'. And Andrew Bolt in Melbourne's *Herald-Sun* wrote a long column claiming Costello had deliberately used the Medicare safety net issue to humiliate Tony Abbott and destroy him as a potential leadership rival. Rightly or wrongly, that article was widely seen as the result of a briefing from the Costello camp – tit for tat for an alleged anti-Costello leak by Abbott to *The Age* to which Bolt pointedly referred.

All that, and more, in just one week. The leaks and counter-leaks show that, behind the scenes, the contest is becoming very willing. The Nelson speech is further evidence. He roamed well beyond his portfolio, discussing everything from taxation reform to Aboriginal welfare to the virtues of nuclear energy, putting on display his credentials for a leadership role. And from some quarters in the party the reaction was hostile. Abbott supporters, seeing Nelson as a threat to their man's hopes of becoming deputy leader, were particularly angry. As one of them put it: 'He's trying to run past Tony while he's down.' Another said that Nelson was showing naked opportunism 'at a time when most Liberals realise it's a time to circle the wagons'.

One of the most vivid TV images of the 1993 federal election campaign was Nelson, four days before the poll, shouting at a crowd: 'I have never voted Liberal in my life.' Not long after the election, he started trailing his coat for a seat, but for some time refused to reveal which party he wanted to represent. In 1994, the then-AMA vice-president, David Weedon, said most members of the AMA would expect Nelson to become an ALP candidate. Asked at that time if it was true that he had joined the Liberals, Nelson replied: 'I'm not prepared to say…It's like asking somebody to show you their tax return.'

But the following year Nelson made his lunge for Liberal preselection, announcing that his 'I have never voted Liberal' statement was a lie. He had told the lie, he said, because he was 'being physically jostled, abused and at one stage spat upon' at the time. His new claim was: 'I have voted Liberal in every election since 1987, even though in 1988 I rejoined the Labor Party.' Why, then, had he retained ALP membership? 'I was trying to push things important to the AMA. There was a Labor government in Canberra so it didn't do any harm to remain in the party.'

Another line that stood out in the Nelson oration was this: 'Although we admire talent, it's character that really counts.' That makes the story of Nelson's move into the Liberal Party even more interesting and relevant.

Political miracle

6 July 2005

Workplace Relations Minister Kevin Andrews said of the government's planned rewrite of industrial relations laws last weekend: 'This is not radical change.' Earlier he had asserted that the proposals amounted to the most significant change since the *Conciliation and Arbitration Act* of 1904. Both statements cannot be right. Similarly – as Australian Workers Union national secretary Bill Shorten has pointed out – unions cannot be both 'a critically important problem and so irrelevant as to be facing extinction', as the government would have us believe. The coalition is talking a fair bit of nonsense in the growing IR debate. It had better hope the punters don't notice.

Cardinal George Pell has put his finger on the central weakness in the push to turn Australia's IR system upside-down. 'We've had a long period of prosperity in Australia,' he told *The Australian Financial Review*. 'I think that means that the necessity for radical change needs to be established.' Trade union and ALP figures have made the same point, but coming from Australia's most senior Catholic Church leader – a man with no axe to grind and who would be considered a friend of the Prime Minister – it has extra impact. The Australian economy has enjoyed an unprecedented period of growth. Inflation is low, interest rates are low, unemployment is at a very low level and still apparently falling, the government boasts about all the new jobs that have been created, and industrial disputation is just about non-existent.

So why tamper with a system that seems to be working? If it ain't broke, don't fix it. The government should be required to show where the system is broke and how the proposed repairs will improve things, but it has hardly even pretended to make a serious case for change. One result is a large degree of scepticism in the media about its intentions. Even *The Australian*'s Dennis Shanahan, the press gallery journalist regarded as closest to John Howard, penned a piece under the heading: 'A rude shock may await the PM if he doesn't temper his labour market reforms.' Shanahan's warning – that the IR campaign 'could do more damage to the government than its commitment to Iraq' – should give Howard pause for thought.

Throwing himself into the fight against the IR changes has given Kim Beazley a boost. Being cheered by 100 000 workers at a Melbourne rally is a great antidote to the whingeing and whining of Harry Quick and other disaffected members of caucus. Suddenly the Labor leader is seen to be standing for something, fighting for something. While the likes of Mark Latham and John Faulkner undermine him by focusing attention on Labor's problems, Beazley is doing what opposition leaders are supposed to do: he is getting stuck into the government. One senior ALP figure says: 'This is an issue that will galvanise the labour movement. Kim's critics will be starved of oxygen.' Perhaps. Certainly Beazley, probably more than anyone else in caucus, understands trade unions. And his speeches at the rallies against Howard's IR legislation showed passion and commitment. They were a reminder of how good a performer he can be in a campaign.

There are risks for Beazley, of course. Voters do not like union militancy, and if the ACTU campaign against the legislation results in disruption, the ALP will suffer by association. But union leaders are treating the campaign as a hearts-and-minds exercise, and are being careful not to get the public offside. So far, in terms of consciousness raising, the protest rallies and union-sponsored ads have had an effect. Proof of that is the government's decision to spend millions of dollars of taxpayers' money to counter the union case.

The risks for the government are greater. What is involved is a core living standards issue. Just as the coalition ran an election scare campaign against Labor on interest rates, the ALP and the unions now have the opportunity to run an equally tough scare campaign on a threat to penalty rates, shift allowances and other important employment conditions. Like tax, this is bread-and-butter stuff to millions of Australians. Howard will be hoping that the economy continues to thrive while he gets the IR changes into law and bedded down. While economic growth continues and employers are hiring, the potential downside of the changes will be masked. But if growth slows and jobs become scarcer, downward pressure on wages and working conditions will start to be felt – not just by battlers, but by middle Australia as well – and the politics will get decidedly uncomfortable for the government.

There is concern in some sections of the coalition that Howard, Andrews and Co may have gone into battle without proper preparation. A degree of ad hoccery has been evident in, for example, confusion over whether a 40-hour week or 38 hours would be the baseline. The suspicion is that the government had to throw something together quickly to avoid accusations it was wasting its Upper House majority. Howard's claim that the government has a mandate for the changes is weak – the most contentious aspects were never mentioned before last year's election.

Shorten says: 'This is a 900-day campaign until the next election.' But he also concedes that the ACTU and the ALP are hoping for results before that. If Howard thinks working Australians 'are going to get disturbed by the pace and the size and the radicalism of the changes', he says, 'there's a chance he may back off'.

But IR has been Howard's obsession since he entered politics. His heir apparent, Peter Costello, is even more of a hard liner on the issue. They will not be easily diverted from something so ideologically important to them.

Latham's mind

21 September 2005

It may not have been a close election, but it was too close for comfort just the same. As ALP president Barry Jones reminded us at the weekend, at one point in the months leading up to last October's vote, the opinion polls actually had Mark Latham ahead of John Howard as preferred leader. There were moments during the campaign when Latham was seen to be doing well and a Labor victory looked far from an impossibility. And in the election itself, it only needed fewer than three more voters in every 100 to cast their ballots for Labor instead of Liberal or National and Latham would now be prime minister.

The weird and ugly mind that penned *The Latham Diaries* would be running the country. The anger, viciousness and near-paranoia evident in the attacks on just about everyone who matters in the Labor Party would have been let loose upon the land. The responsibility for dealing with a terrorist attack or other emergency would be in the hands of a man whose temperament, it now transpires, could not stand up to an election loss or even a bit of intra-party argy-bargy. Our most important alliance, that with the United States, would be in jeopardy under an Australian leader holding the private belief – one which he kept from the electorate – that it is a form of neo-colonialism and should be ditched. It does not bear thinking about.

Barry Jones says you can't 'absolutely' say Latham would have been a disastrous prime minister. Oh, yeah? Tell that to the radio talkback callers disgusted and shocked by the former Labor leader's behaviour. In fact, tell it to just about anyone who watched the Andrew Denton interview. Rarely, if ever, has an election result been so quickly and decisively validated. By his own words and actions around the publication of his poisonous book, the failed and embittered former Labor leader has shown he was not fit to be prime minister. God knows what might have happened if he had made it to the Lodge.

Kim Beazley, at his first news conference responding to Latham's bucket of bile, said: 'If Mark had become prime minister, he would have had around him an absolutely first-class front bench which would have taken care of any emergency situation that arose...If anything went seriously wrong with the leadership while we were in office, we would have dealt with it.' In other words, if Latham had gone off the rails as prime minister, his senior colleagues would have moved to get rid of him. Given how difficult it is to oust leaders, especially in government, that is cold comfort. And the fact that Beazley felt the need to make the point served to underline how flaky the former leader is now perceived to be and how risky a Latham prime ministership would have been.

Labor will not be irreparably damaged by Latham's attacks on the party and on Beazley and other prominent figures. In fact, the immediate result has been to bolster party unity. Even Labor MPs who have been critical of Beazley are now rallying around the leader against a common enemy – one who dismisses caucus members as 'snakes and sewer rats' and describes the party he once led as a 'shitcan'. By launching a highly personal and entirely unconvincing onslaught against the current leader, Latham has strengthened Beazley's position, not weakened it. Muttering about Beazley's performance has largely ceased, thanks to his predecessor's toxic tome. The anti-Beazley forces were, almost by definition, pro-Latham forces. They are in full retreat. An indication of the change is that Jones, who used to dismiss the Bomber as 'closer to John Howard than...to me' now claims approvingly that 'Beazley, to a very large extent, has reinvented himself'.

But Labor cannot avoid blame for fast-tracking Latham to the top and then trying to foist him onto the nation as prime minister. This is where the real political damage is being done. Many of his caucus colleagues had to know what he was like. Certainly the talkback callers (who all vote) believe so. But no one blew the whistle. To capitalise on the situation, the government does not have to do much more than point to Latham and say: 'This was their prime ministerial candidate.' In the words of a former Labor heavyweight: 'It's hard to shuffle away from that. The only way to deal with it is to say, "Yep. We got it wrong."' It will take a long time for voters to forget and for the party to live down such an ill-judged leadership choice. Every time Latham sticks his head up, the issue will be revived.

There are, in the ALP and the media, people who have tried to set aside the vitriol, the vulgarity, the personal abuse, the blame-shifting, the self-justification, the narcissism and the nastiness of the diaries and the interviews Latham has given to help market his book. Amid all the horrible stuff, they say, 'Mark has a point.' Or rather, two points. One is that the ALP has a poisonous culture, the other that the party is 'irreparably broken' because rank-and-file activism has been crushed and machine men and factions rule. It is an indication of the hypocrisy inherent in Latham's position that he himself could be presented as Exhibit A in support of either point.

A poisonous culture? It is hard to think of an act more poisonous than Latham's use of the death of Kevin Rudd's mother in an attack on the shadow foreign minister in the diaries. Except the way he used the suicide of Victorian Labor MP Greg Wilton five years ago as a weapon in his war against Beazley and Senator Stephen Conroy. Politics does not get much lower.

The headline-grabbing claim in the diaries is that Beazley, 'one of the most indecent politicians I've come across', conducted a six-year campaign of smear and innuendo against Latham based on an untrue allegation of sexual harassment. Beazley, Latham asserts, kept a 'dirt file' on him. The charge against Beazley lacks any credibility, which is a pity, in a way. One of Beazley's handicaps – and this is a complaint made most recently by Bob Hawke – is that he is not as nasty and ruthless as an opposition leader needs to be. Critics of the 'too cuddly' Beazley dearly wish he was the unscrupulous mongrel Latham portrays. But it won't wash. Beazley delivered the coup de grace to the allegation when he challenged any journalist to whom he had smeared Latham to come forward and say so. None did because it had not happened. His 'decent bloke' image will not be seriously damaged by Latham.

An interesting sidelight – which I don't think is mentioned in the diaries – is that Latham himself kept files on a range of people. They included Beazley and a number of other Labor figures, along with various coalition politicians and some business identities. In addition to newspaper cuttings, the files contained notes from Latham recording snippets of information or gossip he had picked up. This helped make Latham the master of the personal attack. He had a particularly voluminous file on commentator Gerard Henderson, which formed the basis of a parliamentary character assassination. If Labor has a poisonous culture, Latham was in it up to his neck.

As for the decline of rank-and-file influence and the dominance of the factions…This is a matter on which Latham can claim genuine expertise. In terms of rank-and-file involvement, the most important ALP body in each seat is the Federal Electorate Council. Branches send representatives to the FECs, which then debate both policy and party machine issues. But in Latham's seat of Werriwa, the FEC did not meet for nearly three years. A party official who raised the matter with Latham claims to have received the reply: 'Fuck the members. What would they know?'

Latham relied on the right-wing factional heavies of the NSW ALP to protect him in Werriwa because he did not have the numbers in his own branches. Head Office in Sydney's Sussex Street had to intervene in three successive elections – in 1998, 2001 and 2004 – to ensure his preselection. This was done through the use of what are known as 'N.40 ballots', under which branch members cast half the votes and the Administrative Committee the other half – guaranteeing the result faction leaders want. But in the last preselection, the only votes cast were from the Administrative Committee. For the first time in party history, there was no local component at all because Latham had allowed the Werriwa FEC to collapse. So much for his condemnation of factions and his commitment to democratic processes within the party.

The main victim of Latham's diaries is Latham himself. In the process of self-destructing, he has damaged the ALP, but not nearly as badly as he intended. NSW Premier Morris Iemma had been concerned that the Latham fallout would seriously affect Labor's vote in three state by-elections held while the diaries were dominating the media. In the event, however, the Latham impact was clearly minimal and the results were about what might have been expected, given the way the NSW government has been travelling. 'We got through Billy Hughes,' says a frontbencher. 'We got through Bert Evatt. We got through Arthur Calwell. We'll get through this.'

Low-key dangers

26 October 2005

Should we be worried about the likelihood of mistakes, abuses and unjustified infringements of civil liberties under John Howard's new anti-terrorism legislation? Absolutely. Anyone who doubts that need only reflect on the recent history of the immigration department. The horror stories that have emerged – the deportation of Vivian Alvarez and the detention of Cornelia Rau chief among them – show what can happen (one might almost say will happen) when bureaucrats wield great power with a minimum of scrutiny.

Both former federal police commissioner Mick Palmer, in his findings on the Rau case, and former Victoria Police chief Neil Comrie, in the Ombudsman's report on the Alvarez outrage, were scathing about the 'culture' within the department. Officers, according to Comrie, 'failed to take into account the basic human rights obligations that characterise a democratic society'. That culture, he found, developed while Philip Ruddock was immigration minister.

Agents of the Australian Federal Police and the Australian Security Intelligence Organisation will have unprecedented powers under the Anti-Terrorism Bill 2005. With national security considerations providing an excuse for – and a spur to – zealotry, they will be subjected to much stronger pressures and temptations than immigration department staff ever faced. The media, for the most part, will be prevented by law from reporting on their activities. And Ruddock, now Attorney-General, will again be the minister in charge. There is every reason to be concerned.

If the immigration department scandals are not enough, the 'children-overboard' affair provides further evidence that trusting politicians and bureaucrats with these new powers carries no small degree of risk. In that episode, a garbled report conveyed second-hand to a meeting of bureaucrats (the grandly titled People Smuggling Task Force) was accepted as fact, without any attempt at checking. It was passed on instantly to a minister – Ruddock again – who wasted no time in calling a news conference to exploit it for election purposes. Howard quickly jumped on the bandwagon. And when it became apparent that a group of asylum-seekers had been shamefully maligned and no children had been thrown overboard after all, a cover-up was put in place. The consequences of that kind of incompetence and cynicism combined with the radical anti-terrorism measures in Howard's legislation do not bear thinking about.

Many people are no doubt reassured by the fact that this bill cannot be dismissed as the kind of 'wedge' politics Howard has practised in the past. State and territory leaders, all of them Labor, are backing the legislation and have agreed to refer the necessary constitutional powers to the federal government. More than that, the premiers initiated the process that produced it. They wrote to Howard immediately after the London bombings proposing a special meeting of the Council of Australian Governments (COAG) to give urgent consideration to new anti-terrorism measures and a more coordinated federal–state approach. That makes the proposed legislation a bipartisan measure, even if the federal Labor Party is anything but enthusiastic about some aspects of it.

The motives of the state leaders, however, are not entirely pure. It may be true that, like ACT Chief Minister Jon Stanhope, they were taken aback by the ASIO and AFP briefings Howard turned on for them at the COAG meeting. Nevertheless, cynical electoral politics played a big part in their calculations. The letter requesting the terrorism summit was drafted by the then-NSW premier, Bob Carr, and Victoria's Steve Bracks. Carr, in particular, had decided long ago that national security issues could be exploited just as easily by a premier as by a prime minister. He became even more hairy-chested than Howard on terrorism, and other state Labor leaders followed his lead. Carr announced his retirement as premier the day after the letter to Howard was dispatched, confident that he had left his successor, Morris Iemma, in a strong position to continue making political capital out of the terrorism threat. Iemma has done exactly that.

The result is that Kim Beazley and federal Labor have been 'wedged' by their state allies as well as by Howard. The difficult position federal Labor would be placed in by the legislation was discussed by the premiers and chief ministers. 'Bugger them!' was the attitude. Now federal Labor MPs cannot oppose Howard on the issue without creating a split – or at least the impression of one – in the ALP. Even if it was his inclination, Beazley could not attack the civil liberties implications of what the Prime Minister is proposing because that would also be an attack on his own state colleagues. All federal Labor can do is argue around the edges.

Howard sounded fairly half-hearted about the idea of an anti-terrorism summit when the premiers wrote to him in late July. 'I've got to look at what's going to be achieved,' he said. 'I don't believe in having meetings just for the show of having a meeting. I believe very much in seeing if we can add value.' But Howard is not one to mess around when opportunity beckons. By the end of the first week in August, he had agreed to call COAG together and was previewing tough new counter-terrorism laws that he had apparently not thought necessary a fortnight earlier.

Perhaps we'll be lucky. Perhaps the cops and spooks and bureaucrats and politicians who administer the new laws will prove themselves exceptional people and always take account of – in Comrie's phrase – 'the basic human rights obligations that characterise a democratic society'. I wouldn't bet on it, though.

2006

Howard's growth

7 March 2006

One of John Howard's most treasured mementoes is a small shifting spanner. It was given to him by Dame Pattie Menzies in 1987, during his first stint as opposition leader when everything seemed to be going wrong. 'Keep on working away,' Dame Pattie said as she slipped it into his hand. From then until he became prime minister nine years later, Howard kept the spanner in his briefcase, taking it everywhere. Howard still keeps the spanner close by, and he has never forgotten Dame Pattie's words. They became his credo.

'Keep on working away.' It is what got him to the prime ministership, and it is what has kept him there for a decade. Work and persistence. Oh, yes. There is one other thing. He just happens to have been the smartest politician of his generation. There were plenty of doubters in the 1980s and early 1990s. Paul Keating, the man he was to displace from the Lodge, had dismissed him as 'a bowser boy from Canterbury'. There are few doubters now.

Keating was undoubtedly clever. As treasurer and then prime

minister, he drove the economic change that set Australia up for 15 years of growth – the growth that, to Keating's disgust, has done so much to sustain Howard in office. Friends say Keating still finds it hard to understand how someone he held in such contempt came out on top. But he didn't have Howard's smarts when it came to listening to the electorate and speaking the language of ordinary voters. And – especially in his final three years – the self-styled Placido Domingo of politics lacked energy and interest and could not be bothered to keep working away.

Keating warned in the election campaign that sent him to political oblivion that 'when the government changes, the country changes'. He was right. Australia has changed under Howard, and not only because we now have a GST and the idea of 'mutual obligation' is part of the welfare system and radical new industrial laws are about to make their presence felt. We have become a less questioning, cockier nation confident in our conservative values.

In his book *Postcode: The Splintering of a Nation*, shadow treasurer Wayne Swan recalls a conversation with a former Labor voter after the party's 1996 defeat. 'Labor leaders need to understand that Australians are not all gay, Asian or Aboriginal or belong to some kinky lobby group,' the former rusted-on battler told him. 'The majority are pretty straight, honest and want to work for a living.' Howard plugged into that sentiment 10 years ago, and remains plugged in. His priorities reflect it.

While Howard is clever, he is not as good as some of the more glowing tributes marking his 10th anniversary in office would suggest. He is capable of mistakes, and has made plenty of them. In his first attempt at leadership, in fact – like his hero, Sir Robert Menzies – he was a dismal failure. There were excuses. Joh Bjelke-Petersen's bizarre push to become prime minister, splitting the federal coalition in the process, was hardly Howard's fault. But he was too stubborn, too ideological, and a lousy manager of people. Even he would probably admit that today.

Howard learns from his mistakes, however, and this has been crucial to his success. By the time he got his second chance at leadership, he was far more relaxed and comfortable (to coin a phrase), a lot less edgy and dictatorial.

And Howard Mark 2 was considerably more pragmatic. In 1988, he had landed in hot water – and divided his party – by arguing that a slowing of Asian immigration would be in the interests of Australia's social cohesion. Even when it was clear the issue was seriously damaging his leadership, he would not back off. 'I am not budging. Definitely not. Is that clear?' He had just returned from a trip to London where, in a tête-à-tête at 10 Downing Street, he had received a pep talk from Margaret Thatcher. The Iron Lady told him the secret of political success was to adopt a policy position and then stick to it no matter what. 'Never waver,' she warned. The conversation, Howard's confidants said at the time, had a profound influence on him.

But in January 1995, the new Howard was for turning on the Asian immigration issue, deliberately arranging interviews with *The Australian* and the Nine network's *Sunday* program to admit not only that the comments had been clumsily expressed but also that he had been wrong to make them. Howard had been told by Liberal powerbrokers that disowning the comments was a price he had to pay if he was to return to the Liberal leadership. By then he had decided off his own bat it was something he needed to do anyway. Howard's use of the dog whistle as prime minister has been more subtle.

At about the same time he did an even more spectacular backflip on Medicare. In 1987, it was 'a total disaster' and he pledged that he would 'take a scalpel to it'. By 1996, he was Medicare's best friend, telling me on the *Sunday* program: 'There's no law in politics that says you should never ever change your view.' Thatcher would not have been impressed, but the voters were.

Part of Howard's genius is to look like a reasonable man even when he is engaged in the rankest political opportunism. He is certainly a politician of substance, but style has been central to his success. Howard never had many airs and graces anyway – working in his father's service station as a kid probably saw to that. But he seems to have deliberately studied Keating's style – manner, language and behaviour – and gone to the opposite extreme. Where Keating was up himself, Howard is carefully humble. Where everything Keating did and said was extravagant and colourful, Howard makes a virtue of being boring. It works a treat.

'The times will suit me,' Howard said before he became PM. He was right. Public concern over boatloads of asylum-seekers played into his hands. And the al-Qaeda attacks on New York and Washington put national security at the centre of the Australian political debate. Labor would say Howard exploited these issues. That is simply another way of saying that a majority of Australians approved of the way he handled them.

The main thing that underpins Howard's grip on power might be characterised as 'the economy, stupid!'. It is true that the Hawke and Keating governments laid the foundations for the economic success for which Howard and his treasurer, Peter Costello, now claim credit. But the pair have not squandered the gift Labor bequeathed to them. They have been careful economic managers, and – while critics claim they have not done enough – economic reform has continued under their stewardship. While economic success continues, Labor is shut out.

In his book, Swan writes: 'Labor remains caught between the ghost of Keating and the shadow of Howard.' His point is that the policy changes that opened up the economy under Labor, while good for the nation, had a political cost. They alienated many voters. Howard exploited that disaffection, embraced those voters as 'Howard's battlers', and locked them in to the coalition. Labor now clings to the hope that the industrial relations changes Howard achieved courtesy of the one-vote Senate majority achieved at the last election will push the battlers back its way.

Despite the impression given by some of the tributes in the last week, Howard is far from infallible. Remember the memo – leaked to *The Bulletin* – from then Liberal president Shane Stone to the PM in February 2001 warning that the government was in deep trouble because it had been 'too tricky' on issues such as GST on caravan park fees, beer and fuel. There was a belief among Liberal MPs that the government was dysfunctional and out of touch and that it had to be 'dragged screaming' to fix its mistakes, Stone wrote. In the community, the government was seen as mean and out of touch. The way Howard reacted to the warning and moved dramatically to remedy the situation was impressive, but he was the one who had allowed it to develop. It is a reminder – if Howard needs it – of how easily things can go wrong in politics.

Howard has implemented the agenda he set for himself, and achieved much on top of that. As he basks in all the praise, however, he may reflect that there is one more thing for him to accomplish. He needs to ensure that he manages the succession. If he can organise the process of transition to the next generation smoothly, without rancour, his legacy will be secure. Various pundits, having read the spate of anniversary interviews Howard has given, have concluded that he will probably stay on for another term. They may be right, but it ain't necessarily so. What Howard has said – that he still enjoys the job and is full of energy and enthusiasm – he would say whatever his intentions. Bob Carr was saying similar things right up to the day he announced that he was quitting as NSW premier.

After the welter of 10th anniversary commentary, Howard knows exactly how he will be regarded if he bows out soon. What happened to Thatcher is relevant. She had won three elections and been prime minister for 11½ years. Her intention was to fight one more poll. But, to her astonishment, she was pushed out. Howard, a strong admirer, has studied her career. And perhaps learned from it that, if you hang around too long, someone can always throw a spanner in the works.

The modern witless

21 March 2006

Perhaps the saddest thing about the Labor Party's current brawling is that today's witless men – and women – are not fighting over anything of substance. In the 1950s and '60s, when internal strife helped keep the ALP in the wilderness for a generation, at least the issues were big and important. The threat of Communism. The American alliance. Government aid for Catholic schools. When Doc Evatt took on the Groupers, it was a fiercely ideological battle. The question of whether US bases should be allowed on Australian soil sparked Gough Whitlam's jihad against the faceless machine men of the party's federal conference. Blatant sectarianism provoked Whitlam's explosive confrontation with the national executive which almost resulted in his expulsion from the ALP.

What are the matters causing Simon Crean, Julia Gillard, Kim Beazley, Stephen Conroy, Bill Shorten and the rest to trash their party's prospects? Personal advancement. Who gets what seat. Who can be best positioned for a future crack at the leadership. Who can exert power over whom. Whose advice the leader should heed most. And in the mix is that least admirable motivator, revenge.

No issues of significance are involved. Principle does not get a look in. Ideology is completely absent. It is all about looking after number one. Me, me, me. Squabbling over the spoils of opposition. It is tawdry, depressing and stupid. The despair of Labor voters can only be imagined. If the party is not careful it will whittle its support base down to the kind of people referred to in the US as 'yellow dog Democrats'. A yellow dog Democrat is a Texas Democrat who would vote the party ticket even if it was headed by a yellow dog.

Beazley is not a yellow dog, but he is starting to look and sound like a whipped one. Every time he gets a bit of momentum going – he had been pretty effective in attacking the government over the AWB scandal, and Labor was up in the polls – a party crisis derails him. The truth is that, even when he performs well, a large part of the caucus – including some in his own support group – cannot convince themselves that he has a real chance of winning next year's election. 'Everyone hopes Kim can do it,' says one of his backers. 'But they're worried. If there was someone obviously better than Kim, they'd have left him already.' Small wonder discipline is non-existent.

Kevin Rudd is portrayed as the fallback, but he has no chance of assuming the leadership unless the powerful NSW Right decides to abandon Beazley and back him. So far, despite his high-profile and energetic pursuit of the government in his area of foreign affairs, the people who matter clearly do not believe a Rudd leadership would make much difference to Labor's chances. That would change if there was a sustained dive in the party's poll ratings, which may well happen after this latest lunacy. Meanwhile, Rudd has wisely concentrated on doing his job and played a dead bat on internal party matters.

Gillard obviously smells Beazley's vulnerability, and is going flat out to build name recognition. A colleague puts it more bluntly. 'Her strategy is to turn herself into the public's darling.' That may not be enough to make her a viable leadership candidate, but it could force the party to put her into the deputy leadership down the track. Hence her double whammy in Labor's horrible week – highlighting Beazley's shortcomings while displaying her own wares on ABC-TV's *Australian Story*, and then putting factionalism up in lights in a Sydney Institute address 24 hours later. The resentment generated inside the caucus is palpable.

That resentment was no doubt behind a leak to Sydney's *Sunday Telegraph*, which led to a story headed: 'Gillard's gamble – left-wing star tried to switch factions'. It quoted senior ALP sources claiming Gillard, through an intermediary, approached NSW party secretary Mark Arbib in January last year about the possibility of moving from the Left faction to the Right to boost her chances of becoming leader. That amused those who recalled a report in *The Australian* on January 18 last year headed: 'Gillard resists Right's career-switch carrot'. That version said: 'Julia Gillard has rejected recent overtures from the ALP's Right faction to switch allegiances in a move designed to boost her chances of further promotion.'

The botched attempt by Beazley's factional ally Stephen Conroy to oust Crean in a preselection ballot was a dreadful miscalculation. Crean went from failure to folk hero overnight, and it is hard to blame him for rubbing Beazley's nose in it. Beazley would not be human if he did not feel a bit sorry for himself, and he clearly does. There he was on Brisbane radio, for example, at the end of the disastrous week, complaining that all the 'navel gazing' had drowned out his 'genuinely bold' policy to deal with climate change. He was right. The policy was worthy and should have made an impact, but it sank without trace because Labor infighting dominated the news.

But when he has finished licking his wounds, Beazley might consider the fact that he was at least partly to blame. The Crean ballot was always going to create awful headlines. Whether the move against him succeeded or failed, it was inevitable that Crean and allies such as Gillard would lash out. The date of the ballot had been known for weeks, and yet Beazley decided to launch the policy the following day. Brilliant! It is that sort of thing that gives ammunition to his critics.

Liberal moderates?

2 May 2006

John Howard's government went to a lot of trouble to protect the orange-bellied parrot. It vetoed a proposed wind farm at Bald Hills in Victoria, even though it was estimated that a collision between one of the rare birds and a turbine on the site would be a once-in-a-thousand-years event at worst. By contrast, the Prime Minister did nothing to protect Petro Georgiou, despite the fact that Liberal moderates are also an endangered species – probably more endangered. There are 200 orange-bellied parrots left in the wild. You would be pushed to find a dozen genuine moderates – small 'l' Liberals with the guts to stand up for their beliefs – in the parliamentary ranks of today's Liberal Party.

Howard paid lip-service to the convention that the leader supports sitting members in preselection contests, but lip-service is all it was. Georgiou's opponent in the battle for the blue-ribbon seat of Kooyong, the young Josh Frydenberg, was a former Howard staffer who also worked for Alexander Downer for a time. The Foreign Minister was clearly Frydenberg's sponsor, and Howard gave his cause a nudge wherever possible. The PM clearly approved when three of his ministers from Queensland – members of the faction run by strong Howard ally Santo Santoro – came out publicly in support of Frydenberg. Neither the PM nor Downer has much time for moderates. Neither of them would have been pleased at Georgiou's emphatic preselection victory.

It was Peter Costello who did for Georgiou what Environment Minister Ian Campbell did for the orange-bellied parrot. Costello, who controls the dominant faction in the Victorian branch, joined forces with the group identified with former premier Jeff Kennett to crush the challenge.

Had Costello gone the other way, Georgiou might well have been a dead parrot. It was a surprising alliance – Kennett and Costello loathe each other. Kennett is a mate of Georgiou's. Costello, however, could hardly be described as a fan – not since Georgiou knocked back a parliamentary secretaryship offered after Costello persuaded Howard he should be promoted.

Costello's motives are complex. For a start, as the senior Liberal in Victoria who takes his power in the party organisation seriously, he obviously did not like what he saw as an attempt by Downer to move into his bailiwick. 'This result makes it clear that the Victorian Liberal Party is not going to take instructions from interstate,' says a Costello loyalist. Then there is the vexed matter of the leadership succession. The Costello forces see Downer as trying to build numbers to deal himself into the game – perhaps as leader, but more likely as deputy. On top of that, with Howard still playing cat and mouse over whether he intends to retire this year, the Kooyong preselection vote sends a message that Costello should not be trifled with.

But there was a more straightforward and equally powerful reason for Costello to act as he did. 'Peter doesn't believe you should rub somebody out just because you disagree with them,' a Victorian Liberal said after the ballot. 'That's what they do in NSW. We don't operate that way here.' The reference to NSW – Howard's home state – was pointed. There, the hardline right-wing faction run by Upper House MP David Clarke is conducting a war against moderates – and their definition of a moderate is nothing if not broad. This is occurring under Howard's benign gaze.

The most important NSW moderate in danger of being rubbed out by the Clarke forces is Senator Marise Payne. Like Georgiou, she holds strong views on detention of asylum-seekers and other matters involving human rights. Like Georgiou, she is not afraid to express them. Like Georgiou, she believes the philosophy of those who founded the Liberal Party makes it legitimate for members to exercise their consciences on important matters of principle. Payne is coming up for preselection. The Right has the numbers to do her in. They are sounding out potential candidates. Payne will survive only if Howard, and those who operate on his behalf within the NSW Liberal Party, make it clear that she should be looked after. On Howard's past form, you'd have to say that's unlikely.

Costello made it clear after the vote that he did not see Georgiou's win as an endorsement of the dissident role he had played in the party over asylum-seekers and mandatory detention. One of the preselectors said: 'Petro won in spite of that, not because of it.'

But Georgiou did not back away from his principles and his determination to follow them when he addressed the preselection committee. 'The responsibility of a good parliamentarian is not to silently accept every new bill, but to work within the party honestly and with integrity to improve the legislation and initiate reform,' he said. He also declared that compassion and tolerance were signs of strength, not weakness. And he strongly defended his stand against indefinite detention and the confinement of children behind razor wire.

Those who endorsed Georgiou this time did so in full knowledge of where he stands and what can be expected from him. He might have much in common with the orange-bellied parrot, but no one should be surprised in future when he refuses to simply parrot the party line.

To obfuscate

27 June 2006

Under the NSW Shop Employees Award, workers in Spotlight stores were entitled to a 17.5 percent holiday loading. Under the Spotlight Australian Workplace Agreement, they receive no holiday loading. Like overtime, penalty rates, public holiday rates, meal and uniform allowances, it is a condition they lose in return for the measly 2 cents an hour that Labor has seized on to dramatise the way workers can be screwed under the government's radical reshaping of the industrial relations system.

But there is no point questioning John Howard about any of this. He obfuscates. (The perfect word. *The Macquarie Dictionary* says it means 'to confuse or stupefy'.) On the *Sunday* program, I asked the PM about agreements under which workers 'lose their penalty rates, their holiday leave loadings, public holidays' in return for very little money. 'Did you say annual leave?' he asked. 'Annual leave loadings,' I replied. Ignoring that, he proceeded to explain at length that workers could not lose their annual leave. 'I seize on that as an example of the way in which, in a fairly glib fashion, allegations are being made that aren't correct.'

The fact that I'd made no such allegation was irrelevant. The real reason the PM seized on it was to confuse the issue and stupefy both interviewer and audience. It enabled him, as he always does, to avoid the central issue in the debate over his WorkChoices laws – that a lot of people are going to be worse off. Howard says he is confident that many will be better off because a freer labour market will mean more jobs. But he flatly refuses to address the matter of those who lose out. So does Treasurer Peter Costello, an ardent advocate of this kind of workplace reform since his days as a young barrister.

Costello was tackled on the issue in an interview on Sydney radio with Alan Jones, the man who turned up the heat on the proposed Snowy Hydro privatisation to a point where Howard had to buckle. Now Jones is taking an interest in some of the unfair consequences of the new IR laws. He went for the Treasurer, and got waffle in reply. Sample:

Jones: *I have had a young bloke come to see me here to say, 'If I don't get penalty rates and I am not given overtime, my current take-home pay will drop by 40 percent and I can't survive.' What do you say to that person?*

Costello: *I have no doubt that in a growing economy with a better system of industrial relations, those people will have a better chance of a job and higher wages.*

Jones: *He has got a job.*

And a little later:

Jones: *He can, he will be paid less.*

Costello: *Yes. I have no doubt that as time goes by in a profitable economy that man's wages under a contract will grow faster than they would have under any award because under an award in a stagnant economy...*

Jones: *He has to make his mortgage payment next week.*

So it went on. By refusing to deal squarely with the questions Jones raised, by attempting to use the 'confuse and stupefy' technique, Costello came off sounding not only devious but also out of touch and even a bit thick. But anything, it seems, is preferable to admitting that the ACTU's campaign against WorkChoices has a pretty solid basis in fact.

Cardinal Pell is right to be concerned. These laws will lead to lower pay and worse conditions for a not insignificant number of workers. The government has known it all along. It lied in claiming otherwise. This is the context in which Kim Beazley's promise to abolish AWAs has to be seen. The Labor leader has been bagged in the press and accused by Howard of doing a backflip and kowtowing to the unions. (Given his Snowy backflip and his kowtowing to Jakarta, the PM can be said to have some expertise in this area.) But in reality, there was no choice. As a businessman complained to a Labor frontbencher: 'These bastards [the government] have given AWAs a bad name.'

Had Beazley decided on some halfway house – keeping AWAs but restoring a 'no disadvantage' test, for example – the argument would have been so complex that he'd have crippled himself politically. This way he has a simple argument that voters will easily understand. What Beazley did was what the labour movement overwhelmingly wanted. The caucus dissenters quoted anonymously in the media are a very small minority. And for a Labor leader to adopt a policy favoured by trade unions is no worse than a Liberal leader introducing the sort of open slather IR system the business lobby has been craving. Beazley would have made his decision well aware that big business and sections of the media would turn on him. It took – dare one say it? – ticker.

The WorkChoices issue on its own is not going to win next year's election for Labor. But it gives the party a chance, something to build on. Howard did, after all, give what he called a 'rock-solid guarantee' in 1996 that: 'Under no circumstances will a Howard government create a wages system that will cause the take-home pay of Australians to be cut. Under a Howard government, you cannot be worse off.' Tell that to the Spotlight workers, Alan Jones's mate, and all the others who find themselves on the losing end of AWAs in Howard's brave new world of employer-friendly IR laws. Howard's decade-old promise is now Beazley's.

Risky decision

8 August 2006

It was as though a huge weight had been lifted off the coalition and the government. When Liberal MPs received the faxed letter from John Howard's office on Monday morning announcing he was staying on to fight another election, the relief was palpable. Not only had uncertainty about the leadership and tension between Howard and Peter Costello been a distraction. A torpor had settled over ministers and MPs while they waited for the situation to be sorted out. Howard could not even focus on the question of a ministry reshuffle until he got the leadership issue out of the way.

And even though it had been glaringly obvious for a fortnight that Howard had lost any interest he might have had in retiring, formal confirmation sent a frisson of excitement through coalition ranks. It was game on. Effectively, the campaign for the 2007 federal election began with the Howard letter. The government once more had a sense of direction. Backbenchers who had been considering their own futures knew where they stood.

Also, Kim Beazley knew who he'd be fighting. The opposition leader had been thumping his chest and challenging Howard to stay and face the voters over his new industrial relations laws, and he continued his public show of bravado. But in private Beazley would have been cursing (were he the cursing type). The Labor Party was convinced the coalition would be more vulnerable with Costello as PM, just as it was certain – only to be proved wrong – that directing much of its campaign venom at Costello in the last two elections would pay off electorally.

It was impossible not to feel sorry for Costello when he uttered that plaintive line at a book launch in Melbourne on Sunday. 'Inside every MP is a glorious prime ministership wanting to get out – if only they are given the chance,' he said. That very evening, the Treasurer had the chance of a glorious Costello prime ministership snatched away from him yet again. He would not have been even slightly surprised when Howard phoned him to say: 'I'm staying on.' The PM's intention had been well and truly telegraphed, and by then the long-suffering heir apparent knew that he had no choice but to grit his teeth and accept the situation. The strength of pro-Howard feeling among Liberals meant Costello would be totally humiliated if he challenged for the leadership, carved up if he stacked on a blue. But he didn't have to like it.

Costello's mood was dark. His own actions – effectively calling Howard a liar over the broken December 1994 undertaking to hand over the leadership – had pushed the Prime Minister into an early decision. And the upsurge of support for Howard, inside and outside the Liberal Party, guaranteed the decision would not be the one that Costello wanted. Howard had no trouble interpreting the adulation sparked by the row with Costello as proof that the Liberal Party cannot do without him. He is not the first leader to decide that he is indispensable, and will certainly not be the last.

When politics junkies look back on Howard's decision in years to come, however, they may conclude that it was a mistake. Howard should, perhaps, have adapted a memorable line from the late Kerry Packer. You only get one Mark Latham in your lifetime. The Liberals cannot expect to do as well in the next election as they did in the last. The 2004 result – big swing, big majority, control of the Senate – was the high-water mark. About as good as it gets.

Next time around, the coalition will almost certainly go backwards. The IR laws continue to hurt the government. The punters may well maintain the rage over petrol prices. The promise to keep interest rates low is starting to look a touch hollow. Anecdotal evidence from senior people in business suggests the economy is slowing. The government itself is predicting a rise in unemployment. The redistribution of electoral boundaries in NSW and Queensland has helped Labor and made life harder for the coalition. Iraq goes from bad to worse. And our troops have now been sent to a particularly dangerous area of Afghanistan where casualties are regarded as inevitable.

Had he bowed out now, Howard would have been guaranteed hero status by the Liberals, up there with – perhaps even ahead of – his own idol and the party's founder, Robert Menzies. Now that has all been put at risk. If he were to acknowledge this, Howard would no doubt argue that it proves he is willing to put the party's interests ahead of his own. It can be argued, though, that it actually demonstrates the opposite.

By remaining in the leadership and squashing Costello's ambitions again, Howard may give the coalition a small boost in 2007, but there's a real chance that it will be to the Liberal Party's longer-term disadvantage.

I have written before that the best time for a leadership transition is when things are going well. It makes sense to put a new captain on the bridge when the good ship Liberal Party is seaworthy and going full steam ahead, rather than waiting until it starts taking water. Howard's decision ensures that the leadership changeover will now occur, not when the coalition is riding high, but when its fortunes have taken a turn for the worse.

Halfway through the next parliamentary term, what's more, Costello will be a considerably more jaded and battle-scarred figure than he is now, less youthful and dynamic. The chance to give the government a fresh look, new life, will have been missed. Costello may even be burnt out altogether after another three grinding years as treasurer, in which case the prime ministerial baton will have to be passed to someone with less talent and experience. In years to come, when the consequences are more apparent, this alone may be enough to tarnish the Howard legacy.

Not a holy war

12 September 2006

The reaction was extraordinary. John Howard did nothing more than state the bleeding obvious about a small section of the Muslim community in Australia that is 'very resistant to integration'. Fully integrating, he said, 'means accepting Australian values, it means learning as rapidly as you can the English language if you don't already speak it, and it means…people who come from societies where women are treated in an inferior fashion have got to learn very quickly that that is not the case in Australia'. Motherhood stuff, you might think. But Muslim leaders went off their faces, accusing the Prime Minister of marginalising Muslims and risking more Cronulla-style riots. 'Muslims seethe at PM's stance', was a typical headline. They demanded he apologise.

It was on again a few days later when Peter Costello dared to utter a few home truths about the terrorist risk in Australia. 'I think there is a minority in the Islamic community that has been radicalised and seeks to prey upon young people with a very radical and dangerous ideology,' the Treasurer said. 'It is very important that the moderate leaders speak out quite plainly and quite clearly against those radicals.' Again, nothing inflammatory. A statement so obviously factual that it is hard to see how anyone could argue with it. But the Muslim leadership went into knee-jerk mode anyway. The chairman of the Muslim Community Reference Group, Ameer Ali, for example, claimed the remarks were 'provocative, divisive and mischievous'. 'Muslim anger at Costello call to renounce terrorism', was the front-page headline in *The Age*.

These people, apparently, do not realise the damage they do to their own community by overreacting in this way. By trying to suppress unexceptionable political comment that reflects views widely held in Australian society they gain nothing. They do, however, add to the impression that they are more concerned about criticism of anything to do with the Muslim community than they are about acts of terrorism perpetrated by Muslim extremists. If calls to renounce terrorism make Muslim leaders angry, then non-Muslim Australians have a right to be angry at those Muslim leaders. They should – to use the Australian vernacular – take a good, hard look at themselves.

There was similar ire from Muslim leaders in February when Costello spoke about Australian citizenship at the Sydney Institute. Anyone who actually read the speech would have been impressed by the reasoned argument. Costello's starting point was the Australian Citizenship Oath or Affirmation: 'From this time forward (under God) I pledge my loyalty to Australia and its people, whose democratic beliefs I share, whose rights and liberties I respect and whose laws I will uphold and obey.' That, he said, was a summary of Australian values. Anyone who did not hold democratic beliefs and was unwilling to respect the rights and liberty of others as well as the rule of law should not come here. Respect for the rights and liberty of others meant accepting equal rights for women. The words of the oath ruled out adherence to a second Islamic set of laws, as some Muslim clerics had advocated.

'It will be a problem if we have a second generation – the children of immigrants who have come to Australia – in a twilight zone where the values of their parents' old country have been lost but the values of the new country not fully embraced,' Costello said. 'To deal with this we must clearly state the values of Australia and explain how we expect them to be respected.' To that, most Australians would cry: 'Hear, hear!' But not only did a string of Muslim leaders rush in to condemn Costello, so did some non-Muslims who should have known better. Queensland Premier Peter Beattie accused Costello of 'trying to appeal back to the 1950s'. A prominent history professor accused the Treasurer of launching an 'utterly unAustralian' attack on 'the political value of tolerance'. Nonsense, all of it. I have, from time to time, criticised Howard's involvement in 'dog-whistle' politics, but on this matter his statements have been measured and sensible. So have Costello's.

Australians only have to look at what is happening in Europe to be concerned about the ability and willingness of some Muslim immigrants to integrate. The issue is of particular importance in Europe which – as a result of immigration, high Muslim birth rates, and a shrinking non-Muslim population – is likely to have a Muslim majority before the end of the century. A poll taken just two years ago indicated that 60 percent of British Muslims want to live under Sharia law in the UK. A prominent Muslim cleric in Belgium is campaigning to have Arabic adopted as an official language. A Dutch film-maker was murdered two years ago over a film critical of Islam's treatment of women. In some French schools Muslim girls are informally banned from participating in team sports and – according to an Education Ministry study – their conduct is monitored by young men acting as a kind of religious police force. A survey of young Turkish Germans nine years ago found a third believed every country should be Islamic and violence against unbelievers was justified in the interests of Islam.

There have been European efforts to give integration a push. They range from the French government's ban on headscarfs to proposals in the Netherlands for the development of a more 'homegrown' brand of Islam. A recent poll showed that 80 percent of the Dutch population wants stricter measures to *force* integration.

It is sensible to try to head off such problems in this country before they become a major issue. That is what Howard and Costello are about, and it would be reassuring if leaders of the Muslim community in Australia stopped being so defensive and showed more enthusiasm for the cause.

Sorrow the leader

15 December 2006

On the day Kim Beazley was cut down, his old foe John Howard summed up the situation best. 'It's a brutal game, politics,' the Prime Minister told parliament. Beazley was candid about his feelings immediately after Labor MPs voted to oust him from the leadership. 'I'm heartbroken,' an emotional Bomber told the party room, barely managing to hold himself together. The famous dictum had been borne out yet again: most political careers end in tears.

The last federal leader of a major party to leave politics in relatively happy circumstances was Sir Robert Menzies, way back in January 1966. Ming chose his own time for retirement, handed over to long-time deputy Harold Holt, and spent his final years doing some leisurely writing, enjoying cricket, and revelling in the title bestowed on him by his beloved Queen – Lord Warden of the Cinque Ports.

Holt's brief period as prime minister ended tragically when he drowned off Portsea in Victoria a few days before Christmas in 1967. He had just copped a Senate election drubbing from Labor's new leader, Gough Whitlam, mutterings about his leadership were starting to be heard, and he was said to be depressed. Holt's successor, John Gorton, incurred the wrath of powerful forces – including Liberal premiers and a certain media proprietor – and was brought down in a party room coup. Gorton suffered the indignity of having to use his casting vote against himself. Billy McMahon, who took over, was quickly exposed as a liar and an incompetent (Menzies had called him 'a contemptible squirt') and was a national joke by the time Whitlam beat him in the 1972 election.

Whitlam's fate is well known – sacked by the governor-general after a hostile Senate refused to pass Supply bills, then twice rejected by voters in anti-Labor landslides. Malcolm Fraser, whose ruthlessness destroyed Whitlam, was himself ambushed when Labor changed leaders on the day the 1983 election was called. Fraser's moist eyes and trembling lip as he conceded victory to Bob Hawke on election night have gone down in folklore.

Bill Hayden's career as Labor leader had to be brought to a painful end to accommodate Hawke's ambitions. Hayden's opponents (he had foolishly thought some of them friends) used psychological warfare to force him out. Hawke in turn was viciously undermined and then voted out by caucus – despite being Labor's most electorally successful leader ever – because Paul Keating decided it was his turn to be prime minister. And Keating was humiliated in a massive election loss to a man for whom he had the utmost contempt – John Howard. The once-cocky Keating has become a sad and shrivelled figure as a result.

A brutal game indeed.

Howard *thought* his career had hit the wall when he was dumped as Liberal opposition leader in 1989. Andrew Peacock lost the Liberal leadership in ignominious circumstances in 1985, then regained it, only to be defeated by Hawke in the 1990 election. John Hewson left politics an embittered man after losing the 'unlosable' 1993 election to Keating and then being rolled in the party room by the so-called 'dream team' of Alexander Downer and Peter Costello. And Downer made such an almighty hash of the opposition leadership that he had to hand the job back to Howard in 1995. Very embarrassing. Fortunately for Downer, he got a chance to rebuild his career as foreign minister.

On the Labor side, Simon Crean did not last long enough as opposition leader to fight even one election. The experience left him shattered and brooding, and set on vengeance against Beazley and the others who tore him down. Mark Latham lost the 2004 election and then imploded in spectacular fashion, exposing the dark and ugly side of his personality when he turned on the party that had tried to make him prime minister. And Beazley, in his second stint as opposition leader, was hacked at and stabbed until he was weak enough to be defeated in a caucus ballot. The Creanites rubbed their hands in satisfaction as the Bomber broke down at a news conference.

Nor is the tears-before-bedtime tradition confined to the big parties. Think Australian Democrats. Janet Powell driven out of the leadership by rumour and innuendo. Meg Lees not only ousted from the top job but effectively pushed out of the party. Natasha Stott Despoja chewed up and spat out and now preparing to retire from the Senate at the next election.

So why do they do it? Why do people embark on a career in which the odds are so clearly stacked in favour of an unpleasant end? And why do they stay long past the point where a relatively civilised and decent departure is possible? One answer is self-delusion. They all tell themselves: 'It won't happen to me.' But it does. Almost always.

Howard knows this, as his comment on Beazley's downfall showed. But that did not stop him deciding in mid-2006 to stay for yet another term, even though he could have retired at the top of his game and the peak of his fame, a hero up there with Menzies in the pantheon of Liberal gods. That decision carried the risk that Howard's career, despite its glories, could still end in tears. If it doesn't, of course, Kevin Rudd's almost certainly will.

2007

Half-baked and ham-fisted

26 February 2007

The wheels of justice might grind slowly, but the wheels of government can sometimes be even slower. Consider, for example, John Howard's plan for the federal government to take over state powers and assume responsibility for the Murray–Darling basin. A big, new idea? So the PM would have us believe. In fact, a similar but even more ambitious plan was first proposed 37 years ago. In 1970, with a coalition government in power in Canberra, a Senate committee recommended that 'the whole task of water resources management could best be undertaken on a national scale'.

The six committee members – two Liberal, one Country Party, two Labor and one DLP – believed that the federal government had the constitutional power to simply move in and take control whether the states liked it or not. According to the report: 'evidence presented to the committee tended to establish firmly that the Commonwealth has, through a coalescence of Commonwealth power in the fields of taxation, defence, external affairs, meteorology, fisheries, quarantine, and other fields, sufficient legislative competence to lay down and enforce a national approach through Commonwealth legislation alone'. However, it said, 'notwithstanding this, the committee believes that, bearing in mind the federal concept of the Constitution, it is preferable to achieve the national approach through the system of concurrent, parallel or complementary federal and state legislation'.

Pollution was the concern then. But the recommendations were ignored at the time, and ignored again when the then-minister for national development, John Carrick, tried to revive them in the later years of the Fraser government when John Howard was treasurer. Now that Australia faces a water supply crisis, and our most important river system is drying up, Howard has seen the merit of what his old political mentor was on about back then. The Murray–Darling is a mess, Howard says. Dead right. Someone has to take control. Right again. The federal government is prepared to do it if the states will relinquish the relevant constitutional powers. Bravo!

Except that Howard has botched the politics. Rattled by Kevin Rudd's momentum, on the defensive over climate change, and desperate to start the election year with a bang, he cut corners. The big idea was fine, but – in a bid to score points against Labor – he pushed it into the public domain before the detail was properly worked out.

It was unusually ham-fisted for Howard. Summoning the premiers to Canberra and expecting them to agree before the plan was properly fleshed out was inviting embarrassment. Going public with a half-baked scheme also gave Rudd and the Labor premiers a chance to play politics. Now, when Howard finally gets the states to sign on the bottom line, what could and should have been a political triumph will have lost much of its gloss.

To try to rush something as complex as this was a serious mistake. It deserved careful thought and consultation. The plan involves a virtual seventh state overlaid across a big section of NSW, Queensland, Victoria and South Australia. Within this new entity, Canberra will not only have responsibility for water management. It will also assume powers dealing with land use, planning, environmental guidelines and so on. The rules will be different on either side of the border to be drawn around the Murray–Darling basin. On top of that, town water supplies within the basin will be exempt from federal control. That

POWER PLAYS

makes a map of the area Howard proposes to take over look like a Swiss cheese – full of holes representing population centres.

The complications involved in all this are not hard to imagine. At a meeting of officials a week or so after Howard's first abortive meeting with premiers on the issue, a state public servant asked a federal bureaucrat exactly what powers Canberra wanted. According to a state source, the reply was that no one was quite sure. In effect, the state officials were told: 'You give them all to us, then we'll delegate those we don't need.' It is hardly surprising that the premiers have been cautious.

The federal government underestimated the states. The assumption was that, with the feds offering the nice round figure of $10bn, the states would grab the money and run. 'All the premiers ever want to know is how much is in it for them,' a federal minister said smugly, after Howard's out-of-the-blue announcement of his proposal. It is now clear the state leaders had other, legitimate concerns that were ignored in Howard's frantic attempts to present himself as bolder and more visionary than the new federal Labor leader.

The Howard plan started with the headline – $10bn over 10 years. It was to be announced at the National Press Club on January 25. Just three weeks before that, Peter Shergold, head of the Prime Minister's department, convened a meeting of officials from relevant departments and agencies to discuss what might be included in the package. A task force was formed to put it together. Despite the huge cost, Treasury was not called in until a week before the announcement. The Department of Finance was kept out of the loop until three days before Howard's speech when – in the words of department secretary Ian Watt – they were 'asked if we would run our eye over, lightly...the costings that had been worked out by the task force'. Cabinet was never consulted.

This is the way the nation is run when Howard has his back to the wall electorally. By throwing the whole thing together in three weeks, Howard at least showed how fast the wheels of government can be made to grind when a PM is in trouble.

355

The two faces of Kevin Rudd

25 June 2007

Let's be honest. Kevin Rudd, at this stage of his career, is not worth one biography, let alone two. The bloke's been opposition leader for five minutes, and before that he'd done nothing particularly significant or exciting. Too many trees are sacrificed in this country for books that should not be published. Consider the paper wasted on tomes about (and by) Mark Latham, a flash-in-the-pan if ever there was one. At least Kim Beazley had a longish ministerial career behind him, plus a couple of years as Labor leader, before anyone took the trouble to put his life between covers.

The big contrast, of course, is John Howard. He's been in public life for 33 years, served as treasurer under Malcolm Fraser, had two periods as opposition leader, found himself at the centre of dozens of political battles and dramas, been counted out and come back time and again, lost one election and won four, become the country's longest-serving prime minister since Sir Robert Menzies, and earned the accolade – from Rudd – of being the cleverest politician of his generation. So far, just one biography has been produced, and a pretty awful one at that. Fortunately, a more substantial book – *John Winston Howard: The Biography*, by Peter van Onselen and Wayne Errington – is due out soon. Howard's life and achievements cry out for book-length treatment.

Rudd's don't. Not yet, anyway. School, university, a few fairly uneventful years as a junior diplomat, a period working in the Queensland bureaucracy, a couple of terms in parliament – hardly scintillating stuff. That has not stopped Robert Macklin and Nicholas Stuart hammering out 532 pages between them on his life and times.

The Labor leader cooperated with Macklin. He and his wife, Thérèse Rein, as well as friends and family, provided interviews for *Kevin Rudd: The Biography*. Nicholas Stuart, on the other hand, got no cooperation – was, in fact, obstructed – in the writing of *Kevin*

Rudd: An Unauthorised Political Biography. The treatment of Stuart says as much about Rudd as anything revealed in either book.

Stuart began trying to get an interview with Rudd last December, but was repeatedly put off over the ensuing months. Then, half an hour after submitting his completed manuscript to the publishers, he got a phone call saying he could interview the Labor leader the next day. Arriving for the appointment, however, he was told: 'Mate, he's too busy.' Another appointment was scheduled, but Rudd did not turn up. According to the book, Rudd also asked other people not to speak to Stuart. A person he consulted about Rudd's period working for Wayne Goss's government in Queensland told him: 'You're not going to get very much because everyone's been leant on pretty heavily...The Rudd machine has gone to work.'

The same Rudd machine that has tried to prevent newspapers publishing material that casts him in a less than favourable light. This is further evidence of Rudd's super-sensitivity about his image. He is a politician ready to go to great lengths to control what is said and written about him. This kind of attempted manipulation casts doubt on his judgment. Cooperating with Macklin achieved the desired result – a book that portrays the Labor leader as he wants to be seen. You have to pore over Macklin's work very closely indeed to find any criticism. But, deprived of the easy route, Stuart has worked harder than Macklin and done more digging. Stuart's warts-and-all study makes Rudd a much more interesting and well-rounded figure, and is likely to do him more good.

So what do we learn about Rudd from these books? For a start, his background was Queensland conservative. By his own admission, Macklin says, his mother probably voted DLP and his father supported the Nationals. Whether Rudd's version of events surrounding his father's death and the family's eviction from their dairy farm is accurate or not, it is clear that he believed it and it helped to shape the views that led him as a teenager to the Labor Party. Stuart informs us that the young Rudd captained the champion Nambour High debating team, and later reached the Australian finals of a public speaking contest called 'Youth Speaks for Australia'.

Even in childhood he was neat, organised, disciplined, determined. At university a lecturer recalls him as having 'an air of quiet certainty about him', adding: 'His was the certainty of the man who knows himself.' Rudd took a year off between school and university, partly to deal with what he describes as 'foundational questions'. After some solid reflection he made an adult decision that he was a believer.

At school he had been fascinated by Thomas More, the English humanist who opposed Henry VIII on a matter of conscience and was executed. At the Australian National University, he chose to do his thesis on political dissent in China because – according to his tutor – he was interested in 'the potential conflict between the individual and the state and whether a person should follow their conscience or the imperatives of the despot'. Jump forward to Rudd's article titled 'Faith in Politics' published two months before his successful leadership challenge against Kim Beazley and designed to show that Christian voters could be as much at home with Labor as with the conservatives. Rudd used the martyrdom of Dietrich Bonhoeffer, the German theologian hanged for actively resisting Hitler and the Nazis, as the starting point for a discussion of 'the proper relationship between Christianity and politics in the modern world'. There is a reassuring consistency in all this.

Both books deal at length with Rudd's period in the Foreign Affairs Department, but of rather more relevance to the current debate over his suitability for the prime ministership is the time he spent as Goss's chief of staff and then as head of the Queensland cabinet office – a key policy coordination role. Howard, Peter Costello, Tony Abbott and the rest of the government head-kickers draw extensively on this part of Rudd's career in their attempts to discredit him. Rudd himself relies heavily on it as evidence that he is not the inexperienced novice the coalition tries to portray him as.

According to Stuart: 'Rudd challenged established structures with his attempts to shake up a deeply entrenched bureaucracy that had long operated without accountability.' After the years of Bjelke-Petersen government, this was necessary. The firm impression is that Rudd was effective in pushing policy agendas through, and he was strong enough to say 'no' to ministers trying to engage in nepotism and favouritism with government appointments.

But Rudd was left to take the kicks when some Labor politicians got cold feet about public service reform. And his managerial style could cause resentment. One public servant from the time is quoted as saying: 'He would intimidate people. It was quite deliberate and very calculated.' But the late Tom Burns, deputy premier at the time, provided Stuart with a spirited defence of the way Rudd operated. 'Other ministers would come along to budget review with their dreams, but they weren't properly worked out,' he said. 'They got knocked back, so who are they going to blame? Kevin. They called him Doctor Death, the Mandarin, a whole lot of things like that. Well, that's because he was tough.'

Both authors agree that, during his time with Goss, Rudd displayed an unwise level of arrogance. He was brought back to earth when he ran for the seat of Griffith in the 1996 federal election and was caught up in the anti-Keating landslide. Defeat was good for him. Macklin says it 'swept away the superior air that had surrounded him...he learned that it was better to listen than to lecture'. Rudd turned himself into a skilful grassroots campaigner – the kind who turns up in a mobile office at a shopping centre in his electorate every weekend. He won Griffith in 1998, and has increased his majority at every election since.

One of the riddles about Rudd is how someone who used to be rather awkward when it came to chatting up voters got to be so good at it. Stuart quotes an associate who provides some insight. 'He's an intellectual and doesn't seem to have a lot in common with ordinary people,' this person says, 'but I think he realised this was a problem, and so he's managed to find a way of making ordinary people interesting puzzles for his mind to keep busy with. That's what's made the difference, because he's become intrigued with us. He's become engaged.'

An area where Stuart's book is clearly superior is in explaining how the Rudd forces ambushed Beazley's roosters and seized the leadership. The key was Julia Gillard's decision to put her own leadership ambitions on hold and swing behind Rudd. They held a series of secret meetings. Gillard did not even tell her own staff about them. Once an accommodation was reached, Beazley's fate was sealed.

So there is some useful material in these volumes. But particularly pertinent is a line from Lindsay Tanner in the introduction to Stuart's book, 'I'm in favour of political biographies being written after, not before, people have been in power,' the Labor frontbencher says. Right on!

Excess baggage

7 July 2007

On a trip to the United States in 1984, Peter Costello found himself standing in a supermarket queue in Mobile, Alabama, watching as a young black mother produced food stamps at the cash register to pay for her groceries. 'Those stamps will not work on this basket,' she was told curtly. Then, with everyone in the queue looking on, the checkout operator inspected the shopping trolley item by item, ostentatiously removing everything – chips, chocolate and other foodstuffs not regarded as essential – to which the vouchers did not apply. The woman was humiliated.

The food stamps program feeds millions of needy Americans, and in that sense it is admirable. But what the 25-year-old Costello saw that day showed that it could also be brutal and demeaning. He decided he would not want to see such a system operating in Australia. That is why the Treasurer was initially reluctant to support proposals to deal with gambling, boozing or drug-addicted parents by quarantining a proportion of family payments to be spent only on food, clothing and other essentials.

The man who turned Costello around was Cape York Aboriginal leader Noel Pearson. During a 2005 visit to the Cape, Costello listened to Pearson's arguments for welfare payments to be redirected from 'bad parents' who blew the money to responsible family members who would use it to feed, clothe and house the children it was meant to benefit. The Treasurer was asked at the time why a system of extracting family payments from welfare cheques going to parents who would misuse them should be confined to Aboriginal communities. He agreed that the principle could and should be applied to non-Indigenous parents as well.

From there, it was only a small step for Costello to back the proposal first put forward by Mal Brough in April last year for a portion of family payments to be 'quarantined' by Centrelink in cases where parents could not be trusted to meet the needs of their children. The Families and Indigenous Affairs Minister told Nine's *Sunday* program back then that he wanted to 'take up the initiative that we have been using up in the Cape on a voluntary basis with some Indigenous communities where money is direct debited through Centrelink'. Brough proposed compulsorily earmarking a fixed percentage of payments to be spent on food, clothing and housing. Costello would not have supported a voucher system, but was persuaded the use of EFTPOS cards could eliminate the worst aspects of what he had seen in the US.

The Costello conversion mirrors what has happened with other senior ministers. It shows that the ground was prepared for quarantining of welfare payments for the benefit of children in Aboriginal communities well ahead of the *Little Children Are Sacred* report on child sexual abuse in the Northern Territory. And it makes clear that the idea of extending the principle to protect children of non-Indigenous parents who waste welfare money is not simply a counter to accusations that the federal government's actions in the NT are racially based.

Costello's experience also demonstrates, again, the influence of Pearson. It was, of course, an emotional Pearson news conference on the child sexual abuse issue that persuaded John Howard of the urgent need for dramatic federal intervention. And all of this gives the lie to claims that what the federal government is doing is, at bottom, just a hastily cobbled together pre-election stunt and an exercise in wedge politics.

That being said, however, mistakes have been made in the implementation of Howard's NT plan that provide ammunition for critics and cynics. The confusion over health checks is a case in point. In his initial announcement, Brough said measures would include 'compulsory health checks for all Aboriginal children to identify and treat health problems and any effects of abuse'. The Prime Minister used the same form of words. But just a week later, when Health Minister Tony Abbott held a news conference, the health checks were compulsory no longer. No one will admit publicly to a cock-up, but the reason for the change was advice that health checks on children without parental consent would constitute assault. That something as basic as this could be overlooked reflects very sloppy preparation.

Equally silly was Howard's claim that the cost of dealing with what he called a 'national emergency' would be 'some tens of millions – it's not huge'. If Howard is fair dinkum – if he is looking past the election to the longer term – the cost won't be tens of millions of dollars; it will be billions. New houses, new schools and new health facilities will have to be built. Many more teachers, doctors and nurses will be needed. More police will have to be employed on a permanent basis. Rex Wild, QC, co-author of the *Little Children Are Sacred* report, wants government to commit the equivalent of the $6bn a year raised from taxes on alcohol.

Howard will have been stung by the Galaxy Poll finding in News Ltd papers that 58 percent of voters believe he is acting on this issue only because of the looming election. That reflects the fact that, after 11 years of clever political ploys and unscrupulous stunts such as the 'children-overboard' affair, Howard has a lot of baggage. Voters are reluctant to take anything he does at face value. They are deeply cynical about his motivations. There were plenty of warnings about this before Howard decided last year to stay on for another election rather than handing over to a new, fresher leader. Which brings us neatly back to Peter Costello...

Hollow the leader

30 July 2007

A major reason for John Howard's political longevity has been his ability to learn from mistakes. At the end of the newly published Howard biography, however, the authors suggest that he may now have made 'the one mistake in politics that he wouldn't be around to learn from – misjudging his optimal retirement date'. As the government's woes multiplied in recent weeks, the question of whether Howard has botched the timing of his exit has dominated discussion among the politerati. It has also been exercising Howard's own mind.

'Is it me?' he is supposed to have asked during a cabinet free-for-all on why the government's electoral support, as measured by the opinion polls, is so disastrously low. In fact, there is considerable doubt about whether the PM did anything of the kind. Peter Costello candidly told a radio interviewer in Dubbo: 'The funny thing is, I was actually in cabinet yesterday...and I actually never heard that said.' Some Costello supporters are alleging a phoney line was fed out so that Howard could claim the leadership issue was raised and he received the full backing of ministers.

But, whether he put the question to cabinet or not, Howard has certainly been asking it of himself. A few months ago, he was sounding out friends and family. More recently he has assiduously studied Liberal Party polling on what voters think of him. (The same polling also shows, of course, what they think of Costello.) The upshot is that, despite the polls and Kevin Rudd's big lead, Howard has convinced himself – as he did a year ago – that it is still in the Liberal Party's best interests that he lead it to another election. To put it another way, he has concluded that a leadership switch to Costello at this stage would not be in the interests of the party. Asked about retirement on radio a few days after the cabinet meeting, Howard responded: 'Mate, it ain't close.'

Publicly, no one is rocking the boat about this. Even privately, most in the Costello camp accept that the leadership team is set and – for better or for worse – Howard will take the party into the election. But there are some Liberal MPs so pessimistic about the government's prospects of electoral survival that they bitterly criticise party officers for not taking action. One says: 'Isn't this the time when the federal director [Brian Loughnane] takes the leader aside and says the jig is up?'

Not surprisingly, the Labor Party has also been considering the possibility that the Liberals might change leaders, but the assessment is that they will opt for the status quo. An ALP strategist puts it this way: 'If you are the Liberal federal director, you can't say that Howard is so much on the nose that he'll definitely lose. And Costello is not doing so well that, if you go to him, you'd be sure of winning. In Loughnane's position I'd come down narrowly on the side of sticking with Howard. A switch would kill off the "man of the past" thing, but it would be a hell of a risk. Costello has a lot of baggage.'

The Treasurer has more baggage now, of course, following publication of *John Winston Howard: The Biography*. By criticising Howard so freely to the authors, Wayne Errington and Peter van Onselen, when he must have known the book would appear in the lead-up to the election, Costello provided ammunition for those who claim he lacks judgment. And some material was obviously provided to the authors by Howard supporters wanting to damage Costello – particularly the revelation that in 1999 he raised the prospect of a double-dissolution election in order to pass the GST package as a whole rather than submit to Democrat demands that food be excluded. 'Howard would have none of it,' according to Errington and van Onselen. 'He knew the government could not win a second election selling the GST and began wondering if Costello had the political nous to win elections.'

But the book wounds the PM more. Costello's assessment that, as treasurer in the Fraser government, Howard 'had not been a great reformer' and 'was not a success in terms of interest rates and inflation' can perhaps be discounted as ancient history. But Costello's portrayal of the contemporary Howard as a profligate PM prepared to engage in unsustainable spending to win votes is manna from heaven for a Labor Party needing to blunt another interest-rate scare campaign.

Howard favourite Jackie Kelly also undermines the PM with her candour over a 2001 conversation with Howard just before he announced the government's decision to stop the *Tampa* entering Australian waters with its cargo of rescued refugees. When Kelly said she'd lose her western Sydney seat of Lindsay unless something was done about the One Nation party's growing support, Howard waved his speaking notes and replied: 'Don't worry, Jackie. That's about to change.' The comment feeds the suspicion that the hard line on *Tampa* was primarily about rescuing the government's electoral fortunes at a time when similar suspicions are being aired about the government's handling of the Mohamed Haneef case.

But what is likely to hurt the government most is the revelation that Howard insisted on pressing ahead with the WorkChoices legislation even though the then-workplace relations minister, Kevin Andrews, warned cabinet that 'there was no getting around some workers losing out under the proposed legislation'. It contradicts Howard's repeated claims and gives legitimacy to the anti-WorkChoices campaign being run by the ACTU.

Howard no doubt thought that a biography setting out his achievements over 11 years in government would be a political plus, but the exercise has backfired. It may be that most people had already factored in the Treasurer's leadership frustrations and the poisonous Howard–Costello relationship, but it does the government no good to have them reminded of it. Many of the book's revelations will confirm and reinforce doubts and concerns the voters already had. And the wide media coverage sucked all the oxygen out of Howard's attempts to counter the bad polls. At the very least, it was a lost week for the government.

So why did the PM, along with his family, friends and supporters – and Costello, of course – cooperate so willingly and speak so frankly? The answer was provided by van Onselen on ABC-TV's *Insiders* program: Liberal Party hubris. 'Kevin Rudd wasn't leader when we were doing these interviews,' he said. 'The party was feeling pretty confident that it was cruising towards a victory at the next election.'

Since the advent of Rudd, though, the coalition has looked more like cruising to defeat. There is precious little hubris around now. Which brings us back to the leadership issue. On the day Costello's latest bagging of Howard hit the headlines, there was widespread anger in the party. Costello was condemned in private by many of his colleagues for irresponsible self-indulgence. He was branded a sook. But, significantly, Alby Schultz, who called on the Treasurer to 'pull his head in', was the only Liberal MP to go public. As the days passed, there was acceptance of the explanation that the Treasurer had made his comments while still bruised and upset following the leadership row in July last year.

Costello's comments in the biography, though, highlight the serious consequences of the Liberal Party's failure to sort out the leadership question. Assuming Howard stays in the job, the issue will not go away. Voters can be in no doubt that it will be on the table immediately after the election, whether the coalition wins or loses. The biography has given Labor a means of stirring the Liberal leadership pot from now until polling day.

Interestingly, some Howard loyalists are prepared to admit Costello might well have been prime minister by now if he had taken a tougher stand last year and resigned from the ministry when evidence emerged that Howard had reneged on a leadership handover deal.

Outside the government on the back bench, they say, he would have been in a much better position to advance his leadership claims and exploit the coalition's dramatic poll slump when it came. Explaining to the authors of the biography why he decided to stay in the tent, Costello said: 'Whatever my ambitions were, the party was always greater than them.' It is just possible, however, that resignation back then might have served both him and the party better.

Send in the clown

1 August 2007

Most governments contain ministers who are not up to the job. John Howard's government is no exception. The public, however, is entitled to expect that those of doubtful competence or ability will not be slotted into important portfolios. When Howard decided a better performer was needed in the electorally crucial industrial relations area, he could and should have hidden Kevin Andrews in one of the less sensitive ministerial posts. Instead, Andrews was transferred to immigration. Now we see the results.

The case of Dr Mohamed Haneef has brutally highlighted Andrews's limitations. The man is a political stumblebum. His own statements make that clear. First there was the extraordinary attack on Kevin Rudd and deputy Julia Gillard. Andrews accused them of 'cheap talk' for saying they believed the government had acted in good faith in the Haneef affair. Yes, that's right. The opposition leadership defends the government and Andrews bags them for it. If his cabinet colleagues were not deeply embarrassed by this clownish behaviour, they should have been.

Then there was Andrews's comment after the Gold Coast doctor left the country to return to India. The case against Haneef had collapsed spectacularly. A red-faced Director of Public Prosecutions had admitted that the charge of recklessly providing a SIM card to a terrorist organisation could not be sustained. Australian Federal Police Commissioner Mick Keelty had raised no objection to Haneef going home to Bangalore. And what does Andrews say? That Haneef's departure 'actually heightens rather than lessens my suspicion'.

Think about it. Haneef had been locked up for a month, all dignity stripped away as he was repeatedly brought to court in Guantanamo Bay-style prison clothes and without shoes. His reputation had been trashed. When a magistrate granted him bail, Andrews intervened to revoke his working visa so that he could be kept behind bars anyway. After his release, when charges were dropped, Andrews's refusal to reinstate the visa meant that Haneef could not return to his hospital job or earn a living in any other way. He had a wife waiting in Bangalore, not to mention a newborn child he had never seen. To top it all off, the government intended to deport him anyway.

Of course Haneef was going to get on the first available plane out of Australia. Any sane person would have done the same. And yet to Andrews this is evidence of guilt. The sooner the bloke is out of the immigration portfolio – preferably out of the ministry altogether – the better it will be. As this case has shown, an immigration minister can wield great power without much accountability. The job requires someone sensible, sensitive and with sure hands. Andrews does not fit that job description.

His most serious error was undoubtedly the July 16 revocation of Haneef's visa. Haneef could have been released and kept under observation by police while they continued investigations. There are indications that this was the course Keelty would have preferred. By effectively overriding the magistrate's decision to grant bail because the prosecution case was weak, Andrews gave weight to suspicions that, on behalf of an embattled government floundering in the polls, he was out to ramp up national security as an issue. It was a turning point. The mood in the media changed. The actions of the government, the police and the DPP were put under closer scrutiny. The whole thing started to unravel.

But the Prime Minister shares the blame for a fiasco that has embarrassed Australia internationally and undermined public confidence in those who administer our anti-terrorism laws. While professing support for the presumption of innocence, Howard – like other senior ministers – was happy to insinuate Haneef's guilt. He gave Andrews the nod for the visa cancellation. Clearly, Howard saw the affair as an opportunity to gain a political advantage. And, if talkback radio is any guide, the government probably did get some political benefit, despite the bungles. Howard knows that fear of terrorism is likely to outweigh concern for civil liberties with many voters. But Labor's refusal to be wedged – Rudd avoided it by backing the government's actions – minimised the electoral impact.

No one comes out of the Haneef affair well. Keelty's reputation has taken a hit and the office of DPP Damian Bugg has been humiliated. Two major errors were made in material put before the court – one the fault of a prosecutor, the other the result of incorrect material provided by the AFP. Keelty has implied that the DPP was too quick to proceed to charges, forcing police to rush their work. At the same time, Keelty's criticism of the role the defence barrister and sections of the media played in exposing the errors in the prosecution case looks self-serving. But the hapless and hopeless Immigration Minister is the player most damaged.

Whether Haneef is a bad egg, as Andrews continues to imply, or an innocent man, the ham-fisted handling of the matter has called the government's national security credentials into question. More importantly, a lot of trust has been squandered, and there will be consequences. For example, the government will face a much tougher political battle now if it tries to argue for a further tightening of anti-terrorism laws. Undoing the damage will not be easy, but getting rid of Andrews would be a start.

The comeback track

13 August 2007

The Prime Minister is supposed to be the tricky one. John Howard gets credit – or perhaps blame – from voters for being clever. He is seen as the smart old dog who always finds a way out of trouble. But a lot of the clever trickery and political smarts actually come out of the back room. The key role played by Mark Textor, the Liberal Party's pollster, has been known to close observers of the political process for a long time. Now the proof of Textor's Machiavellian influence has been spread over newspaper front pages for all to see.

In this context, 'Machiavellian' is not meant to be a derogatory term. Machiavelli may have placed expediency ahead of everything else, but he was hardly Robinson Crusoe in the world of politics. Textor's advice may be cunning, but being cunning is no crime in politics, either. When political parties hire professionals like Textor and his business partner, former Liberal federal director Lynton Crosby, they are not paying for morality lessons. They want to know how to win. Labor luminaries such as party president John Faulkner try to demonise Textor, but they dearly wish he worked for them.

In the past month and a half, Howard has started to get his act together. Even some of the government's toughest critics acknowledge it. 'Howard is back,' wrote Kim Beazley's former chief of staff, Michael Costello, in *The Australian*. 'His palpable uncertainty about the line to take against Labor has vanished.' The leaking to News Ltd's

Malcolm Farr of Textor's confidential June 21 report titled *Federal State of Play – Oz Track 33* provides an explanation. In 2001, the hard-hitting 'Mean and Tricky' memo from then Liberal president Shane Stone gave Howard a blueprint to restore the coalition's electoral fortunes. The Textor document may prove to be the 2007 equivalent.

Look at what Textor says and compare it with Howard's words and actions. The stand-out line from *Oz Track 33* refers to the 'need to emphasise Commonwealth is "bailing out" ineffective and inefficient states'. Howard embraces that in his recent advocacy of what he calls 'actively pragmatic federalism'. That means, he says, that when state governments 'fall down on the job', the feds move in. The federal takeover of a Tasmanian hospital slated for downgrading by the state Labor government is held up as an example of this. Declaring war on the premiers is a Crosby–Textor strategy.

At a more fundamental level is the *Oz Track 33* warning that Howard was being seen as 'increasingly rattled and not responding well under pressure' and the report's advice that the Prime Minister needed to 'reconnect with voters' to counter Rudd's warm reception by the electorate. The PM clearly took note. To quote Michael Costello's perceptive column again: 'After looking rattled, jumpy and on edge all year…Howard is back on his game.'

In the same way that he had to suppress a give-away shoulder twitch once before when he was under pressure, Howard has been carefully projecting an image of calmness and confidence. And he has certainly been working at reconnecting, coming out from behind the lectern and getting among the battlers in shopping centres just about every day. Minders, who prefer an environment they can control, would have been nervous, but the television pictures have projected a warmer, friendlier and more accessible persona.

Like Stone with his pull-no-punches analysis of the government's shortcomings six years ago, Textor has been very frank in his assessment. In both cases, the bad news colourfully expressed was guaranteed to get the Prime Minister's attention. But the government's chances of recovery will not be helped by the leaking of Textor's findings – among them that Howard's age is an issue, that some voters have reframed 'experience' to 'cleverness' to the PM's detriment, and that 'there is significant disillusionment with Liberals on the issue of broken promises and dishonesty'. Also, by attributing the government's poor poll position so heavily to problems associated with the leader, the report raises serious doubts about whether any advice can save the day.

The report urges Howard to use the 'gravitas' of government. But in the situation Howard finds himself, that is more easily said than done. The way he has been running around buying votes – with the Mersey Hospital takeover in the marginal Tasmanian seat of Braddon the most blatant and transparent example – conveys a sense of desperation more than gravitas. 'He's not looking prime ministerial,' says one seasoned political observer. 'He's reduced to being just a candidate with a bucket of money.'

Oz Track 33 also calls on the government to stress its economic management record. No surprise there, and Howard did not need polling and confidential reports to tell him that was the way to go. But pork-barrelling and economic responsibility do not go together easily, especially when distribution of the pork is on such a massive scale and interest-rate pressures are at the forefront of voters' minds. No PR magic can sell the $45m-a-year Mersey Hospital bribe as economically sound. The Tasmanian Labor government had a sensible plan for more economic and efficient use of scarce health resources. By overriding it, Howard locked in inefficiency, waste and duplication to hold on to a seat. Smart politics maybe; irresponsible economics undoubtedly.

Textor, who learned much about the dark political arts from Republican pollsters and strategists in the US, is the best in the business in this country. He has done what he can to show the coalition a way out, and Howard is following the road map. But, if the *Oz Track 33* report is right about the extent of voter disillusionment with Howard and the electorate's favourable opinion of Rudd – 'so just like John Howard but younger' – it may be too late.

Two-headed lame duck

21 September 2007

It was almost as though John Howard had based his new leadership transition plan on Dr Dolittle's exotic two-headed llama, the pushmi-pullyu. Assuming the coalition survived the looming election, the Prime Minister said, he would retire part-way into the new parliamentary term and hand over to Peter Costello. In the meantime, Costello would play a much more prominent role – particularly in the election campaign. By the time the spin merchants had finished with that, pundits were writing about a leadership 'duumvirate' and Costello was being billed almost as a co-PM. Costello would campaign as 'putative prime minister' and the coalition's response to the fresh face of Kevin Rudd, explained *The Australian*. 'Two leaders for the price of one' was a common theme running through the media.

But the two-headed leadership notion was always impractical and desperate nonsense. As with the pushmi-pullyu, which had heads at each end of its body, getting such a beast to move in a consistent direction would be almost impossible. Howard will go into the election as leader, Costello as his offsider. There will be no duumvirate. But the spin was not without purpose.

Because voters appeared to have turned off Howard, and given that his standing and authority were further eroded by the farce of the leadership soundings he requested and then rejected, the aim was to focus more attention on the team. More specifically, on the strongest member of the team – Costello. The plan – insofar as there was a plan – involved making a strength out of the government's best performer. The 'co-PM' furphy is simply a means of ensuring Costello gets more coverage in the campaign than has occurred in past elections. That, the reasoning goes, should help to make economic management the issue which, in turn, might bring in some votes.

And there could be another plus. Howard was scornful of Tony Blair for announcing before the last UK election that he would retire and hand over to Gordon Brown at some stage during the following term. The Howard view was that Blair risked making himself a lame duck. But in the British election campaign, Blair and Brown managed to project a feeling of transition, succession and renewal which worked to the government's advantage. Achieving the same positive feeling here is far more important to the Liberals than the likelihood of Howard becoming a lame duck after the election.

The entire arrangement, though, is an unsatisfactory compromise which gives added point to Labor's election slogan: New Leadership. The unveiling of that slogan at a rally in Sydney's western suburbs mortgage belt was yet another piece of evidence that, in his bid for the prime ministership, Rudd has luck on his side. It came at the end of 10 days of leadership speculation and turmoil in the Liberal Party, so the timing was exquisite. But it was also accidental. The slogan launch, at an event designed as a dress rehearsal for Labor's official campaign opening when Howard calls the election, had been planned well before the PM got into a funk about *Newspoll* and set the leadership hares running.

Rudd and the apparatchiks fine-tuning Labor's campaign machine might be clever, but no one could have predicted that a politician as canny as Howard would so stupidly shoot himself in the foot. With the assistance of Alexander Downer, Howard did enormous damage to the Liberal Party and its election prospects. Did it not occur to Howard, when he asked Downer to consult cabinet members about the leadership, that a majority – as alarmed as he was by a disastrous poll – might favour a change? Did it not occur to Downer, when he convened a meeting of senior ministers to canvass opinion on whether Howard should stay or go, that once you get eight people in a room, there is no chance that the outcome will remain secret? Howard, with a little bit of help from his friends, created his own leadership crisis. For sheer dopiness, it was reminiscent of the day back in 1985 when then Liberal leader Andrew Peacock clumsily tried to sack Howard as his deputy and ended up being replaced by Howard in the top job.

Something has gone badly awry with Howard's political judgment. That was again evident in his public justification for remaining leader against the wishes of his colleagues. 'My level of personal support is significantly higher than the party's,' he told a radio interviewer. 'If the party's level of support in the opinion polls was as high as mine is, it would be a different story.' In other words, it is not Howard's fault the government looks to be heading for defeat; everybody else is to blame. The resulting front-page headline in Sydney's *Daily Telegraph*, the PM's favourite newspaper, summed up the arrogance of the statement. 'You're Nothing Without Me', it read.

Howard clearly hated admitting he would not serve another full term as prime minister if he won the election. He did it through gritted teeth in the party room, and on television his reluctance was palpable as he announced he would 'probably...certainly' retire part-way through. But he had no choice. Voters knew he would not run again in his seventies, and had already factored that into their thinking about the election. And any attempt to persist with the old formula – 'I will remain as leader for as long as the party wants me to' – would have been treated with contempt once the results of the cabinet soundings leaked.

After dismissing the majority cabinet view brought back to him by Downer, and vowing to stay on as leader anyway, Howard can no longer pretend that he puts the Liberal Party's interests ahead of his own. He had better win the election now, or he will inevitably be portrayed as the villain. His legacy will be seen through the prism of the past few months and massively diminished as a result.

The Embassy Rooftop Strategy

6 November 2007

The document put together in secret by a small group of ALP hard-heads in the dying days of the Keating government was titled 'What To Do When Labor Loses'. But it was referred to by those in the know as 'The Embassy Rooftop Strategy'. That was an allusion to the evacuation of more than 1000 Americans and some five times that number of South Vietnamese from the US embassy in Saigon as North Vietnamese troops occupied the city on April 30, 1975. Relays of helicopters plucked them from the embassy roof and flew them to ships of the US 7th Fleet in the South China Sea. Choppers had to be tipped overboard from some ships to make room on deck for others to land.

'You save what you have to save,' a Labor figure involved in the 1996 operation told me once. 'That's the situation we were in.' The group came to the conclusion a few weeks out from the election that there was no prospect of Paul Keating pulling off a victory. Normally in election campaigns, no matter how hopeless things look, everyone focuses on how to win. They do not allow themselves to prepare for the worst. But this handful of Labor MPs, officials and staffers did the unthinkable.

They were prompted to act by memories of a conversation after the defeat of Barrie Unsworth's Labor government in NSW in 1988. Several of those involved in setting up the new opposition under Bob Carr had a long discussion about what should have been done before the election to prepare for the political equivalent of a nuclear winter. Their conclusions formed the basis for what happened in Canberra eight years later as it became clear that the coalition forces were about to take power.

'What To Do When Labor Loses' was a highly sensitive document, for obvious reasons, so it had a very small circulation. Only Labor's core leadership group – excluding Keating – and a very few others were aware of its existence. The aim was to help set Labor up for opposition. The thinking was that the early months of opposition would be crucial to the party's recovery. It is fair to say that the secret blueprint laid the groundwork for Kim Beazley's near-win in 1998.

In light of the opinion polls, it would be interesting to know if there is a similar group in the Liberal Party now, drawing up and quietly implementing its own Embassy Rooftop Strategy. Just as Rudd has a team working on 'transition to government', is there a Liberal team working on 'transition to opposition'? Are there people who have read the wind, decided that the party is headed for defeat and appointed themselves custodians of its future?

The starting point for 'What To Do If Labor Loses' was that nothing must happen in ministerial offices in the final days that would stress or stretch the caretaker protocols. Care was taken to ensure no major decisions were taken, appointments made, contracts renewed or obligations locked in that might cause embarrassment to Labor after the election. If Labor was to be up and running quickly in opposition, there must be no hidden time bombs from the period of pre-election desperation.

A crucial part of the strategy was to make sure that all documents to which ministers were entitled were boxed and quietly removed from parliament. Shredders were not to be used because it was realised that information contained in the documents would be gold to opposition MPs cut off from public service assistance. Staff lists and mailing lists were included because of their potential value in allowing shadow ministers to establish themselves quickly. Boxes were transported to ALP national headquarters.

The process caused considerable distress among some ministerial staff who were approached to help. 'But we haven't lost yet,' was a frequent complaint. Not all cooperated. Keating's office could not be 'sanitised' (that's the word that was used) because a senior staffer – knowing how angry the PM would be – flatly refused permission. But he did not dob in those behind the exercise, and Keating remained blissfully ignorant of what was going on.

And the documents proved their worth over the next two years, providing background that enabled the new Labor opposition to put new ministers under pressure quickly. Alexander Downer, for example, was embarrassed over the Export Market Developments Grants scheme as a result of information from documents that had been removed from the office of Labor's trade minister, Peter Cook.

The 'What To Do' strategy also stressed that, where possible, arrangements should be made for Labor staffers who had come from the public service to be slotted back in. Before polling day (and therefore before coalition ministers had a say), key staffers were quietly advised to approach departmental heads to discuss what positions they could move to after the election.

And hard decisions were made about staff to be employed in opposition. It was agreed that most of those who had worked for ministers should not get jobs because government and opposition required different skill sets. A good speechwriter for a treasurer is not necessarily the right person to be jack-of-all-trades in a shadow treasurer's office. Quite a few of those judged to have the right stuff for opposition, however, were locked in before the change of government.

The final – and hardest – decision was to hold back $2m that could have been spent on Labor advertising in the final week. It was agreed the money would be better saved for the next campaign, rather than thrown away on a lost cause. These are the kind of issues Liberals face this time around if the polls don't improve quickly.

Election that changes everything

28 November 2007

On the Saturday evening before the election, Kevin Rudd was in Melbourne. It was an opportunity for some time off, an early night after five weeks of tough campaigning. Instead, Rudd went onto the streets to visit a soup kitchen and talk to the homeless people who rely on it. And he spent time at a homeless shelter, listening to the stories of the residents. There were no cameras, no reporters. The media were not told about the outing. It was not about votes. But it said a lot about the man who would be swept into the prime ministership a week later.

As part of the most negative campaign ever seen in this country, John Howard and his lieutenants had tried to portray the Labor leader as a politician bereft of genuine beliefs. Tony Abbott, shameless as always, even tried to cast doubt on Rudd's Christian faith. But Australia's new prime minister has strong principles. Christian principles. He believes in good works, and he practises what he preaches.

During the campaign, when he might have been expected to be focused totally on winning the election, Rudd also made quiet visits to shelters in Brisbane and Sydney. He had been appalled at Census statistics indicating that there are 100 000 homeless Australians, including 10 000 kids, an unknown number of whom are sleeping rough. He learned that centres set up to provide emergency accommodation are so short of beds that some have to turn away four out of every five people who ask for help.

Rudd gave a campaign commitment to provide $150m for extra emergency housing, but he did not make a big thing of it. The plight of the homeless was not something likely to be a vote-changer in middle Australia. But it looms large in the mind of the man about to move into the Lodge.

With federal coffers brimming with money, his conscience will compel him to use some of it to help those who have no voice and no political clout. 'You'll see a lot of activity on this, and fairly early in the life of the government,' says a source close to Rudd. Those who dismiss Labor's new hero as a cold, emotionless technocrat misread him badly.

Rudd is not one for high-blown rhetoric about Labor tradition and lights on the hill. As he said during the campaign, he is not an ideologue. He will be a strict manager, as he was when he earned the nickname 'Dr Death' for his cost-cutting zeal as head of the Queensland cabinet office under Wayne Goss.

And he is no saint. He is ruthless and calculating. As Machiavellian as any successful politician. Just ask Kim Beazley, who did not see Rudd's leadership takeover coming. Ask Wayne Swan, the former close mate who found out the hard way that Rudd does not put friendship ahead of ambition. Or ask Howard, supposedly the shrewdest and trickiest politician of his era, repeatedly out-thought and out-manoeuvred by Rudd over the past 12 months. You don't get to the top of the greasy pole in politics by being nice all the time.

But the bloke offering 'new leadership' also has the kind of concerns Labor leaders are supposed to have. Rudd is certainly, as he claims, an economic conservative, but he nevertheless has more in common with Tim Costello than with Peter. And the commentary suggesting he is a John Howard clone – a younger version of the PM the voters have so emphatically rejected – is mistaken.

Rudd's victory speech on election night made that clear. Howard was a polarising prime minister, routinely using wedges to divide Australians to gain a political advantage. Australia's 26th PM promises the opposite. He wants to banish the old political battles and divisions. He believes he can achieve his aims through consensus and cooperation. 'The future is too important for us not to work together,' he said. It is a style Howard would not recognise.

Part of the Rudd attempt at consensus will be a move towards a more civilised, less combative political discourse. It worked for him in the campaign. And he will have noted the way Australians reacted against the mean-spiritedness of the coalition's behaviour: the over-the-top ads, the exaggerations of Howard and Costello, the personal nastiness of Abbott and Alexander Downer, and – the event that symbolised it all – the racist Lindsay phoney flyer fiasco.

If an unexpected degree of altruism is likely to be a mark of Rudd's prime ministership, the election result has drawn attention to Howard's selfish approach to his own party. The charge of selfishness is being levelled at the rejected PM now by a whole swag of Liberal Party figures, including many who used to be ardent and uncritical supporters. The hollowness of Howard's mantra – that he would remain leader of the Liberal Party 'as long as the party wants me to and as long as it's in the best interests of the party' – has been exposed for all to see by the massacre inflicted on the coalition by voters who were well and truly over him and no longer impressed by his bag of tricks.

Had Howard been sincere about putting the interests of the party first, he would have accepted an orderly transition to Costello last year. He hung on past his use-by date because he could not bear to let go. As one very senior Liberal said the day after the election: 'He bought himself another 18 months in Kirribilli House, but he blew up the party and he blew up Peter Costello.'

Not that Howard is the only one deserving of blame. The entire cabinet and some of those at the top of the Liberal Party organisation are culpable. Downer, for one, now admits publicly that he had seen the defeat coming for a year. Other ministers make the same confession privately. So why didn't they do something about it? Because they did not want to commit regicide, they say. In which case, they deserved to lose. The Labor Party had no such scruples when it decided Beazley was unlikely to get it back into power.

During the September APEC summit, Downer – at Howard's request – sounded out the cabinet on whether there should be a leadership change. When Howard rejected the almost unanimous verdict – 'He should go!' – Downer lacked the courage to enforce it. According to a high-level Liberal source: 'Janette and his good friend in Washington [George W. Bush] didn't want him to go. So he stayed. And look at the consequences.' Had Costello taken over then, it is argued, he would have signed Kyoto, been persuaded to make WorkChoices more acceptable, ramped up his republican credentials and taken one or two other symbolic actions to show a change of direction, then campaigned on the 'New Leadership' slogan that Rudd appropriated. Abbott, the most loyal of Howard's chorus of 'yes' men, helped persuade him to stay. Now Abbott himself – whose own campaign performance was disastrous – wants the leadership of the party his mentor and hero has all but wrecked.

Costello is copping criticism for announcing that he is not interested in taking on the leadership in opposition. But the truth is that the outgoing treasurer is doing the right thing by himself and by the party. Not that he owes his colleagues anything, anyway. When Howard rejected the 'orderly transition' push last year, most Liberal ministers and backbenchers supported the decision. It was not just Howard who rebuffed Costello. They may regret it, but that's their problem. They did not want him then; he is entitled to a life now.

If Costello became opposition leader, the Labor government would lump him with responsibility for all the alleged wrongs of the Howard years – just as Costello himself pinned on Beazley the blame for all the sins of the Hawke and Keating administrations. It would be impossible for Costello to shake off the Howard legacy. Howard's decision to anoint him as a kind of co-leader for the election campaign guarantees that. What the Liberals need is a new leader less closely identified with Howard's 11½-year reign – someone who can credibly jettison much of the baggage and move in a new direction. Abbott and Downer could not do that.

Malcolm Turnbull, however, could pull it off – especially since the campaign leak revealing that he tried to persuade cabinet before the election to ratify Kyoto. (Most cabinet members agreed, but again they allowed Howard to overrule them.) Turnbull would be able to change direction on WorkChoices, which Liberal federal director Brian Loughnane admits alienated part of the party's core support group.

The new Liberal leader will face an unenviable task. The party is at its lowest point since its formation 63 years ago – out of power everywhere (except the Brisbane City Council). A number of its state branches are dysfunctional, none more so than the NSW branch taken over by right-wing religious zealots. The party's preselection processes badly need changing to frustrate the branch-stackers. And there is a desperate need for new office-bearers at the top of the federal organisation – particularly for a stronger, more effective party president.

Someone will have to grab the party by the scruff of the neck and fix these problems, and that someone should be the new leader. Turnbull is the man most likely. He does not mind treading on toes. And, because he is relatively new to politics, the people in the party who need to be dumped or jolted out of their entrenched ways are not his friends or allies.

But will the party that, lemming-like, allowed Howard to lead it over the electoral cliff see things that way? Have the Liberals learned anything from the defeat? The leadership vote will provide an indication.

Talent quest

7 December 2007

One of the things a desperate John Howard hoped would give him a chance in the election was 'the team'. The coalition, he claimed, had a far stronger team than Labor. Liberal advertising pushed the message that members of Kevin Rudd's front bench lacked not only experience, but talent as well. Pro-Howard commentators hammered the line that no one in Labor's ranks could hold a candle to Peter Costello, Alexander Downer, Tony Abbott or Malcolm Turnbull. This was central to the 'don't take the risk' warning that dominated the coalition campaign in the final week.

It was a hogwash argument that disappeared with the announce-ment of Rudd's ministry. Suddenly even employer groups that had opposed Labor's election were agreeing that Julia Gillard, handed a super-portfolio combining Education with Workplace Relations, was immensely capable. Wayne Swan was being praised by business and most of the financial press for the vision and energy he brings to the job of Treasurer. Stephen Smith's appointment as Foreign Minister earned almost universal praise, here and overseas. John Faulkner's re-emergence in a powerful new role as Special Minister of State and Cabinet Secretary was hailed as a masterstroke.

The truth is that Rudd's team is an impressive one. Unlike the Howard ministry, it contains very little dead wood. Gillard, Swan, Smith, Faulkner, Penny Wong, Lindsay Tanner, Nicola Roxon, Tony Burke, Anthony Albanese, Jenny Macklin and Robert McClelland would compare favourably with the upper echelon of any recent administration – even the first Hawke government, which is often held up as the yardstick.

At the bottom end of Rudd's ministry, there is the youth and enthusiasm of 30-year-old Kate Ellis alongside the steadiness and experience of former NSW attorney-general Bob Debus. And in training as future ministers – in the role of parliamentary secretaries – are the likes of Greg Combet, Maxine McKew, Bill Shorten, Gary Gray and Mike Kelly. The defeated coalition government had nothing like this spread or depth of talent.

And Rudd showed, in the way he shaped his team, the kind of smarts that could make him a formidable prime minister. He defied ALP tradition by picking the ministry himself – and has now given notice that he wants a caucus rule change to formalise this new power. Such was Rudd's authority that there were no leaks. Those who received a phone call to tell them they had been chosen were sworn to secrecy, and when one of them asked if he could pass on the good news to his wife, Rudd responded: 'Why?' The new government structure was tailored to fit the themes of Rudd's election campaign, with Gillard's portfolio – all about boosting productivity and dealing with the skills shortage – the stand-out example. Those who performed well in the run-up to the election – Gillard, Swan, Roxon, Smith, Wong – got the big jobs. Those whose performance disappointed – Peter Garrett the most prominent of them – paid a price.

The weakness of the coalition team was suddenly exposed when Costello declined to take over the leadership. Suitable alternatives were thin on the ground. Downer was unsellable as a leader for the future. Abbott, punchy and gaffe-prone, put up his hand for the job and was greeted by horse laughs. Malcolm Turnbull, the one Liberal who might have had the profile and toughness and cut-through ability to worry Rudd, was vetoed by the conservative wing because he had the sense to realise some of the Howard baggage rejected by voters needed to be dumped. Which left Brendan Nelson.

Ah, Brendan! Where to begin? His party room speech after his three-vote leadership ballot win is as good a place as any. Instead of delivering an inspirational pep talk to inject some fighting spirit into the defeated and demoralised Liberal army, Nelson went all teary. Small wonder Turnbull felt the need to deliver a pep talk in Nelson's office immediately afterwards in an attempt to inject some fighting spirit into the new leader.

Then there is the character issue. Nelson appears to believe in nothing. Or rather, when it suits him, he can believe in anything. He can be Liberal or Labor, moderate or conservative. Former treasury secretary John Stone recently described Nelson as 'like Andrew Peacock but without the substance'. Clever, but Stone actually got closer a few years ago when he dubbed Nelson 'a political hermaphrodite'.

As I have reminded readers of this column several times over the past dozen years, Nelson was identified with the Labor Party for two decades before deciding his political career prospects were better with the Liberals. Four days before the 1993 election, he was captured by TV cameras shouting at a crowd: 'I have never voted Liberal in my life.' Not long after that, he started trailing his coat for a seat in federal parliament, but for some time refused to say which party he wanted to represent. Asked at one point if it was true he had abandoned Labor and joined the Liberals, he replied: 'I'm not prepared to say. It's like asking somebody to show you their tax return.' Then, in 1995, he targeted the second-safest Liberal seat in the nation and announced that his 'I never voted Liberal' statement had been a lie. He had voted Liberal since 1987, he claimed, but had remained in the ALP because 'I was trying to push things important to the AMA. There was a Labor government in Canberra'.

Asked about all this on ABC-TV's *Insiders* program last Sunday, Nelson suggested it might help the Liberal Party to attract 'the people who perhaps move from one side to the other as elections come and go'. Is it possible he doesn't get it? That he fails to see that lies, deception and gross hypocrisy are the issue – not his change of political allegiance? Was he the only one who failed to see the irony in his statement on winning the Liberal leadership – 'It's important for us to stand true to the things in which we believe'?

Good will to all

14 December 2007

When Tony Blair walked into Number 10 Downing Street after being sworn in as prime minister of Britain, he found a bottle of Champagne waiting for him. With it was a message from John Major, the man he'd defeated, saying: 'It's a great job – enjoy it.' There was no Champers for Kevin Rudd, but John Howard left a note saying he hoped the Lodge would prove to be a happy home for the Rudd family. And the outgoing prime minister's media staff put a six-pack of beer in the press office refrigerator for the enjoyment of the new Labor lot when they moved in.

When Julia Gillard arrived in her new office the only trace of her predecessor, Mark Vaile, was a pair of rusty nail clippers in a desk drawer. But waiting on Gillard's new computer was what she calls 'a lovely email – very cute' from Tim Fischer, National Party leader and Howard's deputy for the first three years of the coalition government. Fischer wrote:

Dear Julia,

Congratulations on becoming Deputy Prime Minister of this great country and moving into the best office, in my view. Somewhere in

your new office shelves there should be a small plaque which you
will need to update to announce your occupancy of this suite. One
thing I could never get approval for was to open the windows onto
the forecourt. I wish you well if one day you succeed in this regard.

Tim Fischer

Australia has a fiercely adversarial political system, and most of
the time – especially during election campaigns – the jibes, insults
and accusations fly thick and fast. But when the government changes,
both the victors and the vanquished behave in a remarkably civilised
way. Not always, of course. What Tony Abbott left behind for
Anthony Albanese in the ministerial office occupied by the manager
of government business was a 'Labor Lies' poster pinned to the wall.
But Abbott was the exception.

Outgoing finance minister Nick Minchin had words of
encouragement and advice for incoming treasurer Wayne Swan during
a brief tête-à-tête in the Tally Room late on election night. Even the
acid-tongued Alexander Downer displayed unusual generosity of
spirit in his private farewell address to staff of the Foreign Affairs
Department. Stephen Smith, Downer said, was 'an intelligent, hard-
working MP who will make a very good foreign minister'. Smith
reciprocated within hours of being sworn in, using a speech to the
annual diplomatic corps Christmas Party to praise Downer's 'personal
contribution in our national interest'.

One of the elevating aspects of election night was the generous
way Howard and Rudd spoke about each other. Howard, in a gutsy
and classy concession speech, congratulated the prime minister-elect
and wished him well. Rudd, in claiming victory, said: 'I want to
acknowledge now for the entire Australian nation...Mr Howard's
extensive contribution to public service in Australia...And I want
to wish Mr and Mrs Howard and their family all the very best for
the future.' A low point of election night was the way some Labor
supporters in the Tally Room booed that statement.

Not surprisingly, Labor ministers found their new roles took some
getting used to. Swan, in a car on his way to a function, asked: 'Is
anyone from the government coming to this?' A staffer replied: 'That
would be you.' When US Secretary of State Condoleezza Rice phoned
Smith at his Perth home at 9.40 pm, the new Foreign Affairs Minister's

two teenage children were using computers and playing music. Smith had to take the call in a garage out back, where it was quieter. Gillard, unfamiliar with the workings of the ministerial wing of Parliament House, had trouble getting cleaners to remove a large box of wilting roses. It turned out that the cleaners twigged to something Gillard and her staff had missed – the box also contained chocolates and a bottle of bubbly.

But the transition from one government to another was smooth and astonishingly swift. The bureaucracy hardly missed a beat in adjusting to a new administration and a new set of policy priorities. And the public took the changeover in its stride. 'A fortnight later,' says an amazed Labor MP, 'it's almost as though the other lot had never been there.' Howard, once so dominant, simply faded away.

There is something else about election night worth mentioning. Howard made his concession speech to a crowd of the Liberal faithful in the ballroom of a Sydney hotel. What few people noticed was that all the exit signs had been covered with gaffer tape. Why? Because someone realised that Howard beneath an exit sign on the night of his defeat was the shot every TV cameraman would be after. It was a small act of kindness in a mudslide of humiliation.

In this space a year ago, just after Kim Beazley was toppled from the Labor leadership by Rudd, my theme was the famous dictum that most political careers end in tears. I wrote of what had happened to Holt, Gorton, McMahon, Whitlam, Hayden, Hawke and Keating, and I quoted Howard's own comment in parliament on Beazley's downfall: 'It's a brutal game, politics.' It is indeed. We can now add Howard to the list. Peter Costello too, for that matter. Rudd no doubt tells himself: 'It won't happen to me.' But it almost always does.

In the meantime, though, Rudd clearly agrees with Major that being PM is a great job, and he is quietly putting his own stamp on it. When ministers gathered for lunch at the Lodge immediately after the swearing-in, the first speech was delivered not by the PM, but by local Aboriginal elder Matilda House, who formally welcomed them to Ngunnawal country. The former tenant would certainly not have approved.

Index

POWER PLAYS

57–60
referendum proposed in conjunction
with election 28–30
state governments 49–57
transition to Opposition 138, 149–51
Latham, John 111, 132
Latham, Mark 146, 156, 279–82,
286–7, 287–90, 291–4, 295, 298–9,
302–4, 304–6, 308, 310, 311, 314,
324, 326–9, 346, 352, 356
Lavarch, Michael 100
Lawrence, Carmen 51–2, 54–5, 71, 100,
104–5, 122–4, 177
Laws, John 85, 120, 121, 207–10, 227
Lee, Michael 100, 205
Lees, Meg 258, 352
Lewis, Tom 127
Liberal Party see also Coalition
Elliott as president of 10–13
New Right, and 25–7
One Nation, connection with 187–90,
244–7
Opposition strategies 37–9
religious influences 315–17
Lindell, Geoffrey 251–2
Lindsay, Peter 267
Loosely, Stephen 249
Loughnane, Brian 364, 380
Lynch, Sir Phillip 8, 9
Lyons, Joseph 60, 111, 271

McClelland, Robert 382
Macfarlane, Ian 238
McGarvie, Richard 180
Mackellar, Robin 32
McKew, Maxine 57, 238, 272, 382
MacKinnon, Barry 52, 54
Macklin, Jenny 277–9, 382
Macklin, Robert 356–60
McMahon, William 202, 203, 259,
351
McMullan, Bob 124, 280
Macphee, Ian 20, 25–7
Maher, Robert 50
Maiden, Samantha 298
Matthews, Christopher 81–2
Matthews, Race 258

Mellors, John 169–72
Menzies, Sir Robert 18–19, 37, 38,
39, 60–1, 62, 65, 99, 101, 104, 191,
203, 259, 267, 274, 334, 346, 350,
356
Minchin, Nick 193, 194, 318, 385
Mitchell, Neil 289, 293
Moore, Des 56
Moore, John 174, 187, 188
Moore-Wilton, Max 144, 153–4, 170
Morosi, Junie 126
Morris, Dick 150
Morris, Graeme 161, 171
Moylan, Judi 195, 279
Muldoon, Sir Robert 44
Murphy, Lionel 109, 126
Murray, Andrew 255

Napthine, Denis 252
Nelson, Brendan 117–19, 275–6, 277–9,
320–3, 383
Nogarotto, Remo 215–16

O'Brien, Kerry 107, 206
O'Byrne, Michelle 299, 301
O'Leary, Tony 220, 222
One Nation 227
Liberal Party, connection with
187–90, 244–7
Oss-Emer, Liz 258

Palmer, Mick 330
Parliament House 19–21
Payne, Marise 317, 341
Peacock, Andrew 2–3, 6, 7–9, 11, 16,
30, 39, 73, 107, 111, 124, 174, 192,
194, 203, 204, 351, 383
Pearson, Noel 360, 361
Pell, Cardinal George 323, 344
Powell, Janet 352
Puplick, Chris 30

Ramsey, Alan 112, 177, 261, 262, 263
Randall, Don 300–1
Rau, Cornelia 330
Ray, Robert 35, 72, 102, 186, 249, 311
Reagan, Ronald 81–2, 223
Rein, Thérèse 356